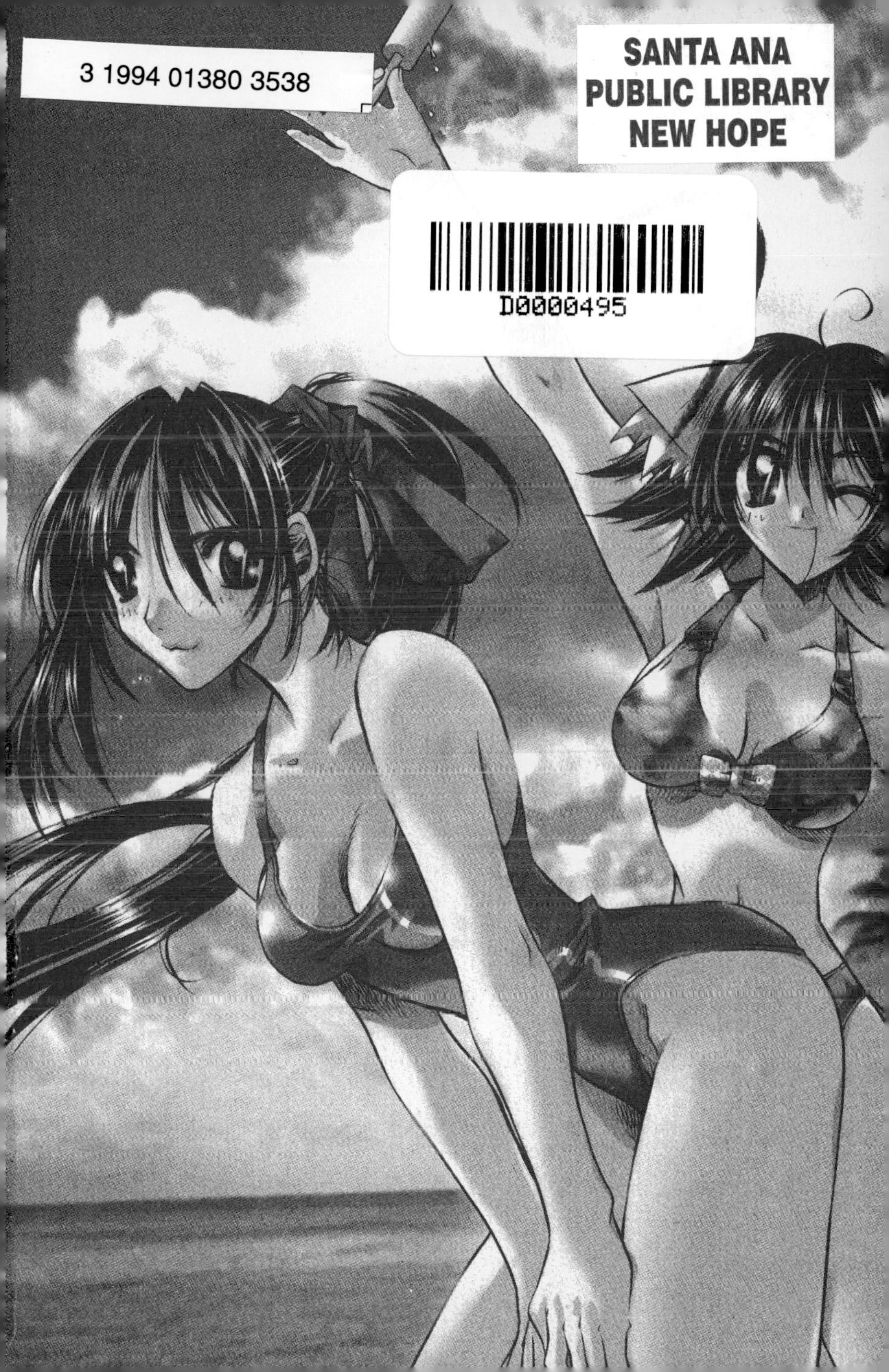

CHRONICLES OF THE CURSED SWORD

Volume 4

Story by
YEO BEOP-RYONG
Art by
PARK HUI-JIN

Los Angeles • Tokyo • London

Translation - Yongju Ryu
English Adaptation - Matt Varosky
Graphic Designers - John Lo & Steven Redd
Copy Editor - Tim Beedle
Retouch & Lettering - Tim Law
Cover Design - Gary Shum

Editor - Paul Morrissey
Managing Editor - Jill Freshney
Production Coordinator - Antonio DePietro
Production Manager - Jennifer Miller
Art Director - Matt Alford
Director of Editorial - Jeremy Ross
VP of Production - Ron Klamert
President & C.O.O. - John Parker
Publisher & C.E.O. - Stuart Levy

Email: editor@TOKYOPOP.com
Come visit us online at www.TOKYOPOP.com

A  Manga

TOKYOPOP Inc.
5900 Wilshire Blvd. Suite 2000
Los Angeles, CA 90036

Chronicles of the Cursed Sword vol. 4
©2000 YEO BEOP-RYONG and PARK HUI-JIN.
First printed in Korea in 2000 by Daiwon C.I. Inc. English translation rights in
North America, UK, NZ and Australia arranged by Daiwon C.I. Inc.

English text copyright ©2004 TOKYOPOP Inc.

ISBN: 1-59182-421-4

First TOKYOPOP printing: January 2004

10 9 8 7 6 5 4 3 2 1
Printed in the USA

Chronicles

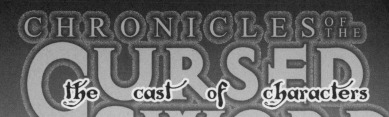

CHRONICLES OF THE CURSED SWORD

the cast of characters

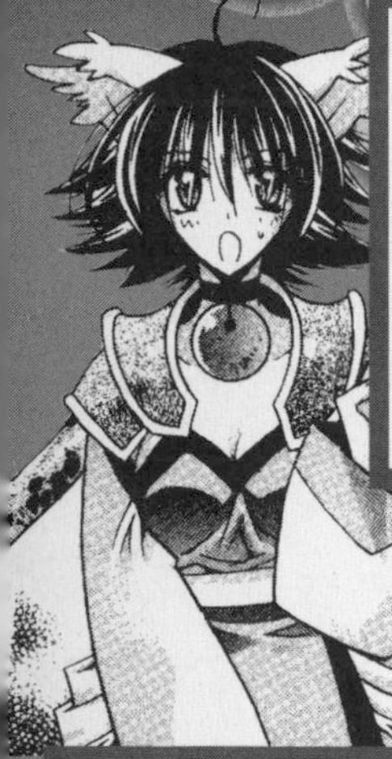

MINGLING

A lesser demon with feline qualities, Mingling is now the loyal follower of Shyao Lin. She lives in fear of Rey who still doesn't trust her.

THE PASA SWORD

A living sword that hungers for demon blood. It grants its user incredible power, but at a great cost-it can take over the user's body and, in time, his soul.

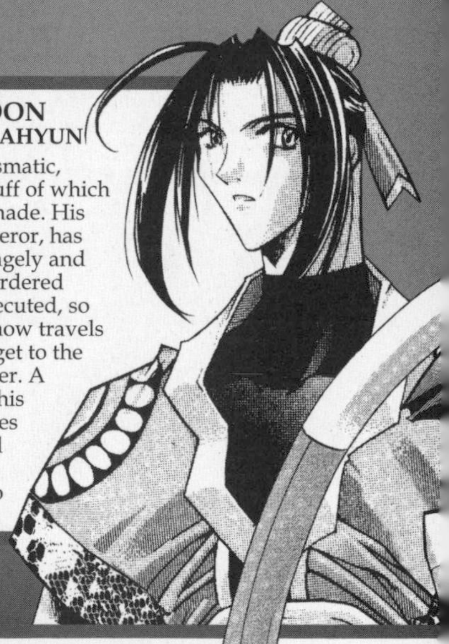

JARYOON
KING OF HAHYUN

Noble and charismatic, Jaryoon is the stuff of which great kings are made. His brother, the emperor, has been acting strangely and apparently has ordered Jaryoon to be executed, so the young king now travels to the capital to get to the heart of the matter. A great warrior in his own right, he does not have magical abilities and is unaccustomed to battling demons.

SHYAO LIN

A sorceress, and Rey Yan's traveling companion. Shyao grew fond of Rey during their five years of study together with their master, and thinks of him as her little brother. She's Rey's conscience—his sole tie to humanity. She also seems quite enamored with the handsome Jaryoon.

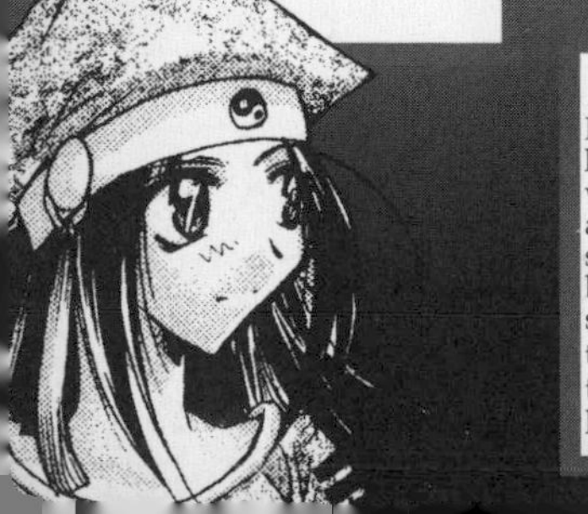

REY YAN

Rey's origins remain unknown. An orphan, he and Shyao were raised by a wise old man who trained them in the ways of combat and magic. After the demon White Tiger slaughtered their master, Rey and Shyao became wanderers. Rey wields the PaSa sword, a weapon of awesome power that threatens to take over his very soul. Under the right circumstances, he could be a hero.

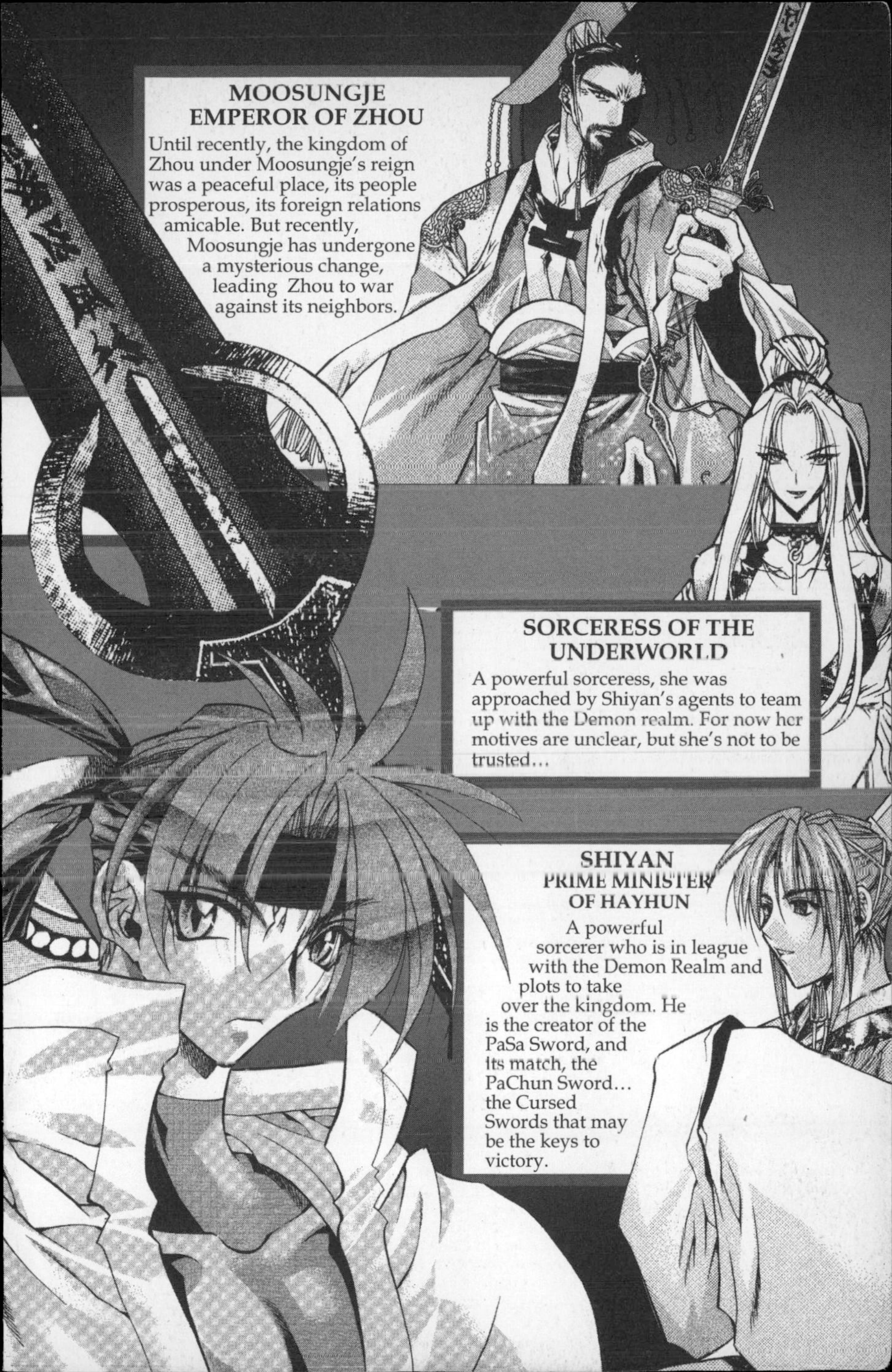
MOOSUNGJE
EMPEROR OF ZHOU
Until recently, the kingdom of Zhou under Moosungje's reign was a peaceful place, its people prosperous, its foreign relations amicable. But recently, Moosungje has undergone a mysterious change, leading Zhou to war against its neighbors.
SORCERESS OF THE UNDERWORLD
A powerful sorceress, she was approached by Shiyan's agents to team up with the Demon realm. For now her motives are unclear, but she's not to be trusted…
SHIYAN
PRIME MINISTER OF HAYHUN
A powerful sorcerer who is in league with the Demon Realm and plots to take over the kingdom. He is the creator of the PaSa Sword, and its match, the PaChun Sword… the Cursed Swords that may be the keys to victory.

When Rey refuses an invite from the Sorceress of the Underworld, her minions kidnap Shyao as bait.

Rey offers to exchange the PaSa sword for her release, inciting the wrath of the sword, which proves to have a life of its own…

…but Rey's true colors shine and he takes back the sword. Joined by Mingling and Jaryoon, he ventures to the Underworld to rescue Shyao.

During his confrontation with the Sorceress of the Underworld, Rey transforms into his "true" demon form…

…and his personality recedes into the back recesses of his consciousness, as a conniving demon possesses him.

The demon possessing Rey conspires with the Sorceress to summon the Demon Emperor by combining the powers of the PaSa and PaChun swords.

Rey awakens safely with Shyao, remembering nothing of his "demon form."

Out of the Sorceress's clutches, Rey encounters Chen Kaihu—a diminutive half-frog, half-human martial arts master who playfully bests Rey in combat…

Meanwhile, Emperor Moosungje madly wields the PaChun sword in battle.

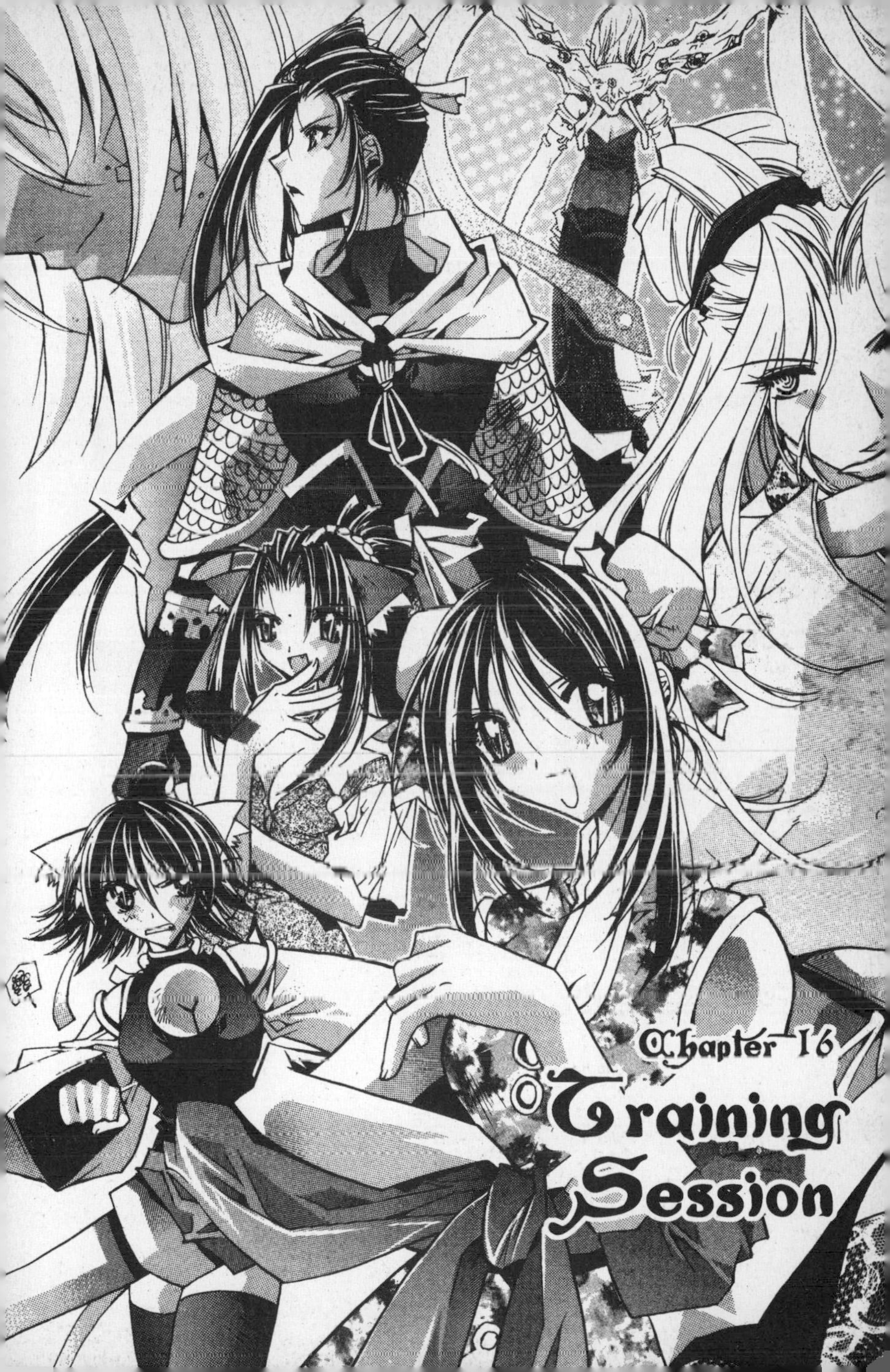
Chapter 16
Training Session

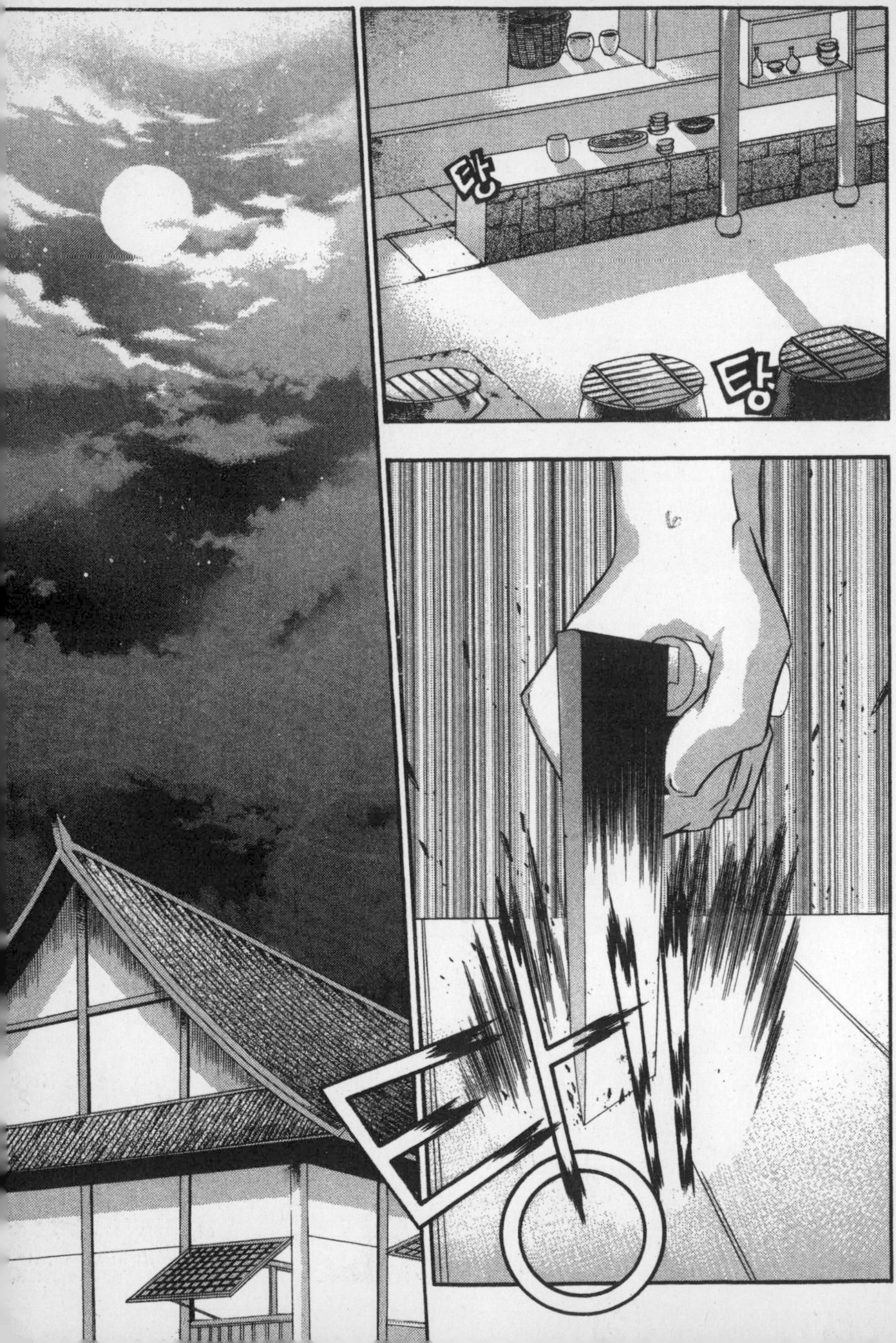
탕
탕
탕

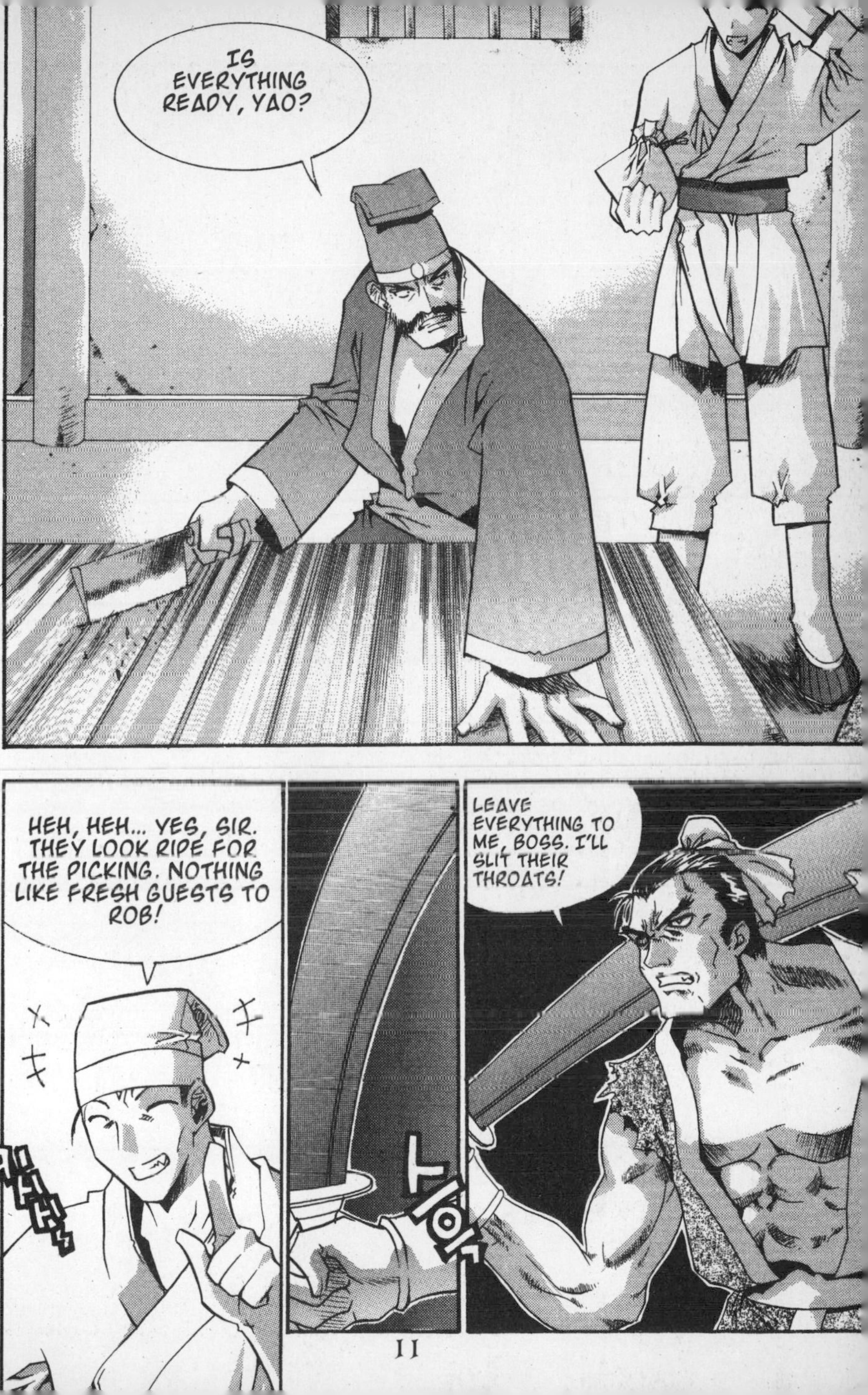
IS EVERYTHING READY, YAO?
HEH, HEH... YES, SIR. THEY LOOK RIPE FOR THE PICKING. NOTHING LIKE FRESH GUESTS TO ROB!
LEAVE EVERYTHING TO ME, BOSS. I'LL SLIT THEIR THROATS!

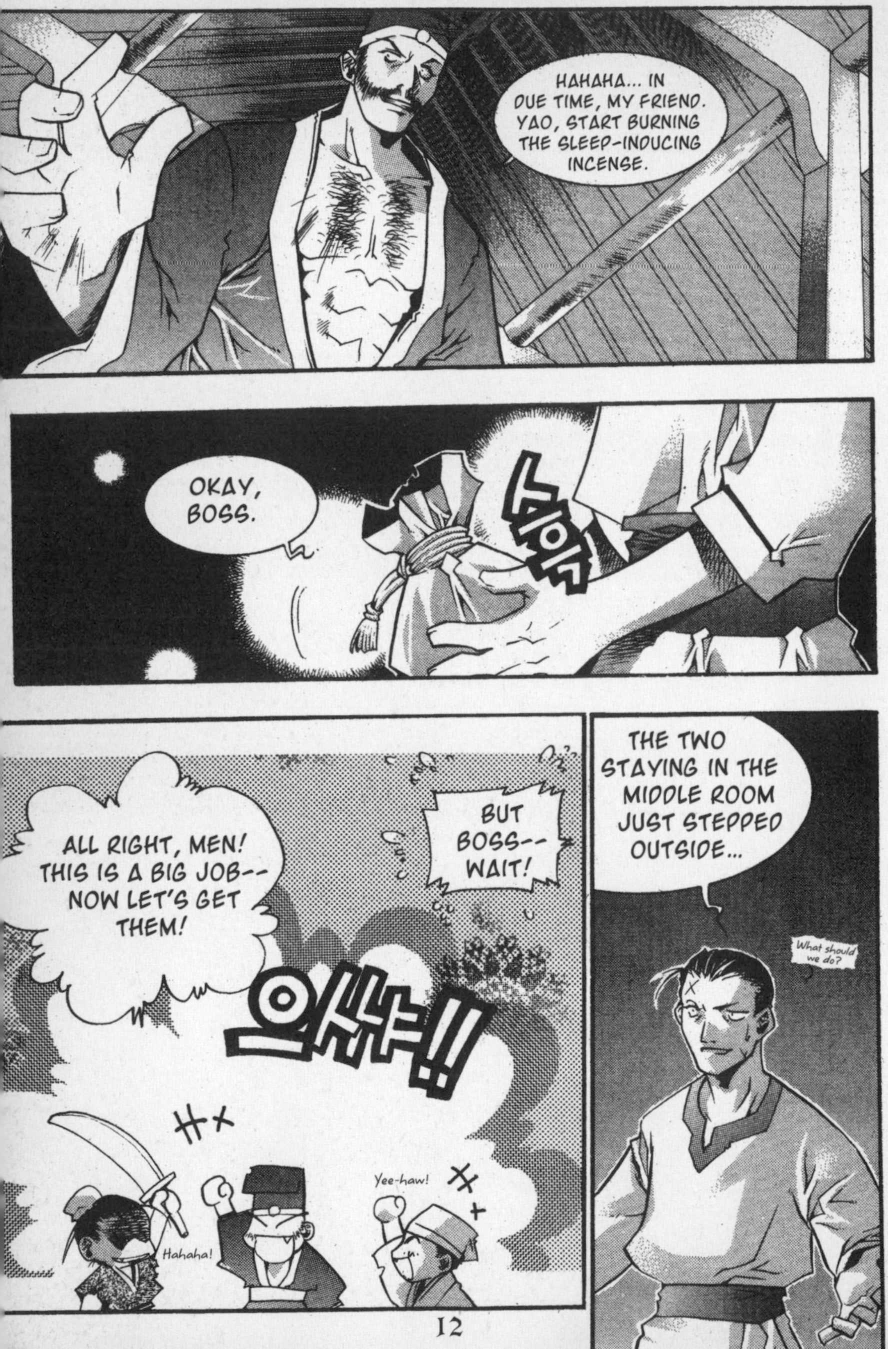

HAHAHA... IN DUE TIME, MY FRIEND. YAO, START BURNING THE SLEEP-INDUCING INCENSE.
OKAY, BOSS.
ALL RIGHT, MEN! THIS IS A BIG JOB-- NOW LET'S GET THEM!
BUT BOSS-- WAIT!
Hahaha!
Yee-haw!
THE TWO STAYING IN THE MIDDLE ROOM JUST STEPPED OUTSIDE...
What should we do?

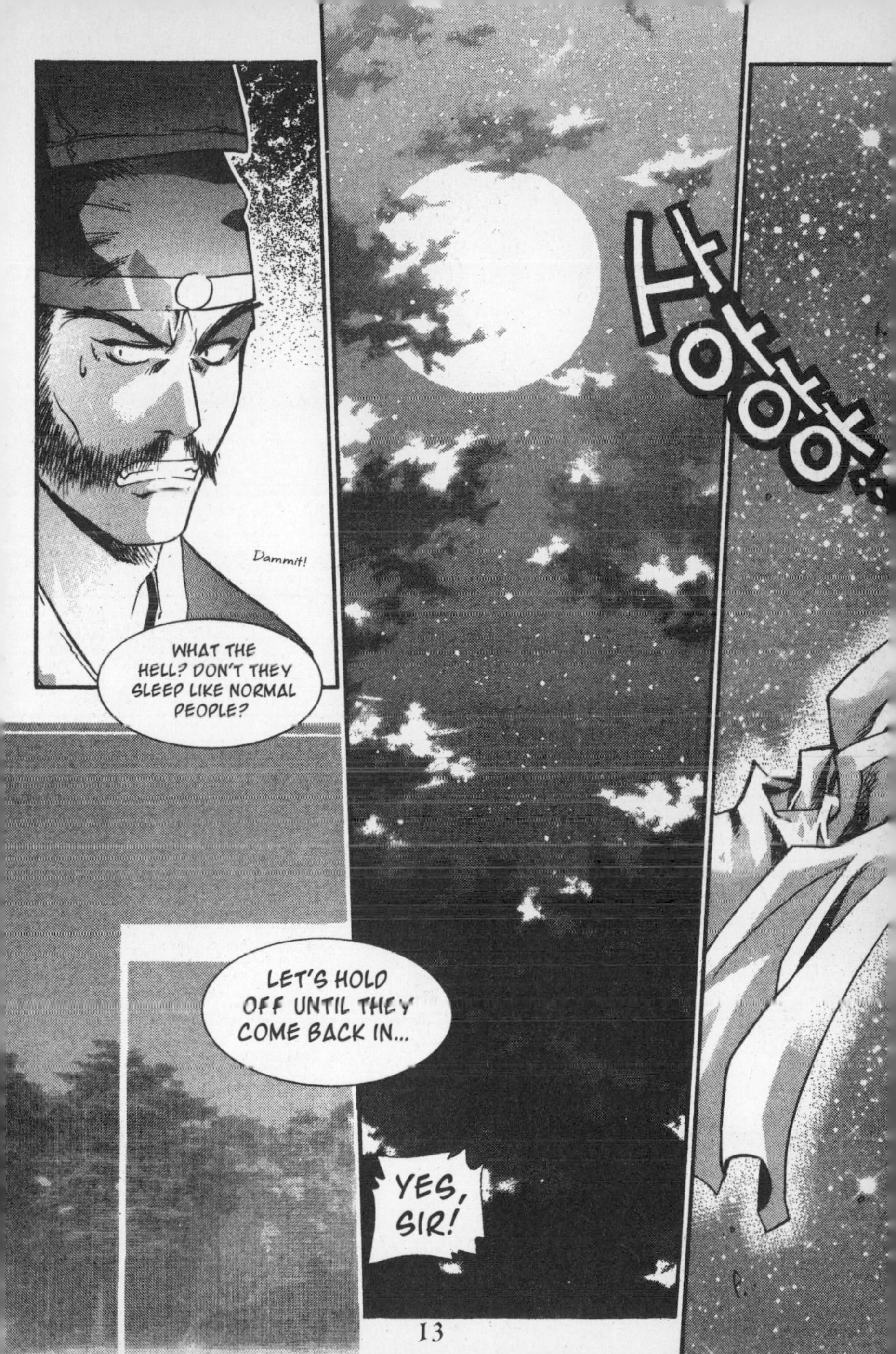
Dammit!
WHAT THE HELL? DON'T THEY SLEEP LIKE NORMAL PEOPLE?
LET'S HOLD OFF UNTIL THEY COME BACK IN...
YES, SIR!

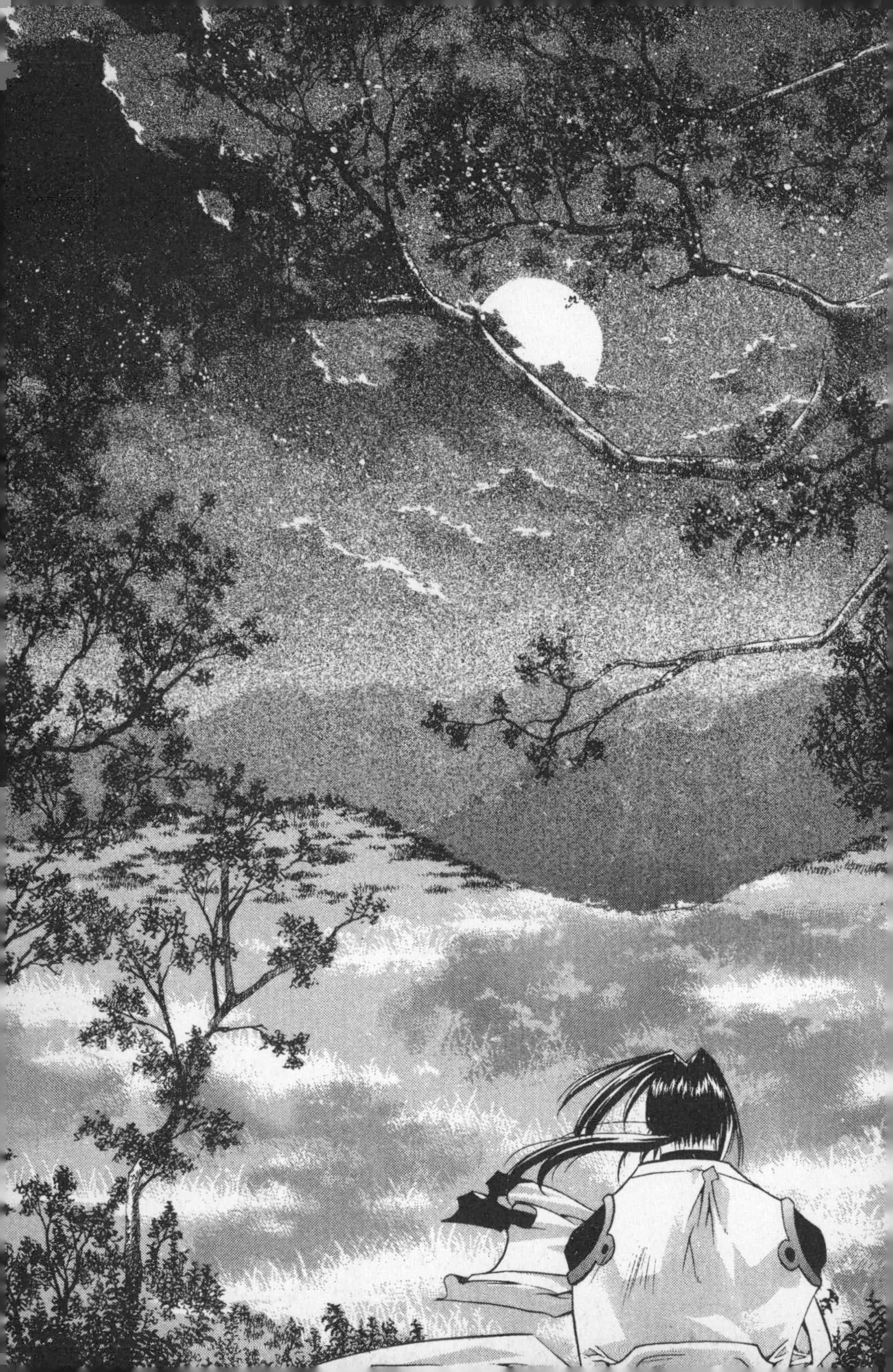

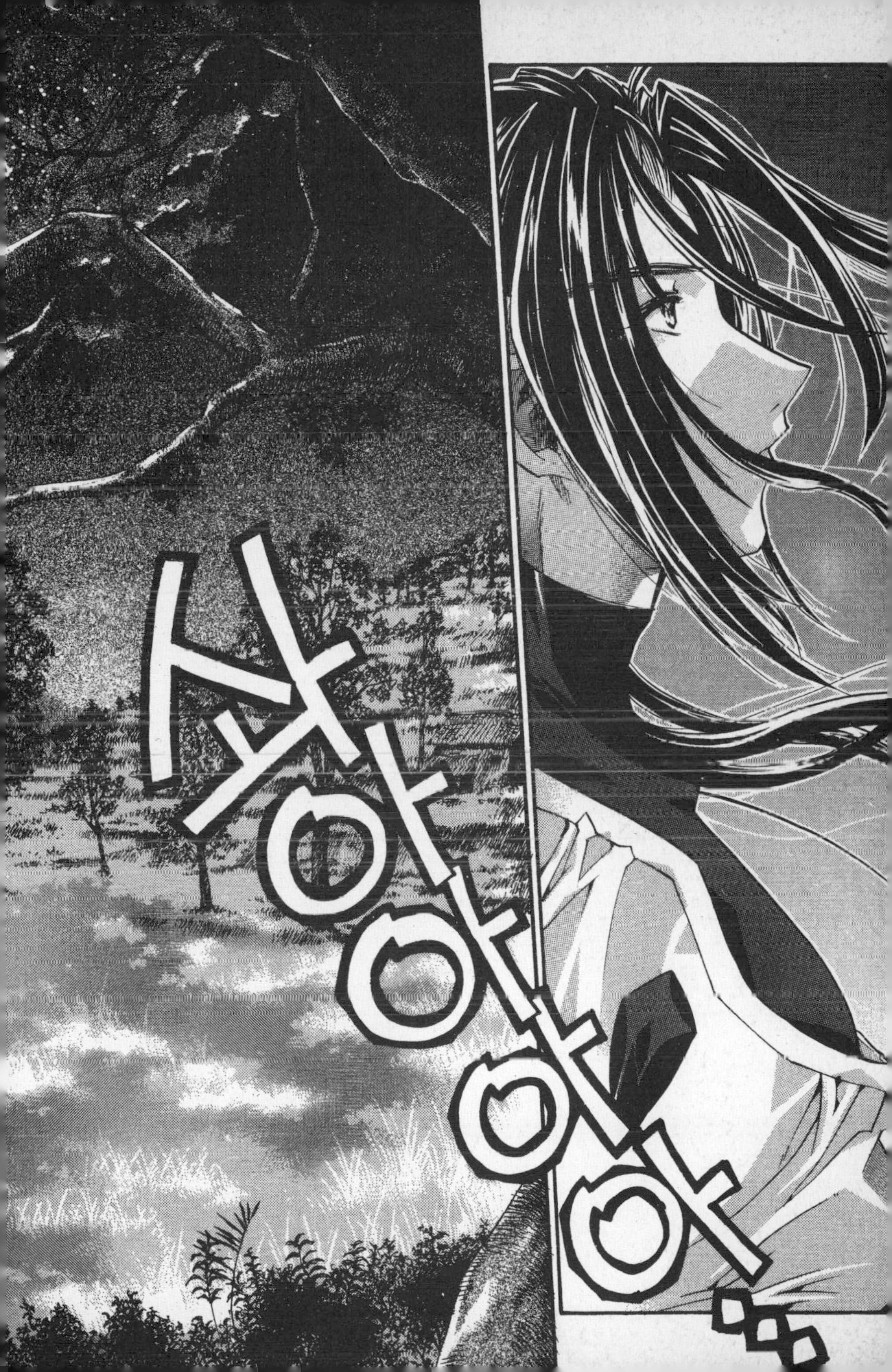
스아아아아…

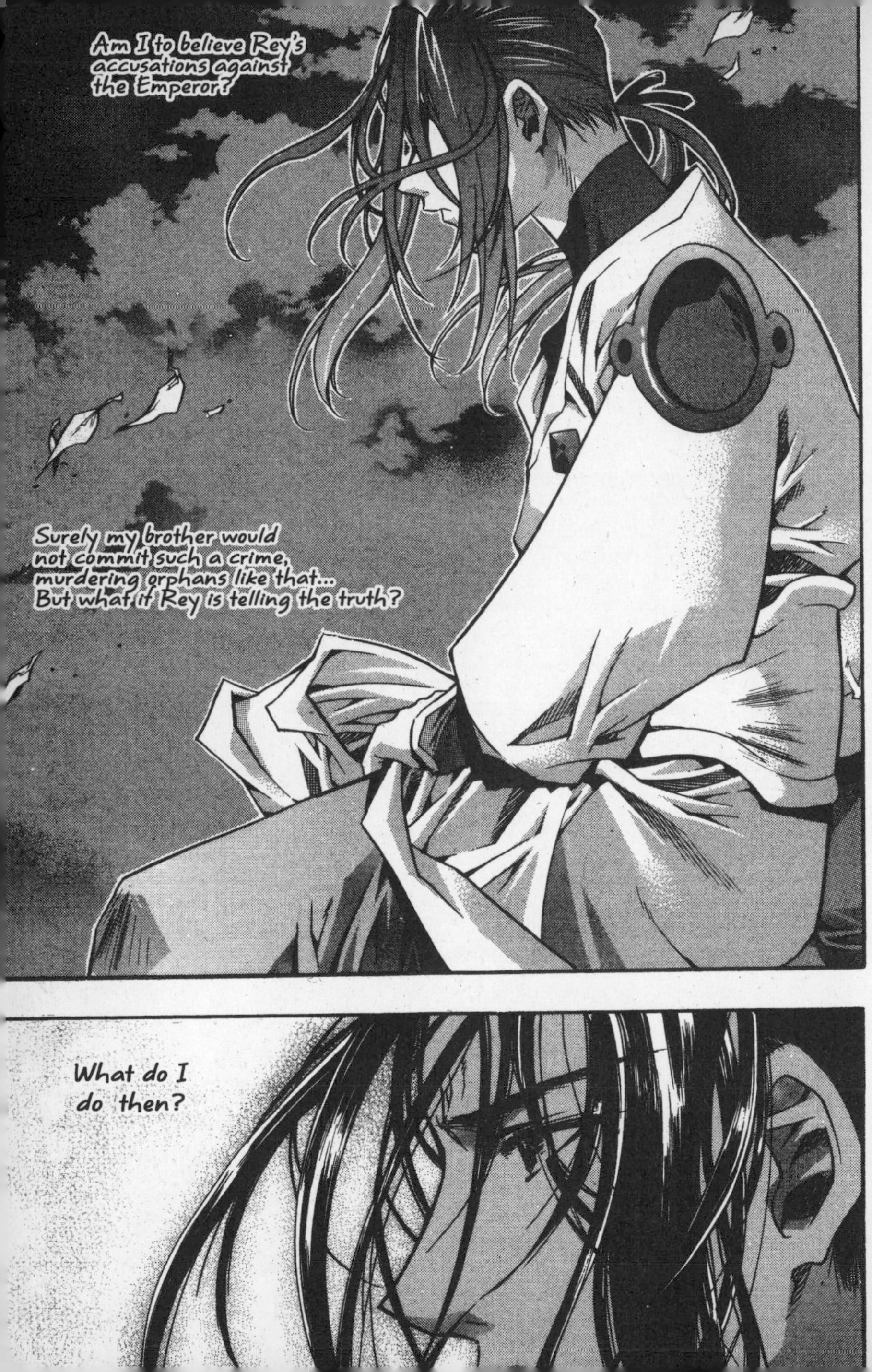
Am I to believe Rey's accusations against the Emperor?
Surely my brother would not commit such a crime, murdering orphans like that... But what if Rey is telling the truth?
What do I do then?

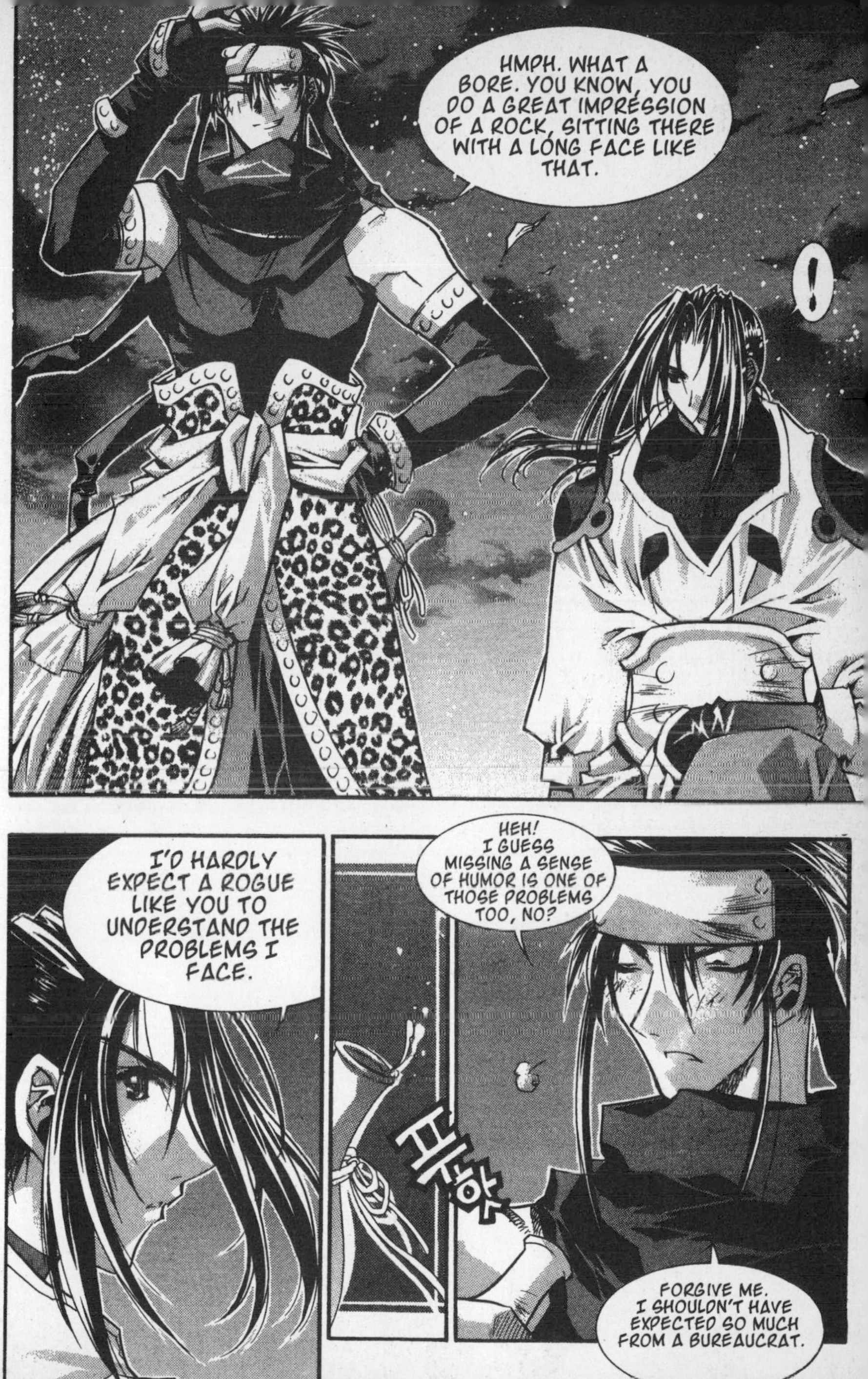
HMPH. WHAT A BORE. YOU KNOW, YOU DO A GREAT IMPRESSION OF A ROCK, SITTING THERE WITH A LONG FACE LIKE THAT.
!
I'D HARDLY EXPECT A ROGUE LIKE YOU TO UNDERSTAND THE PROBLEMS I FACE.
HEH! I GUESS MISSING A SENSE OF HUMOR IS ONE OF THOSE PROBLEMS TOO, NO?
FORGIVE ME. I SHOULDN'T HAVE EXPECTED SO MUCH FROM A BUREAUCRAT.

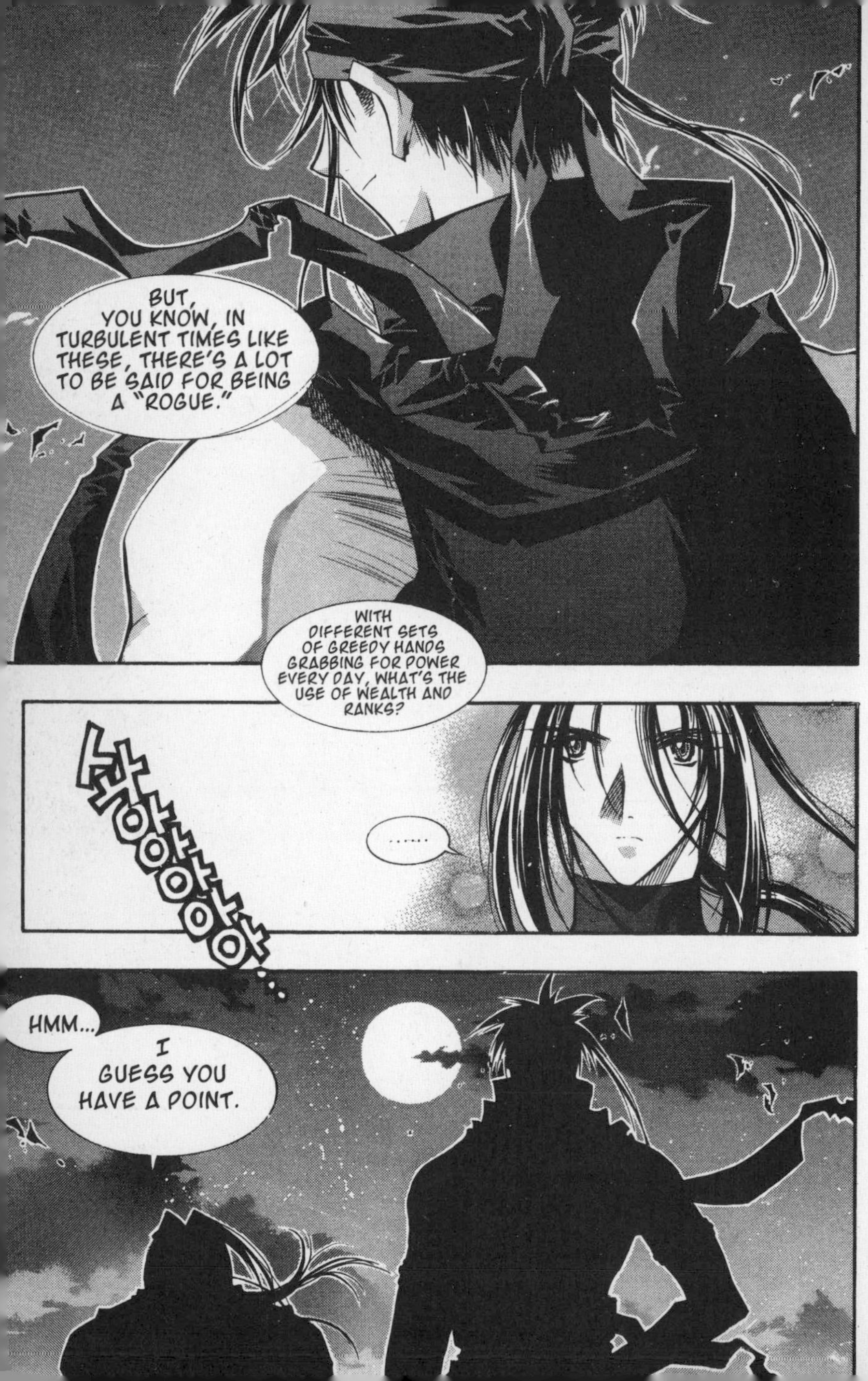
BUT, YOU KNOW, IN TURBULENT TIMES LIKE THESE, THERE'S A LOT TO BE SAID FOR BEING A "ROGUE."
WITH DIFFERENT SETS OF GREEDY HANDS GRABBING FOR POWER EVERY DAY, WHAT'S THE USE OF WEALTH AND RANKS?
......
HMM... I GUESS YOU HAVE A POINT.

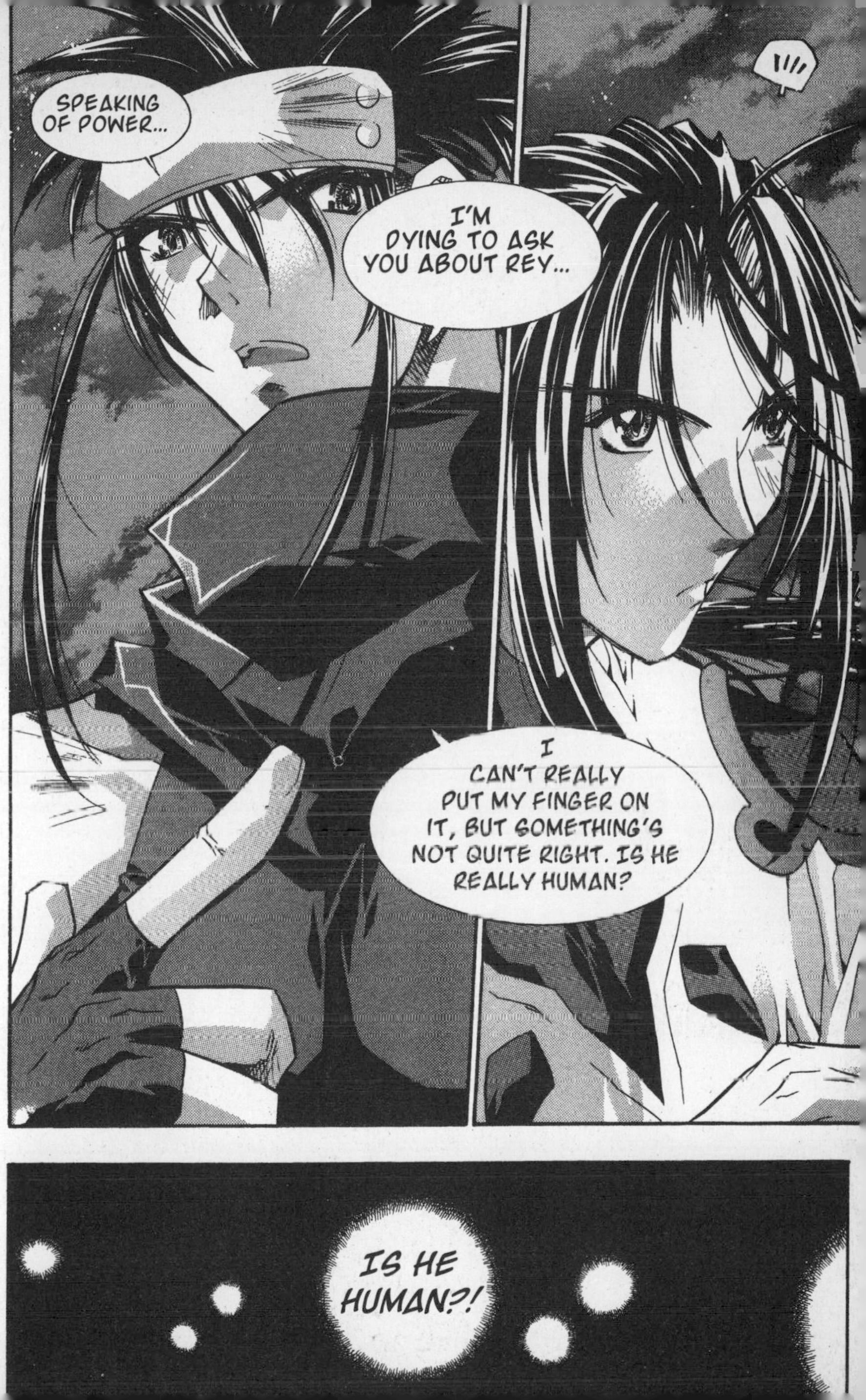
SPEAKING OF POWER...
I'M DYING TO ASK YOU ABOUT REY...
I CAN'T REALLY PUT MY FINGER ON IT, BUT SOMETHING'S NOT QUITE RIGHT. IS HE REALLY HUMAN?
IS HE HUMAN?!

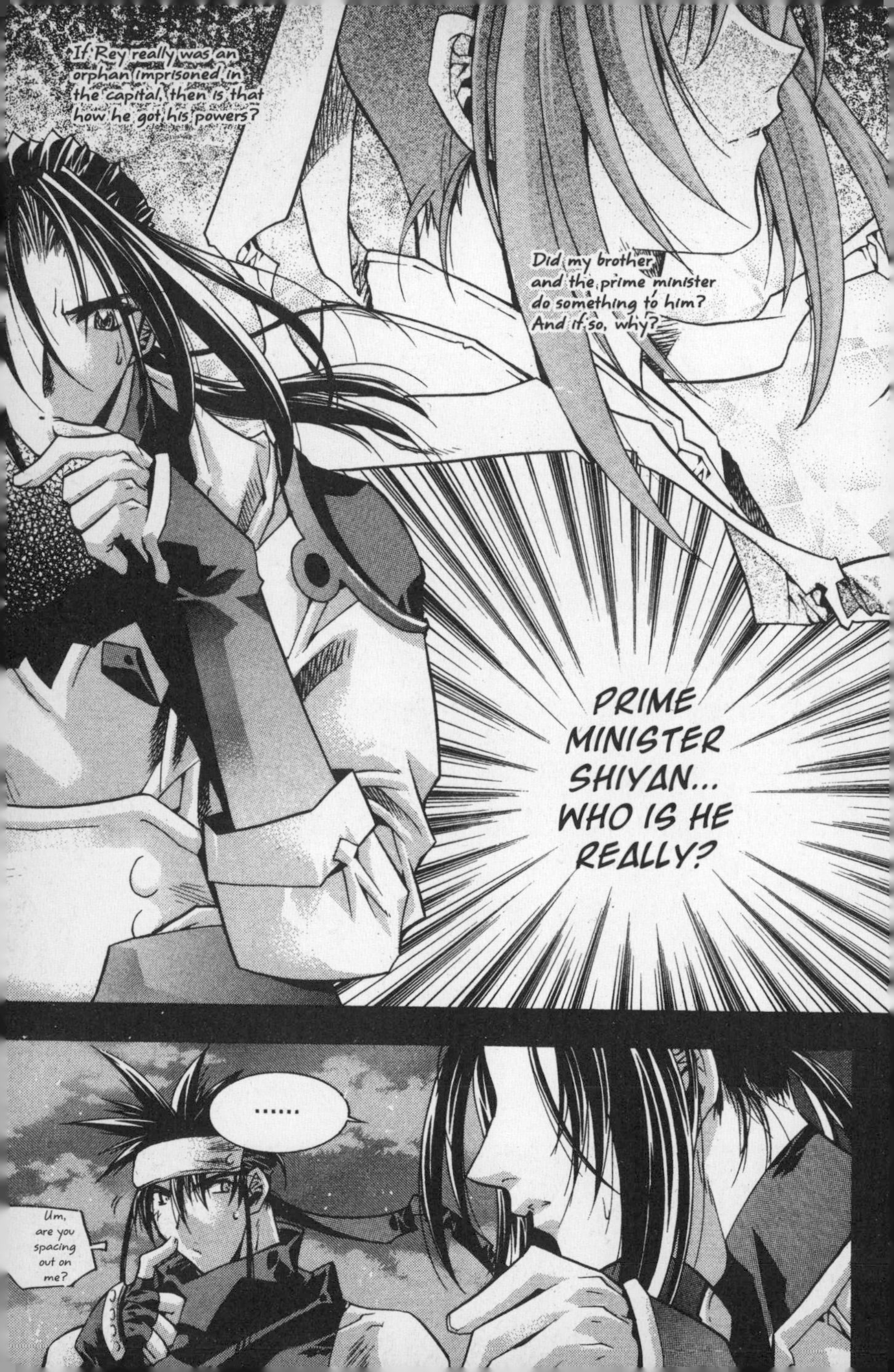
If Rey really was an orphan imprisoned in the capital, then is that how he got his powers?
Did my brother and the prime minister do something to him? And if so, why?
PRIME MINISTER SHIYAN... WHO IS HE REALLY?
......
Um, are you spacing out on me?

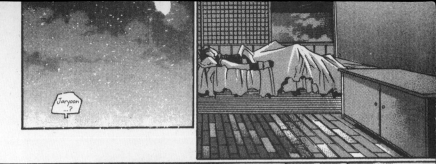

Jaryoon
...?

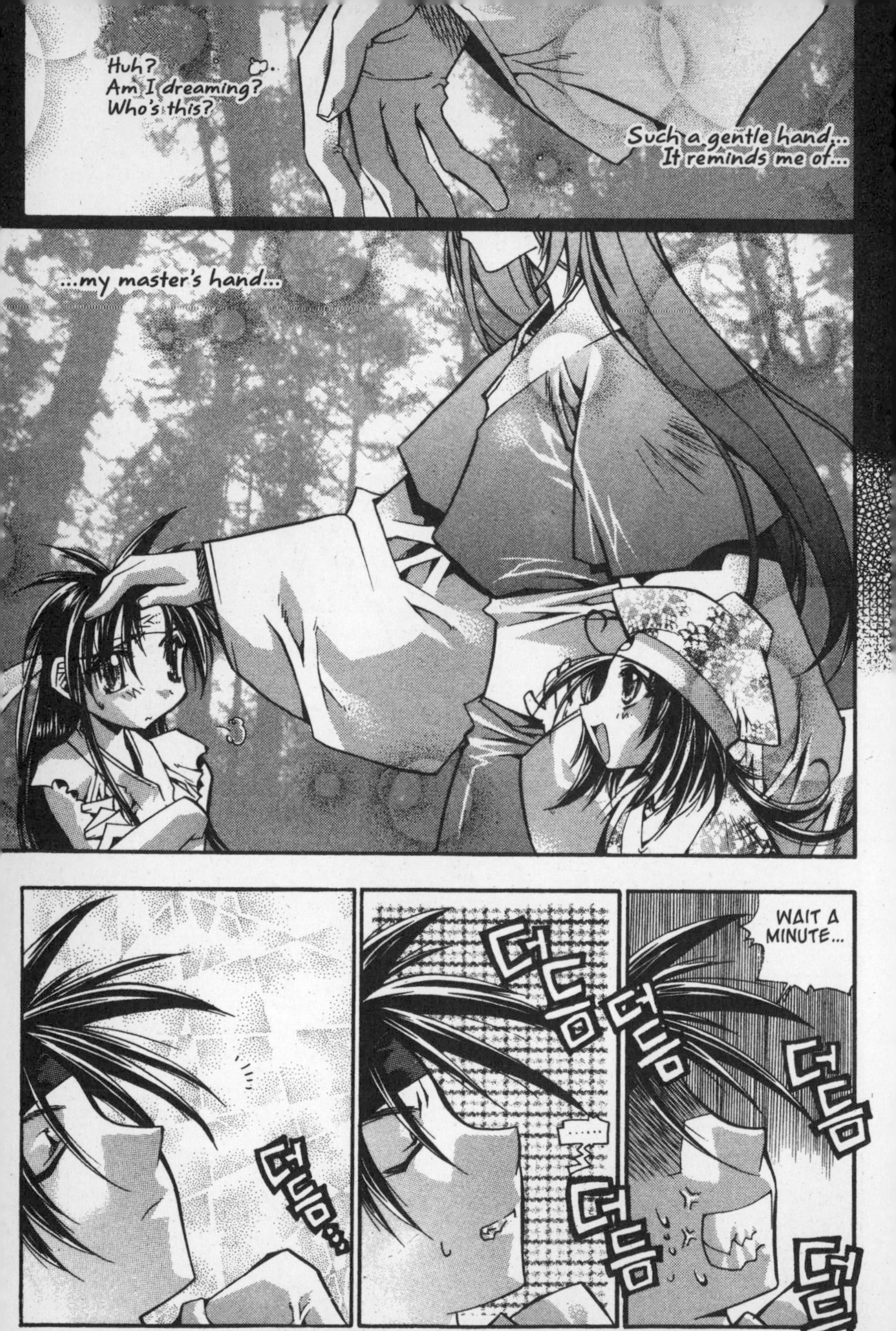
Huh? Am I dreaming? Who's this?
Such a gentle hand... It reminds me of...
...my master's hand...
......
WAIT A MINUTE...

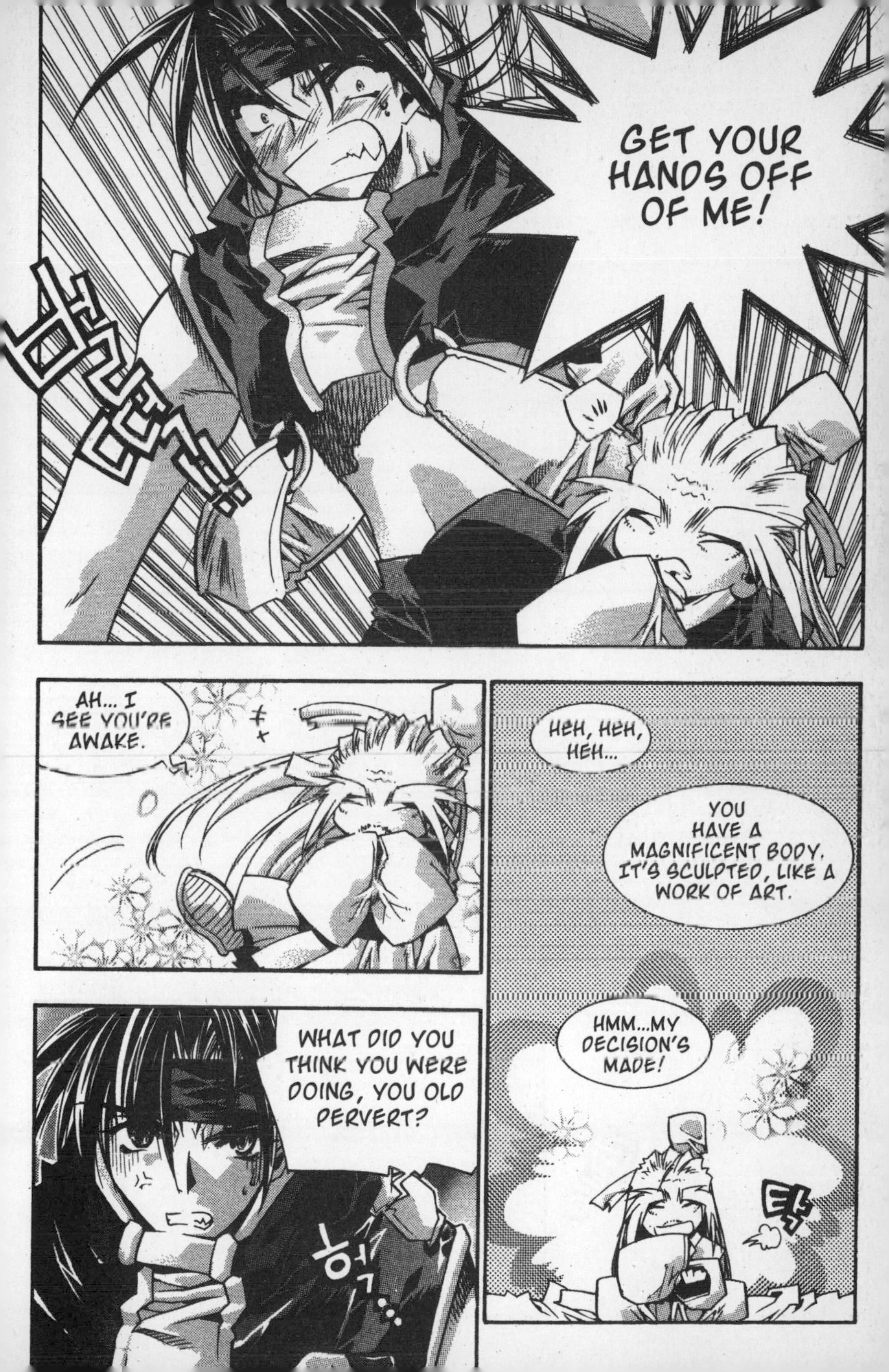
GET YOUR HANDS OFF OF ME!
AH... I SEE YOU'RE AWAKE.
WHAT DID YOU THINK YOU WERE DOING, YOU OLD PERVERT?
헉...
HEH, HEH, HEH...
YOU HAVE A MAGNIFICENT BODY. IT'S SCULPTED, LIKE A WORK OF ART.
HMM...MY DECISION'S MADE!
턱

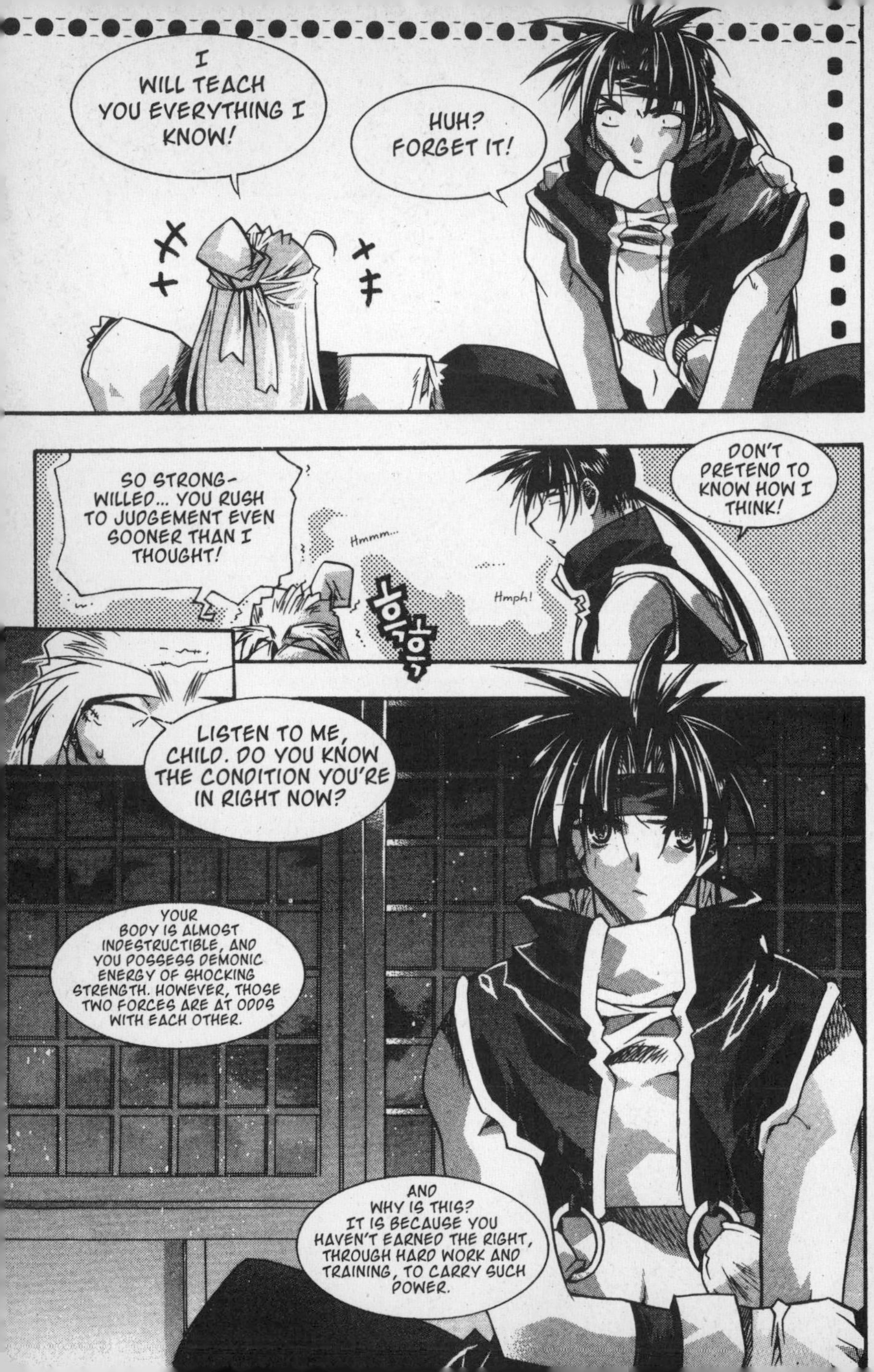
I WILL TEACH YOU EVERYTHING I KNOW!
HUH? FORGET IT!
SO STRONG-WILLED... YOU RUSH TO JUDGEMENT EVEN SOONER THAN I THOUGHT!
Hmmm...
......
Hmph!
DON'T PRETEND TO KNOW HOW I THINK!
LISTEN TO ME, CHILD. DO YOU KNOW THE CONDITION YOU'RE IN RIGHT NOW?
YOUR BODY IS ALMOST INDESTRUCTIBLE, AND YOU POSSESS DEMONIC ENERGY OF SHOCKING STRENGTH. HOWEVER, THOSE TWO FORCES ARE AT ODDS WITH EACH OTHER.
AND WHY IS THIS? IT IS BECAUSE YOU HAVEN'T EARNED THE RIGHT, THROUGH HARD WORK AND TRAINING, TO CARRY SUCH POWER.

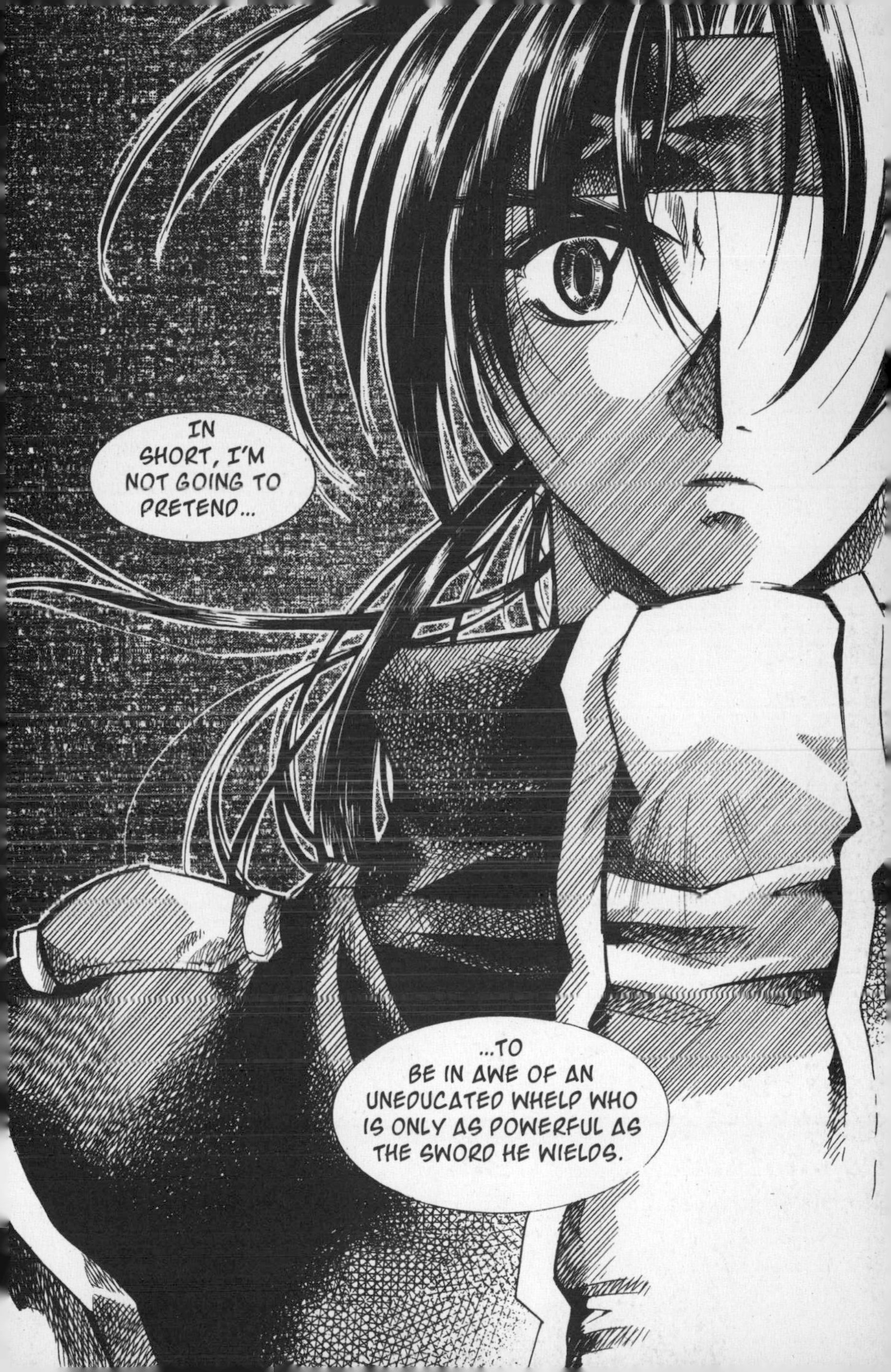
IN SHORT, I'M NOT GOING TO PRETEND...
...TO BE IN AWE OF AN UNEDUCATED WHELP WHO IS ONLY AS POWERFUL AS THE SWORD HE WIELDS.

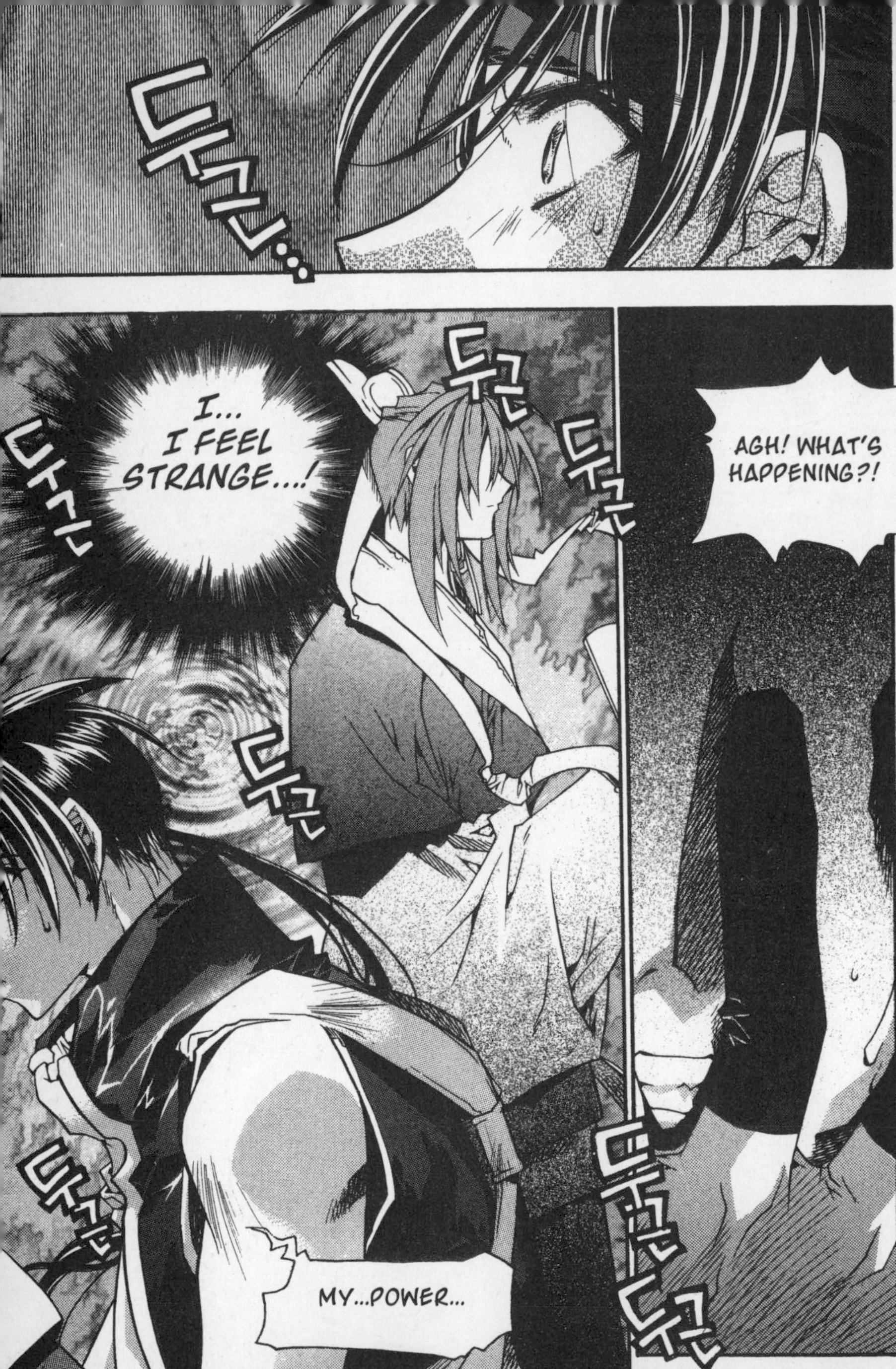
I... I FEEL STRANGE...!
MY...POWER...
AGH! WHAT'S HAPPENING?!

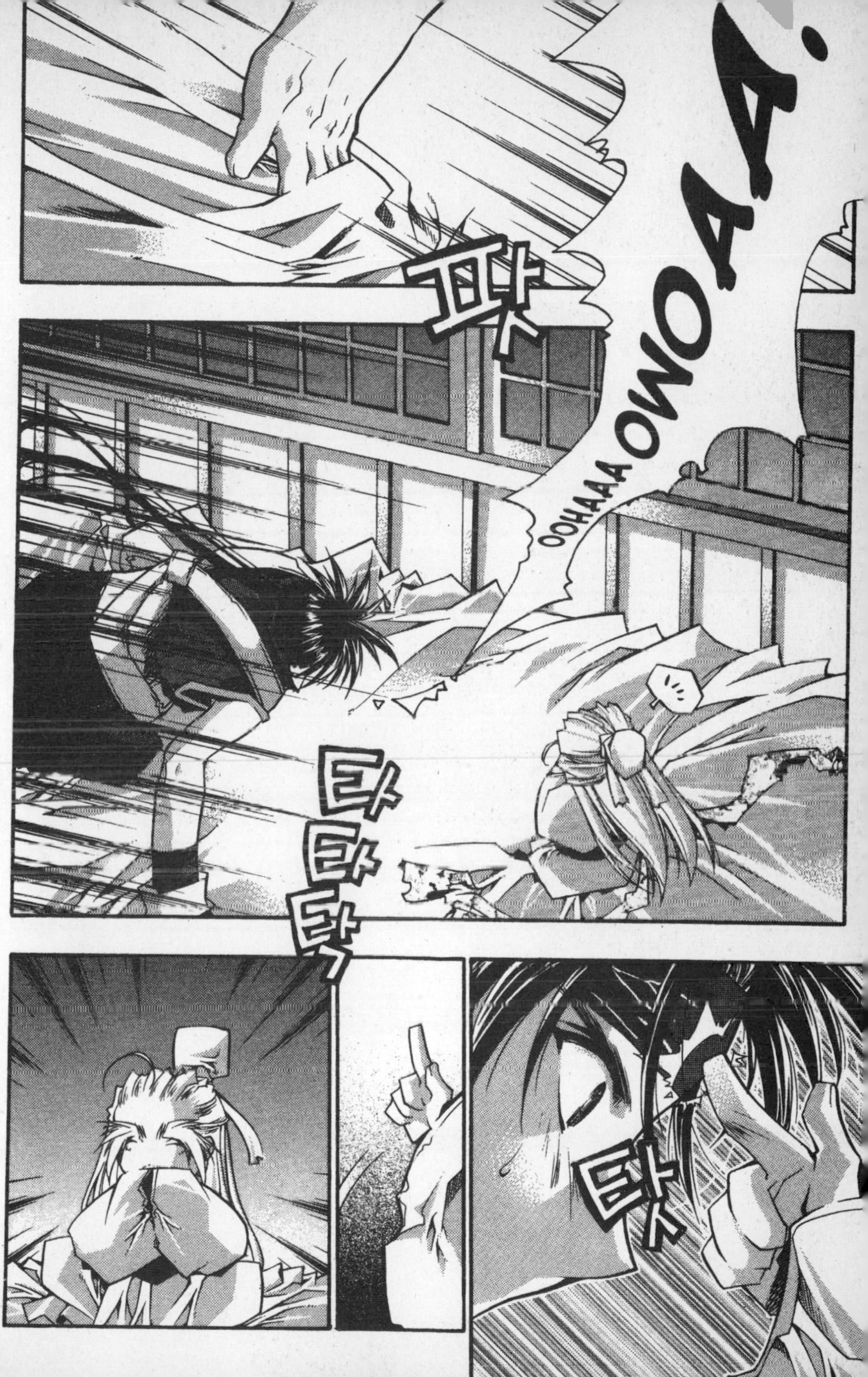

팍
OOHAAA OWOAA!
...
타타탁
탁

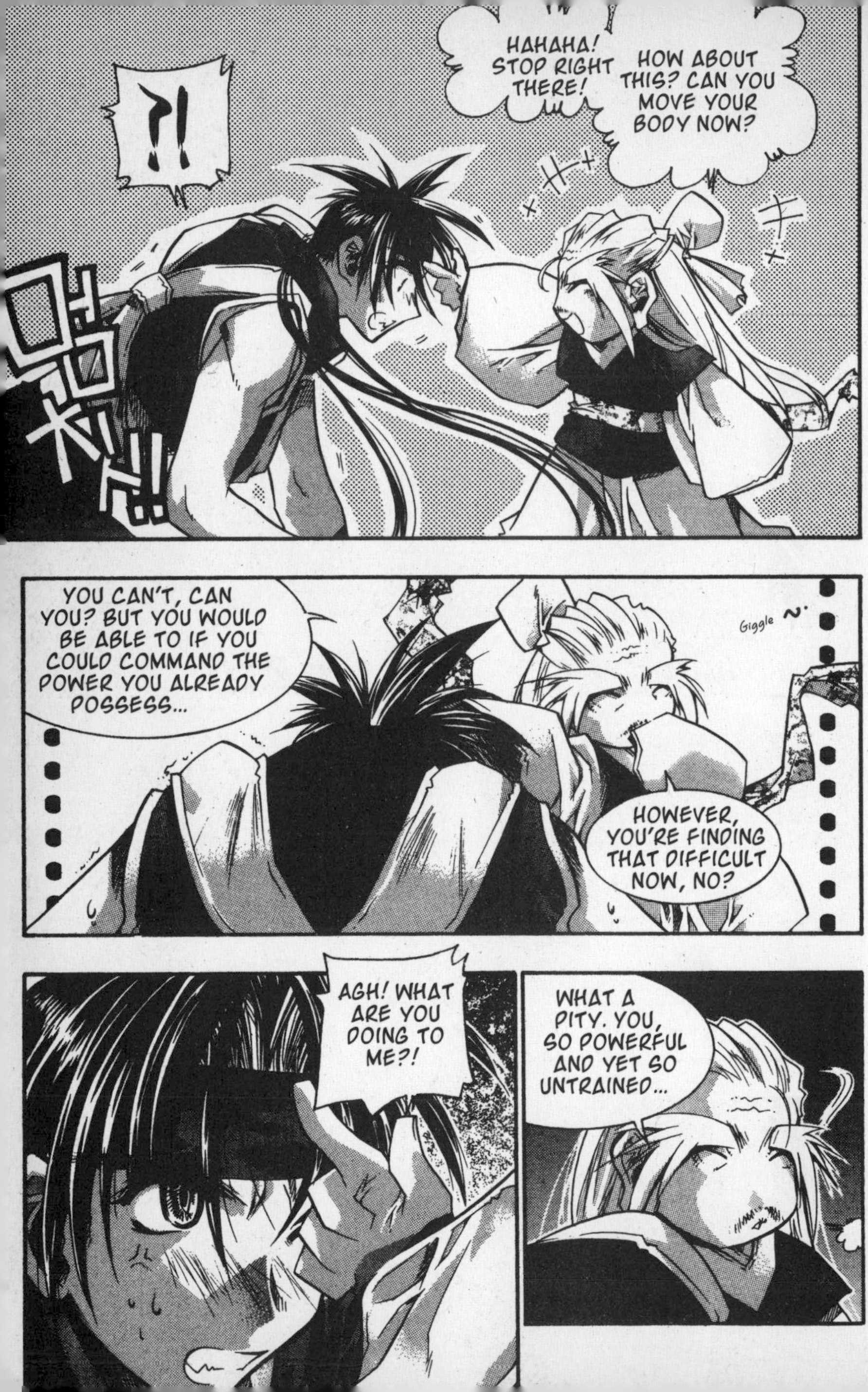
?!
HAHAHA! STOP RIGHT THERE!
HOW ABOUT THIS? CAN YOU MOVE YOUR BODY NOW?
YOU CAN'T, CAN YOU? BUT YOU WOULD BE ABLE TO IF YOU COULD COMMAND THE POWER YOU ALREADY POSSESS...
Giggle ~
HOWEVER, YOU'RE FINDING THAT DIFFICULT NOW, NO?
AGH! WHAT ARE YOU DOING TO ME?!
WHAT A PITY. YOU, SO POWERFUL AND YET SO UNTRAINED...

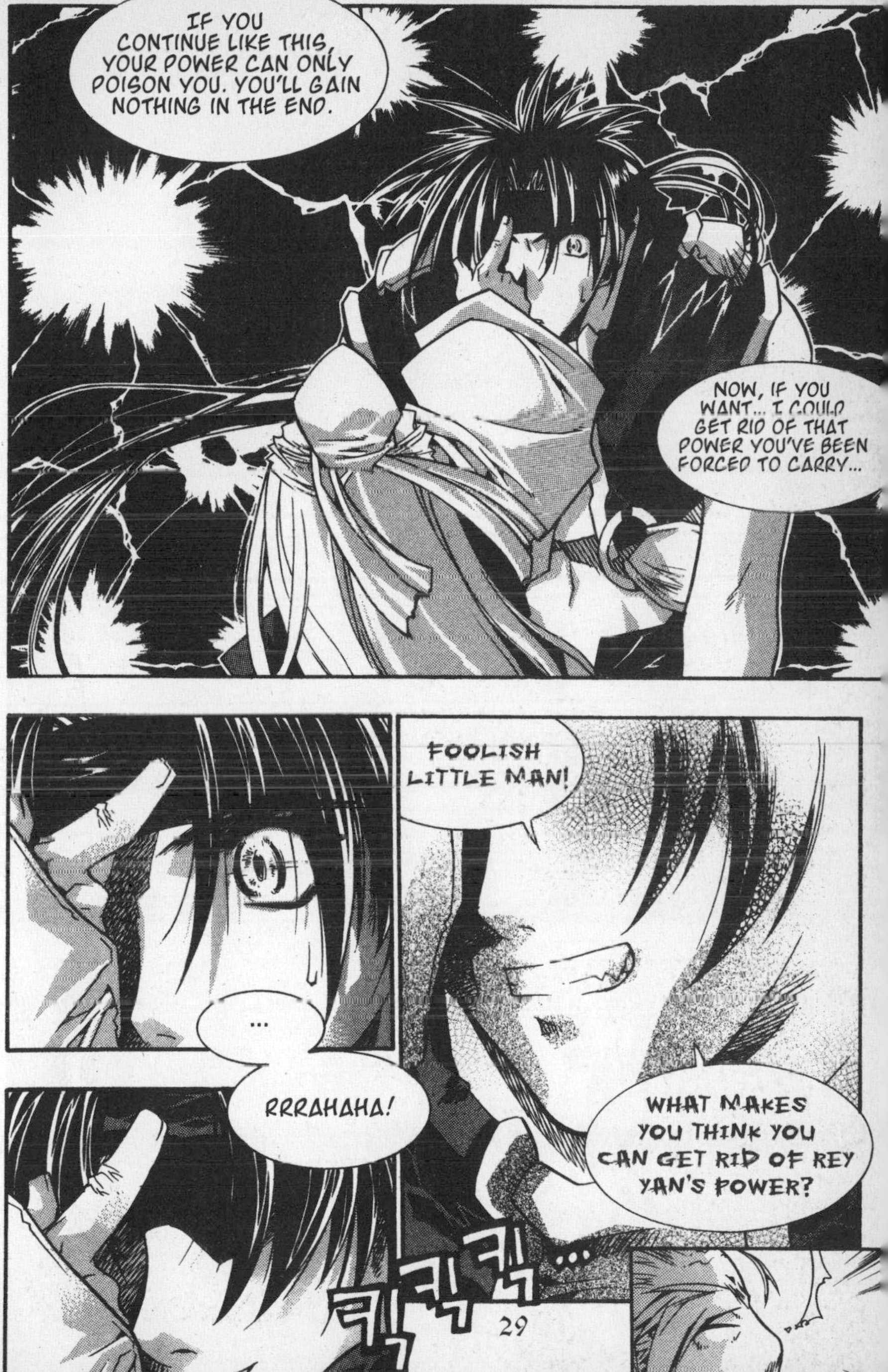
IF YOU CONTINUE LIKE THIS, YOUR POWER CAN ONLY POISON YOU. YOU'LL GAIN NOTHING IN THE END.
NOW, IF YOU WANT... I COULD GET RID OF THAT POWER YOU'VE BEEN FORCED TO CARRY...
...
RRRAHAHA!
FOOLISH LITTLE MAN!
WHAT MAKES YOU THINK YOU CAN GET RID OF REY YAN'S POWER?

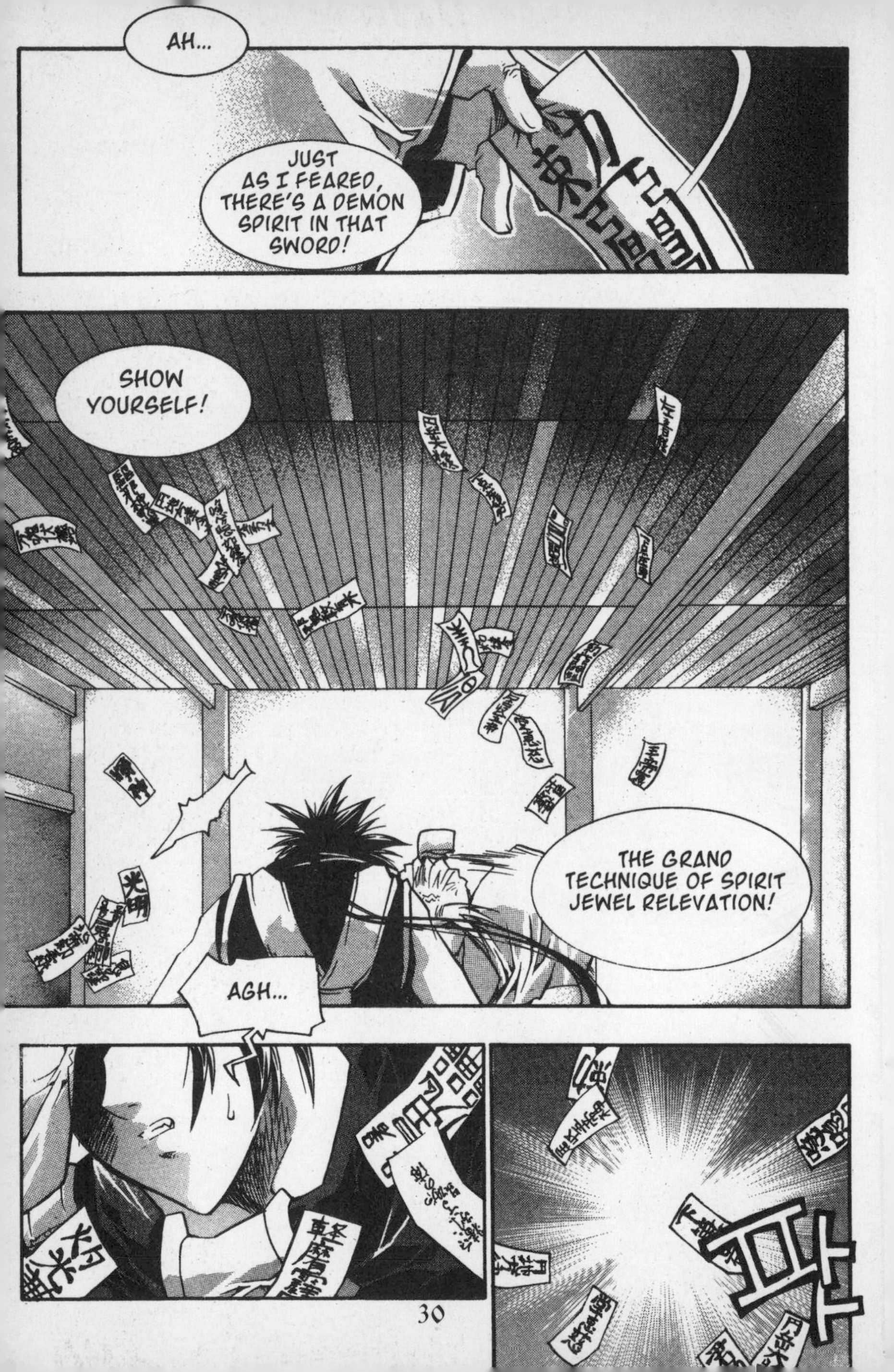
AH...
JUST AS I FEARED, THERE'S A DEMON SPIRIT IN THAT SWORD!
SHOW YOURSELF!
THE GRAND TECHNIQUE OF SPIRIT JEWEL RELEVATION!
AGH...

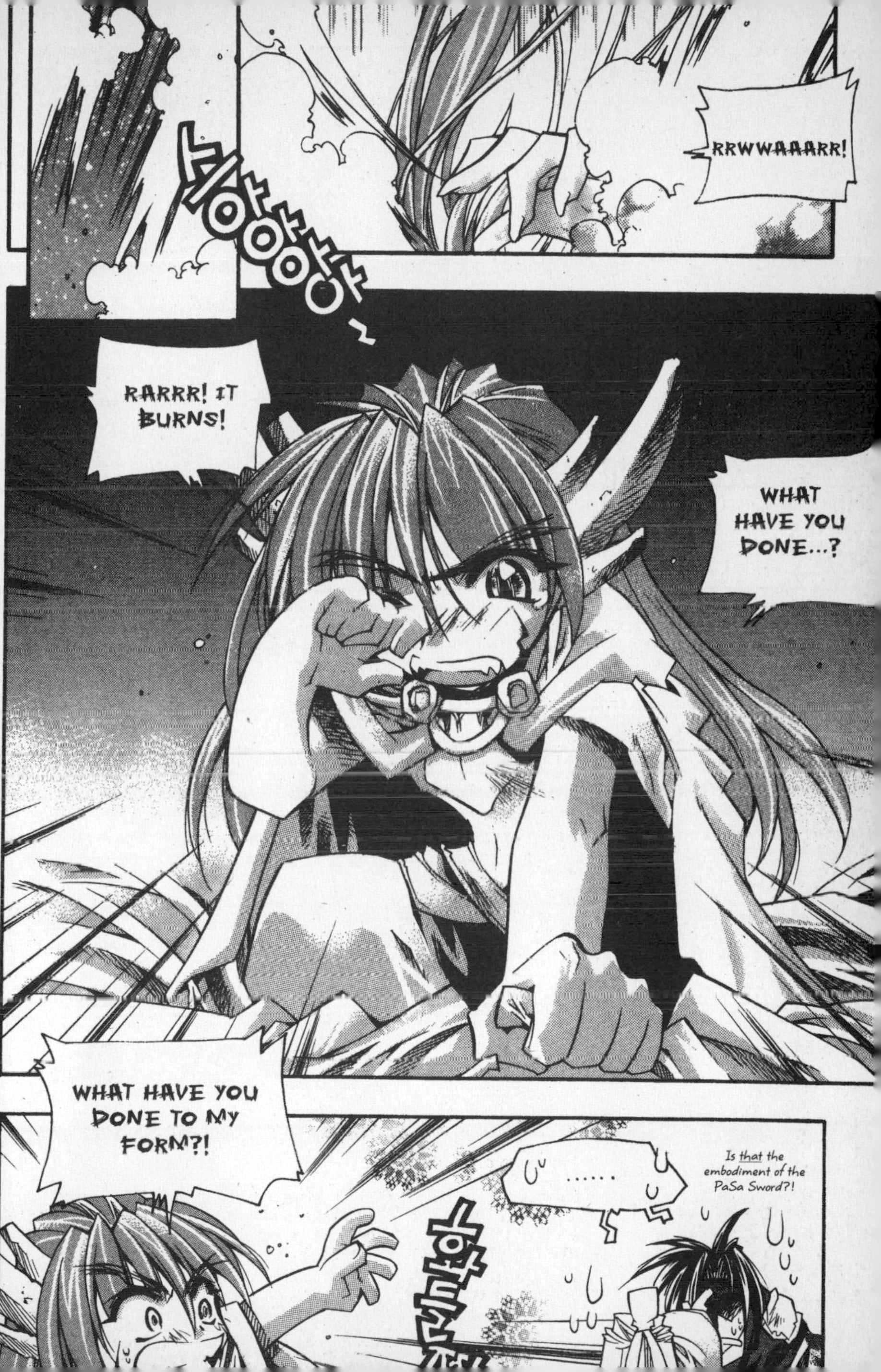
RRWWAAARR!
RARRR! IT BURNS!
WHAT HAVE YOU DONE...?
WHAT HAVE YOU DONE TO MY FORM?!
......
Is that the embodiment of the PaSa Sword?!

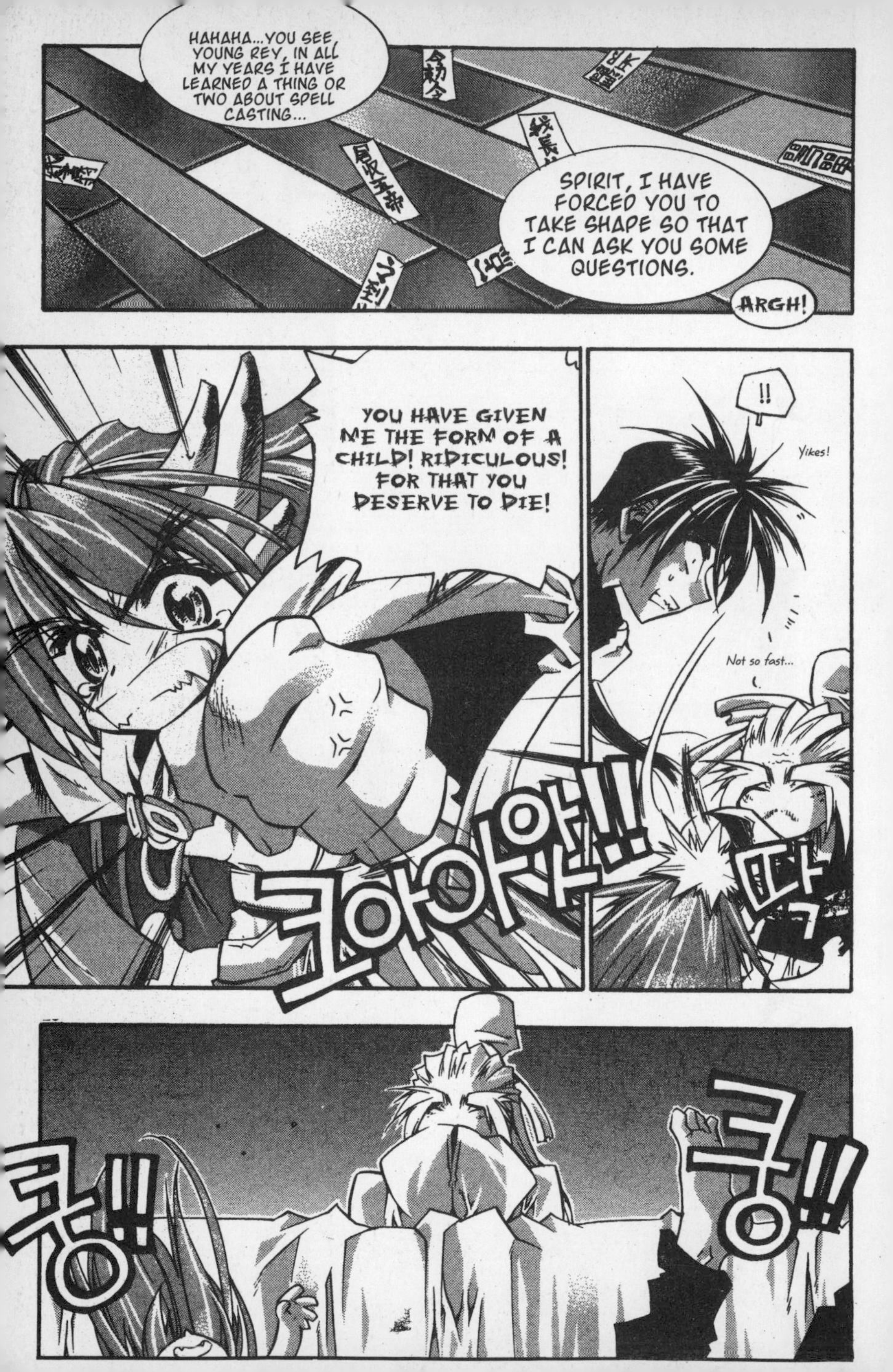
HAHAHA...YOU SEE YOUNG REY, IN ALL MY YEARS I HAVE LEARNED A THING OR TWO ABOUT SPELL CASTING...
SPIRIT, I HAVE FORCED YOU TO TAKE SHAPE SO THAT I CAN ASK YOU SOME QUESTIONS.
ARGH!
YOU HAVE GIVEN ME THE FORM OF A CHILD! RIDICULOUS! FOR THAT YOU DESERVE TO DIE!
!!
Yikes!
Not so fast...
쿵!!
쿵!!

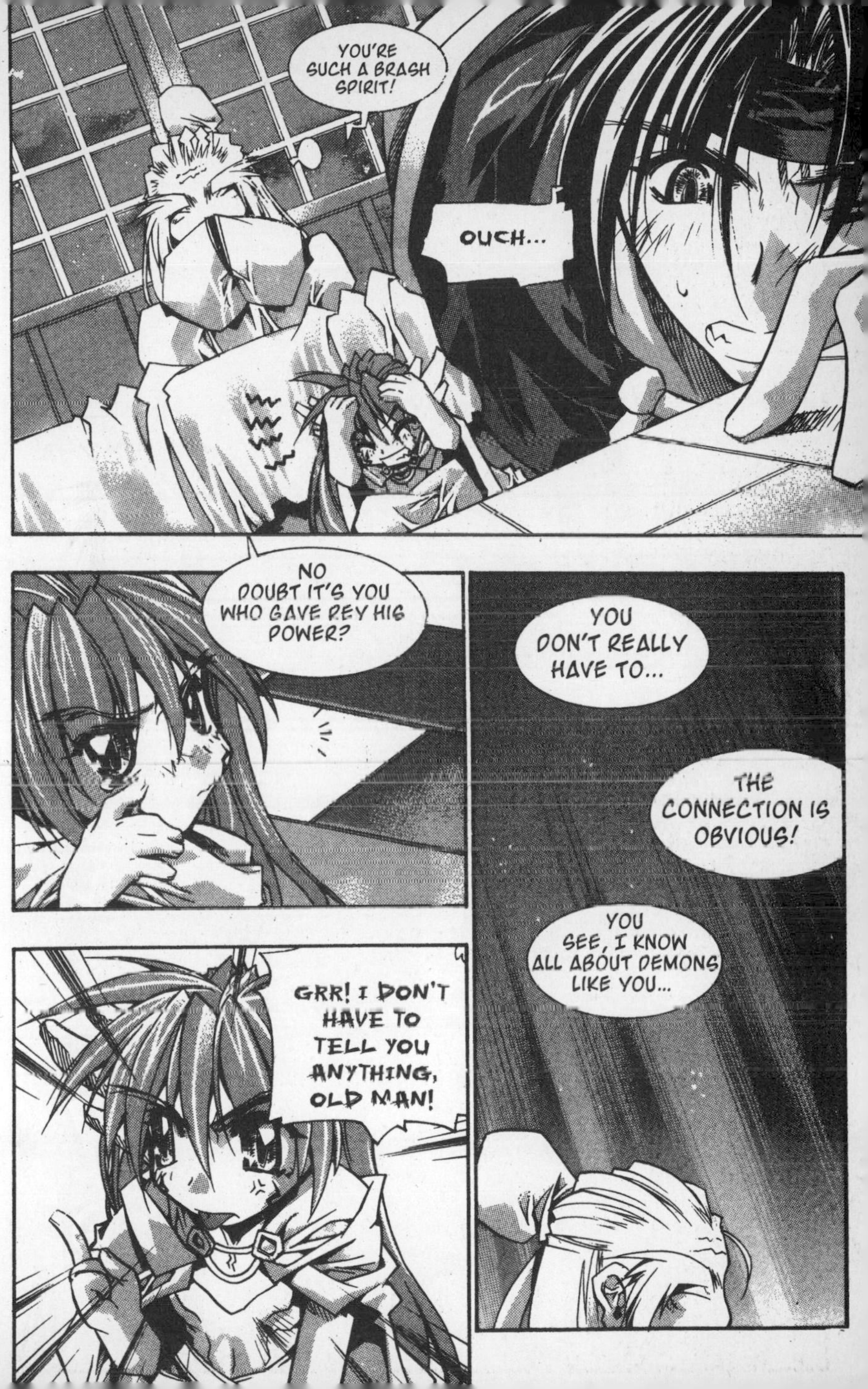
YOU'RE SUCH A BRASH SPIRIT!
OUCH...
NO DOUBT IT'S YOU WHO GAVE REY HIS POWER?
GRR! I DON'T HAVE TO TELL YOU ANYTHING, OLD MAN!
YOU DON'T REALLY HAVE TO...
THE CONNECTION IS OBVIOUS!
YOU SEE, I KNOW ALL ABOUT DEMONS LIKE YOU...

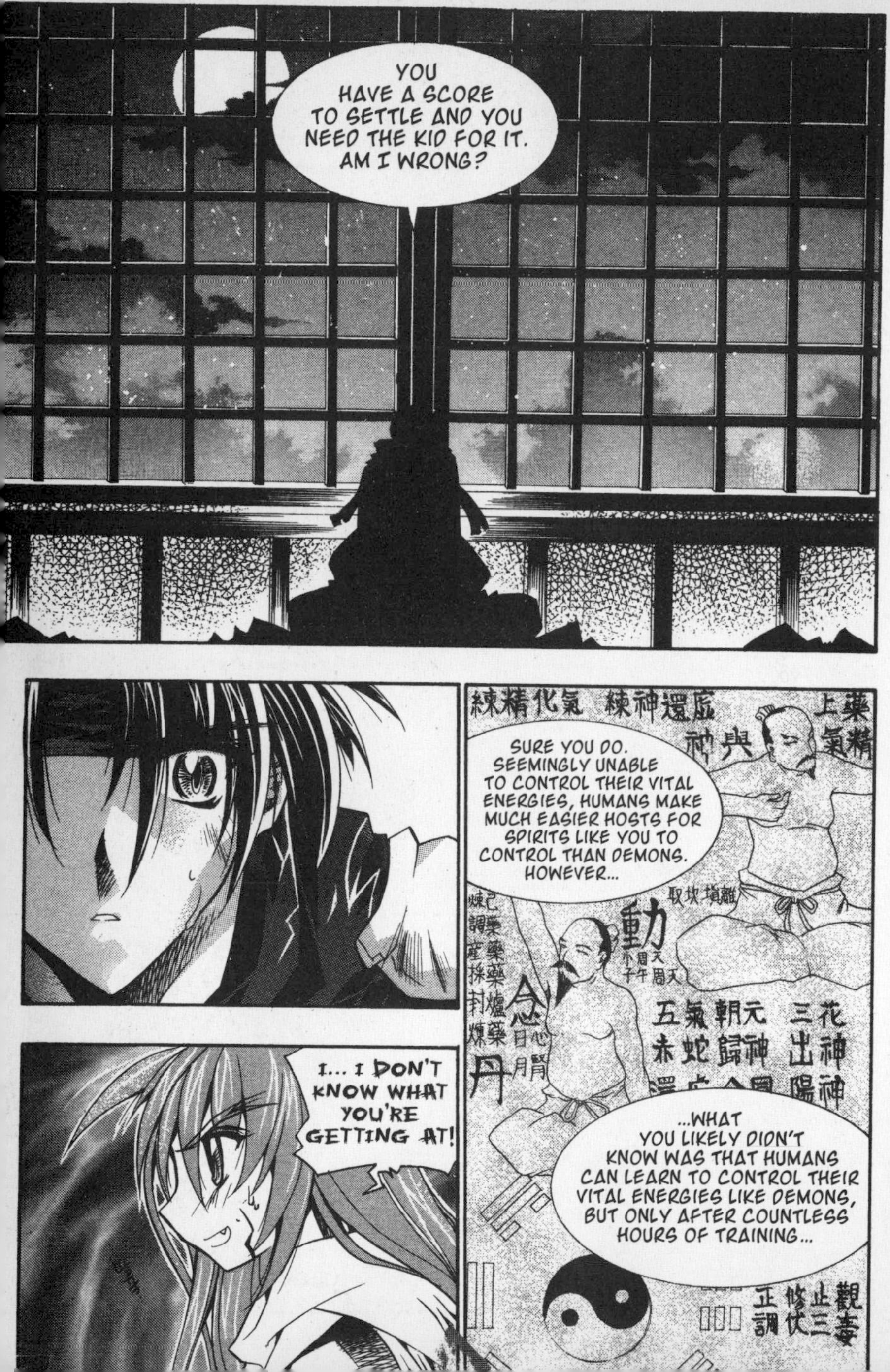
YOU HAVE A SCORE TO SETTLE AND YOU NEED THE KID FOR IT. AM I WRONG?
I... I DON'T KNOW WHAT YOU'RE GETTING AT!
SURE YOU DO. SEEMINGLY UNABLE TO CONTROL THEIR VITAL ENERGIES, HUMANS MAKE MUCH EASIER HOSTS FOR SPIRITS LIKE YOU TO CONTROL THAN DEMONS. HOWEVER...
...WHAT YOU LIKELY DIDN'T KNOW WAS THAT HUMANS CAN LEARN TO CONTROL THEIR VITAL ENERGIES LIKE DEMONS, BUT ONLY AFTER COUNTLESS HOURS OF TRAINING...

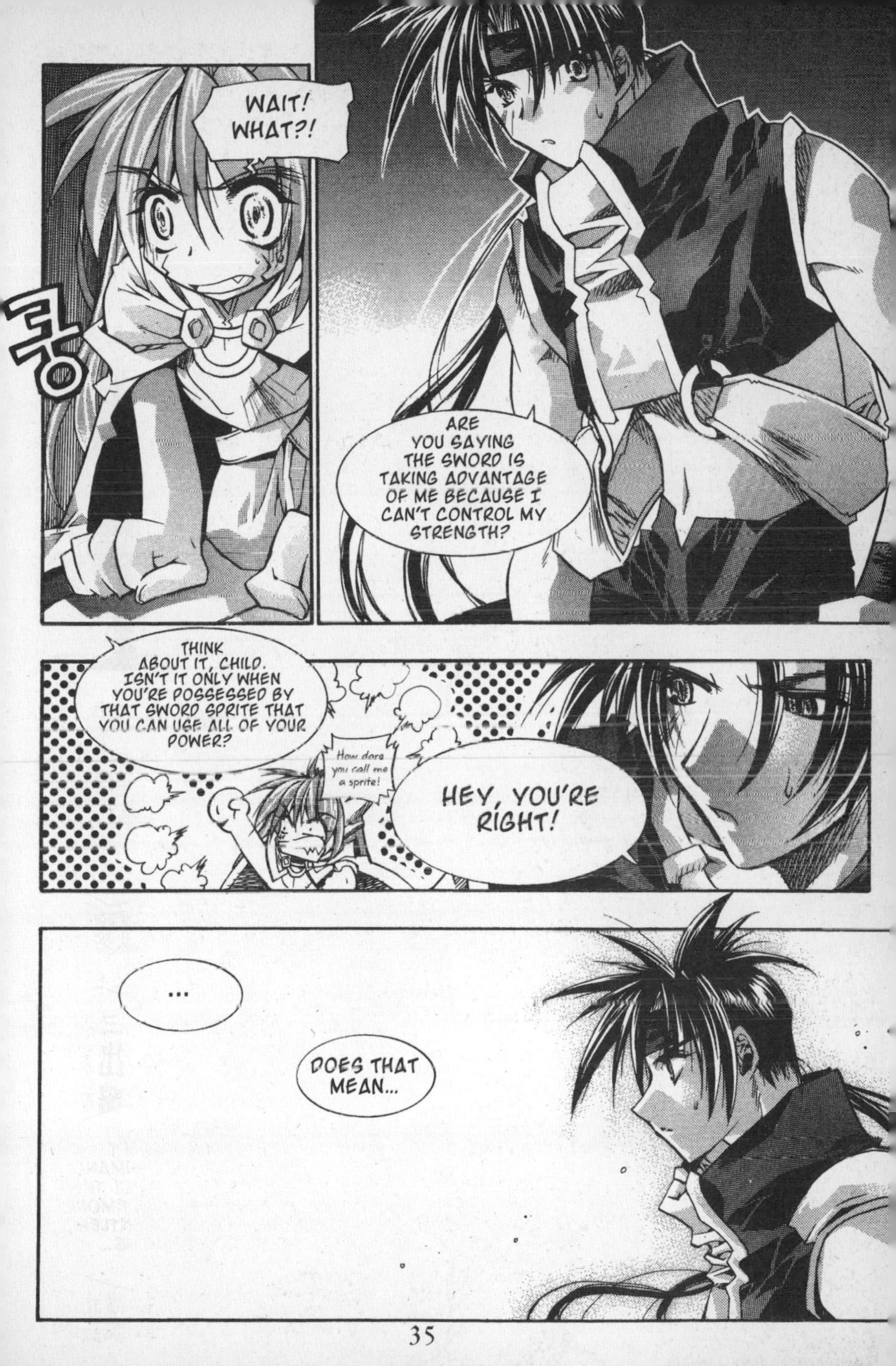
WAIT! WHAT?!
쿵
ARE YOU SAYING THE SWORD IS TAKING ADVANTAGE OF ME BECAUSE I CAN'T CONTROL MY STRENGTH?
THINK ABOUT IT, CHILD. ISN'T IT ONLY WHEN YOU'RE POSSESSED BY THAT SWORD SPRITE THAT YOU CAN USE ALL OF YOUR POWER?
How dare you call me a sprite!
HEY, YOU'RE RIGHT!
...
DOES THAT MEAN...

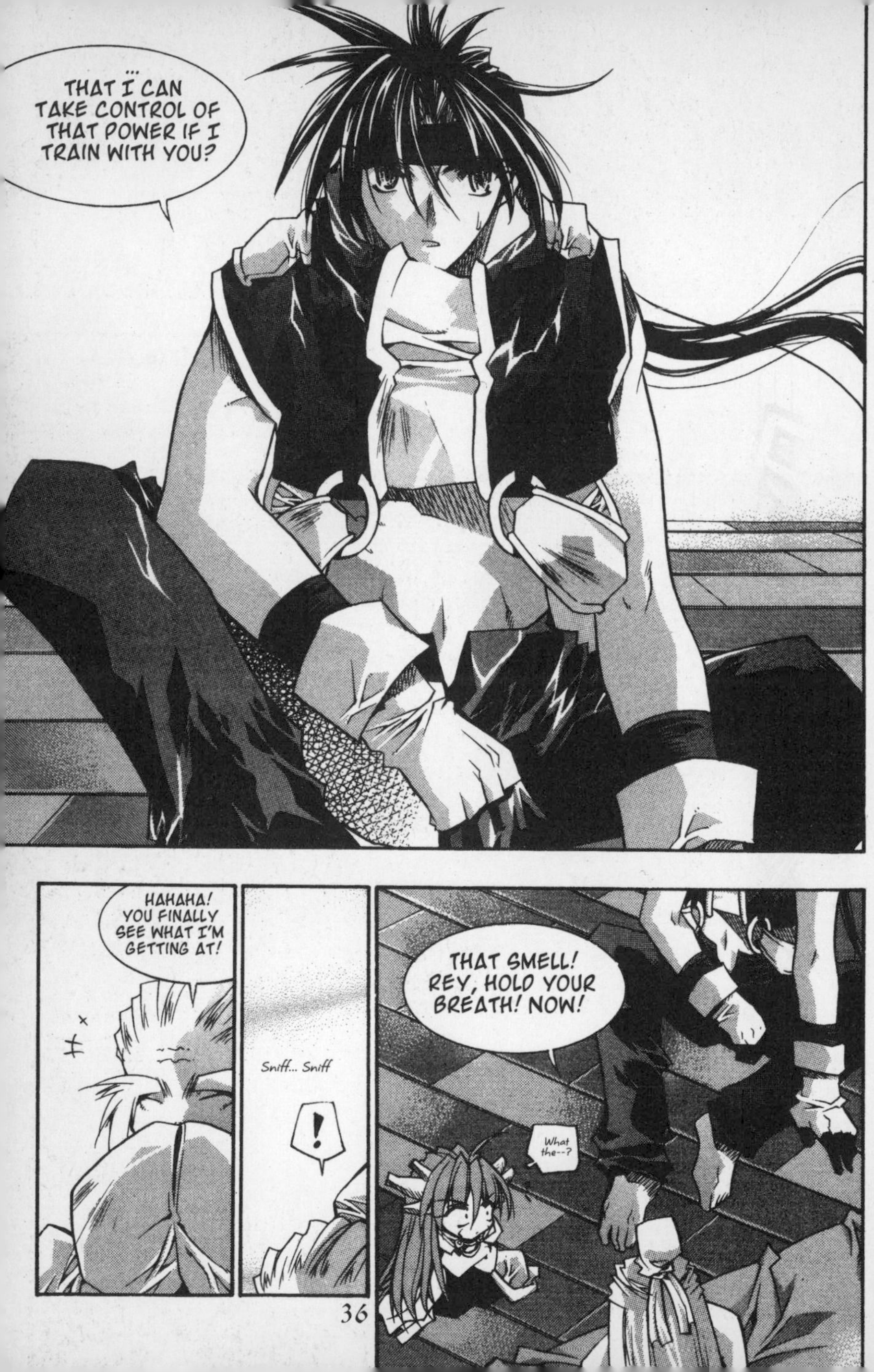
...THAT I CAN TAKE CONTROL OF THAT POWER IF I TRAIN WITH YOU?
HAHAHA! YOU FINALLY SEE WHAT I'M GETTING AT!
Sniff... Sniff
THAT SMELL! REY, HOLD YOUR BREATH! NOW!
What the--?

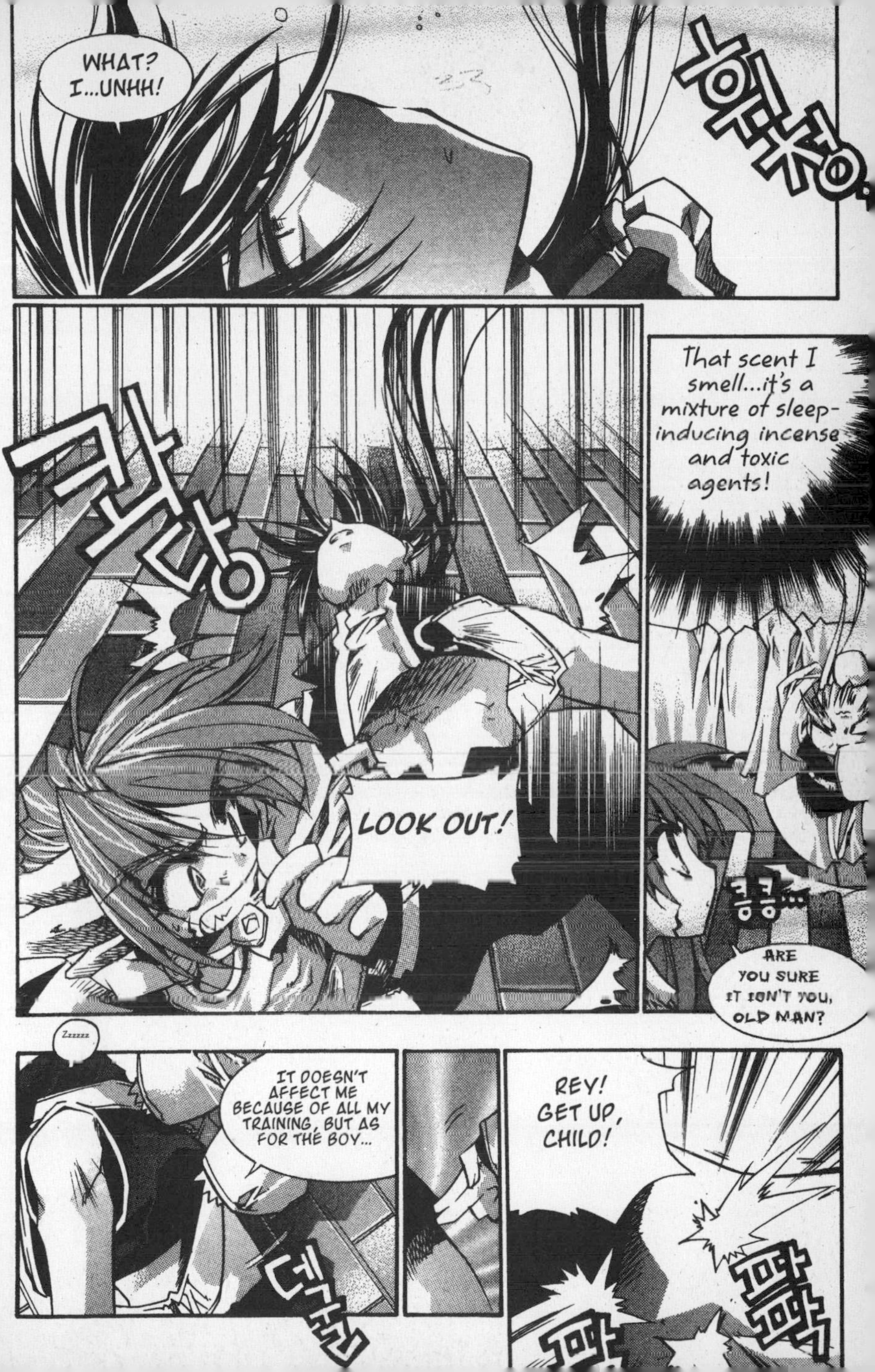
WHAT? I...UNHH!
LOOK OUT!
That scent I smell...it's a mixture of sleep-inducing incense and toxic agents!
ARE YOU SURE IT ISN'T YOU, OLD MAN?
Zzzzzz
IT DOESN'T AFFECT ME BECAUSE OF ALL MY TRAINING, BUT AS FOR THE BOY...
REY! GET UP, CHILD!

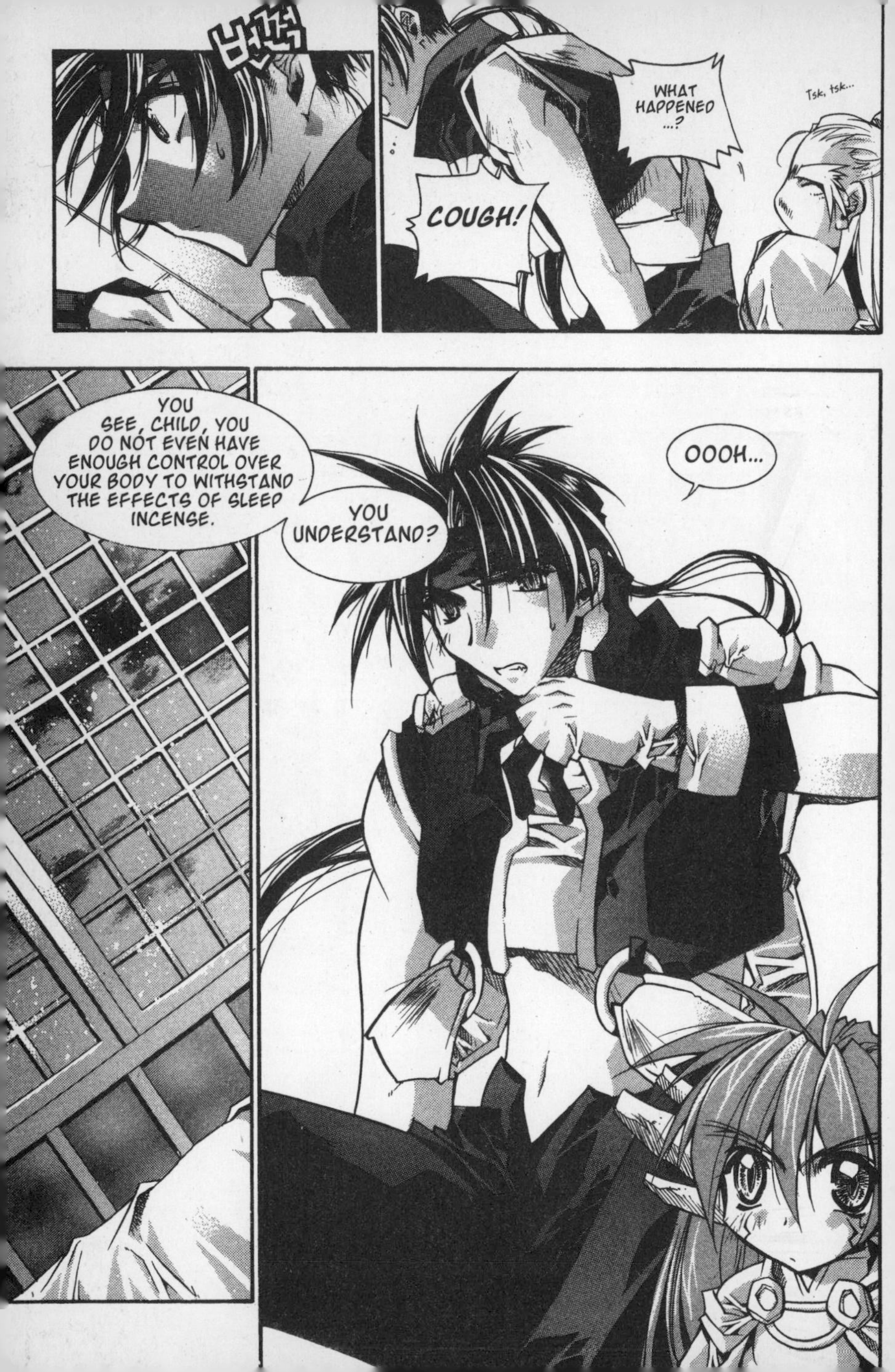
WHAT HAPPENED ...?
COUGH!
Tsk, tsk...
YOU SEE, CHILD, YOU DO NOT EVEN HAVE ENOUGH CONTROL OVER YOUR BODY TO WITHSTAND THE EFFECTS OF SLEEP INCENSE.
YOU UNDERSTAND?
OOOH...

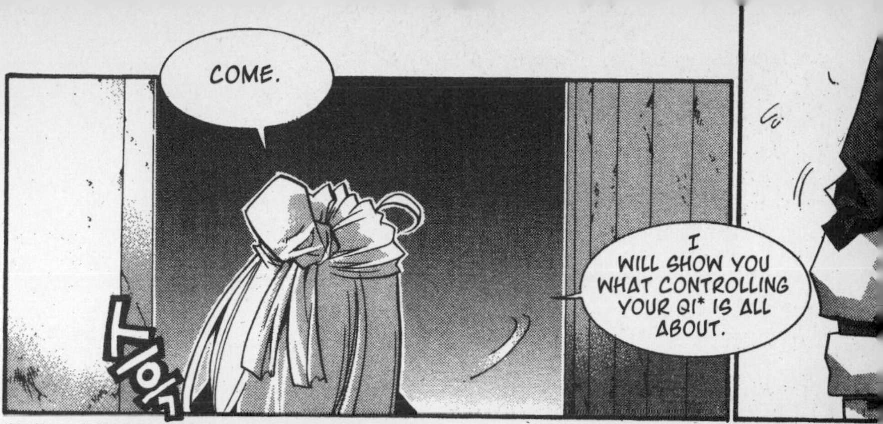
COME.
I WILL SHOW YOU WHAT CONTROLLING YOUR QI* IS ALL ABOUT.

*EDITOR'S NOTE: In Chinese philosophy, "qi" is an essence, a vital life force that can be harnessed for spiritual power and longevity.

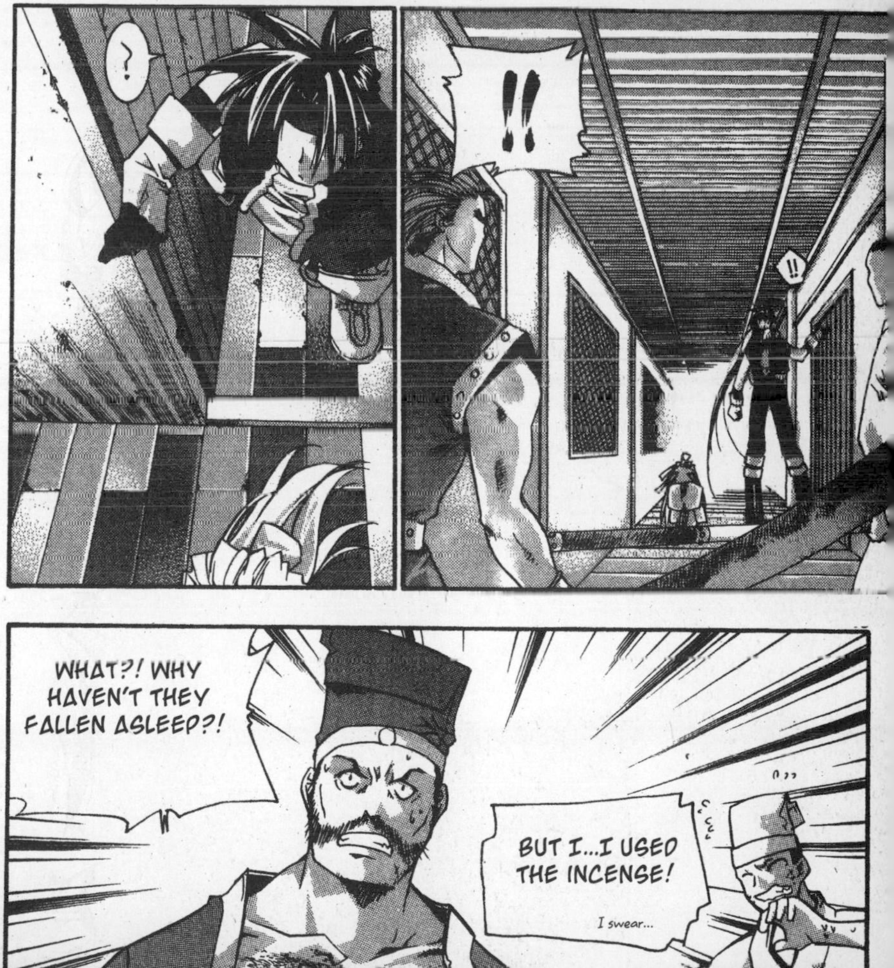
!!
!!
?
WHAT?! WHY HAVEN'T THEY FALLEN ASLEEP?!
BUT I...I USED THE INCENSE!
I swear...

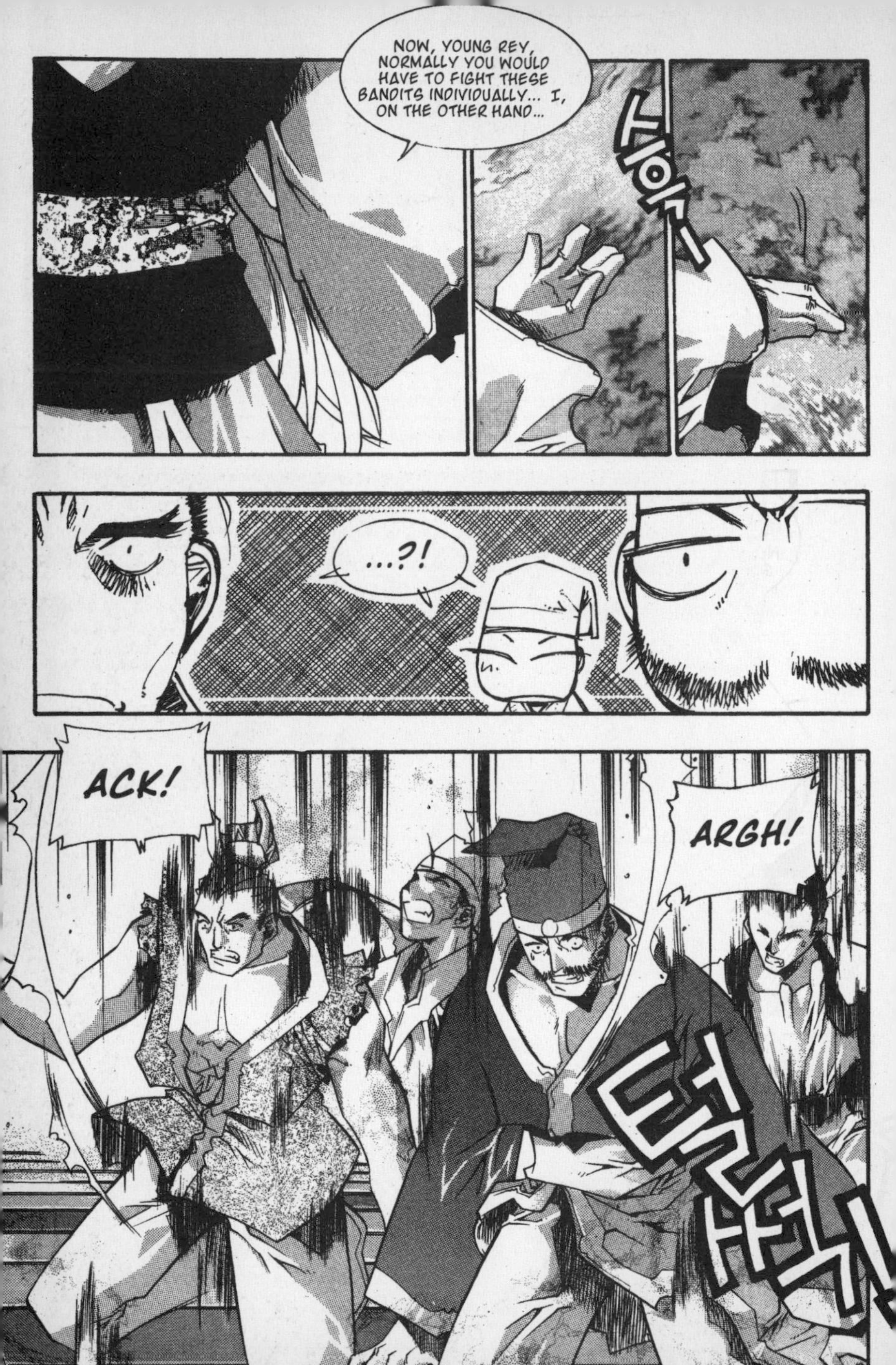
NOW, YOUNG REY, NORMALLY YOU WOULD HAVE TO FIGHT THESE BANDITS INDIVIDUALLY... I, ON THE OTHER HAND...
...?!
ARGH!
ACK!

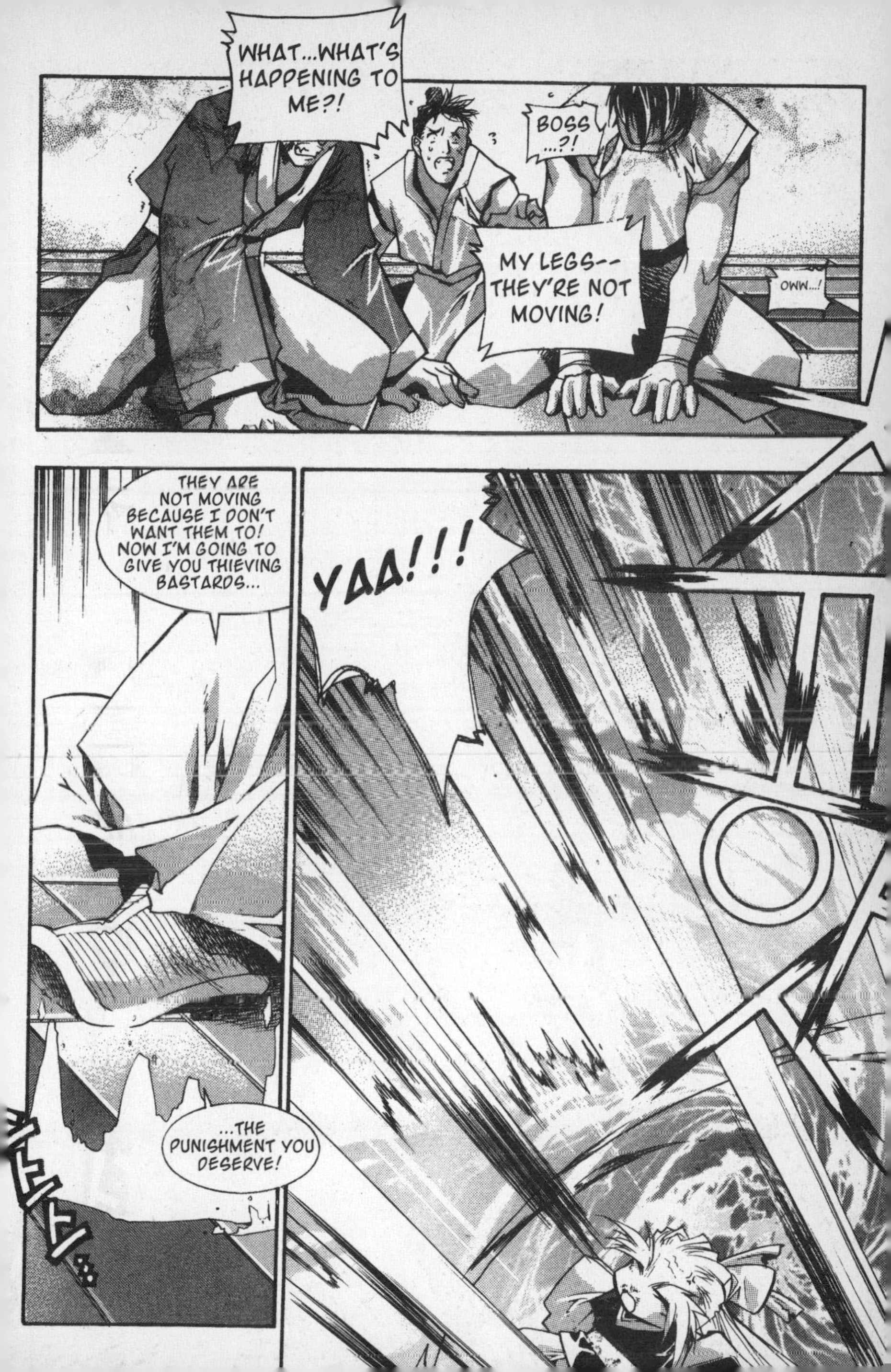
WHAT...WHAT'S HAPPENING TO ME?!
BOSS ...?!
MY LEGS--THEY'RE NOT MOVING!
OWW...!
THEY ARE NOT MOVING BECAUSE I DON'T WANT THEM TO! NOW I'M GOING TO GIVE YOU THIEVING BASTARDS...
...THE PUNISHMENT YOU DESERVE!
YAA!!!

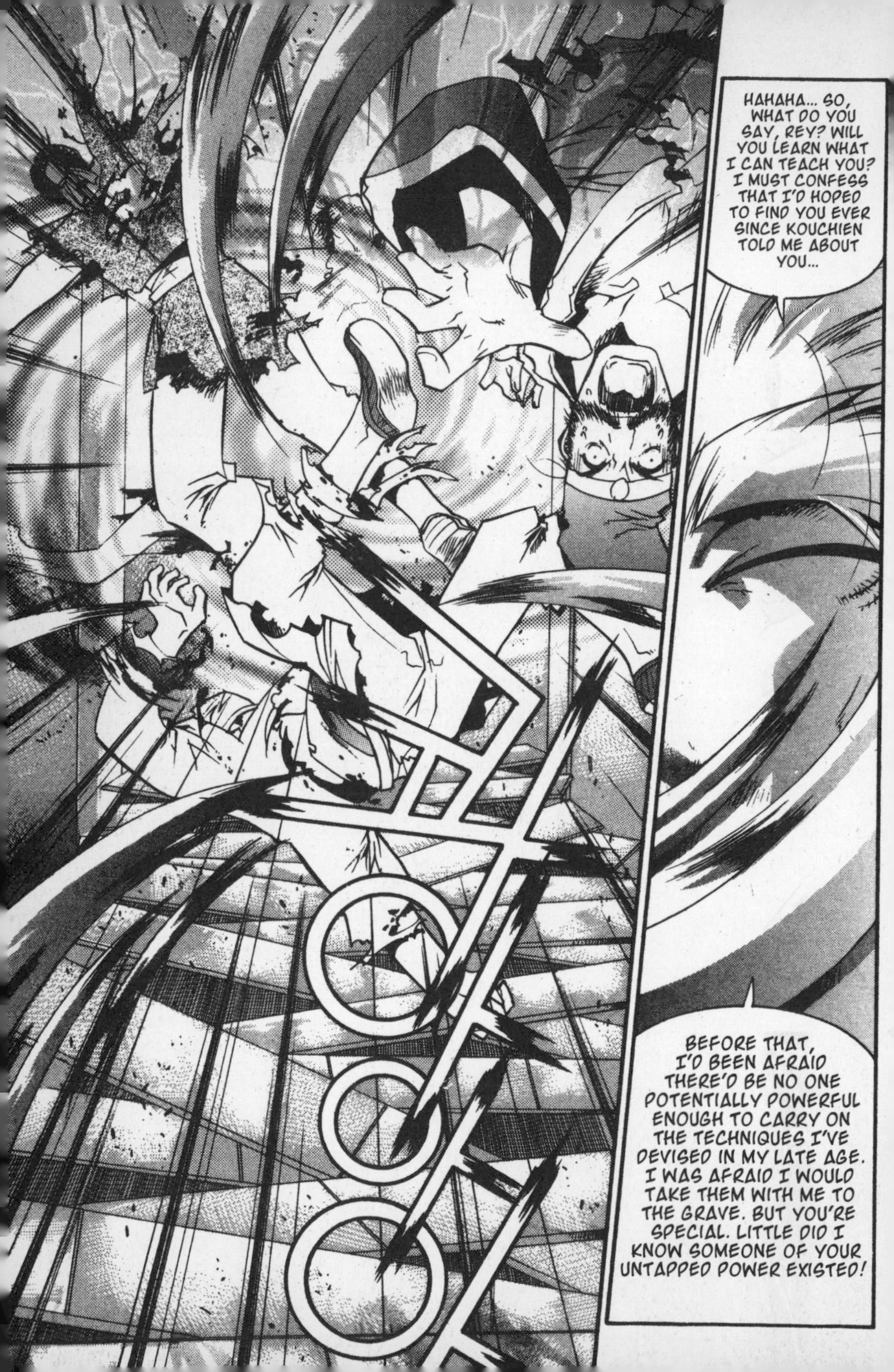
HAHAHA... SO, WHAT DO YOU SAY, REY? WILL YOU LEARN WHAT I CAN TEACH YOU? I MUST CONFESS THAT I'D HOPED TO FIND YOU EVER SINCE KOUCHIEN TOLD ME ABOUT YOU...
BEFORE THAT, I'D BEEN AFRAID THERE'D BE NO ONE POTENTIALLY POWERFUL ENOUGH TO CARRY ON THE TECHNIQUES I'VE DEVISED IN MY LATE AGE. I WAS AFRAID I WOULD TAKE THEM WITH ME TO THE GRAVE. BUT YOU'RE SPECIAL. LITTLE DID I KNOW SOMEONE OF YOUR UNTAPPED POWER EXISTED!

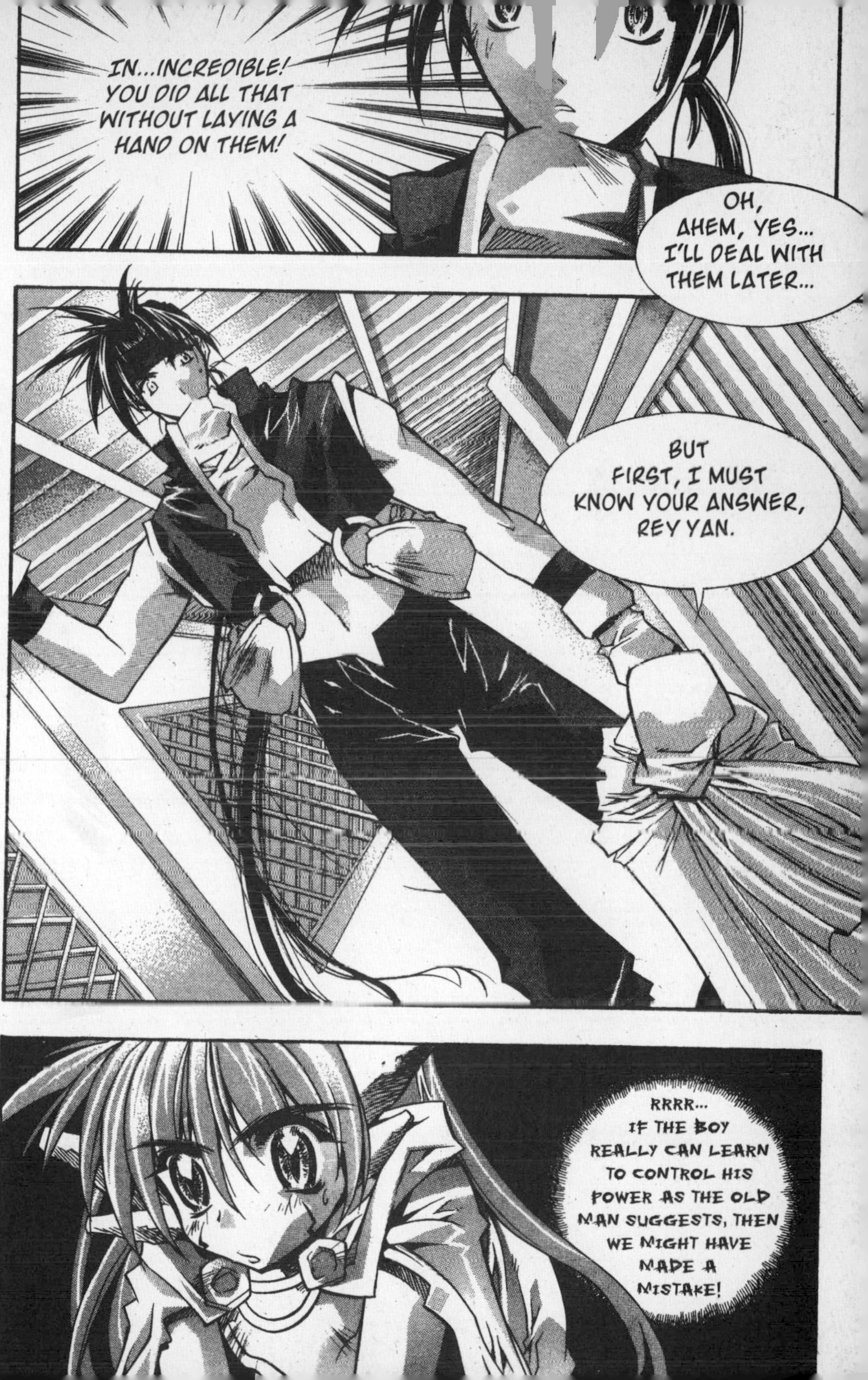
IN...INCREDIBLE! YOU DID ALL THAT WITHOUT LAYING A HAND ON THEM!
OH, AHEM, YES... I'LL DEAL WITH THEM LATER...
BUT FIRST, I MUST KNOW YOUR ANSWER, REY YAN.
RRRR... IF THE BOY REALLY CAN LEARN TO CONTROL HIS POWER AS THE OLD MAN SUGGESTS, THEN WE MIGHT HAVE MADE A MISTAKE!

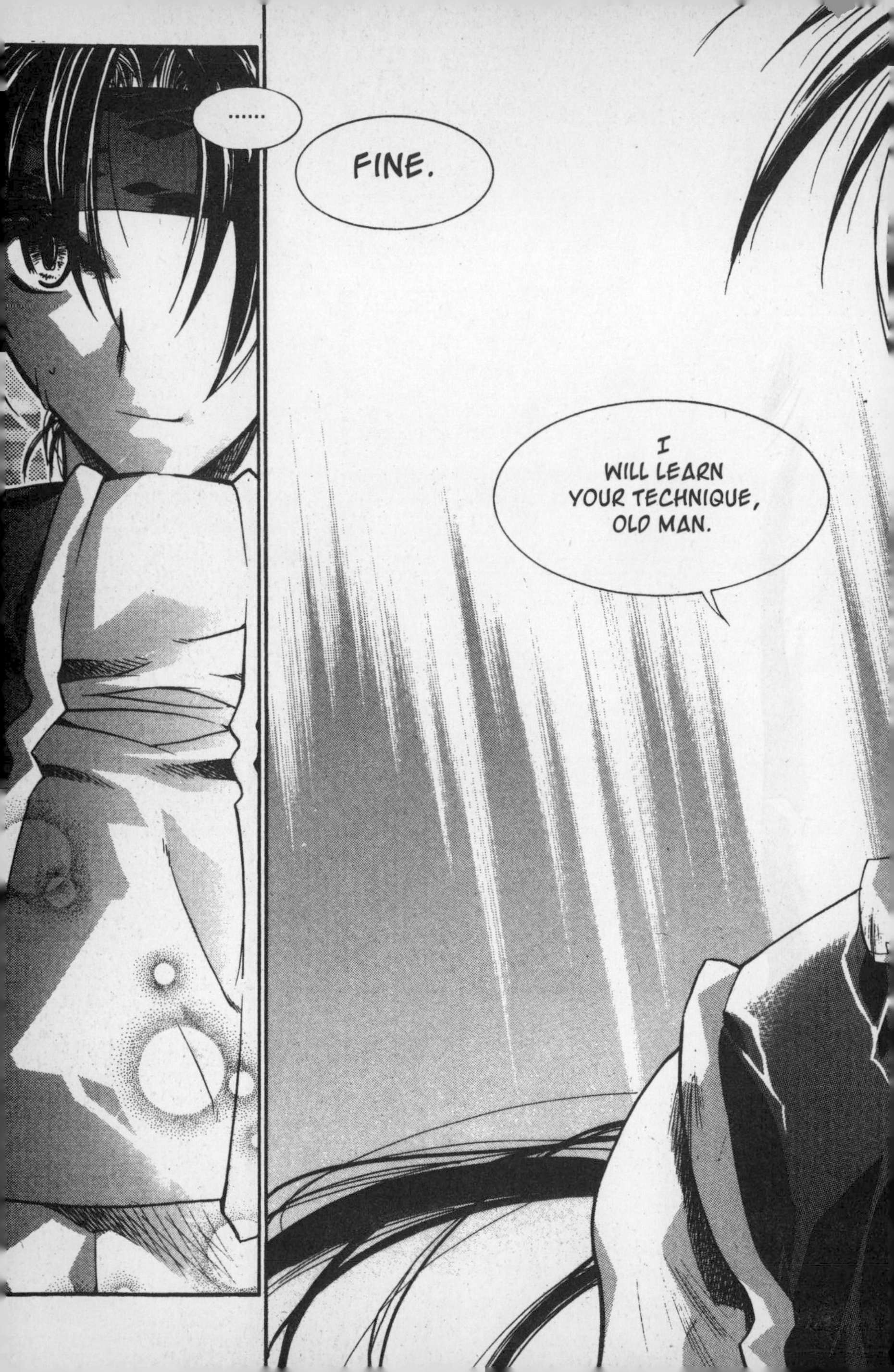
......
FINE.
I WILL LEARN YOUR TECHNIQUE, OLD MAN.

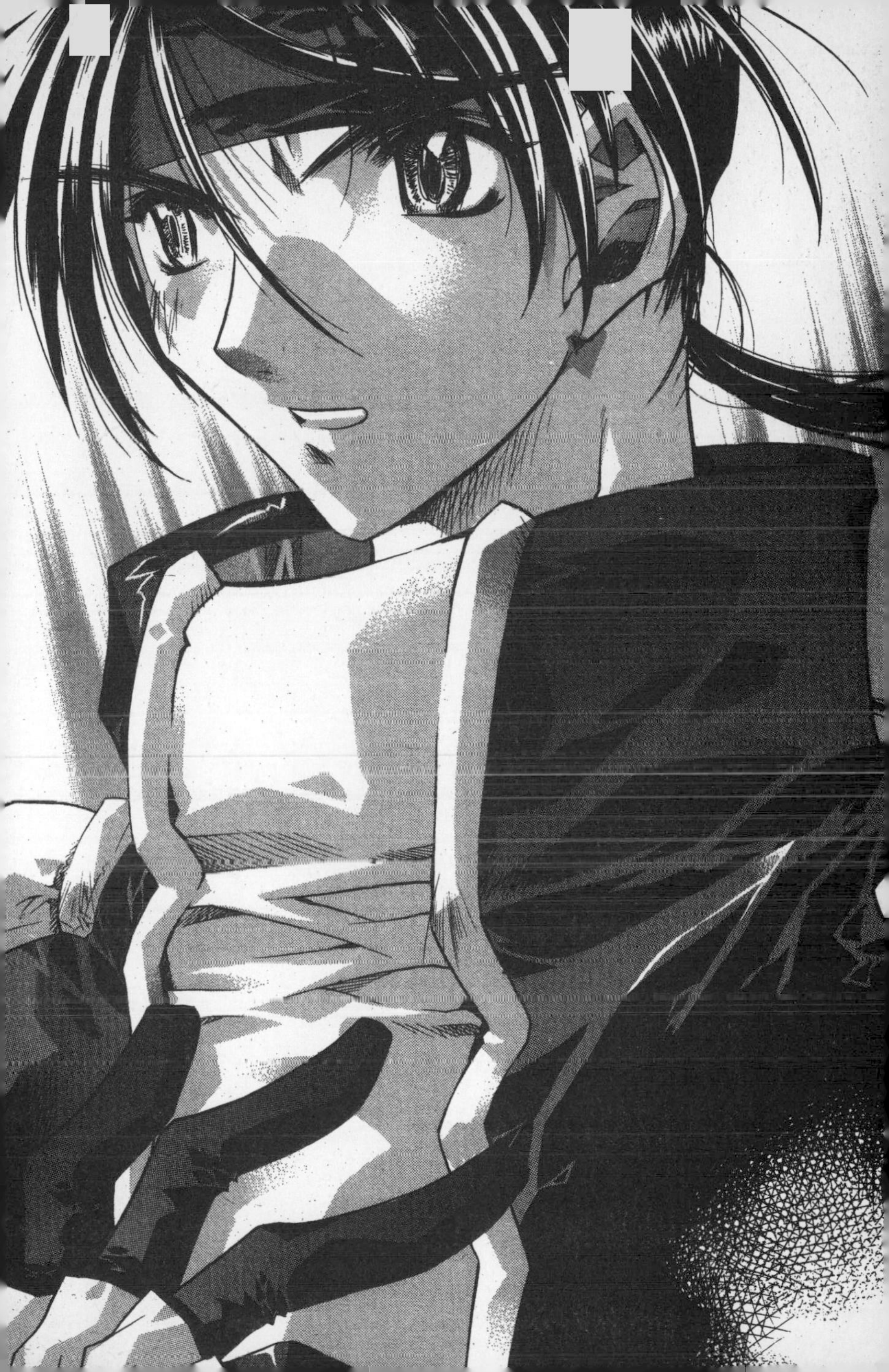

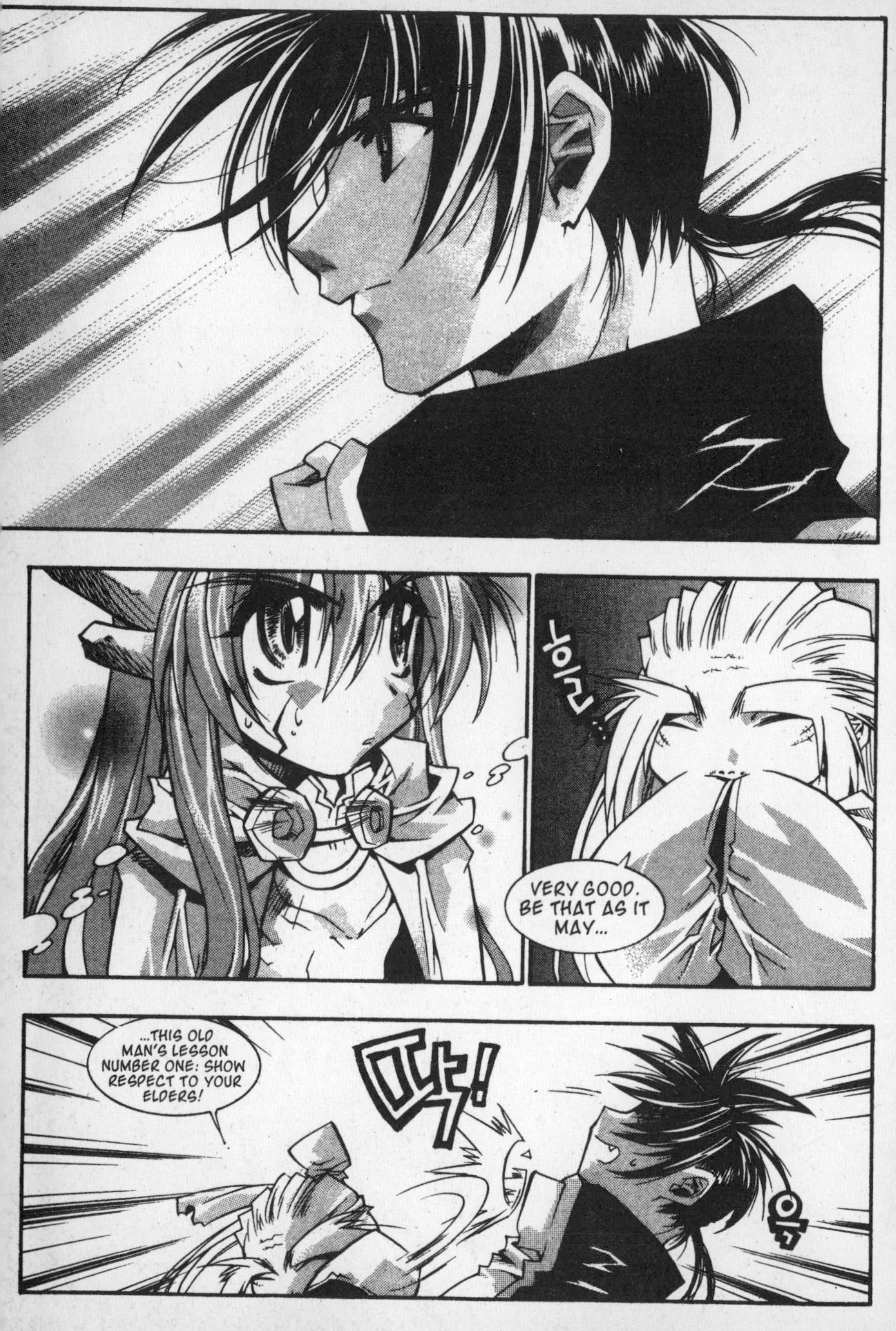
VERY GOOD. BE THAT AS IT MAY...
...THIS OLD MAN'S LESSON NUMBER ONE: SHOW RESPECT TO YOUR ELDERS!

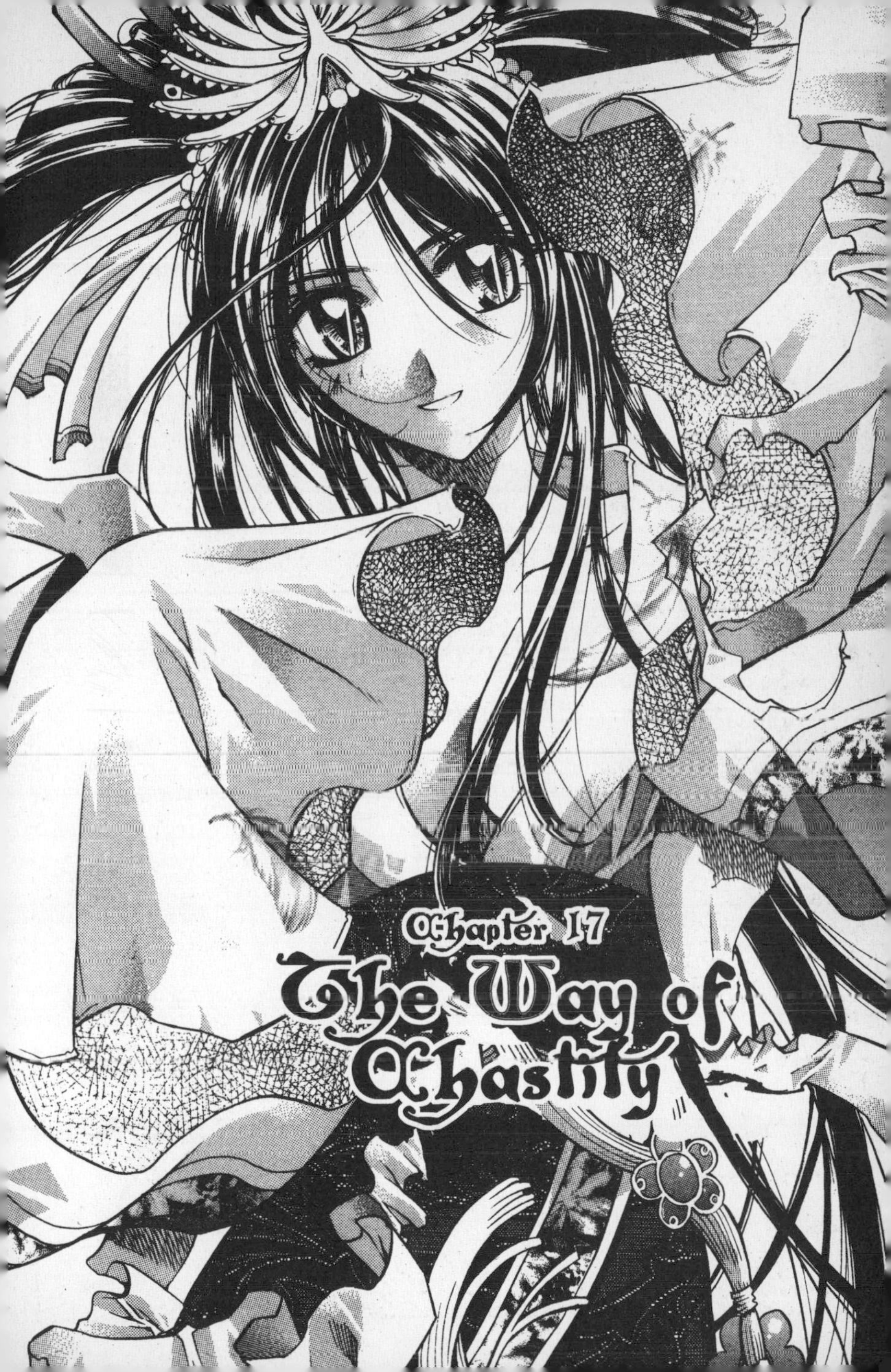
Chapter 17
The Way of Chastity

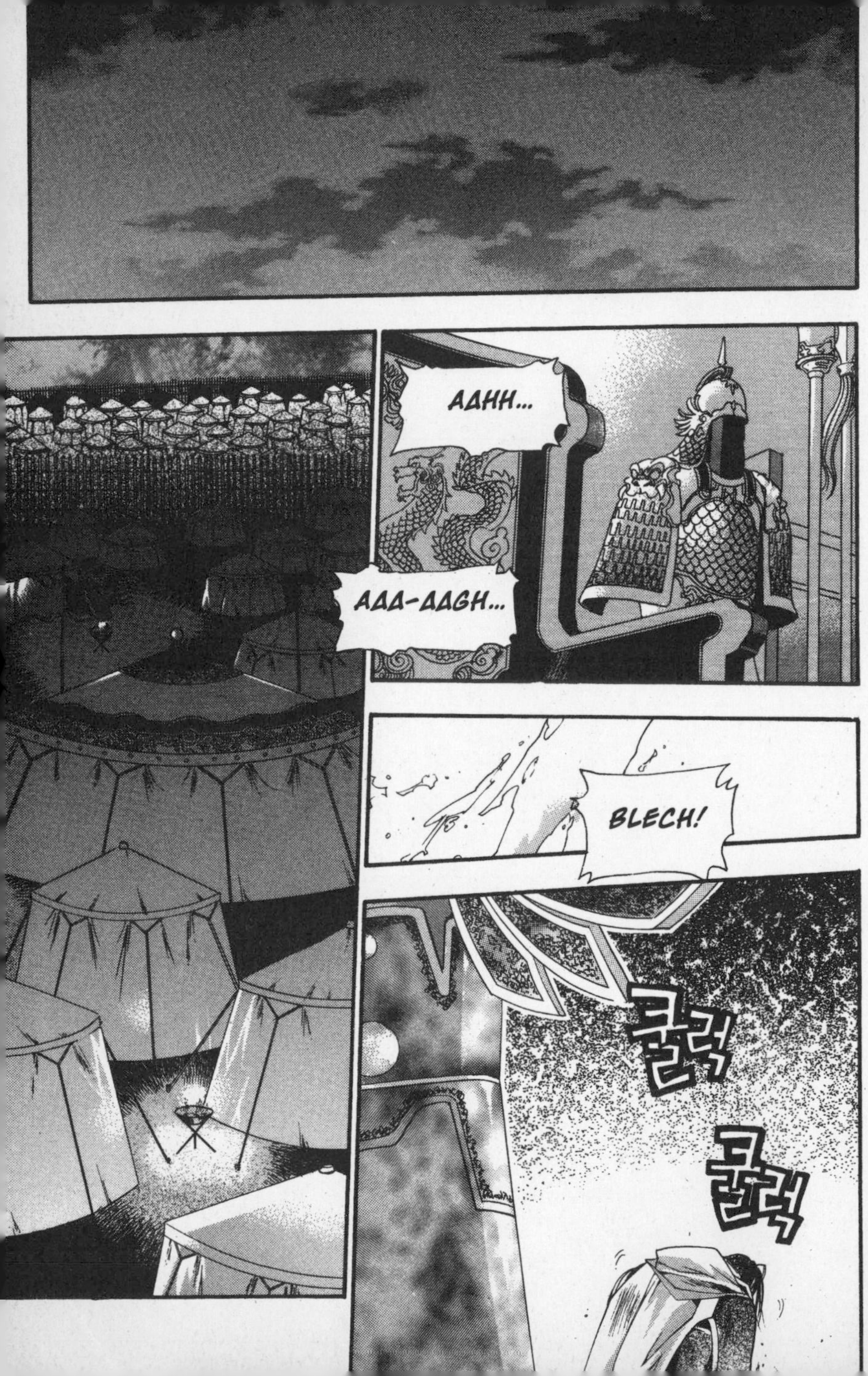
AAHH...
AAA-AAGH...
BLECH!
쿨럭
쿨럭

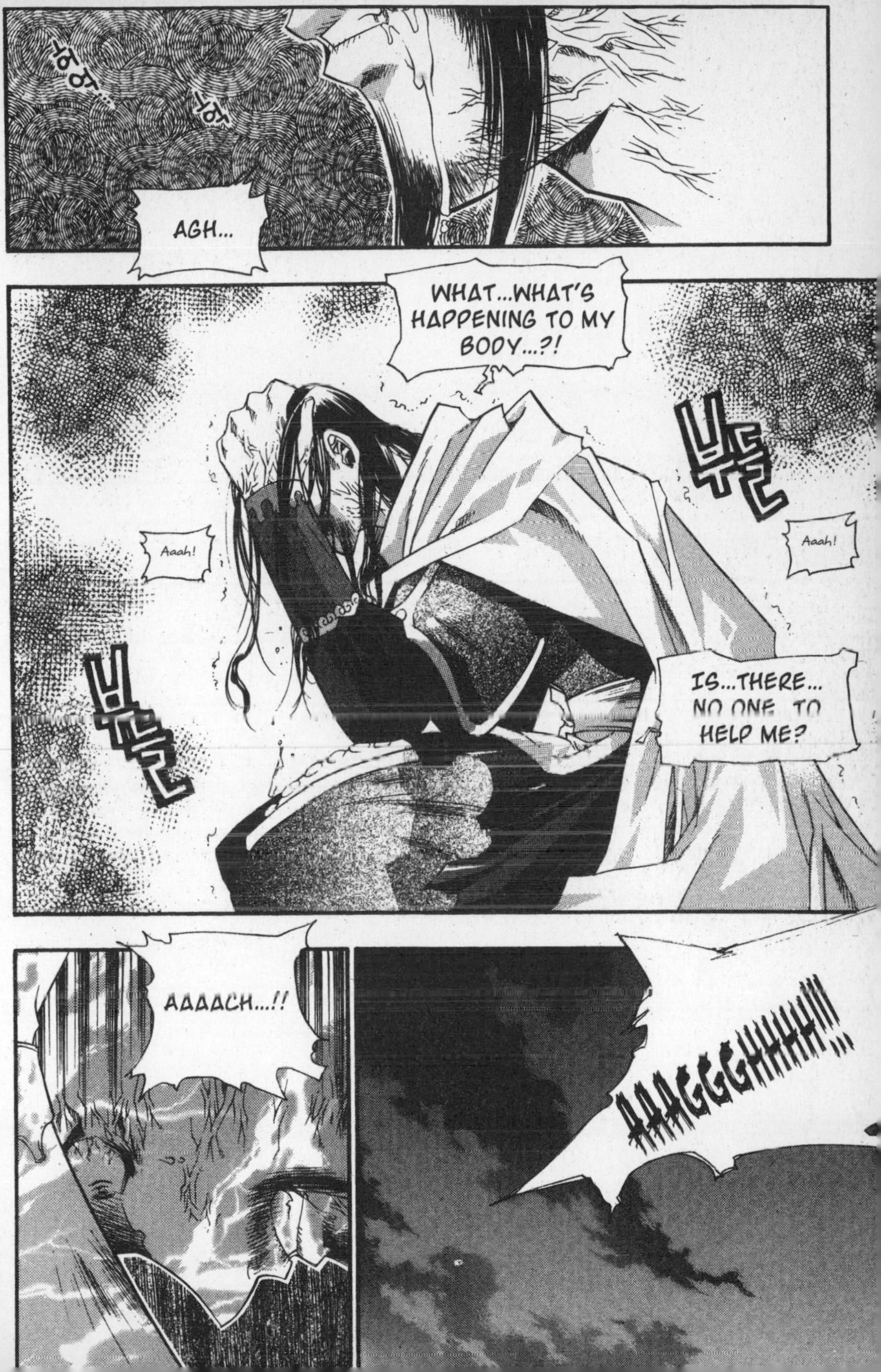
AGH...
WHAT...WHAT'S HAPPENING TO MY BODY...?!
Aaah!
Aaah!
IS...THERE... NO ONE TO HELP ME?
AAAACH...!!
AAAGGHHHH!!!

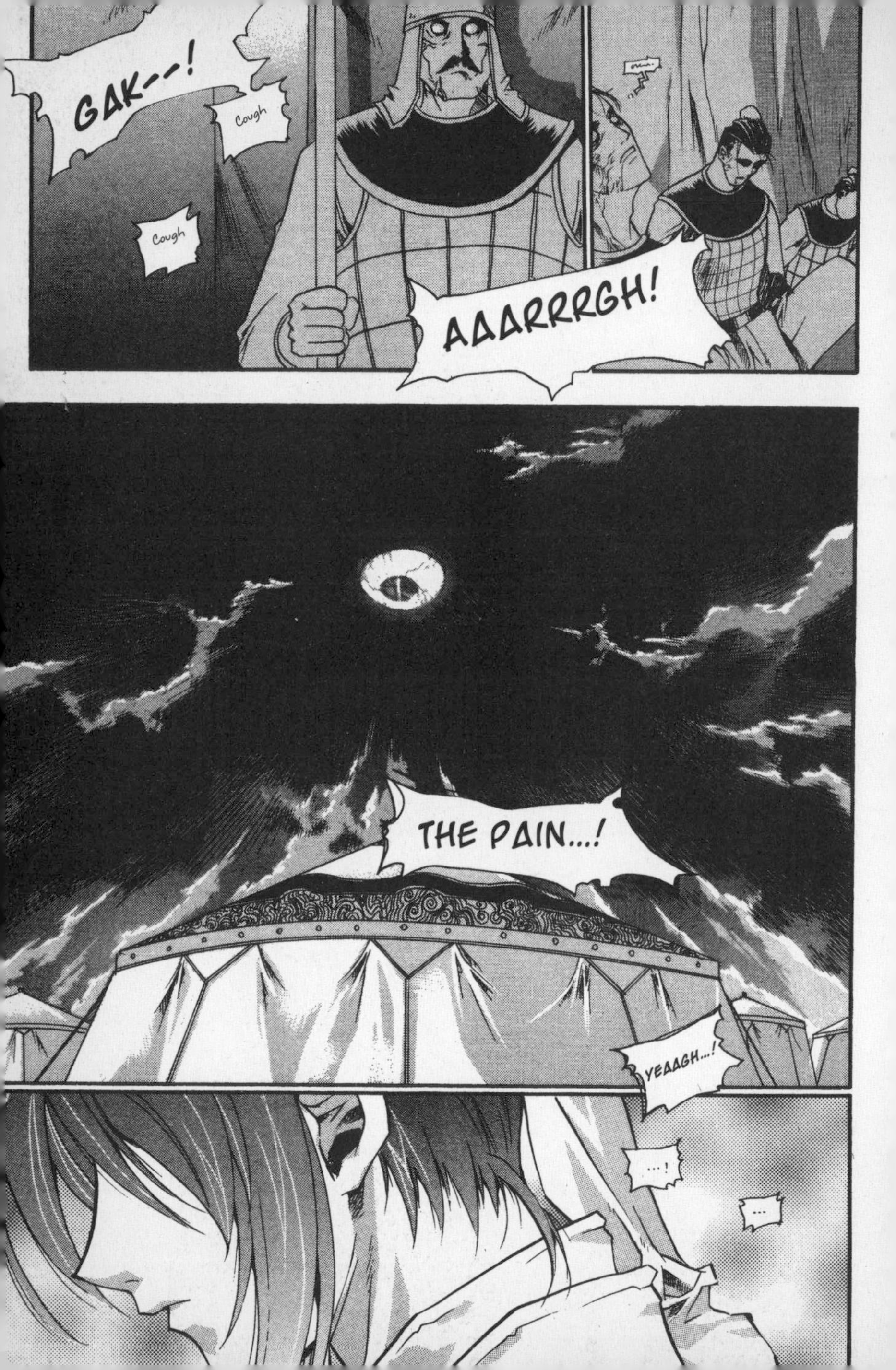
GAK--!
Cough
Cough
AAARRRGH!
THE PAIN...!
YEAAGH...!
...!
...

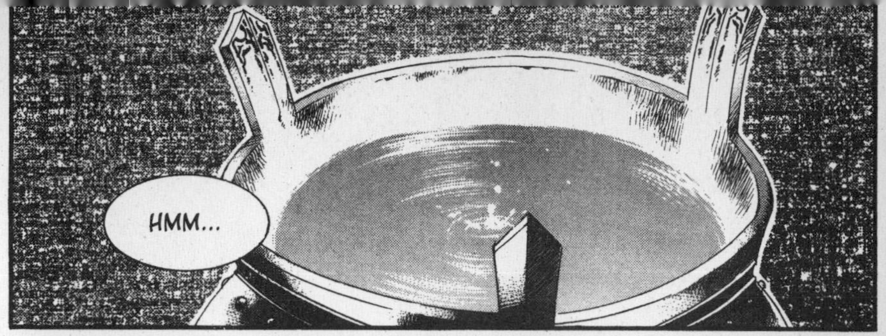
HMM...

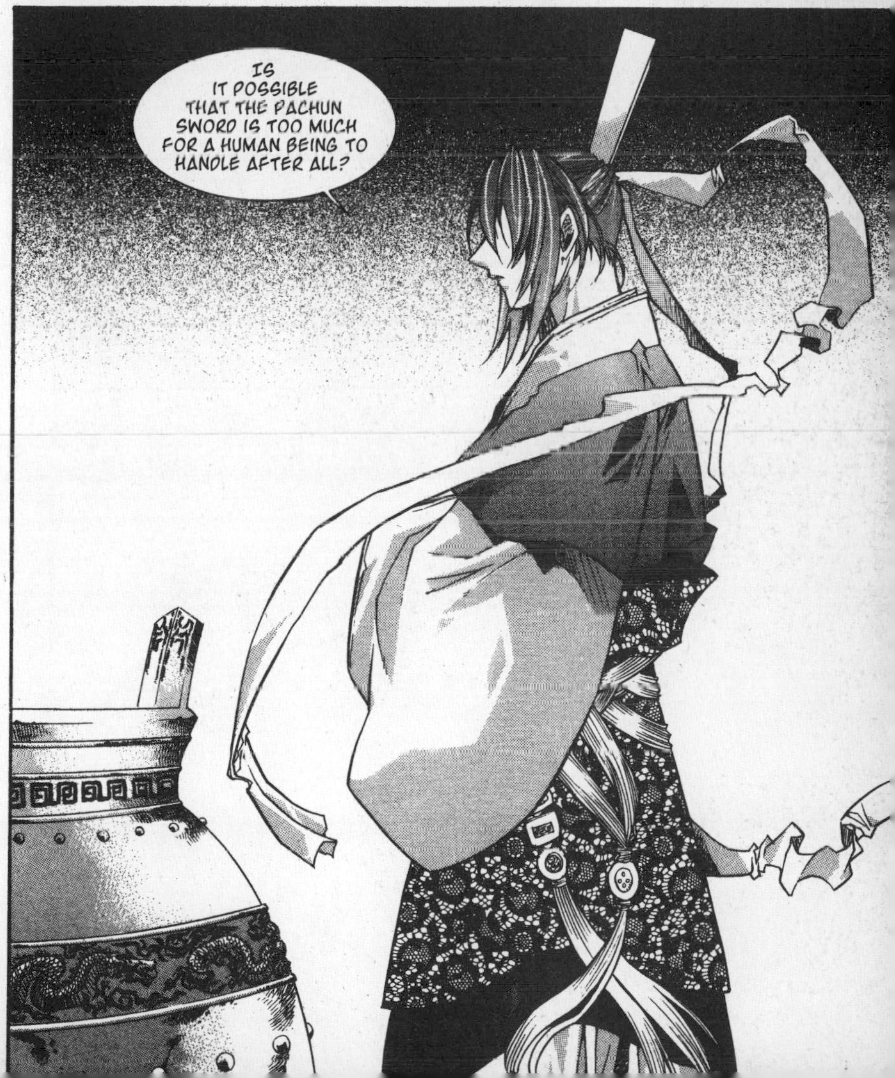
IS IT POSSIBLE THAT THE PACHUN SWORD IS TOO MUCH FOR A HUMAN BEING TO HANDLE AFTER ALL?

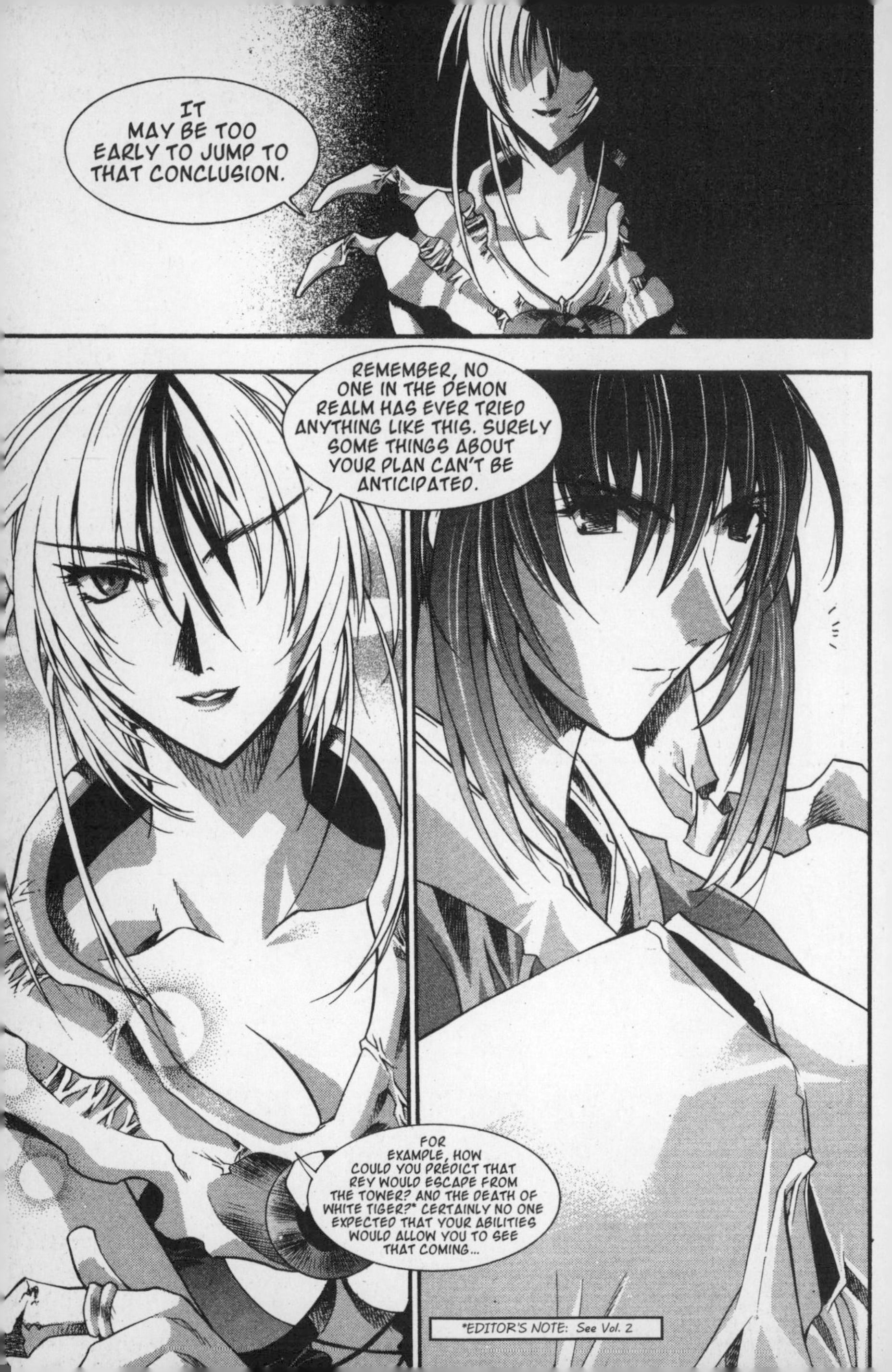
IT MAY BE TOO EARLY TO JUMP TO THAT CONCLUSION.
REMEMBER, NO ONE IN THE DEMON REALM HAS EVER TRIED ANYTHING LIKE THIS. SURELY SOME THINGS ABOUT YOUR PLAN CAN'T BE ANTICIPATED.
FOR EXAMPLE, HOW COULD YOU PREDICT THAT REY WOULD ESCAPE FROM THE TOWER? AND THE DEATH OF WHITE TIGER?* CERTAINLY NO ONE EXPECTED THAT YOUR ABILITIES WOULD ALLOW YOU TO SEE THAT COMING...
*EDITOR'S NOTE: See Vol. 2

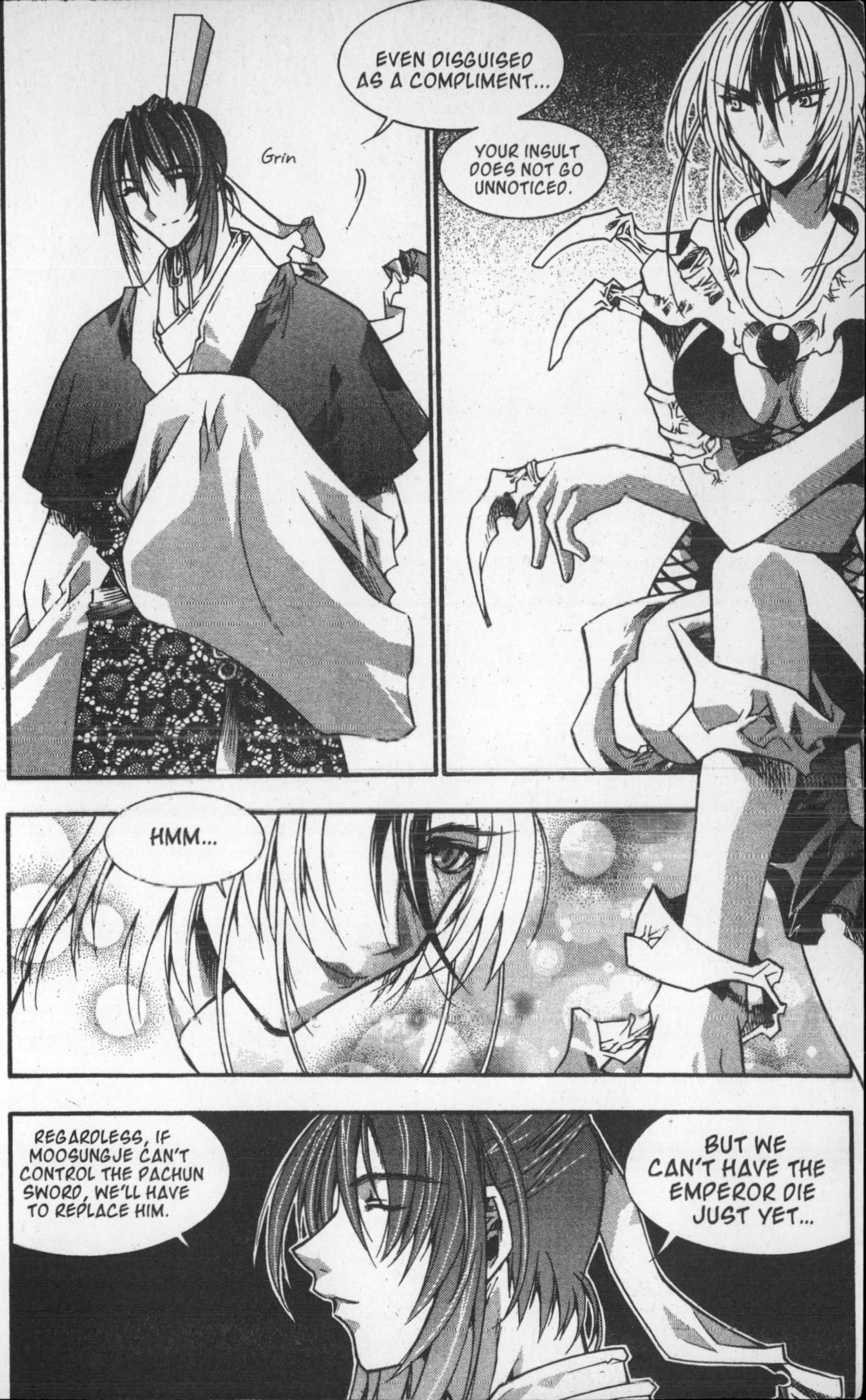
Grin
EVEN DISGUISED AS A COMPLIMENT...
YOUR INSULT DOES NOT GO UNNOTICED.
HMM...
REGARDLESS, IF MOOSUNGJE CAN'T CONTROL THE PACHUN SWORD, WE'LL HAVE TO REPLACE HIM.
BUT WE CAN'T HAVE THE EMPEROR DIE JUST YET...

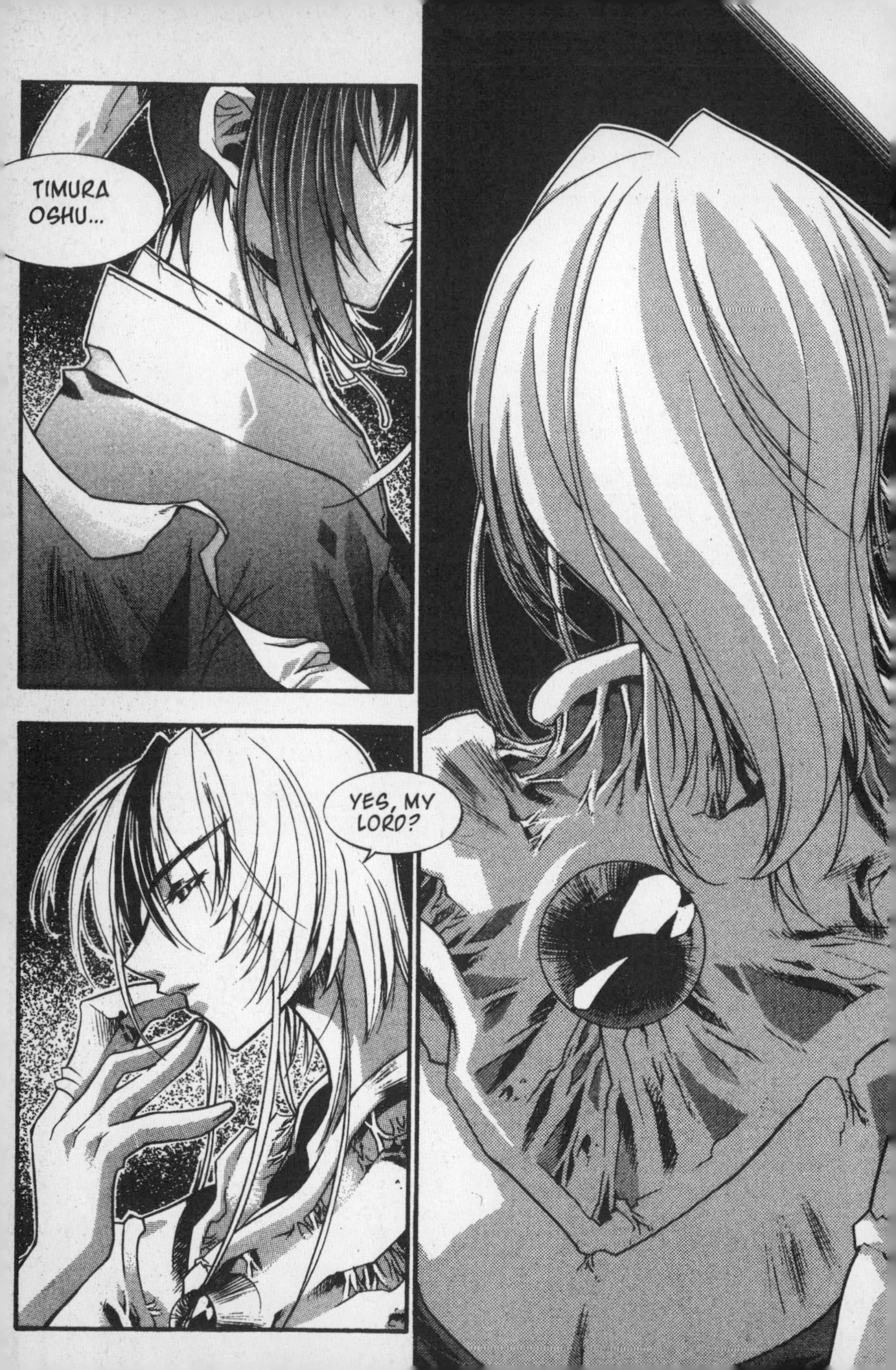
TIMURA OSHU...
YES, MY LORD?

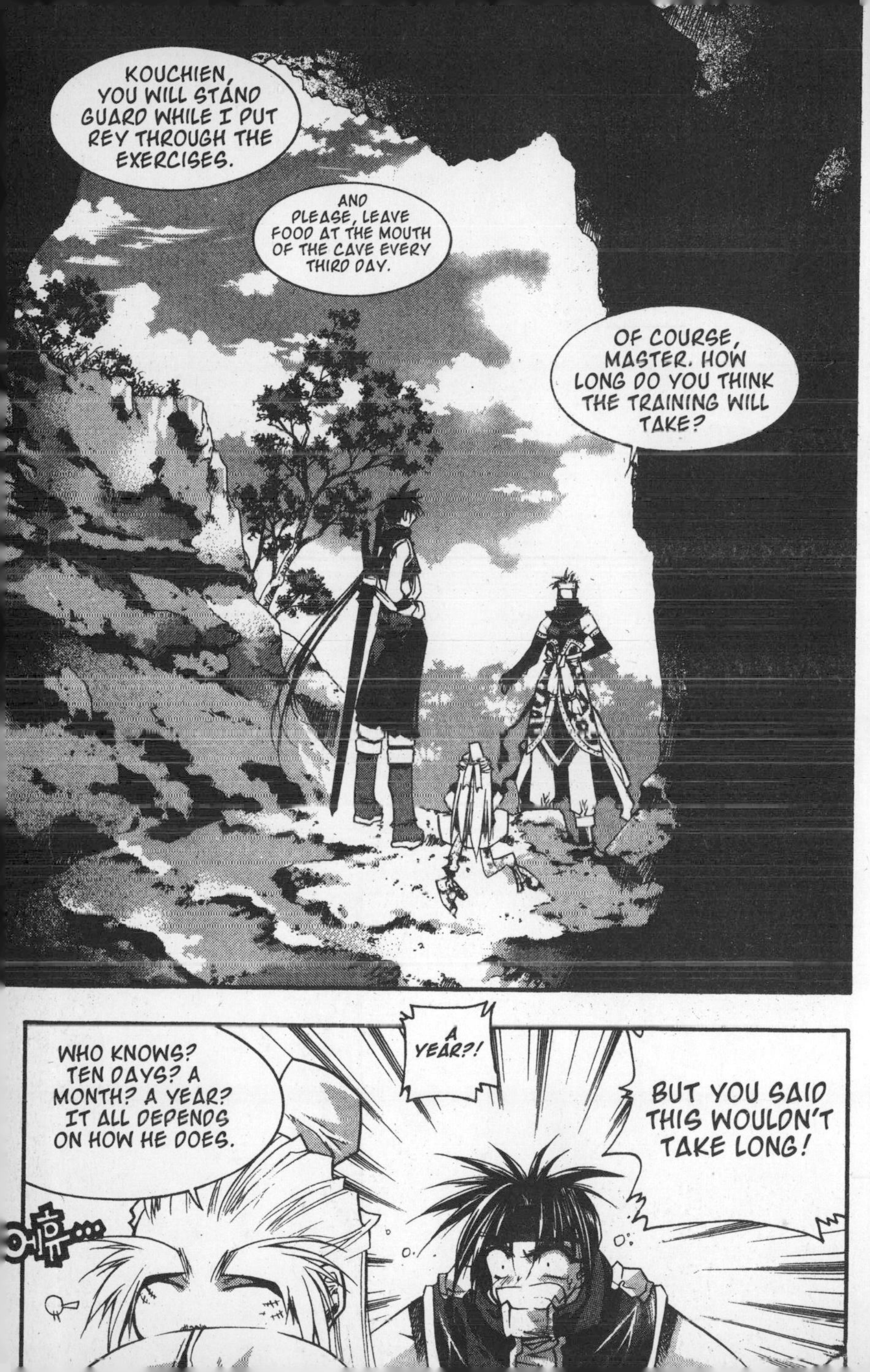
KOUCHIEN, YOU WILL STAND GUARD WHILE I PUT REY THROUGH THE EXERCISES.
AND PLEASE, LEAVE FOOD AT THE MOUTH OF THE CAVE EVERY THIRD DAY.
OF COURSE, MASTER. HOW LONG DO YOU THINK THE TRAINING WILL TAKE?
WHO KNOWS? TEN DAYS? A MONTH? A YEAR? IT ALL DEPENDS ON HOW HE DOES.
A YEAR?!
BUT YOU SAID THIS WOULDN'T TAKE LONG!

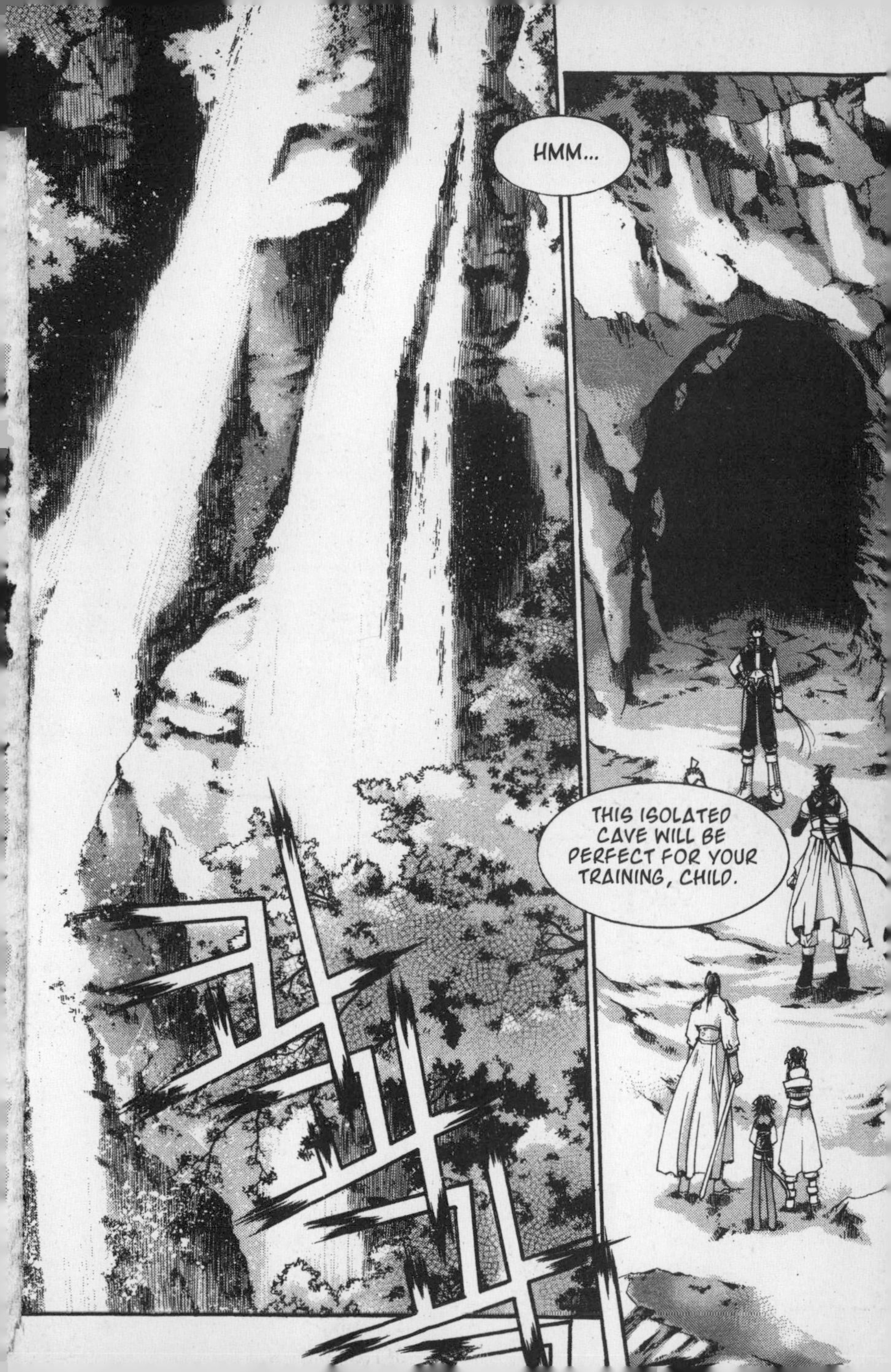
HMM...
THIS ISOLATED CAVE WILL BE PERFECT FOR YOUR TRAINING, CHILD.

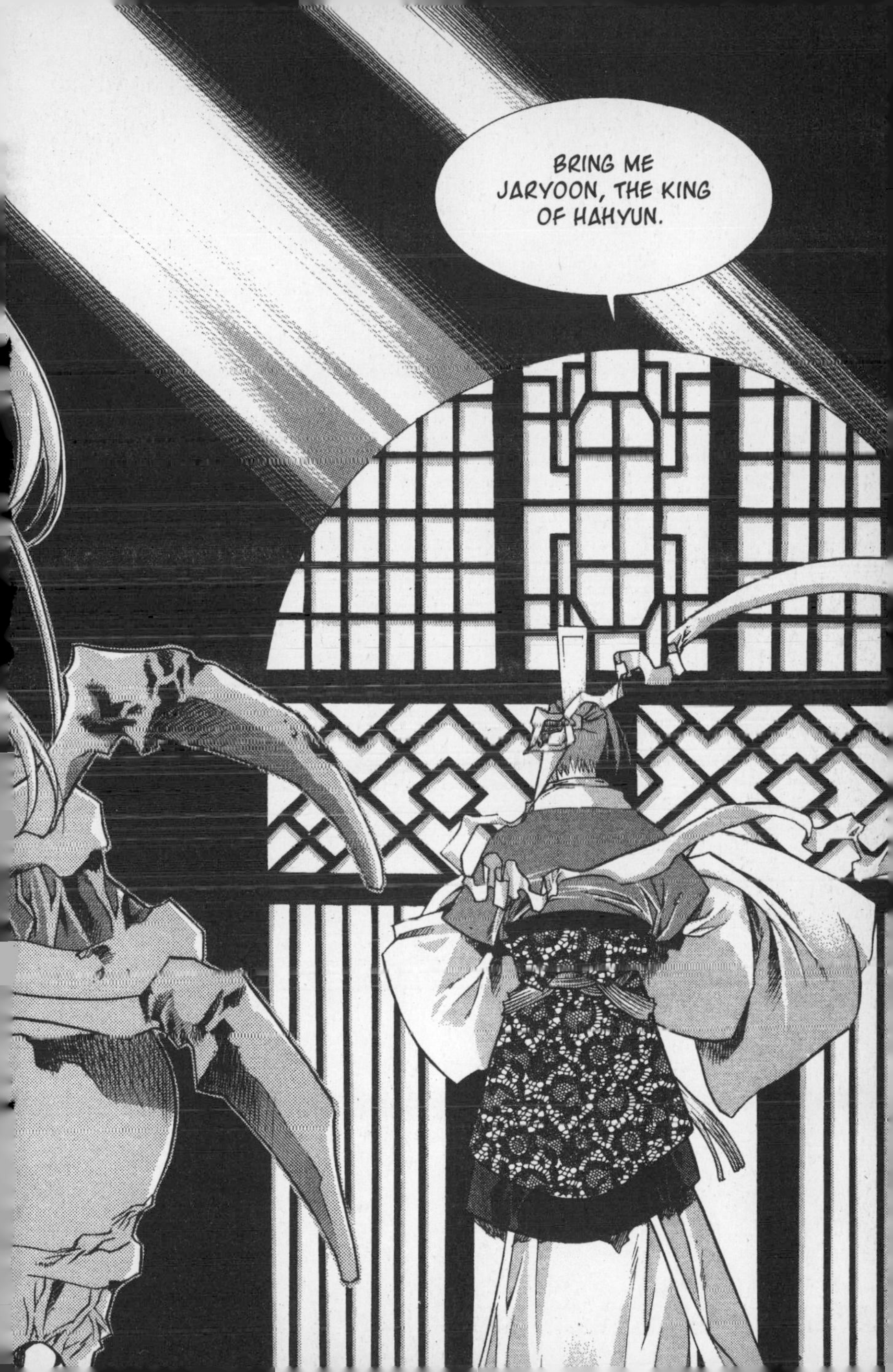
BRING ME JARYOON, THE KING OF HAHYUN.

トン……

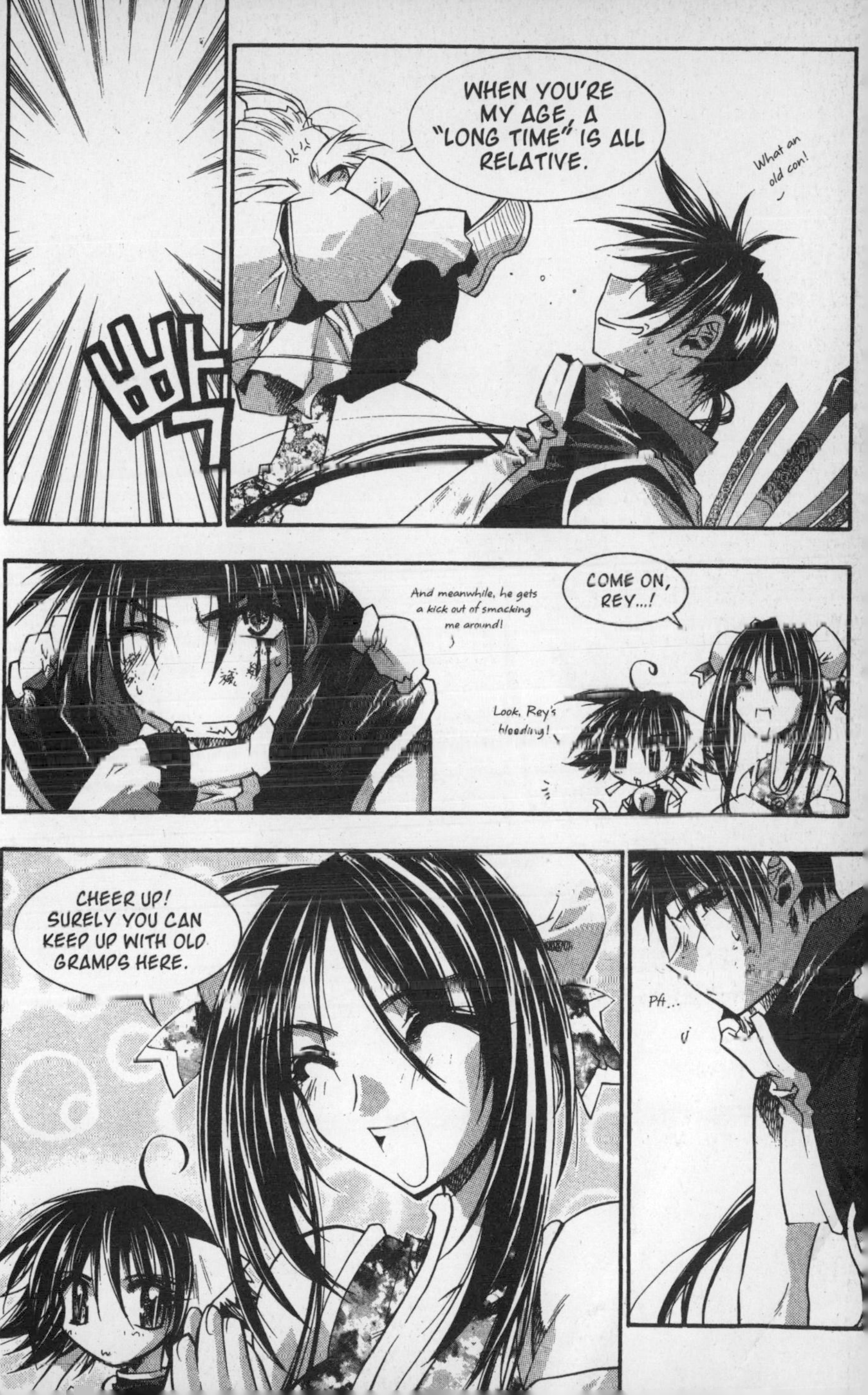
WHEN YOU'RE MY AGE, A "LONG TIME" IS ALL RELATIVE.
What an old con!
And meanwhile, he gets a kick out of smacking me around!
COME ON, REY...!
Look, Rey's bleeding!
CHEER UP! SURELY YOU CAN KEEP UP WITH OLD GRAMPS HERE.
Pft...

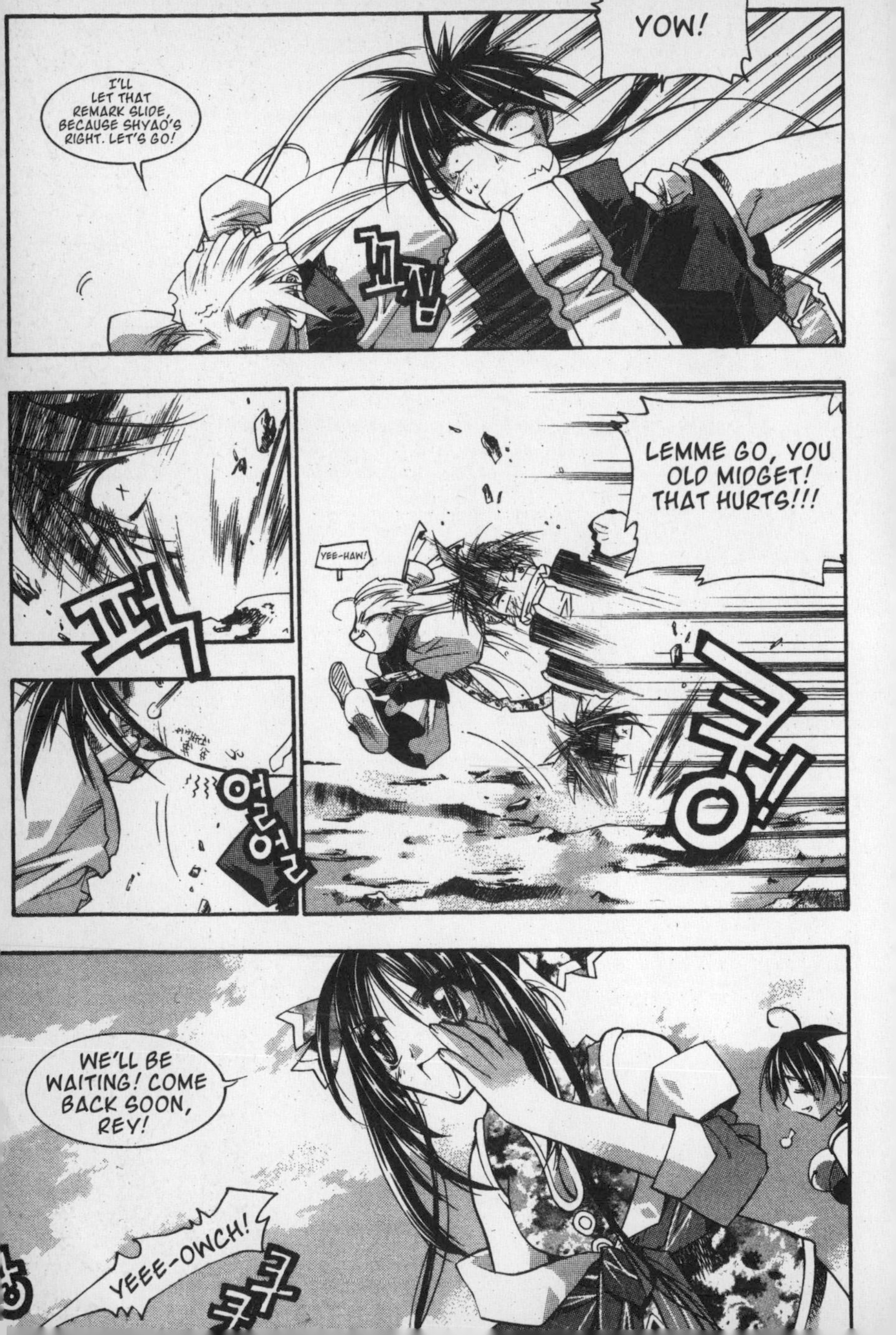
I'LL LET THAT REMARK SLIDE, BECAUSE SHYAO'S RIGHT. LET'S GO!
YOW!
YEE-HAW!
LEMME GO, YOU OLD MIDGET! THAT HURTS!!!
WE'LL BE WAITING! COME BACK SOON, REY!
YEEE-OWCH!

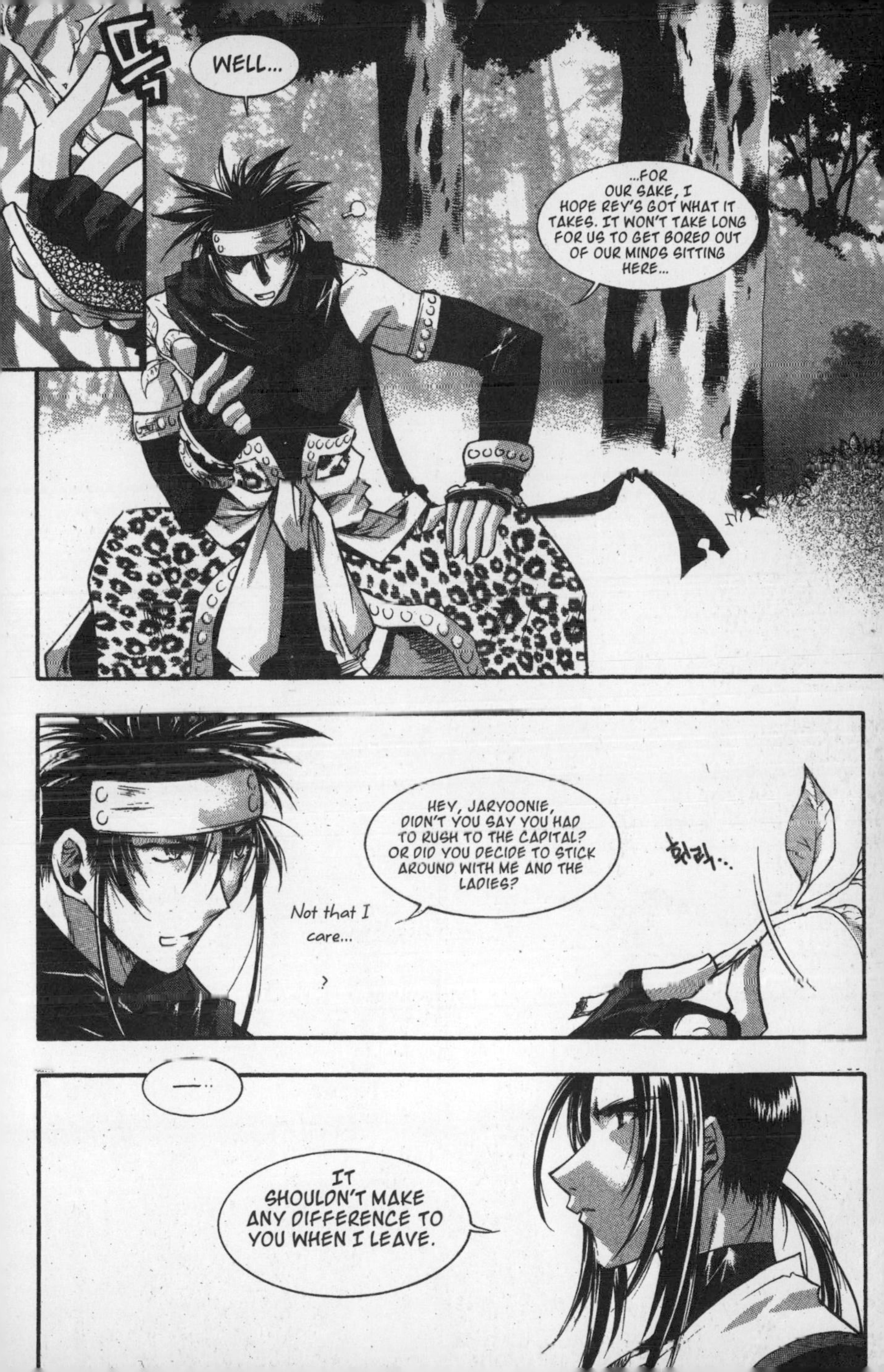
WELL...
...FOR OUR SAKE, I HOPE REY'S GOT WHAT IT TAKES. IT WON'T TAKE LONG FOR US TO GET BORED OUT OF OUR MINDS SITTING HERE...
HEY, JARYOONIE, DIDN'T YOU SAY YOU HAD TO RUSH TO THE CAPITAL? OR DID YOU DECIDE TO STICK AROUND WITH ME AND THE LADIES?
Not that I care...
?
—..
IT SHOULDN'T MAKE ANY DIFFERENCE TO YOU WHEN I LEAVE.

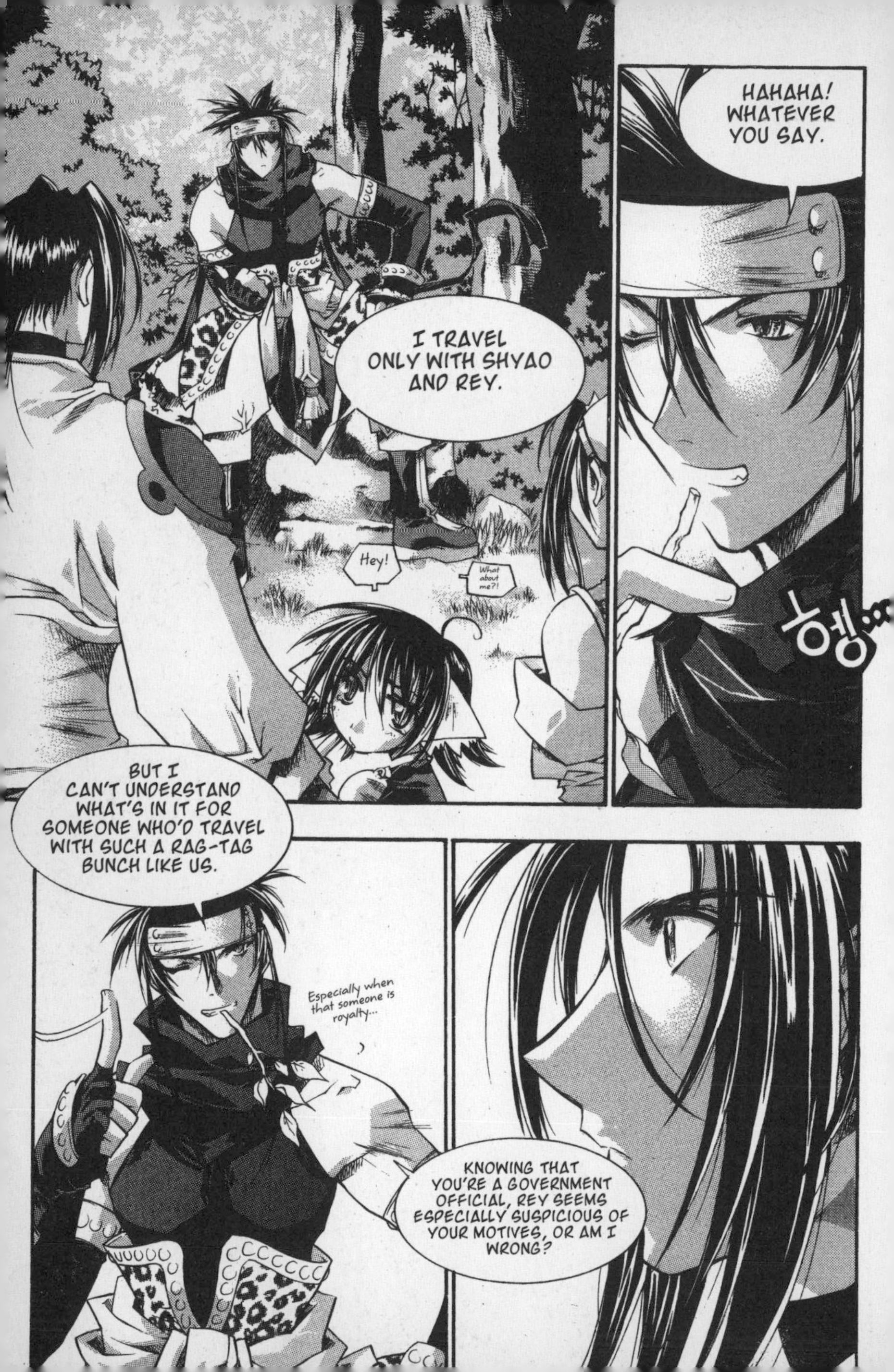
I TRAVEL ONLY WITH SHYAO AND REY.
Hey!
What about me?!
HAHAHA! WHATEVER YOU SAY.
BUT I CAN'T UNDERSTAND WHAT'S IN IT FOR SOMEONE WHO'D TRAVEL WITH SUCH A RAG-TAG BUNCH LIKE US.
Especially when that someone is royalty...
KNOWING THAT YOU'RE A GOVERNMENT OFFICIAL, REY SEEMS ESPECIALLY SUSPICIOUS OF YOUR MOTIVES, OR AM I WRONG?

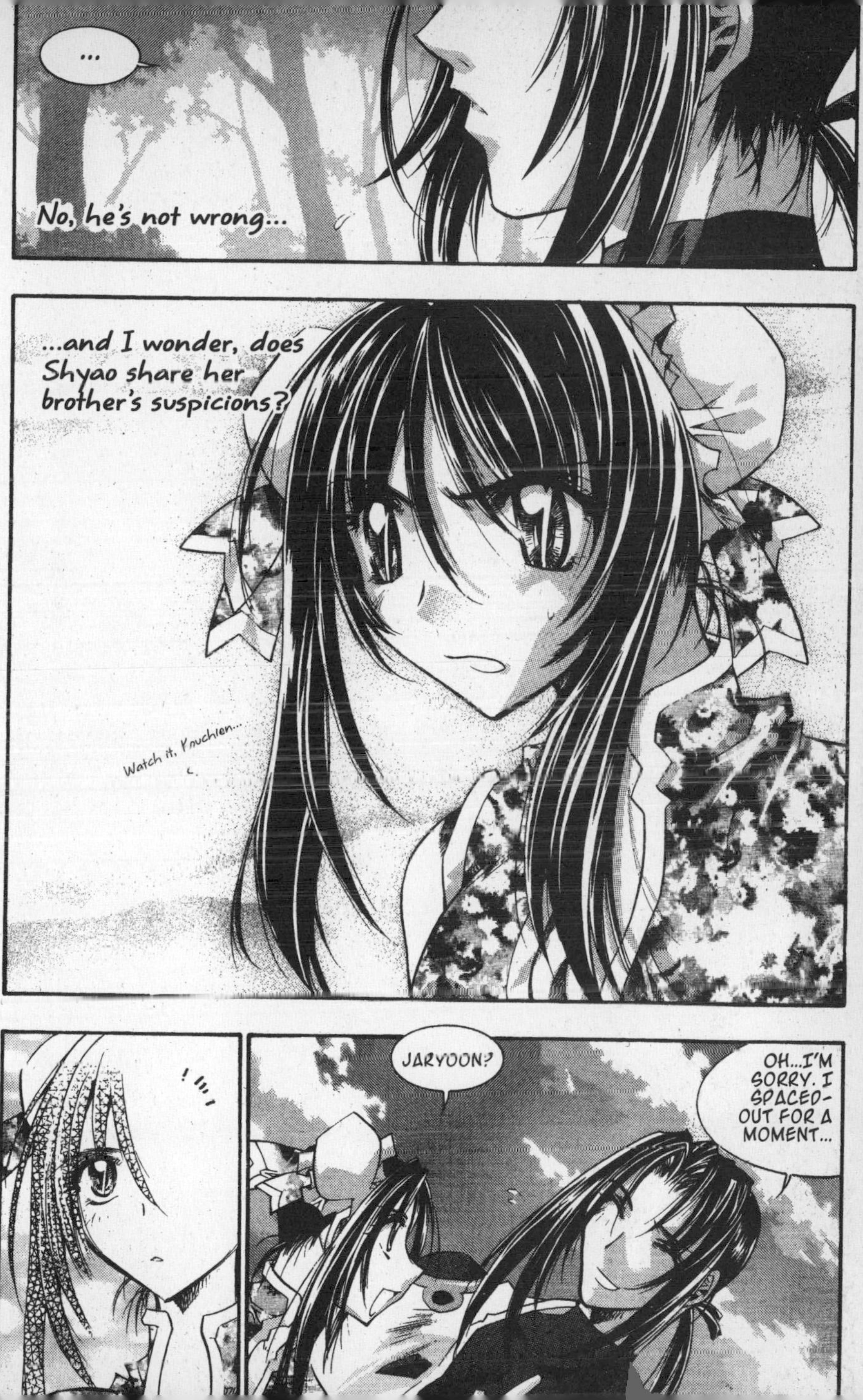
...
No, he's not wrong...
...and I wonder, does Shyao share her brother's suspicions?
Watch it, Ynuchien...
!!!!
JARYOON?
OH...I'M SORRY. I SPACED-OUT FOR A MOMENT...

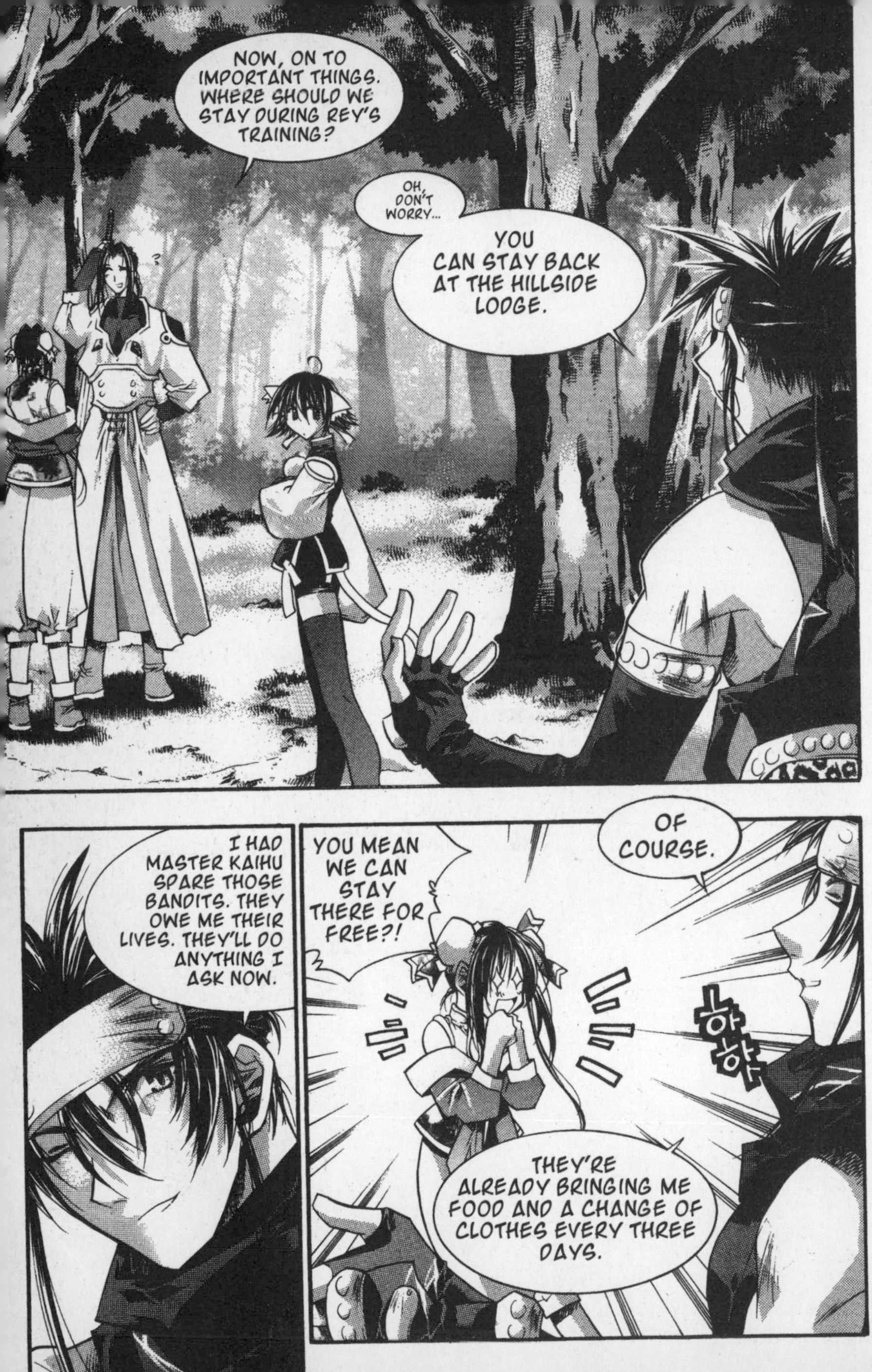
NOW, ON TO IMPORTANT THINGS. WHERE SHOULD WE STAY DURING REY'S TRAINING?
OH, DON'T WORRY...
YOU CAN STAY BACK AT THE HILLSIDE LODGE.
I HAD MASTER KAIHU SPARE THOSE BANDITS. THEY OWE ME THEIR LIVES. THEY'LL DO ANYTHING I ASK NOW.
YOU MEAN WE CAN STAY THERE FOR FREE?!
OF COURSE.
하하
THEY'RE ALREADY BRINGING ME FOOD AND A CHANGE OF CLOTHES EVERY THREE DAYS.

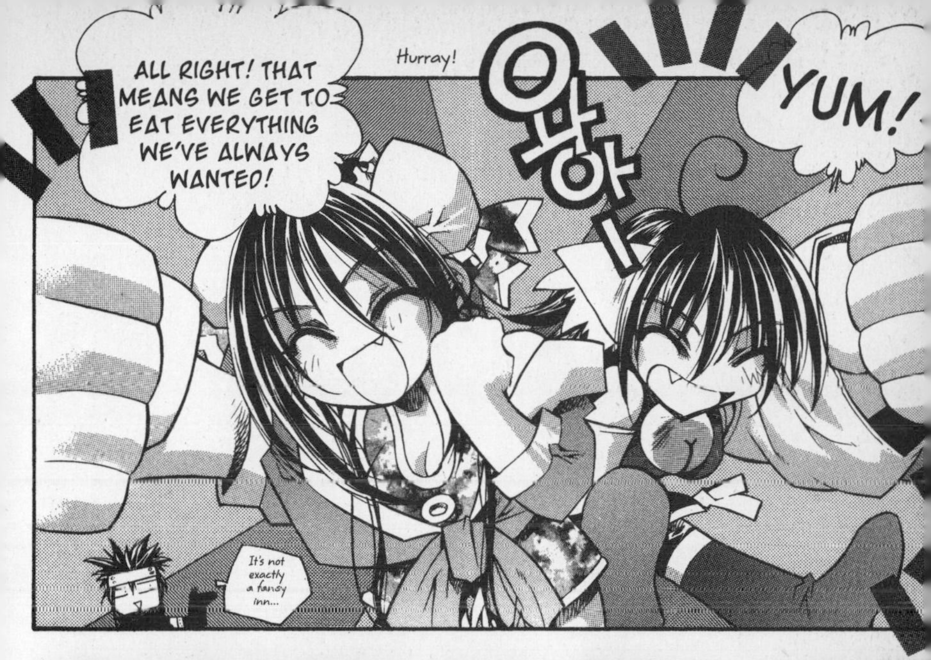
ALL RIGHT! THAT MEANS WE GET TO EAT EVERYTHING WE'VE ALWAYS WANTED!
Hurray!
YUM!
It's not exactly a fancy inn...

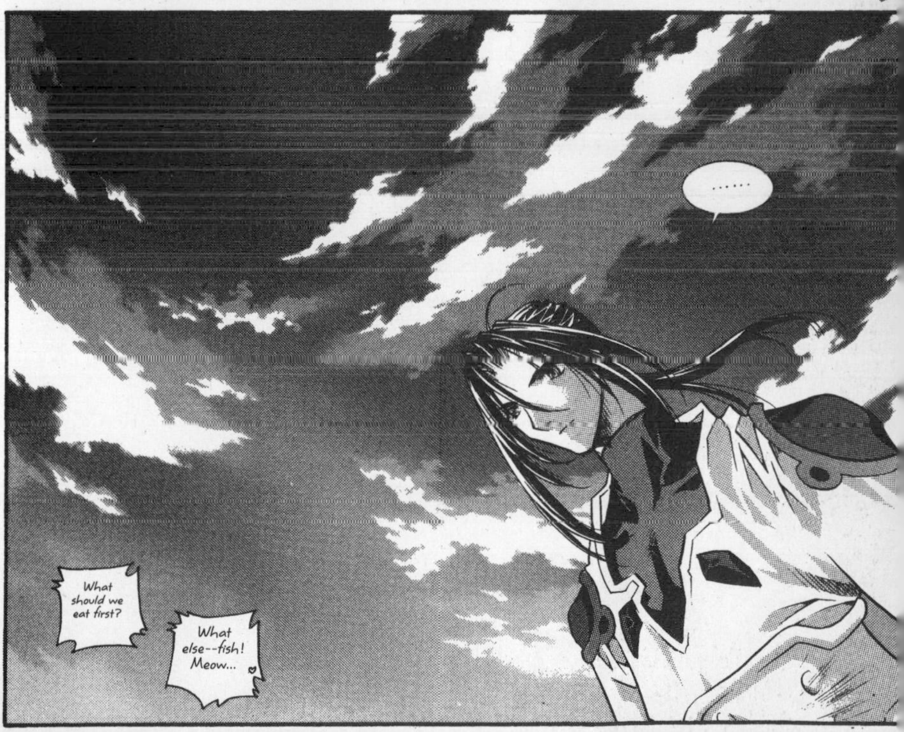
......
What should we eat first?
What else--fish! Meow...

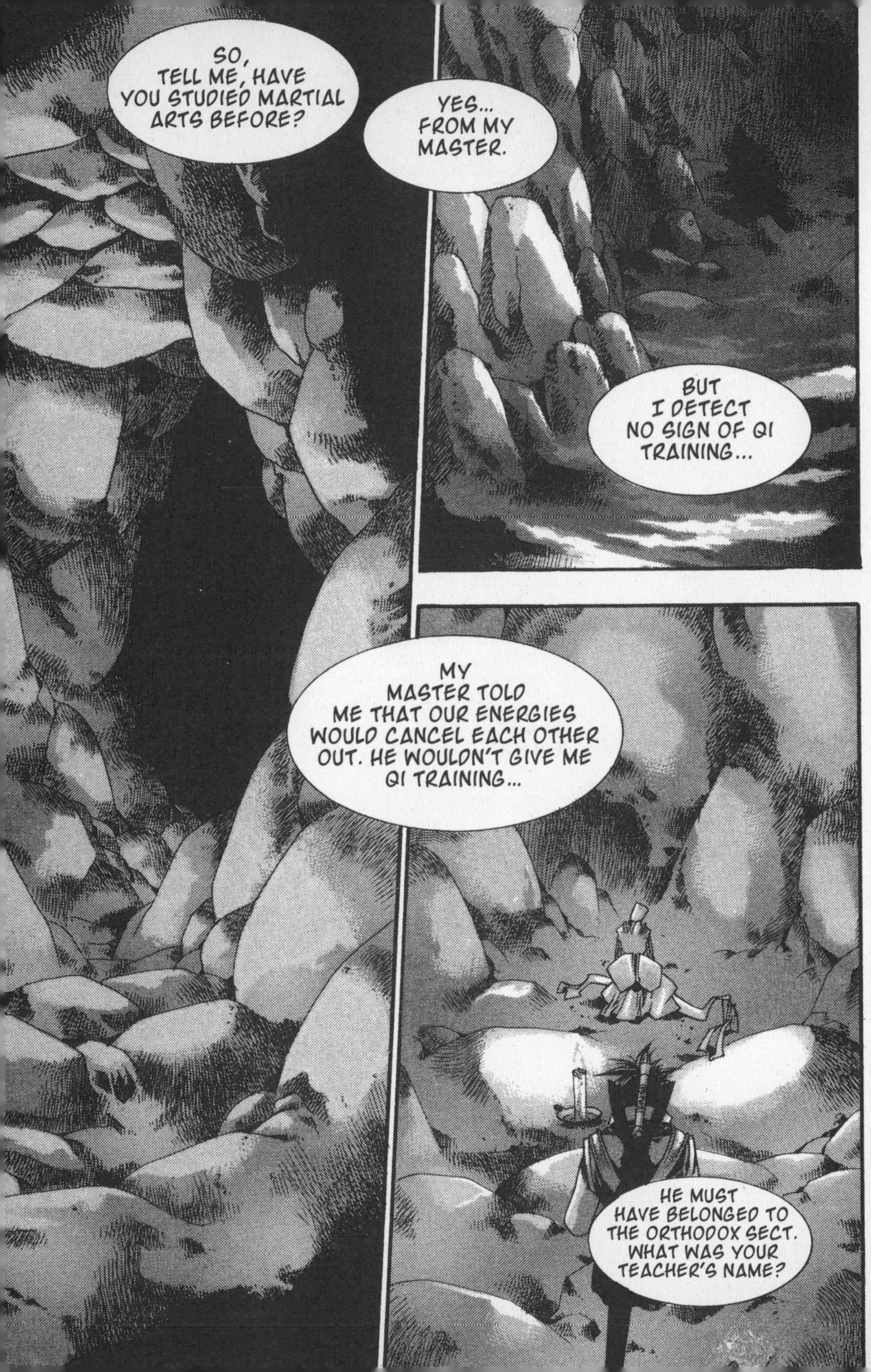
SO, TELL ME, HAVE YOU STUDIED MARTIAL ARTS BEFORE?
YES... FROM MY MASTER.
BUT I DETECT NO SIGN OF QI TRAINING...
MY MASTER TOLD ME THAT OUR ENERGIES WOULD CANCEL EACH OTHER OUT. HE WOULDN'T GIVE ME QI TRAINING...
HE MUST HAVE BELONGED TO THE ORTHODOX SECT. WHAT WAS YOUR TEACHER'S NAME?

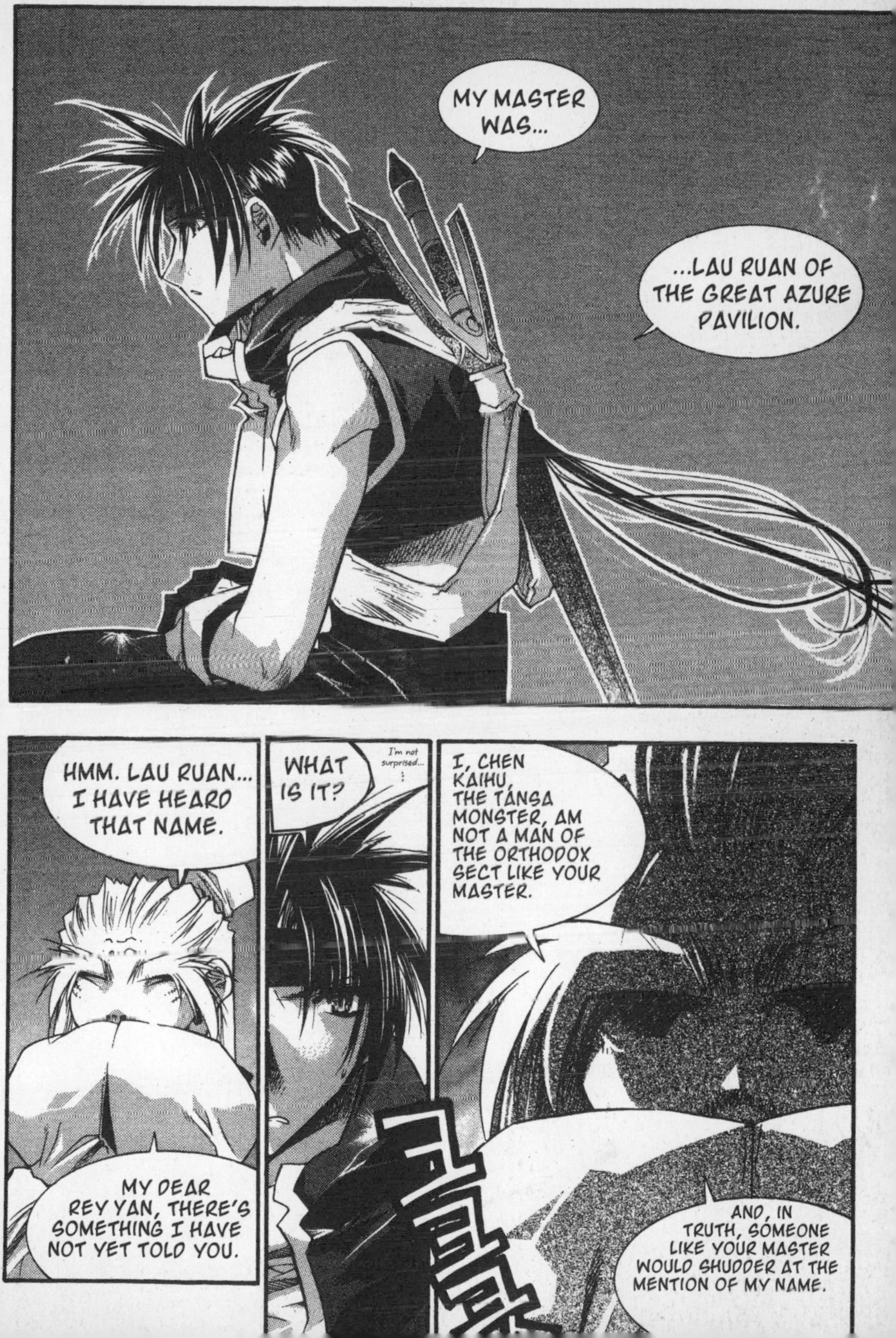
MY MASTER WAS...
...LAU RUAN OF THE GREAT AZURE PAVILION.
HMM. LAU RUAN... I HAVE HEARD THAT NAME.
MY DEAR REY YAN, THERE'S SOMETHING I HAVE NOT YET TOLD YOU.
WHAT IS IT?
I'm not surprised...
I, CHEN KAIHU, THE TÁNSA MONSTER, AM NOT A MAN OF THE ORTHODOX SECT LIKE YOUR MASTER.
AND, IN TRUTH, SOMEONE LIKE YOUR MASTER WOULD SHUDDER AT THE MENTION OF MY NAME.

WHAT DOES THAT MEAN?

LET ME MAKE IT CRYSTAL CLEAR. MY TECHNIQUES ARE DEMONIC IN NATURE. AND, IF NEED BE, THEY MIGHT EVEN REQUIRE YOU TO INVITE IN A DEMON SPIRIT.

OKAY. I GOT IT. JUST TEACH ME.

AND THERE'S ONE MORE THING...

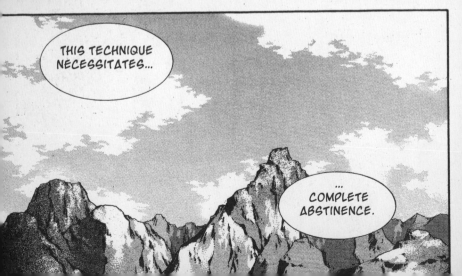

THIS TECHNIQUE NECESSITATES...

...COMPLETE ABSTINENCE.

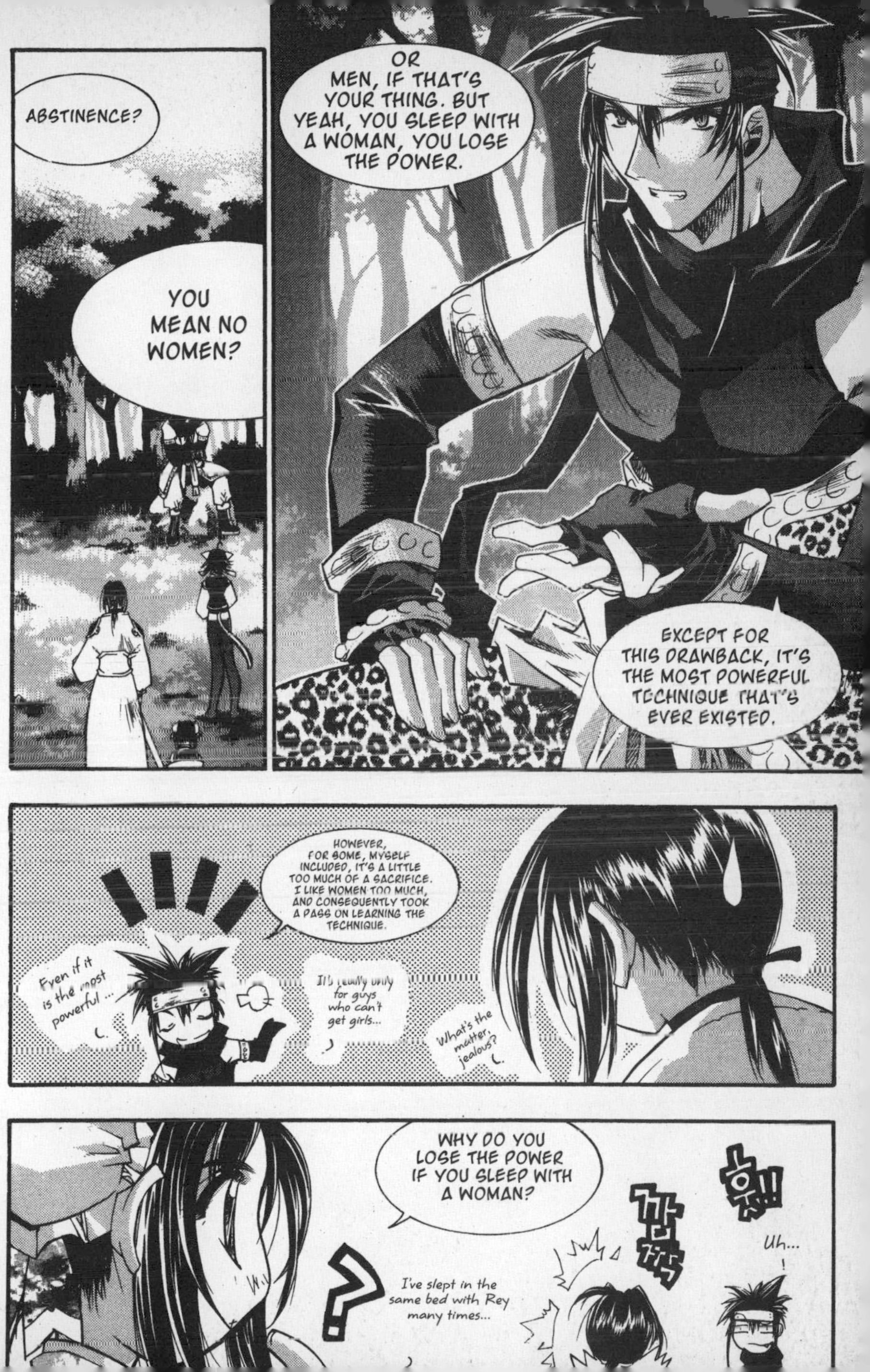
ABSTINENCE?
YOU MEAN NO WOMEN?
OR MEN, IF THAT'S YOUR THING. BUT YEAH, YOU SLEEP WITH A WOMAN, YOU LOSE THE POWER.
EXCEPT FOR THIS DRAWBACK, IT'S THE MOST POWERFUL TECHNIQUE THAT'S EVER EXISTED.
HOWEVER, FOR SOME, MYSELF INCLUDED, IT'S A LITTLE TOO MUCH OF A SACRIFICE. I LIKE WOMEN TOO MUCH, AND CONSEQUENTLY TOOK A PASS ON LEARNING THE TECHNIQUE.
Even if it is the most powerful ...
It's really only for guys who can't get girls...
What's the matter, jealous?
WHY DO YOU LOSE THE POWER IF YOU SLEEP WITH A WOMAN?
I've slept in the same bed with Rey many times...
깜짝
후!!
Uh...
!

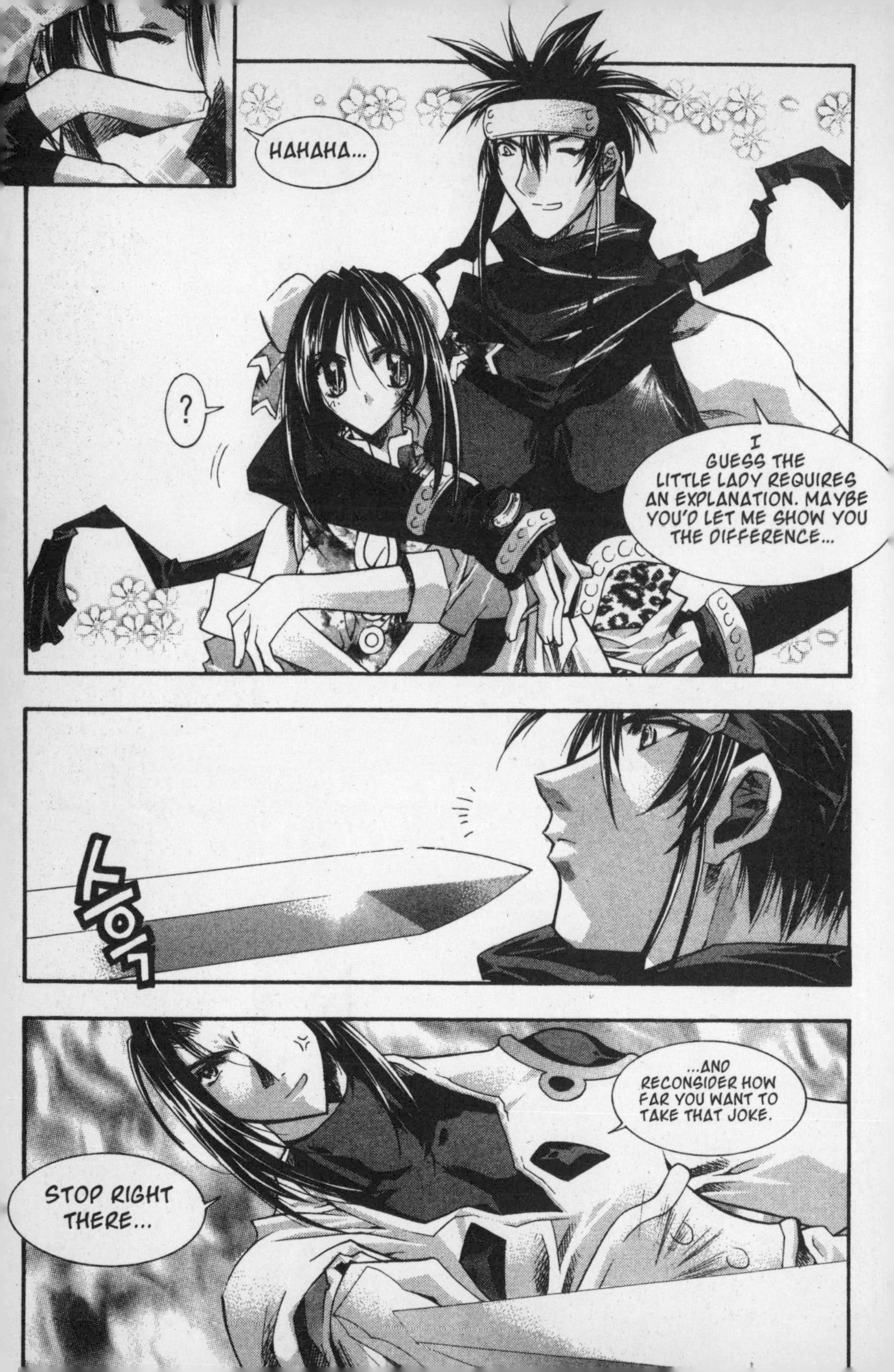
HAHAHA...
?
I GUESS THE LITTLE LADY REQUIRES AN EXPLANATION. MAYBE YOU'D LET ME SHOW YOU THE DIFFERENCE...
STOP RIGHT THERE...
...AND RECONSIDER HOW FAR YOU WANT TO TAKE THAT JOKE.

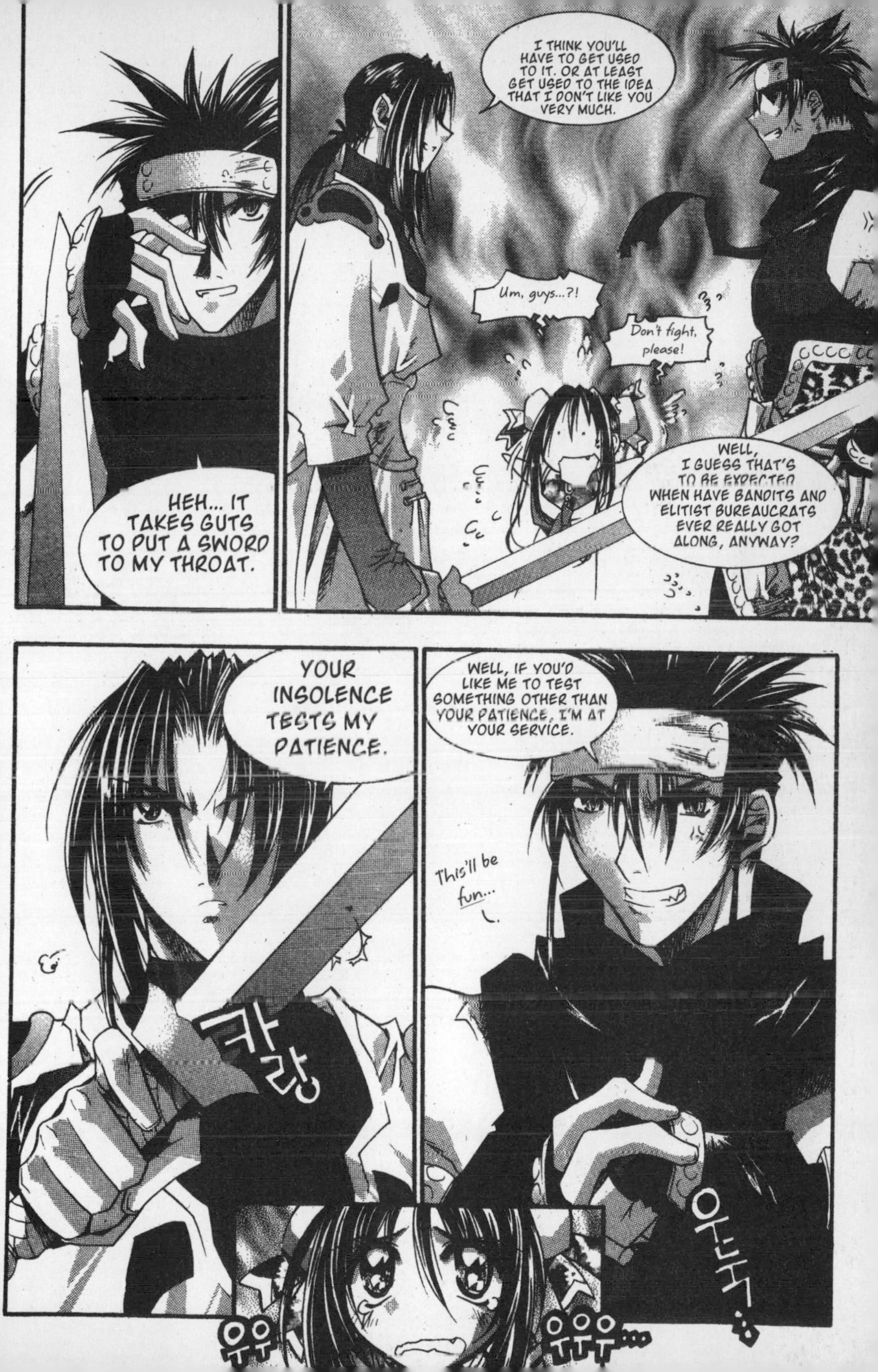
HEH... IT TAKES GUTS TO PUT A SWORD TO MY THROAT.
I THINK YOU'LL HAVE TO GET USED TO IT. OR AT LEAST GET USED TO THE IDEA THAT I DON'T LIKE YOU VERY MUCH.
Um, guys...?!
Don't fight, please!
WELL, I GUESS THAT'S TO BE EXPECTED WHEN HAVE BANDITS AND ELITIST BUREAUCRATS EVER REALLY GOT ALONG, ANYWAY?
YOUR INSOLENCE TESTS MY PATIENCE.
WELL, IF YOU'D LIKE ME TO TEST SOMETHING OTHER THAN YOUR PATIENCE, I'M AT YOUR SERVICE.
This'll be fun...

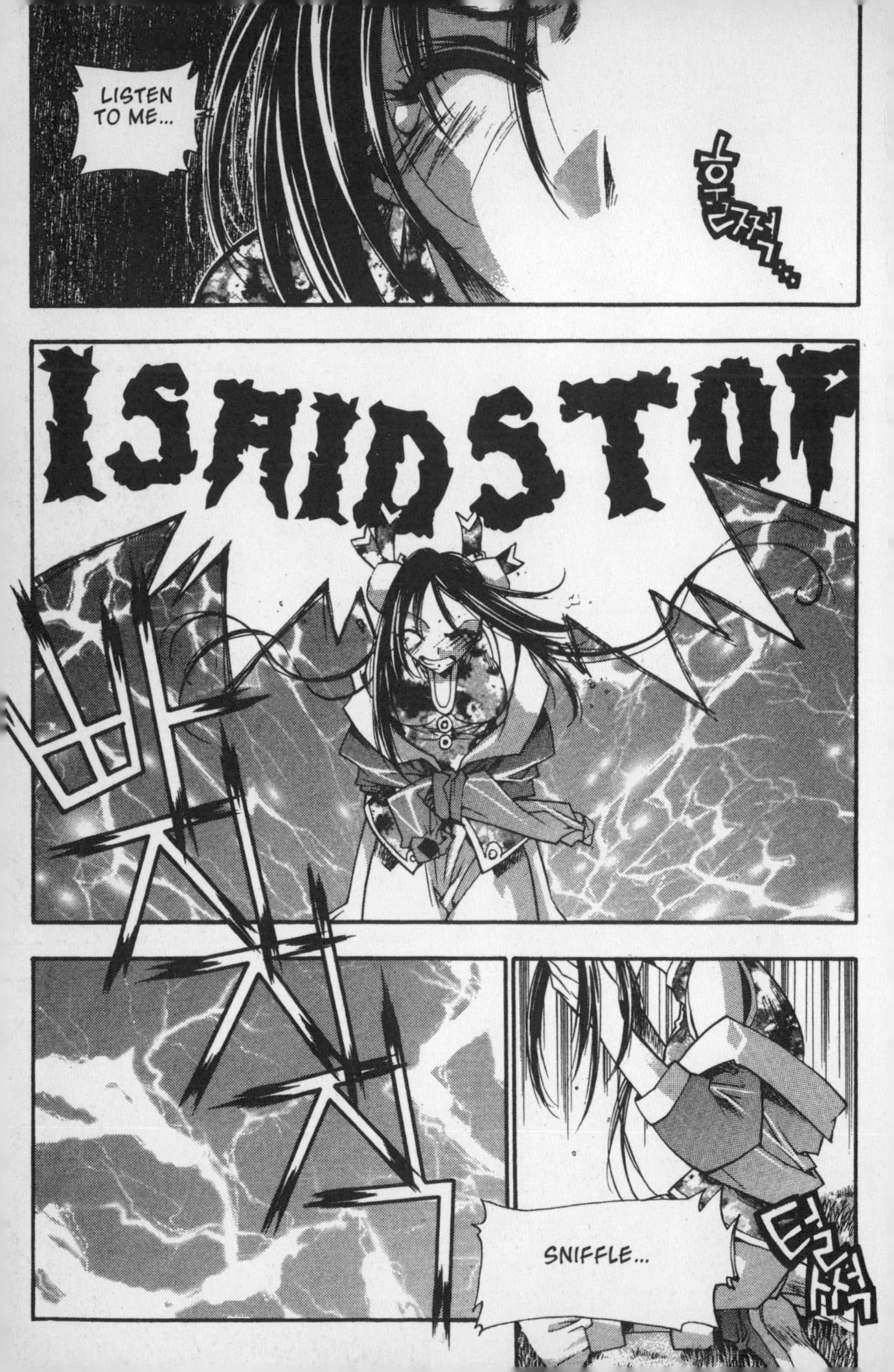
LISTEN TO ME...
훌쩍...
I SAID STOP
SNIFFLE...

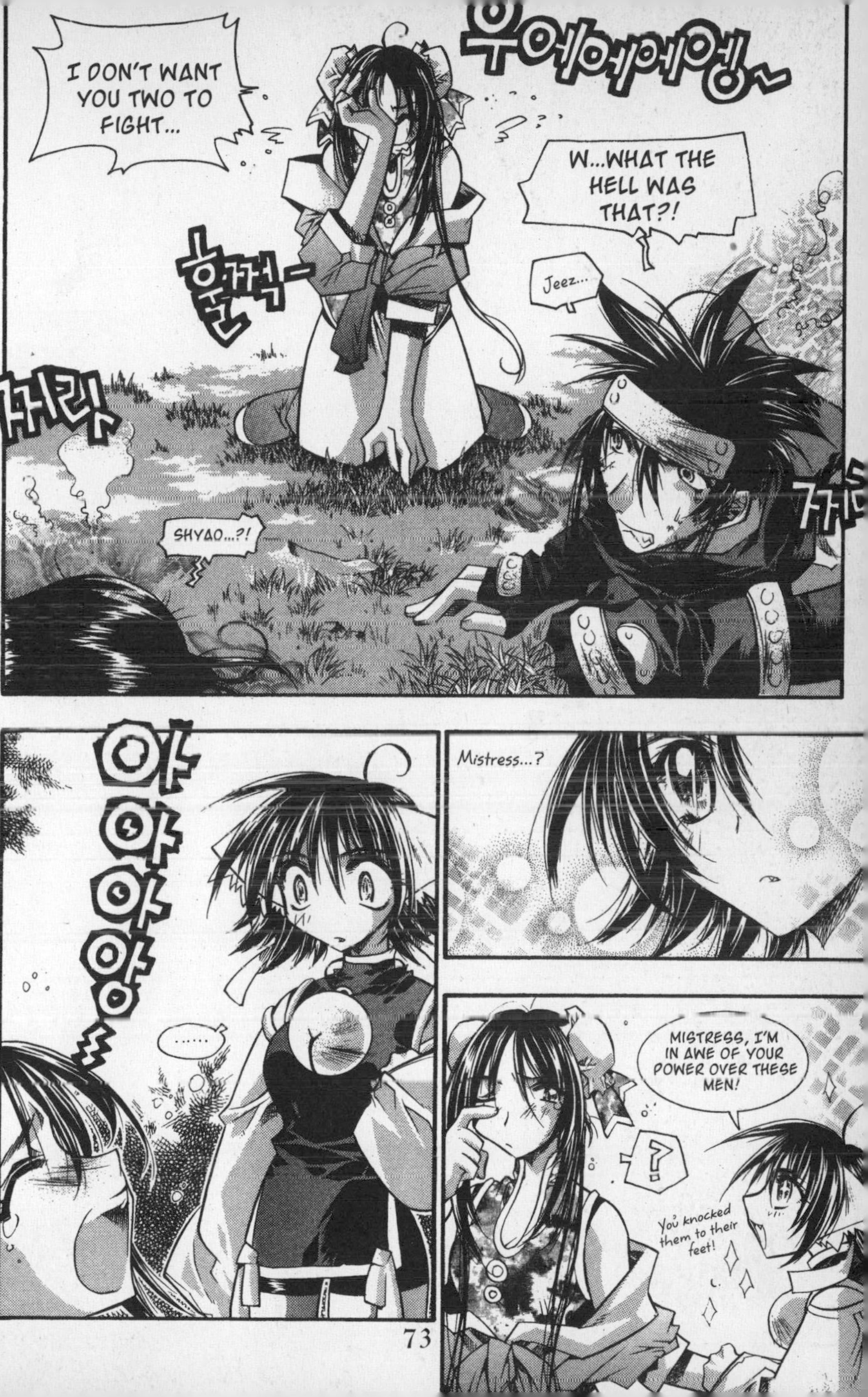
I DON'T WANT YOU TWO TO FIGHT...
우에에에엥~
W...WHAT THE HELL WAS THAT?!
Jeez...
SHYAO...?!
야야야양~
......
Mistress...?
MISTRESS, I'M IN AWE OF YOUR POWER OVER THESE MEN!
You knocked them to their feet!
?

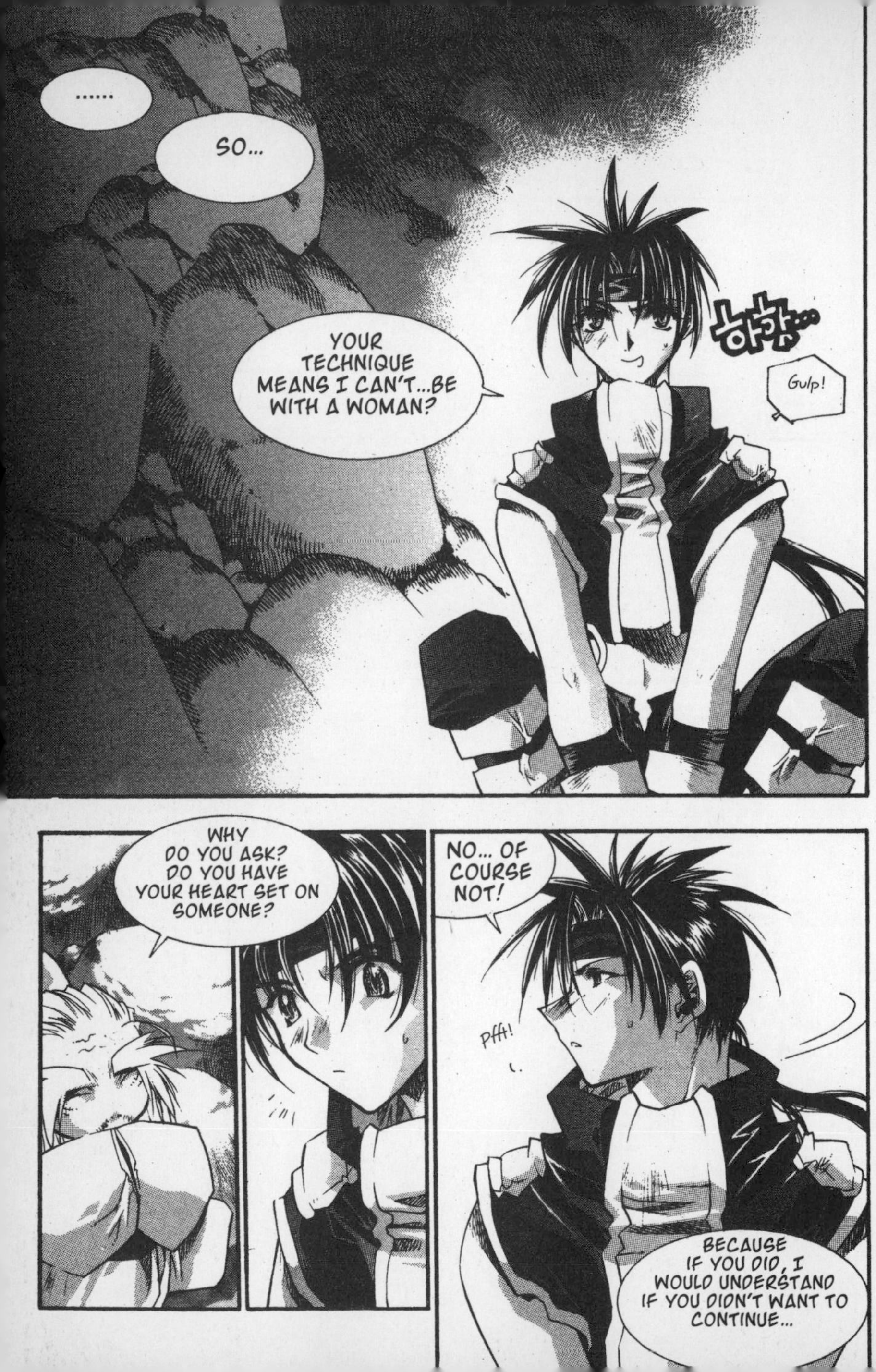
......
SO...
YOUR TECHNIQUE MEANS I CAN'T...BE WITH A WOMAN?
Gulp!
WHY DO YOU ASK? DO YOU HAVE YOUR HEART SET ON SOMEONE?
NO... OF COURSE NOT!
Pfft!
BECAUSE IF YOU DID, I WOULD UNDERSTAND IF YOU DIDN'T WANT TO CONTINUE...

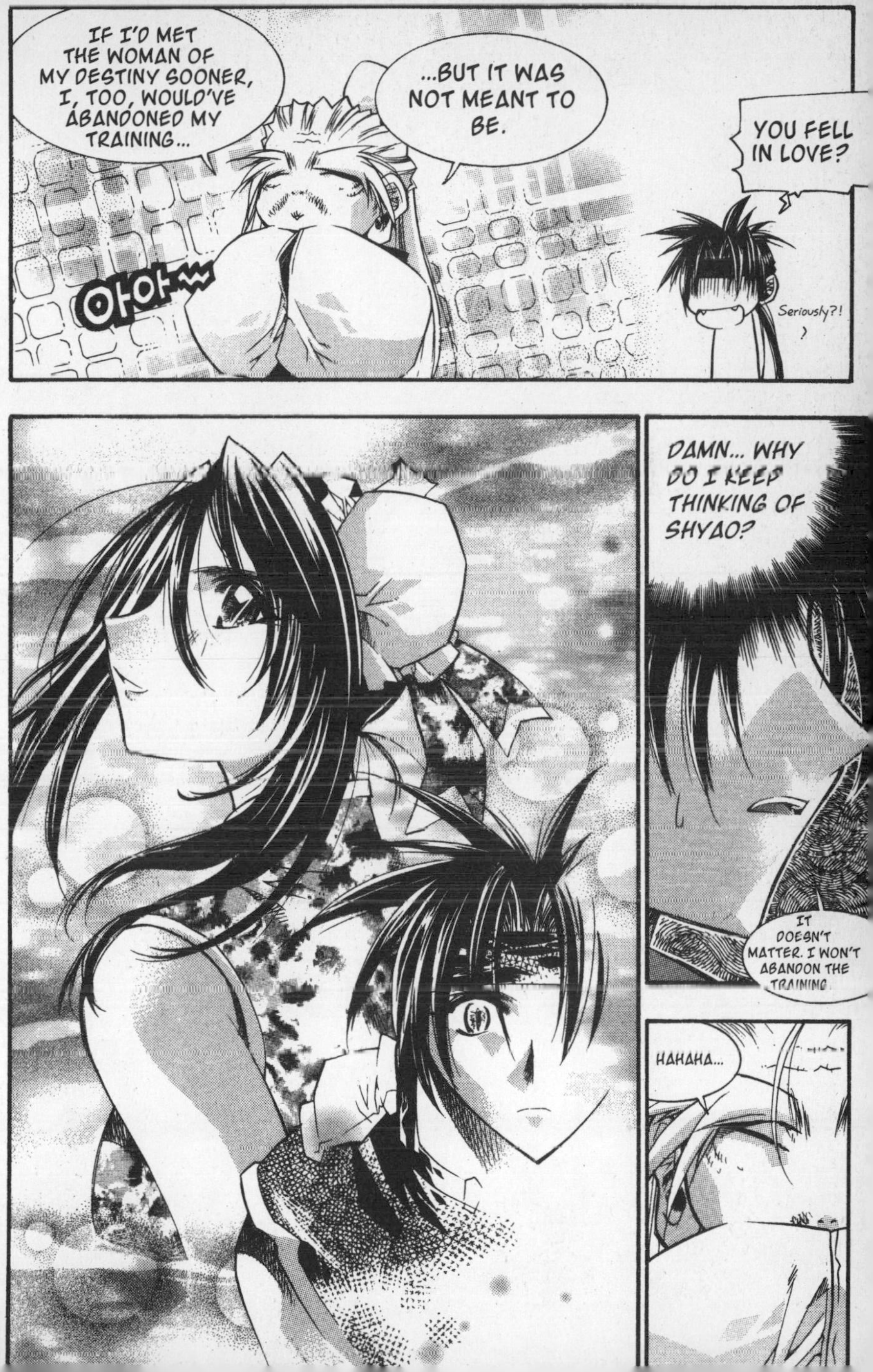
IF I'D MET THE WOMAN OF MY DESTINY SOONER, I, TOO, WOULD'VE ABANDONED MY TRAINING...
...BUT IT WAS NOT MEANT TO BE.
아아~
YOU FELL IN LOVE?
Seriously?!
DAMN... WHY DO I KEEP THINKING OF SHYAO?
IT DOESN'T MATTER. I WON'T ABANDON THE TRAINING.
HAHAHA...

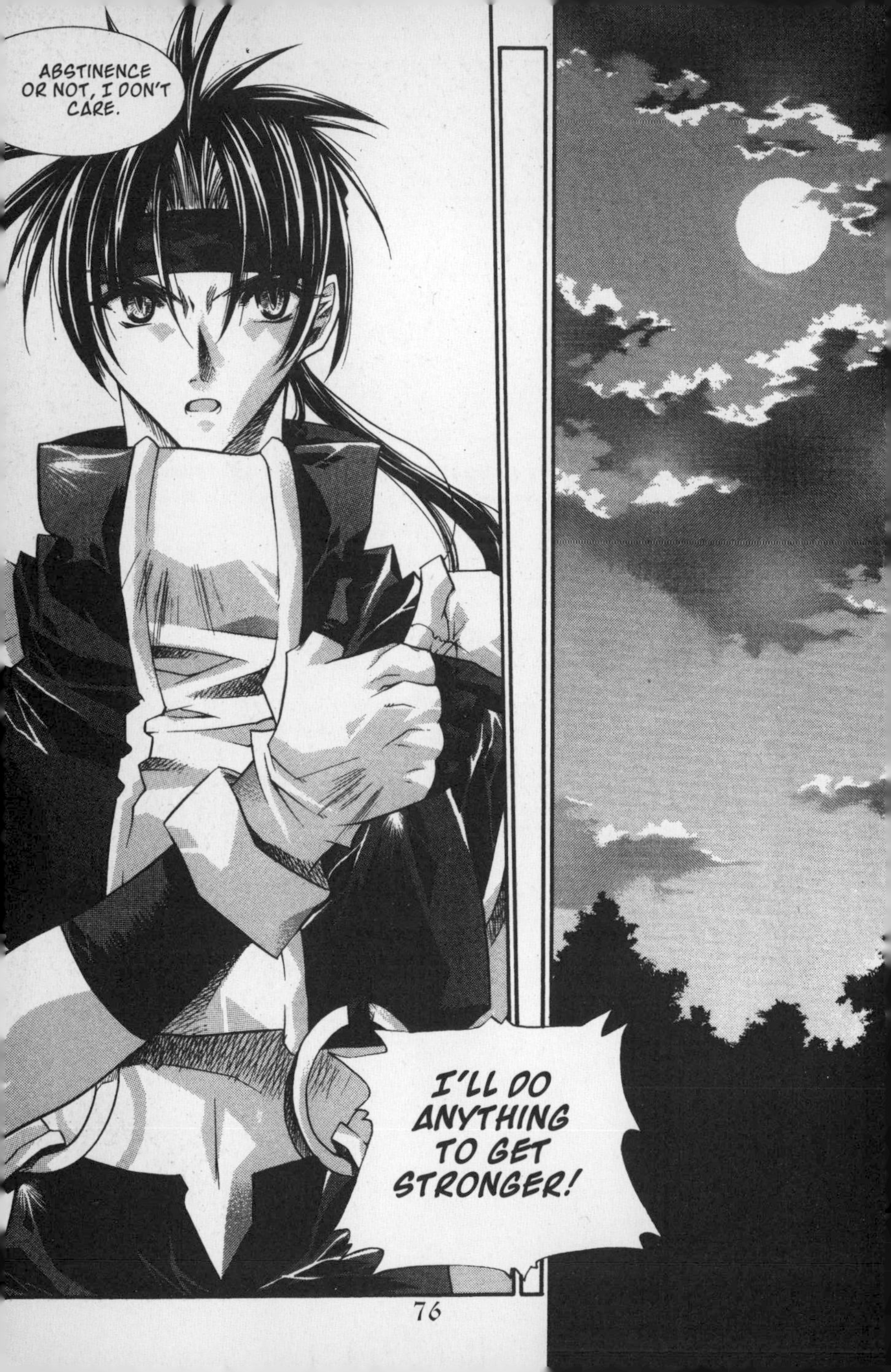
ABSTINENCE OR NOT, I DON'T CARE.
I'LL DO ANYTHING TO GET STRONGER!

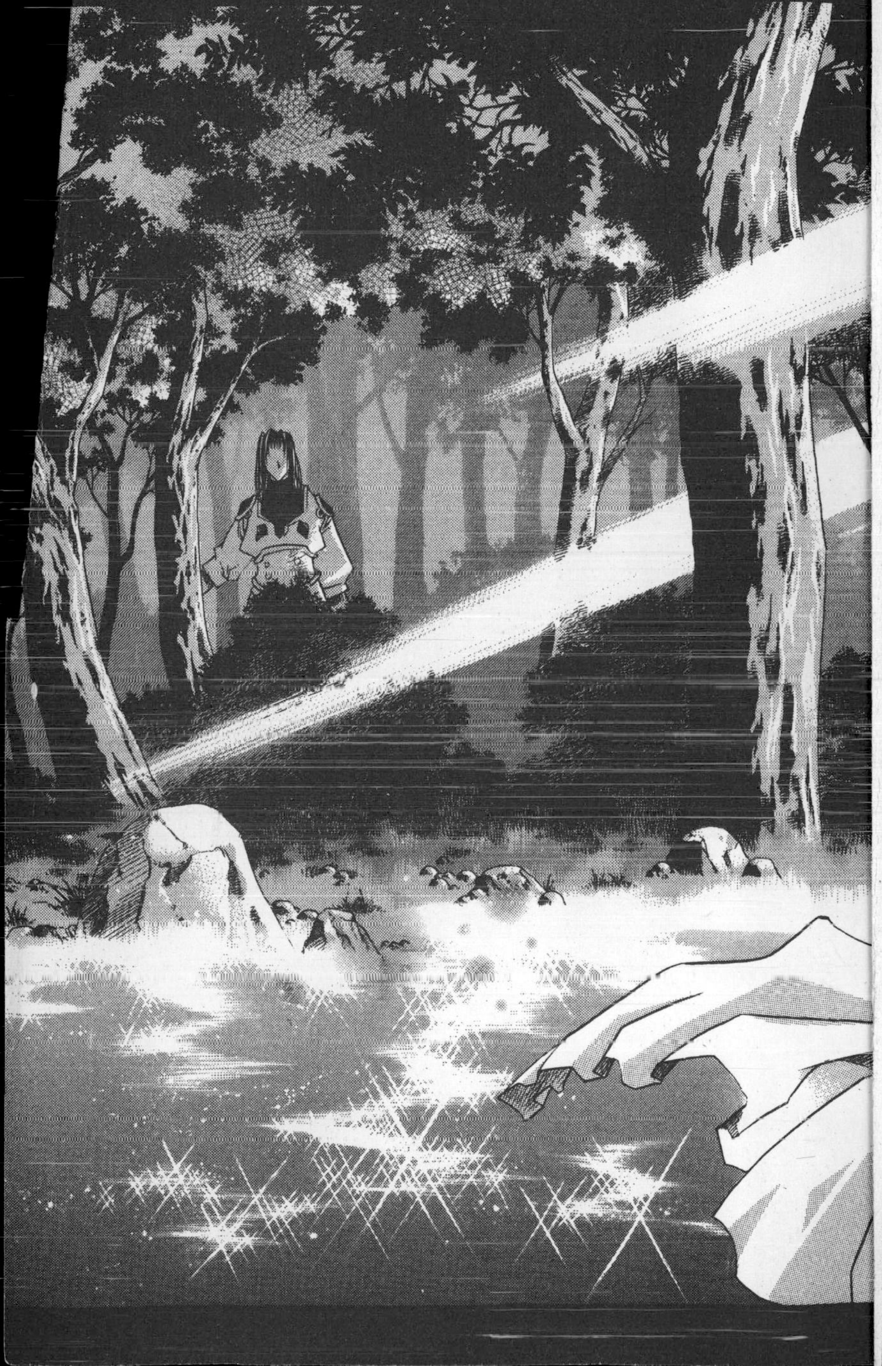

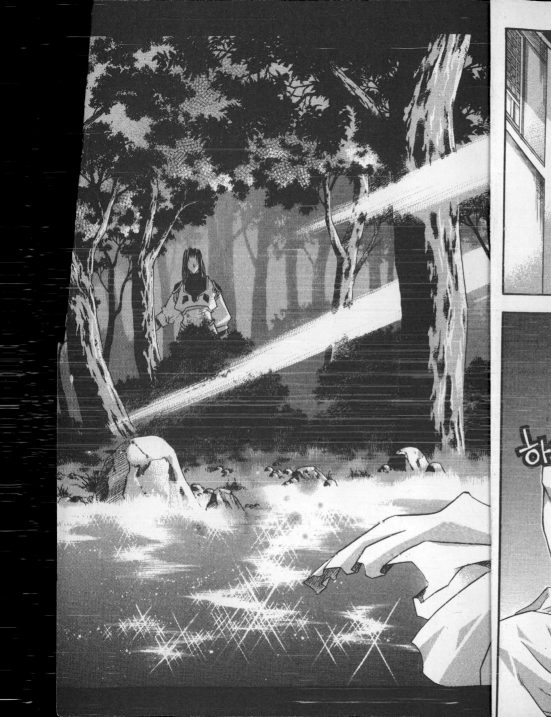

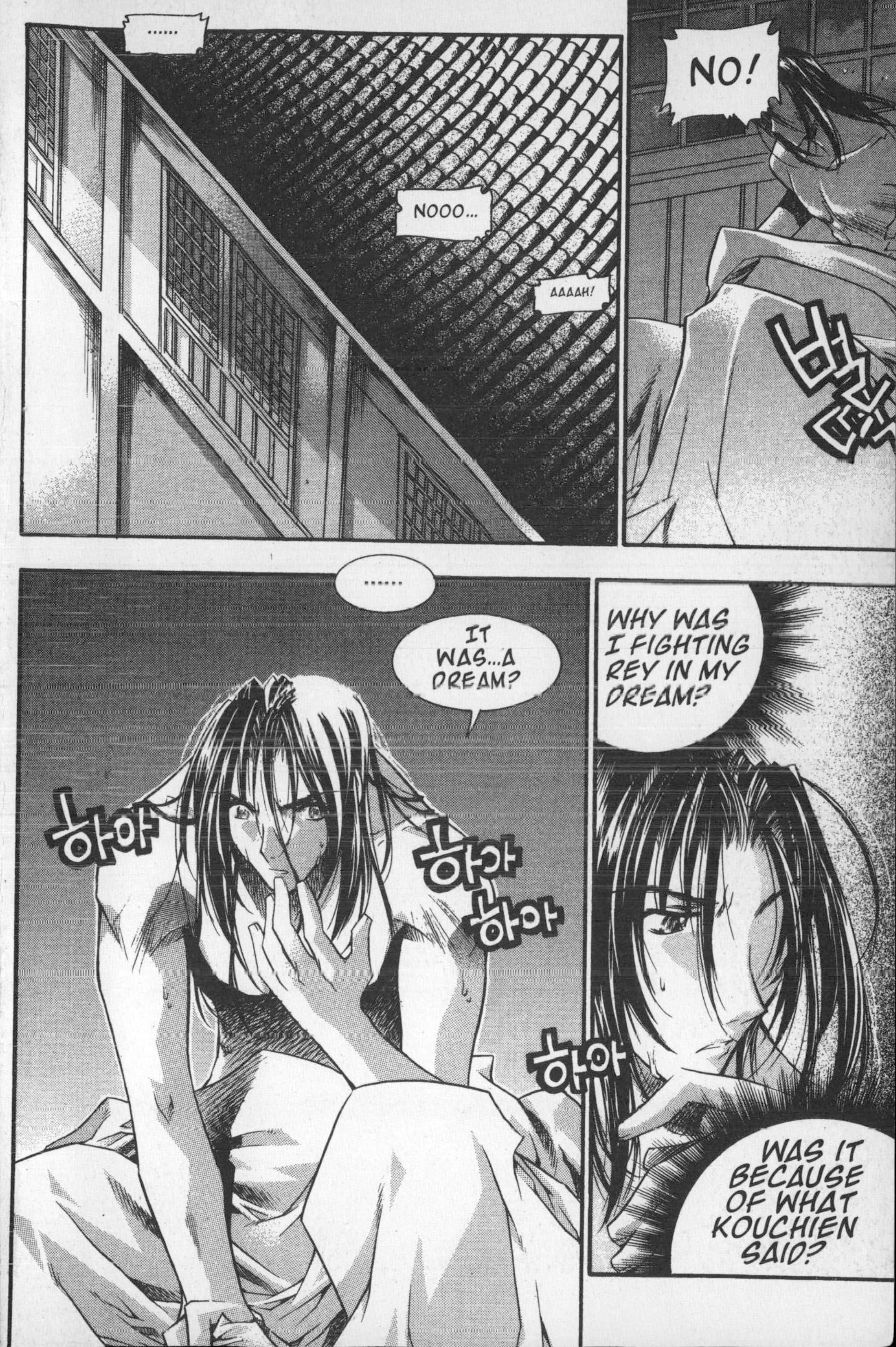
......
NOOO...
AAAAH!
NO!
......
IT WAS...A DREAM?
하아
하아
하아
하아
WHY WAS I FIGHTING REY IN MY DREAM?
WAS IT BECAUSE OF WHAT KOUCHIEN SAID?

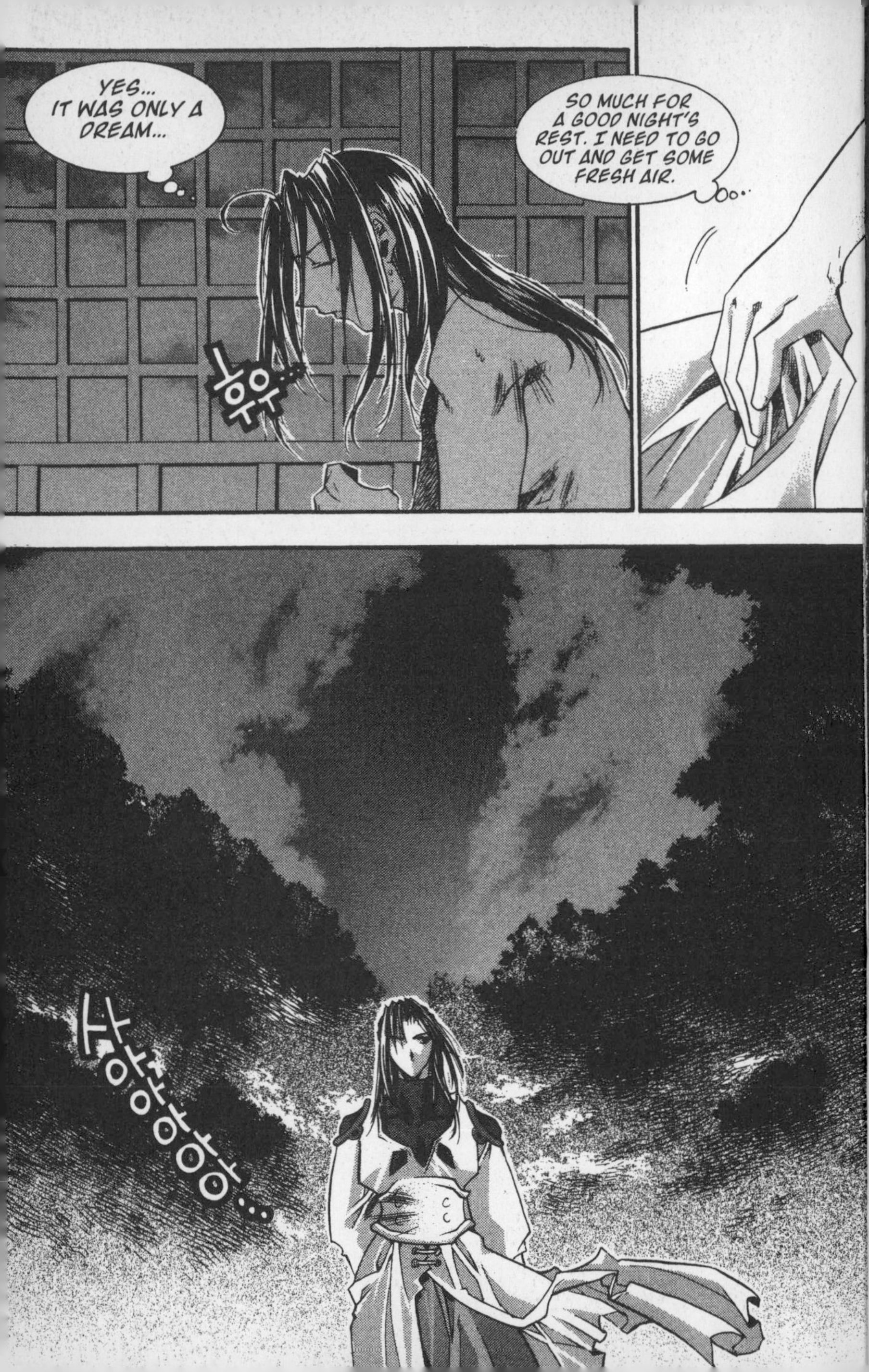
YES... IT WAS ONLY A DREAM...
SO MUCH FOR A GOOD NIGHT'S REST. I NEED TO GO OUT AND GET SOME FRESH AIR.

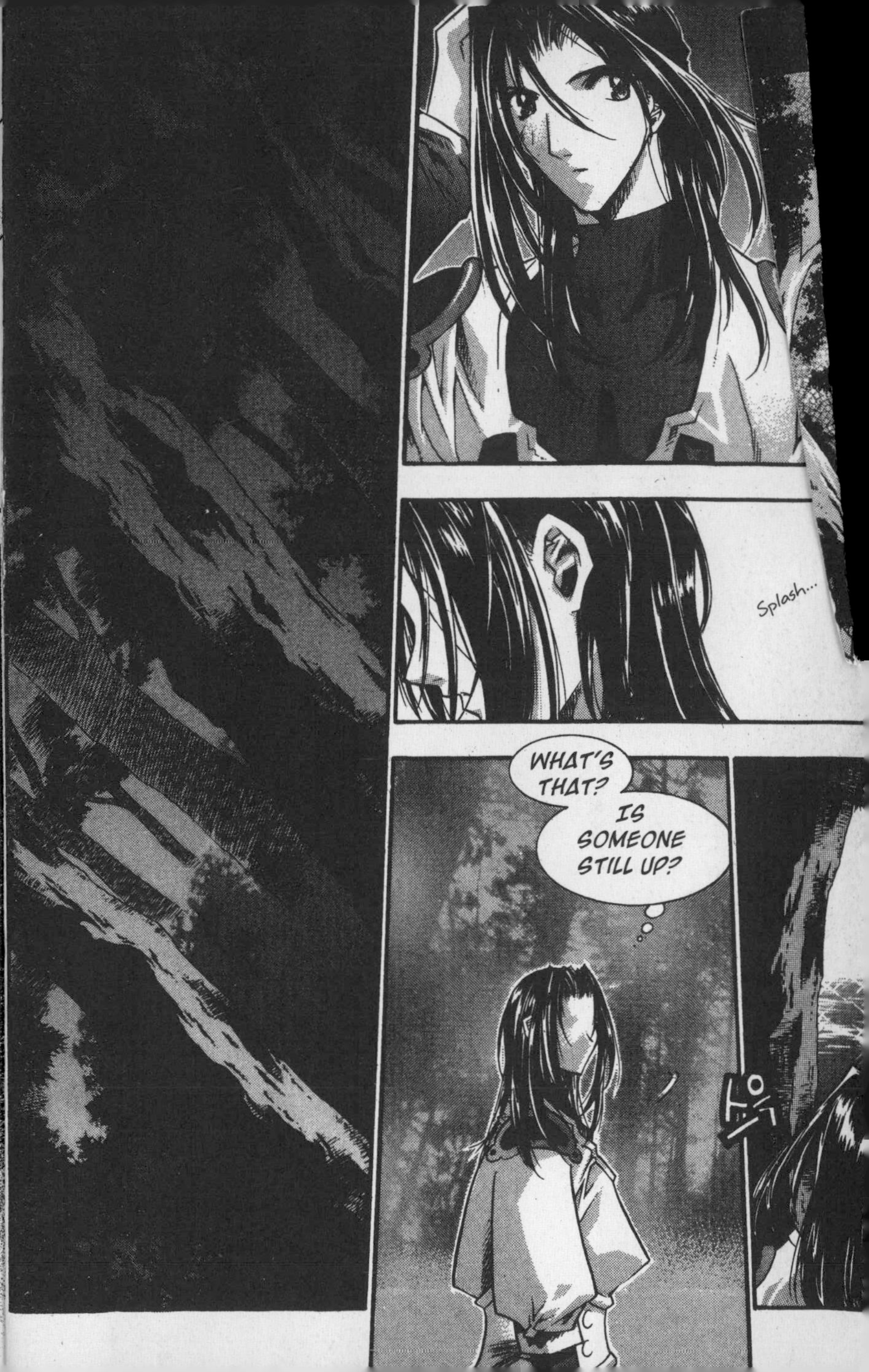
Splash...
WHAT'S THAT?
IS SOMEONE STILL UP?

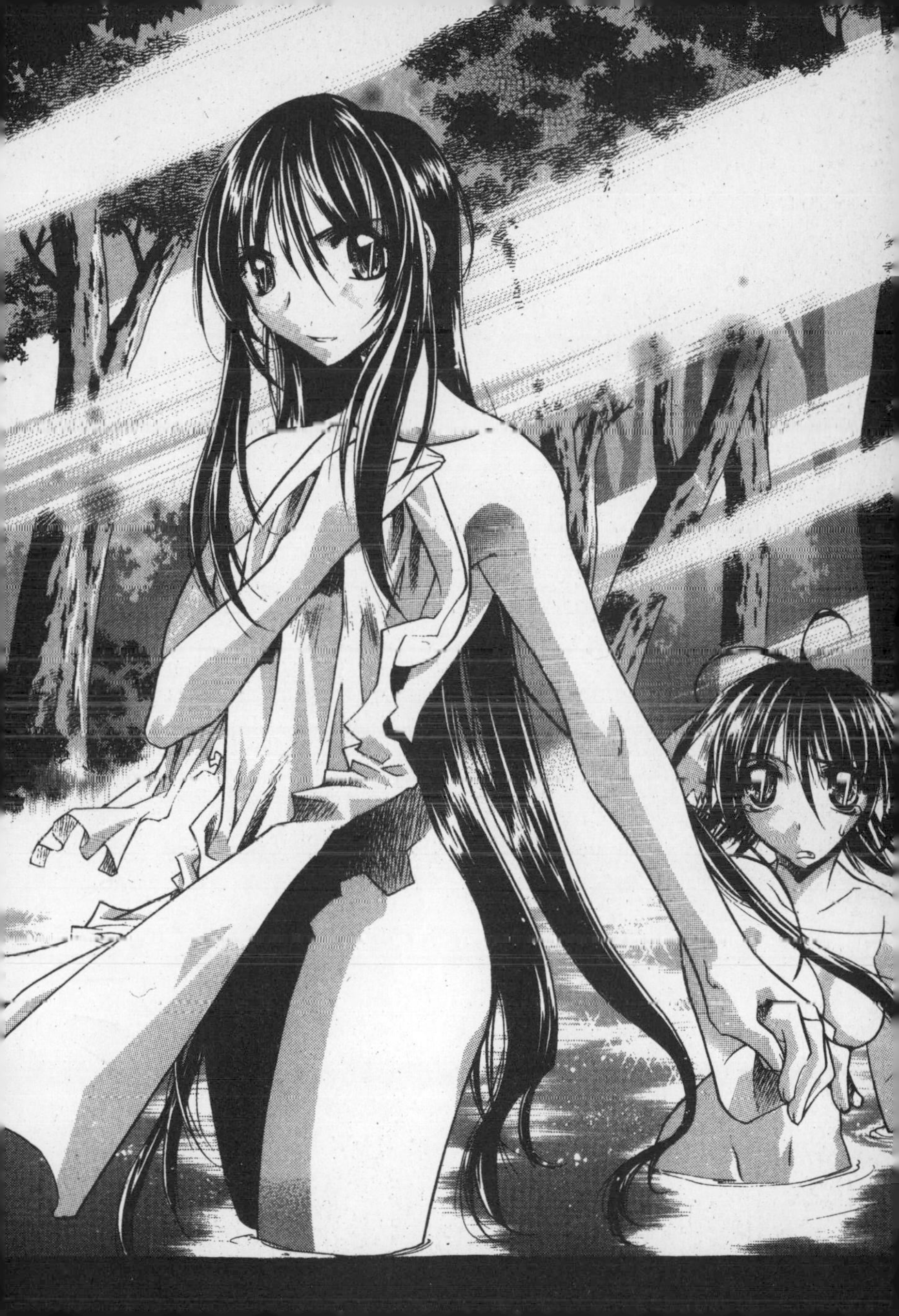

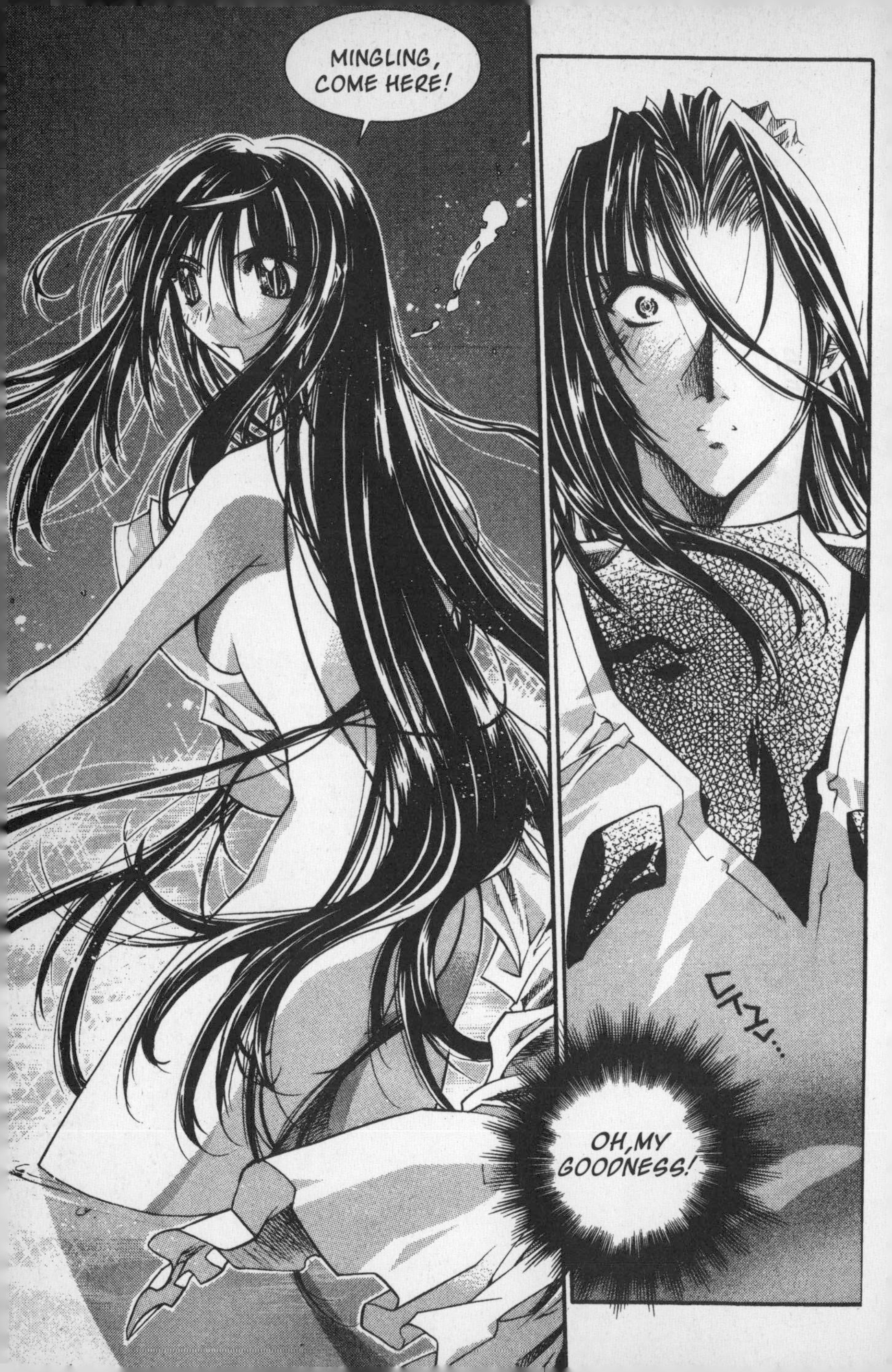
MINGLING, COME HERE!
UKYU...
OH, MY GOODNESS!

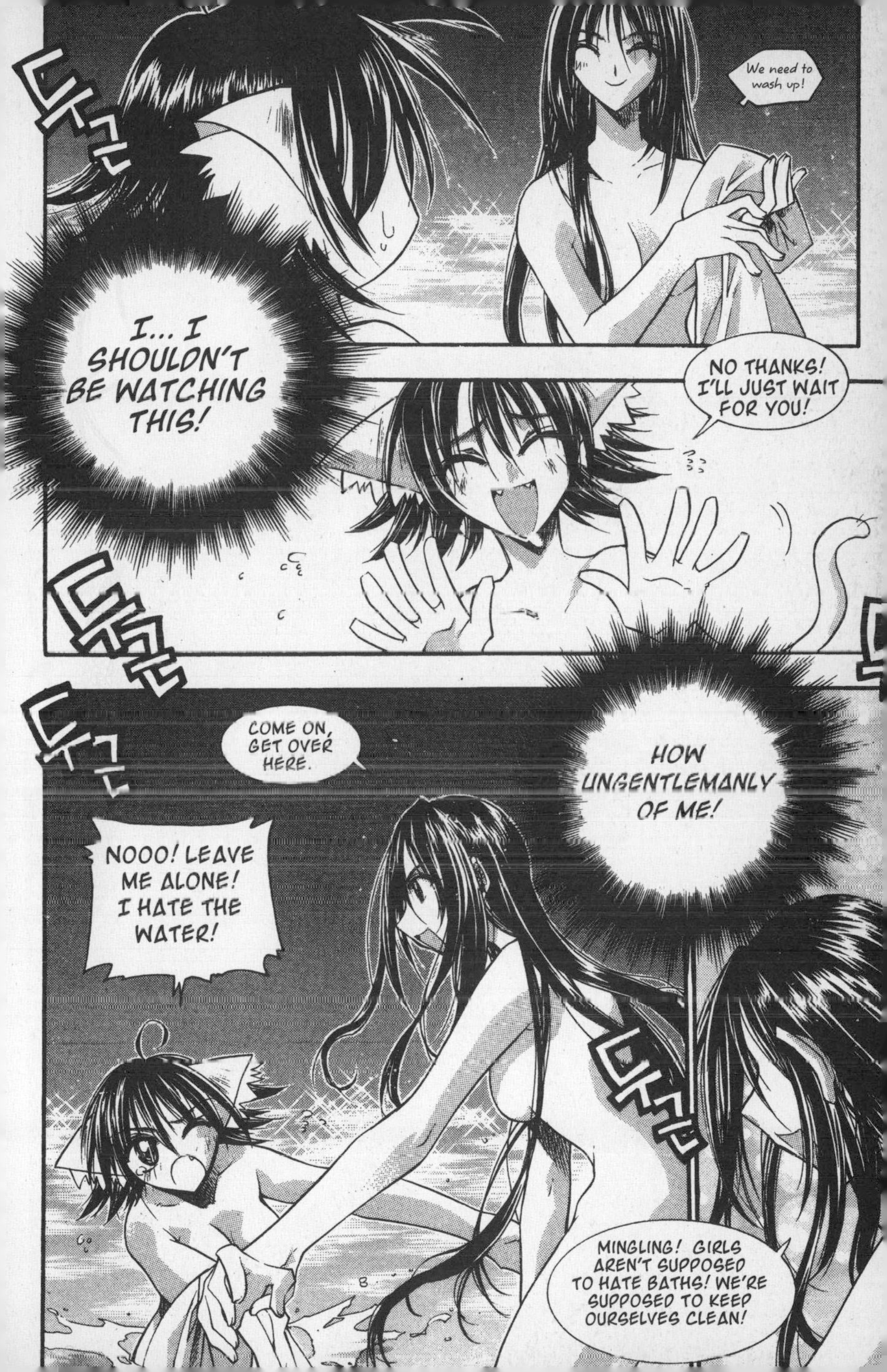
We need to wash up!
I... I SHOULDN'T BE WATCHING THIS!
NO THANKS! I'LL JUST WAIT FOR YOU!
COME ON, GET OVER HERE.
HOW UNGENTLEMANLY OF ME!
NOOO! LEAVE ME ALONE! I HATE THE WATER!
MINGLING! GIRLS AREN'T SUPPOSED TO HATE BATHS! WE'RE SUPPOSED TO KEEP OURSELVES CLEAN!

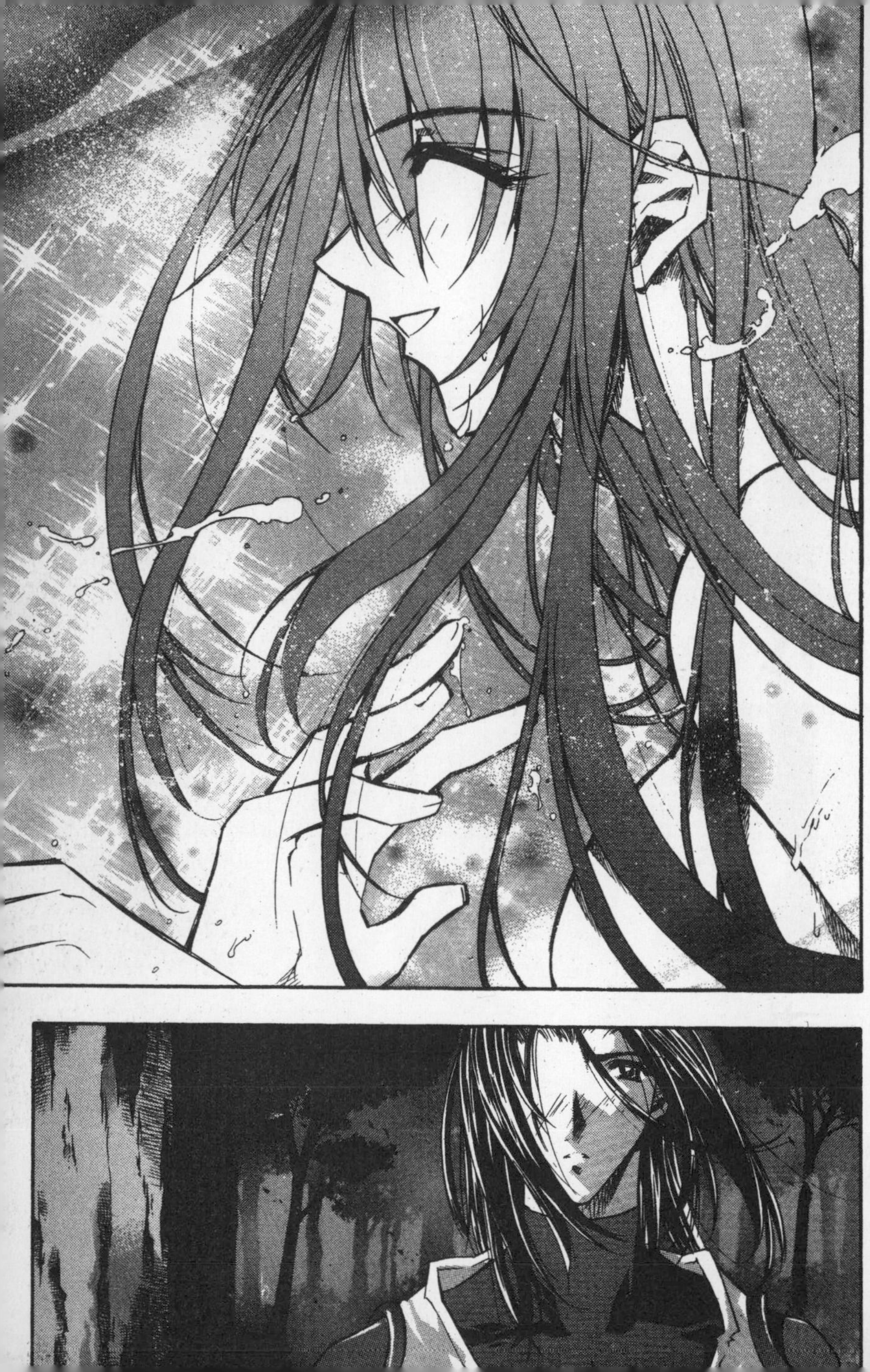

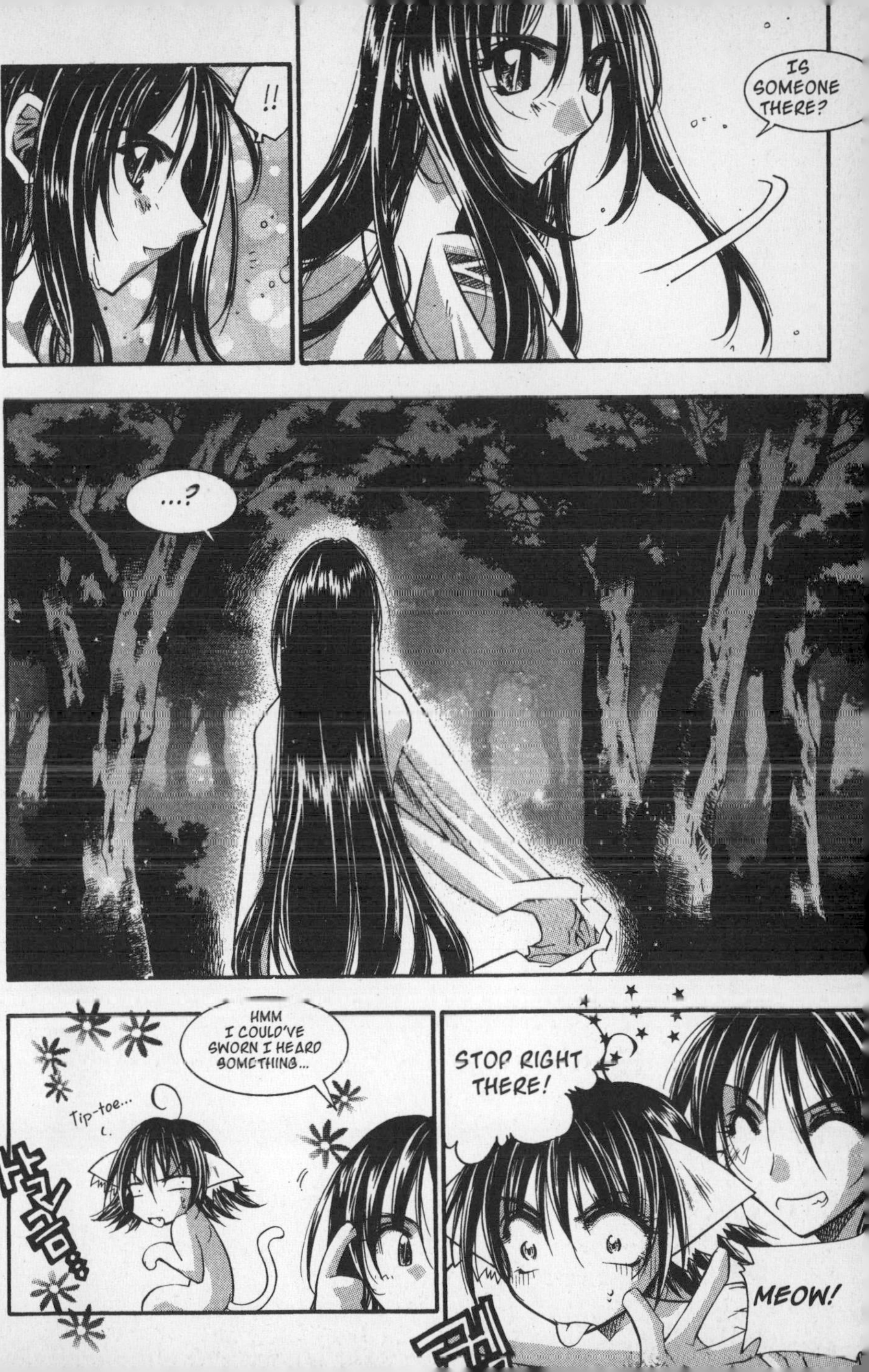
!!
IS SOMEONE THERE?
...?
HMM I COULD'VE SWORN I HEARD SOMETHING...
Tip-toe...
STOP RIGHT THERE!
MEOW!

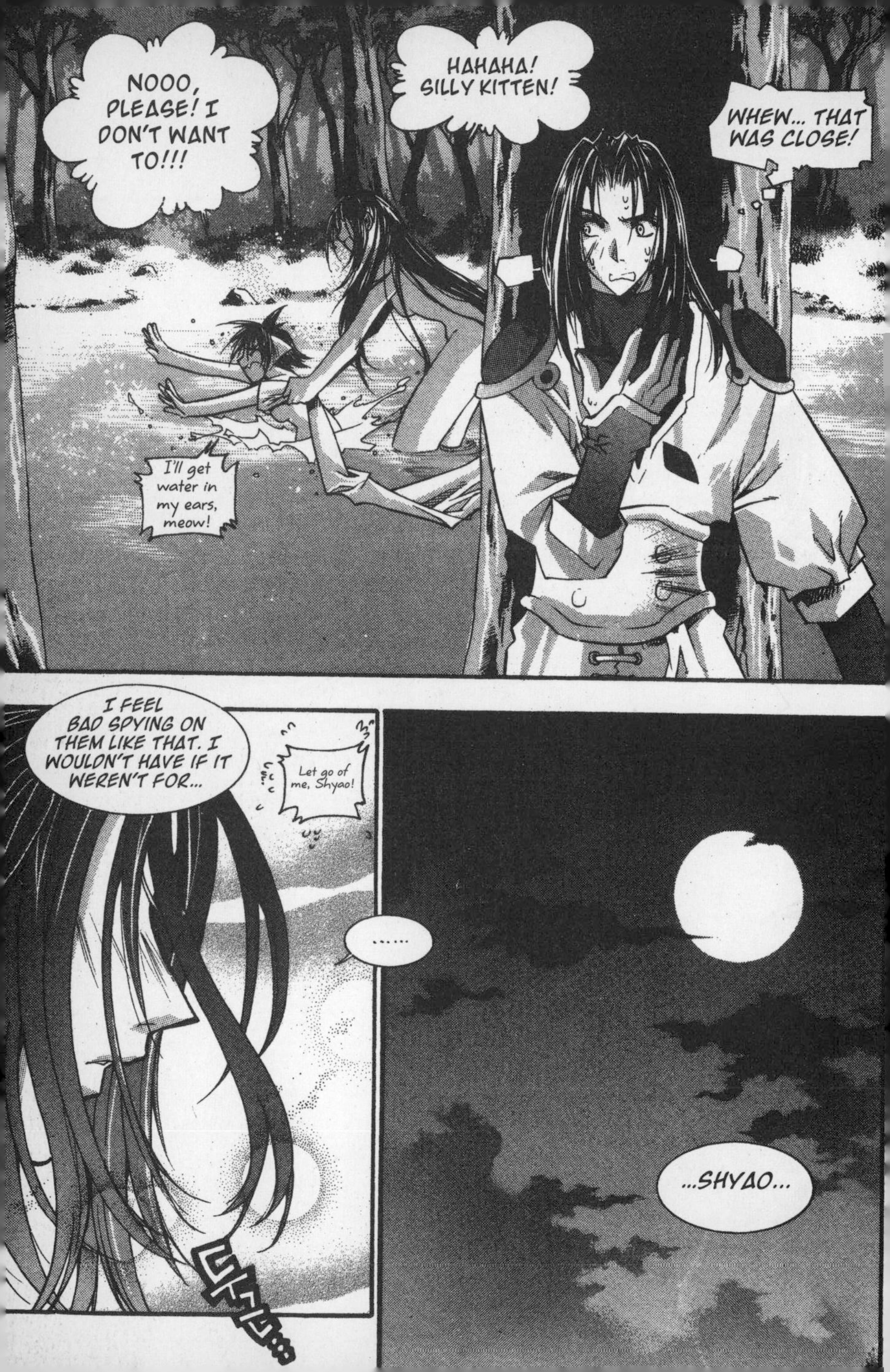
NOOO, PLEASE! I DON'T WANT TO!!!
HAHAHA! SILLY KITTEN!
WHEW... THAT WAS CLOSE!
I'll get water in my ears, meow!
I FEEL BAD SPYING ON THEM LIKE THAT. I WOULDN'T HAVE IF IT WEREN'T FOR...
Let go of me, Shyao!
......
...SHYAO...

Chronicle 18

Timura Oshu

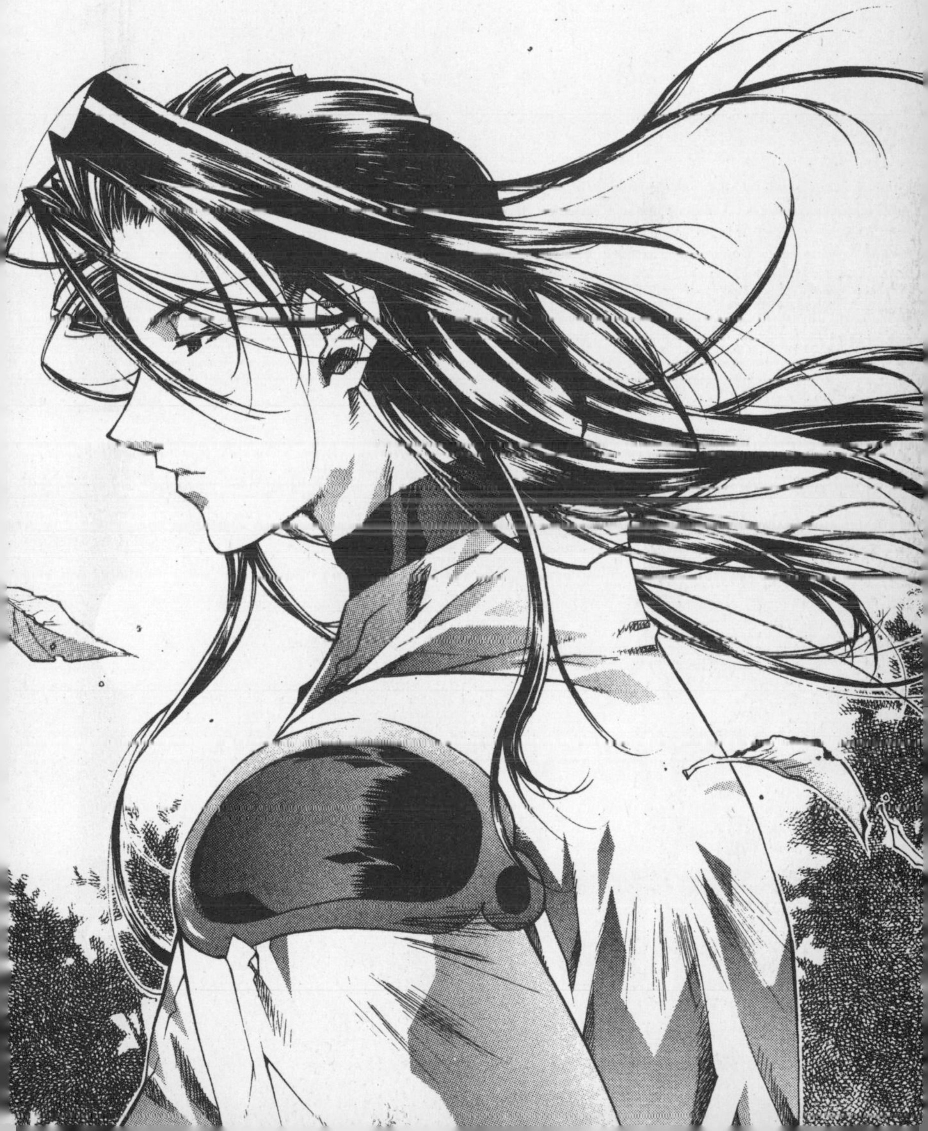

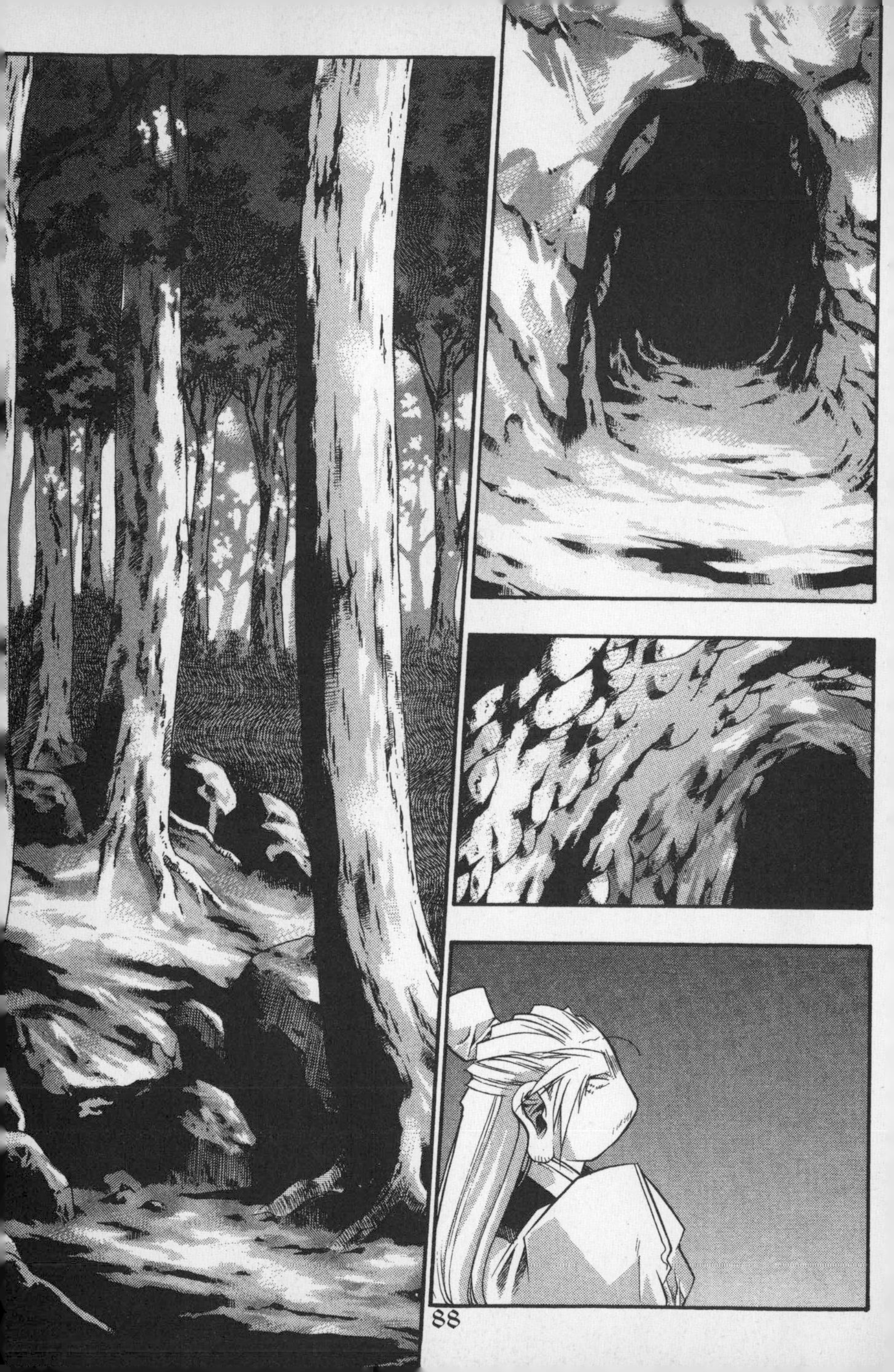

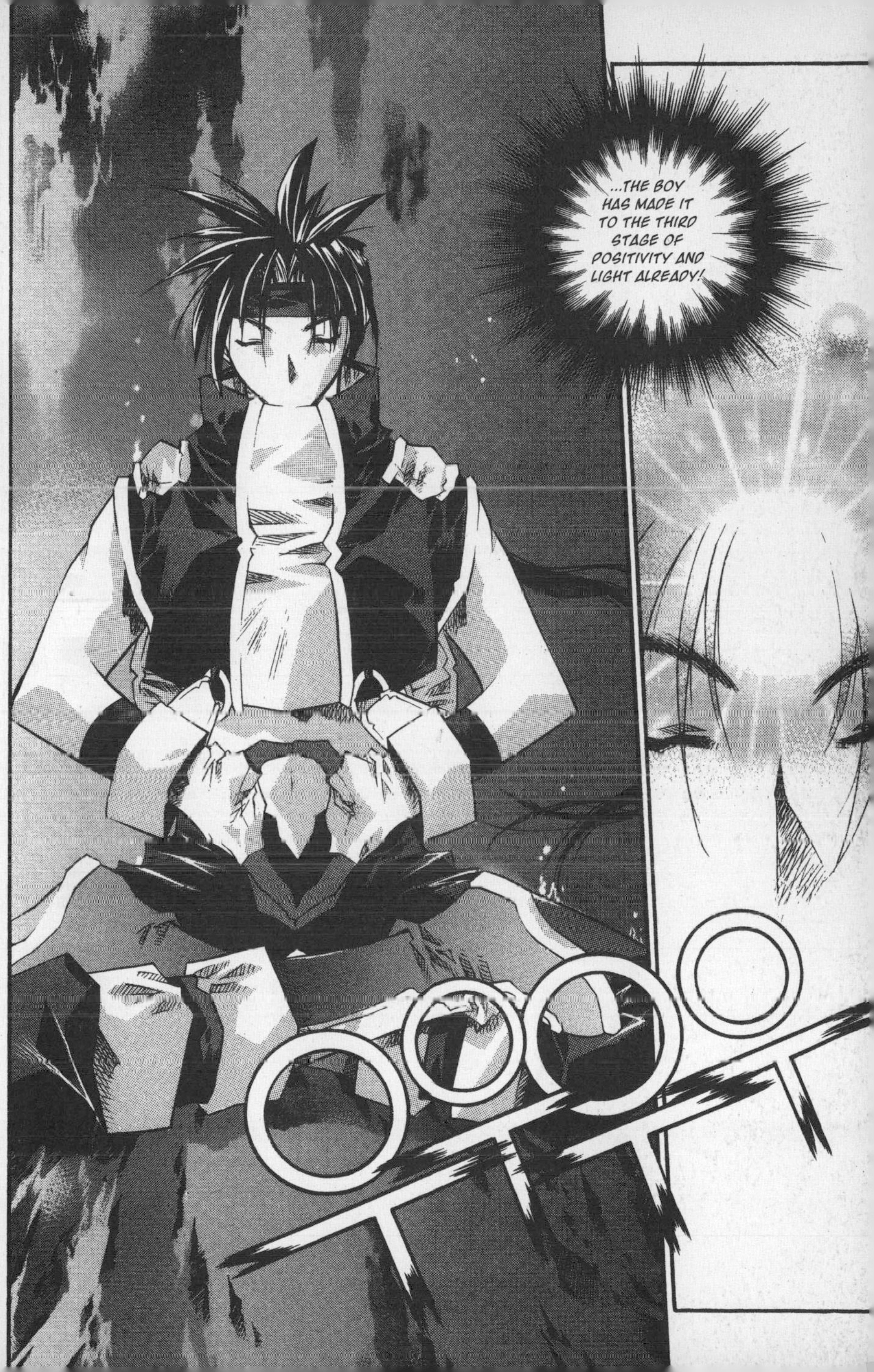
...THE BOY HAS MADE IT TO THE THIRD STAGE OF POSITIVITY AND LIGHT ALREADY!

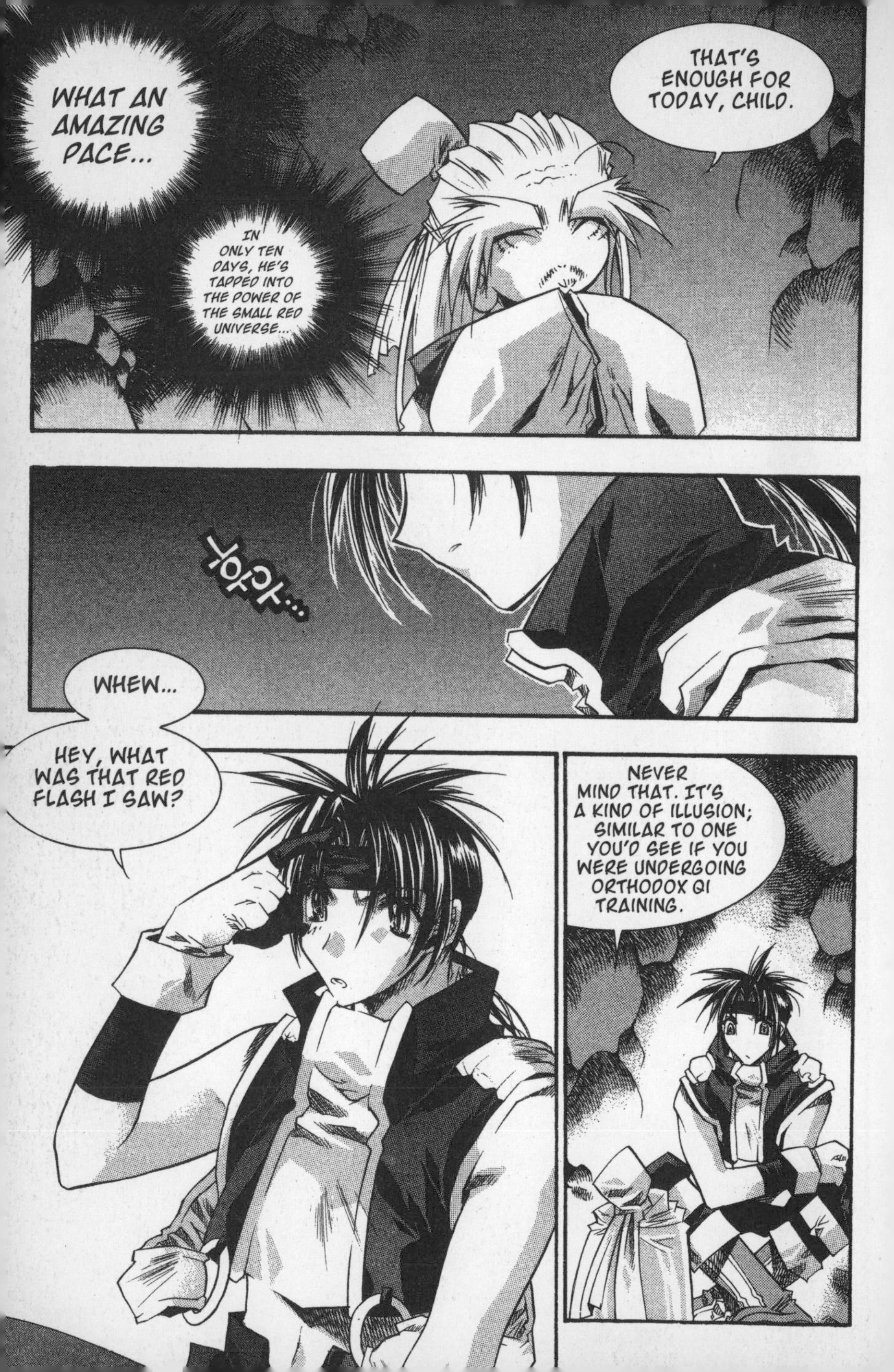
WHAT AN AMAZING PACE...
IN ONLY TEN DAYS, HE'S TAPPED INTO THE POWER OF THE SMALL RED UNIVERSE...
THAT'S ENOUGH FOR TODAY, CHILD.
WHEW...
HEY, WHAT WAS THAT RED FLASH I SAW?
NEVER MIND THAT. IT'S A KIND OF ILLUSION; SIMILAR TO ONE YOU'D SEE IF YOU WERE UNDERGOING ORTHODOX QI TRAINING.

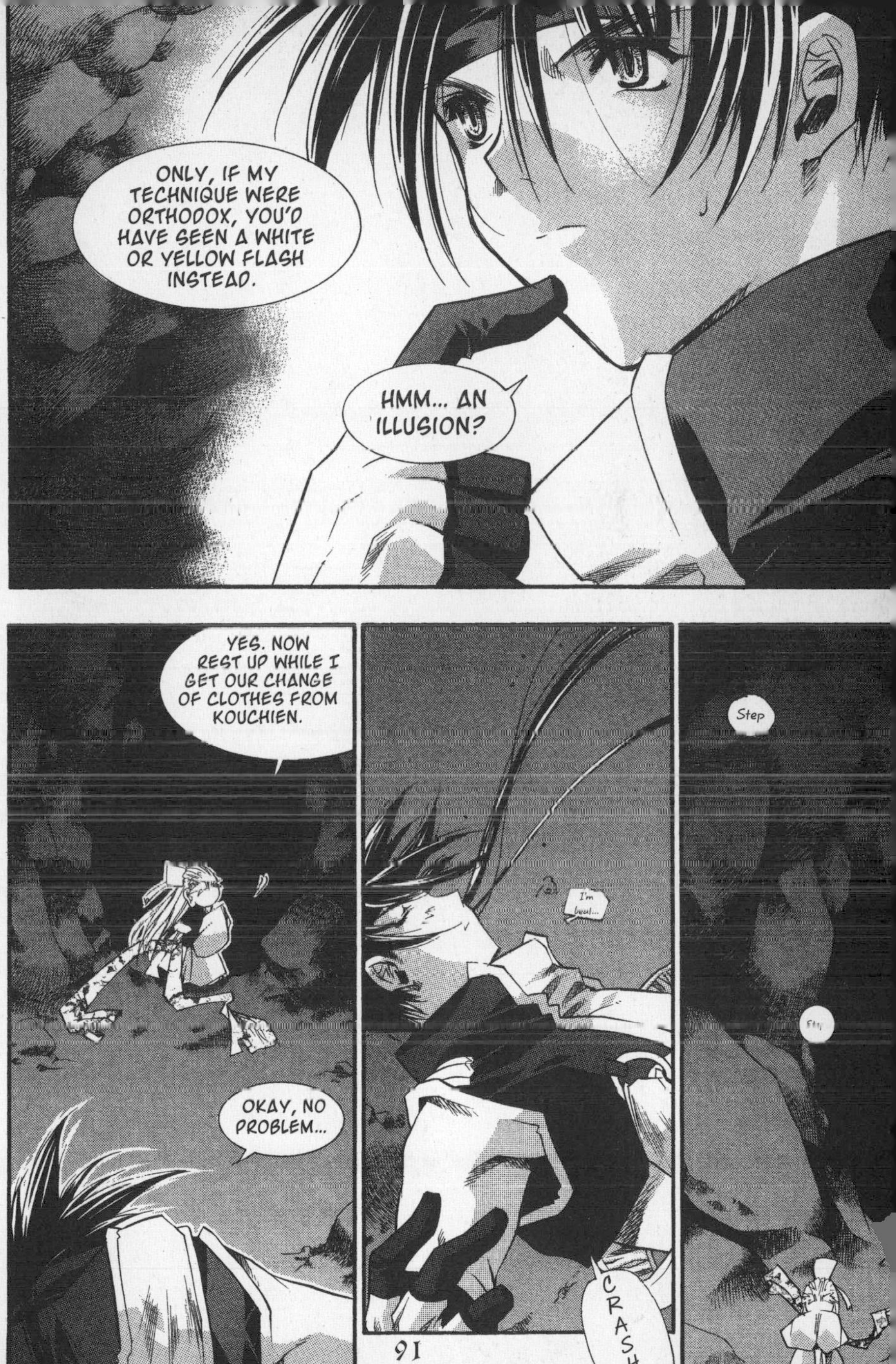
ONLY, IF MY TECHNIQUE WERE ORTHODOX, YOU'D HAVE SEEN A WHITE OR YELLOW FLASH INSTEAD.
HMM... AN ILLUSION?
YES. NOW REST UP WHILE I GET OUR CHANGE OF CLOTHES FROM KOUCHIEN.
OKAY, NO PROBLEM...
I'm beat...
CRASH
Step

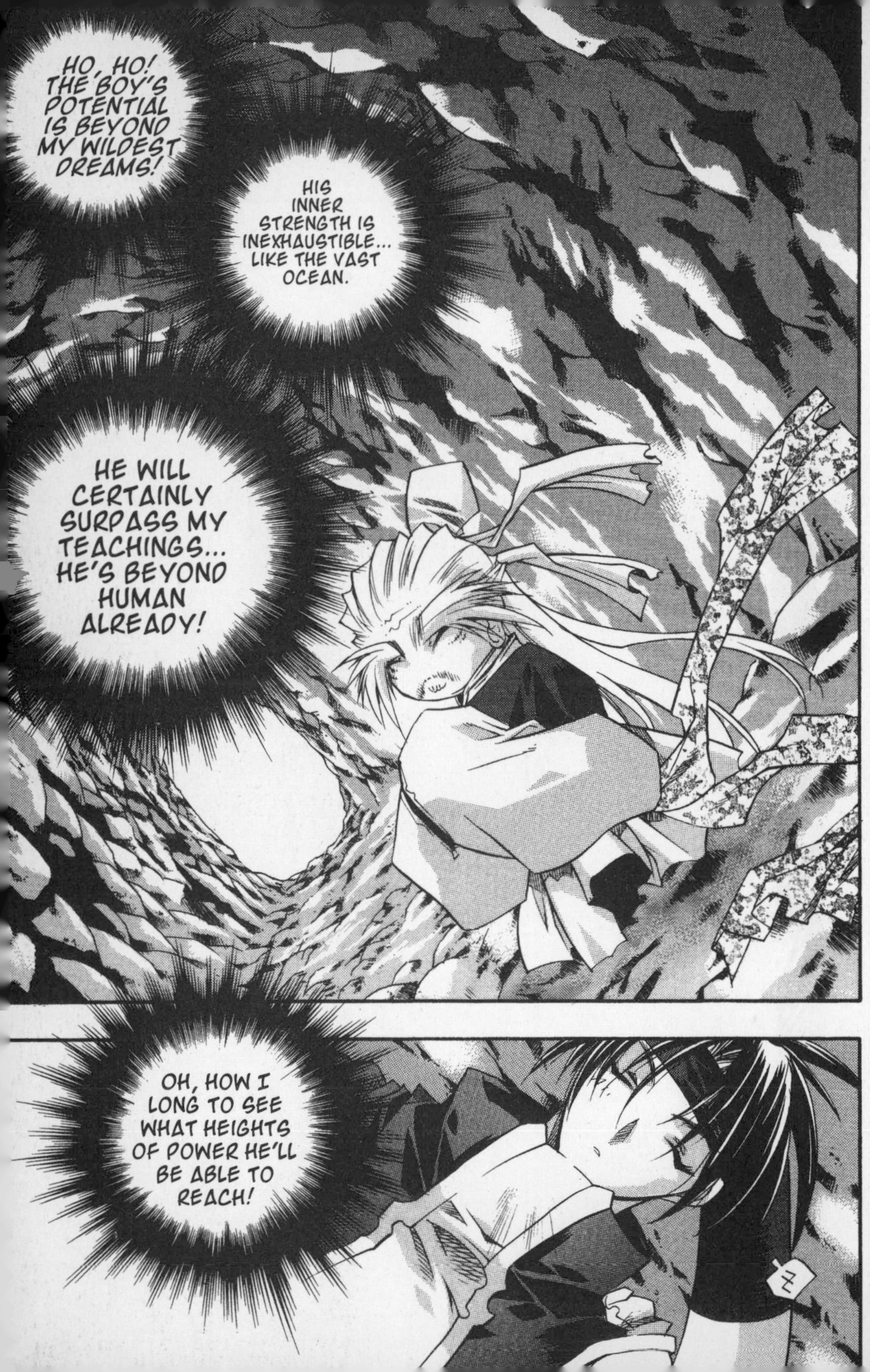
HO, HO! THE BOY'S POTENTIAL IS BEYOND MY WILDEST DREAMS!
HIS INNER STRENGTH IS INEXHAUSTIBLE... LIKE THE VAST OCEAN.
HE WILL CERTAINLY SURPASS MY TEACHINGS... HE'S BEYOND HUMAN ALREADY!
OH, HOW I LONG TO SEE WHAT HEIGHTS OF POWER HE'LL BE ABLE TO REACH!

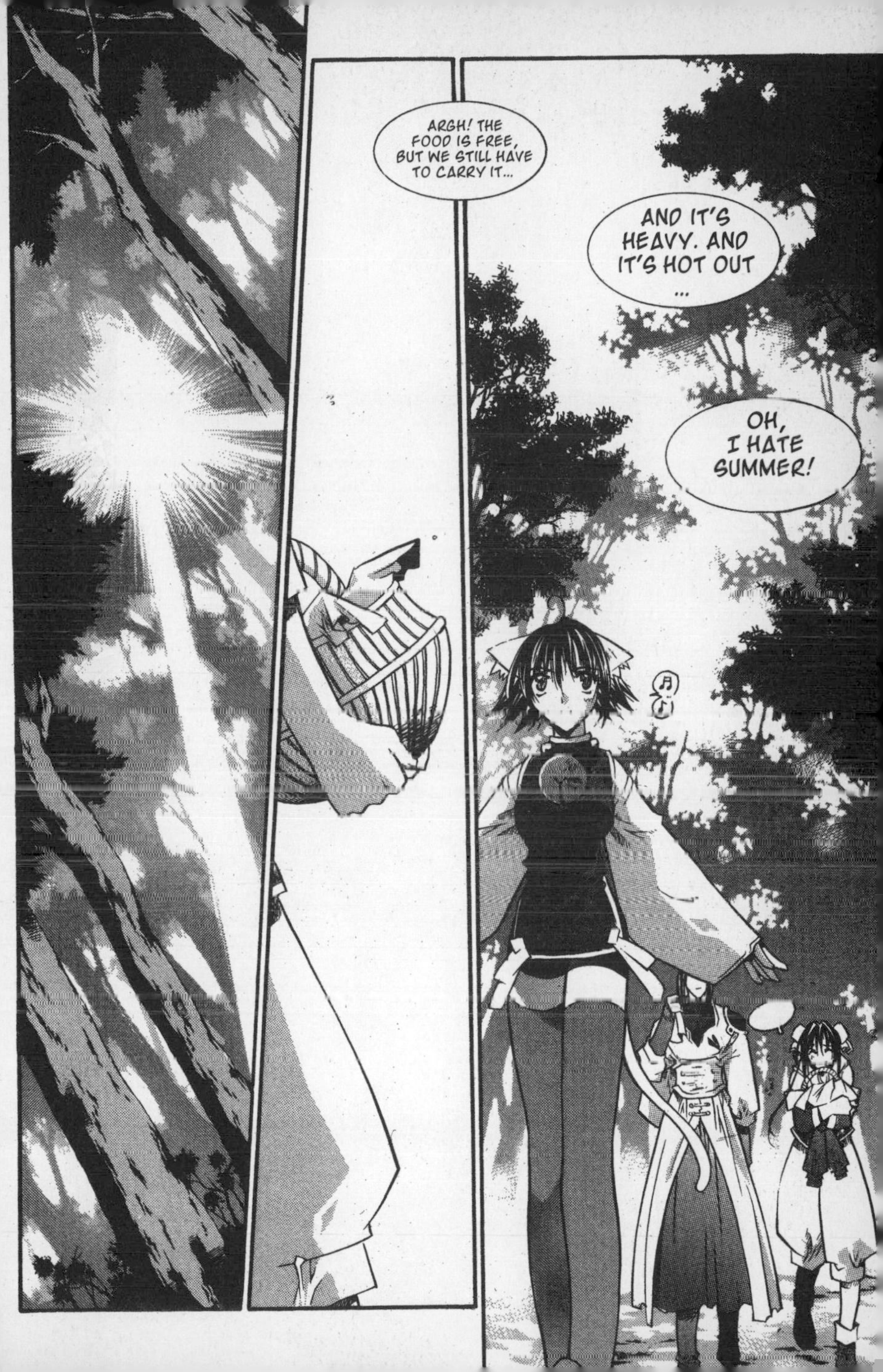
ARGH! THE FOOD IS FREE, BUT WE STILL HAVE TO CARRY IT...
AND IT'S HEAVY. AND IT'S HOT OUT ...
OH, I HATE SUMMER!

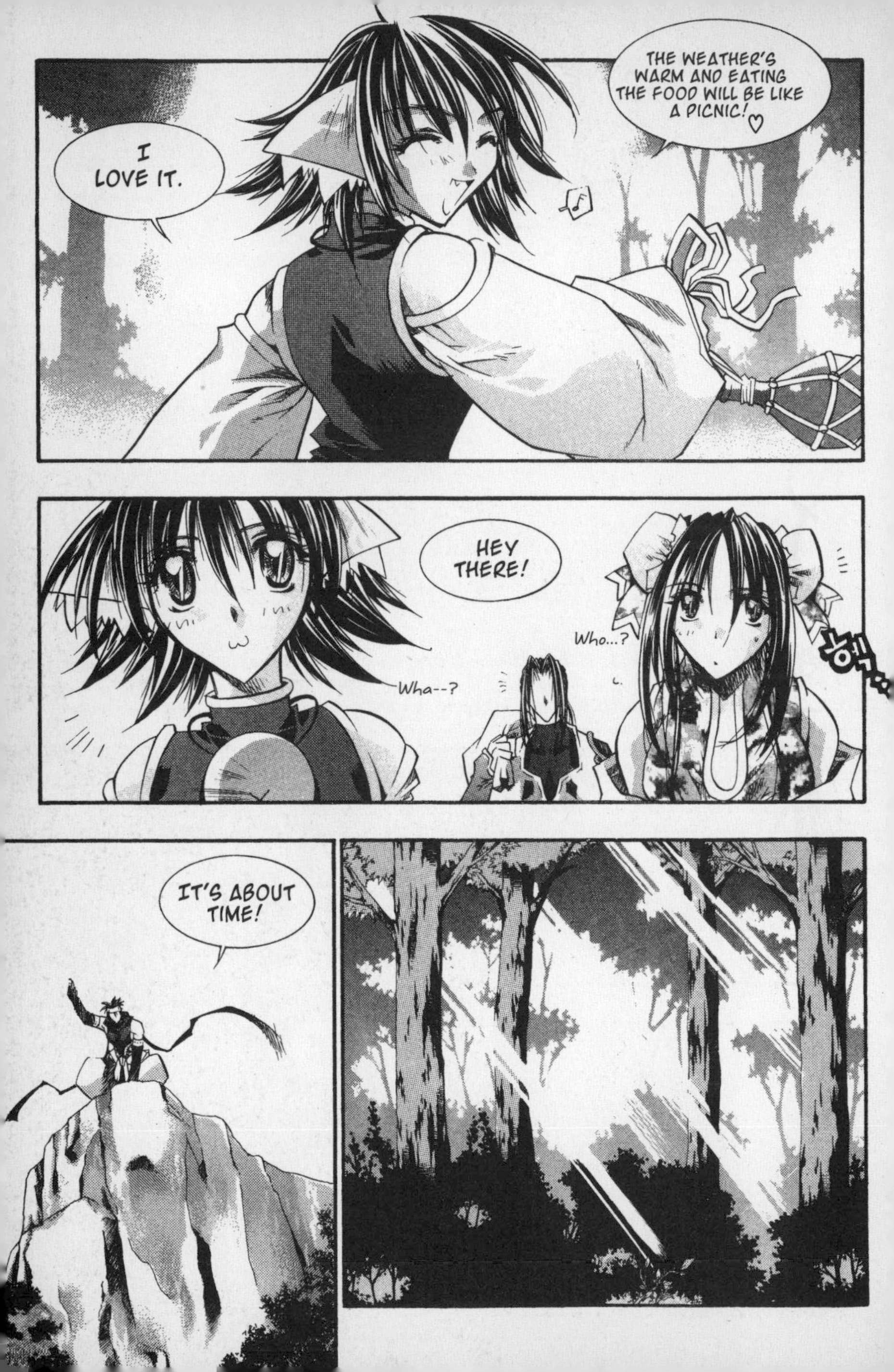
I LOVE IT.
THE WEATHER'S WARM AND EATING THE FOOD WILL BE LIKE A PICNIC! ♡
HEY THERE!
Wha--?
Who...?
IT'S ABOUT TIME!

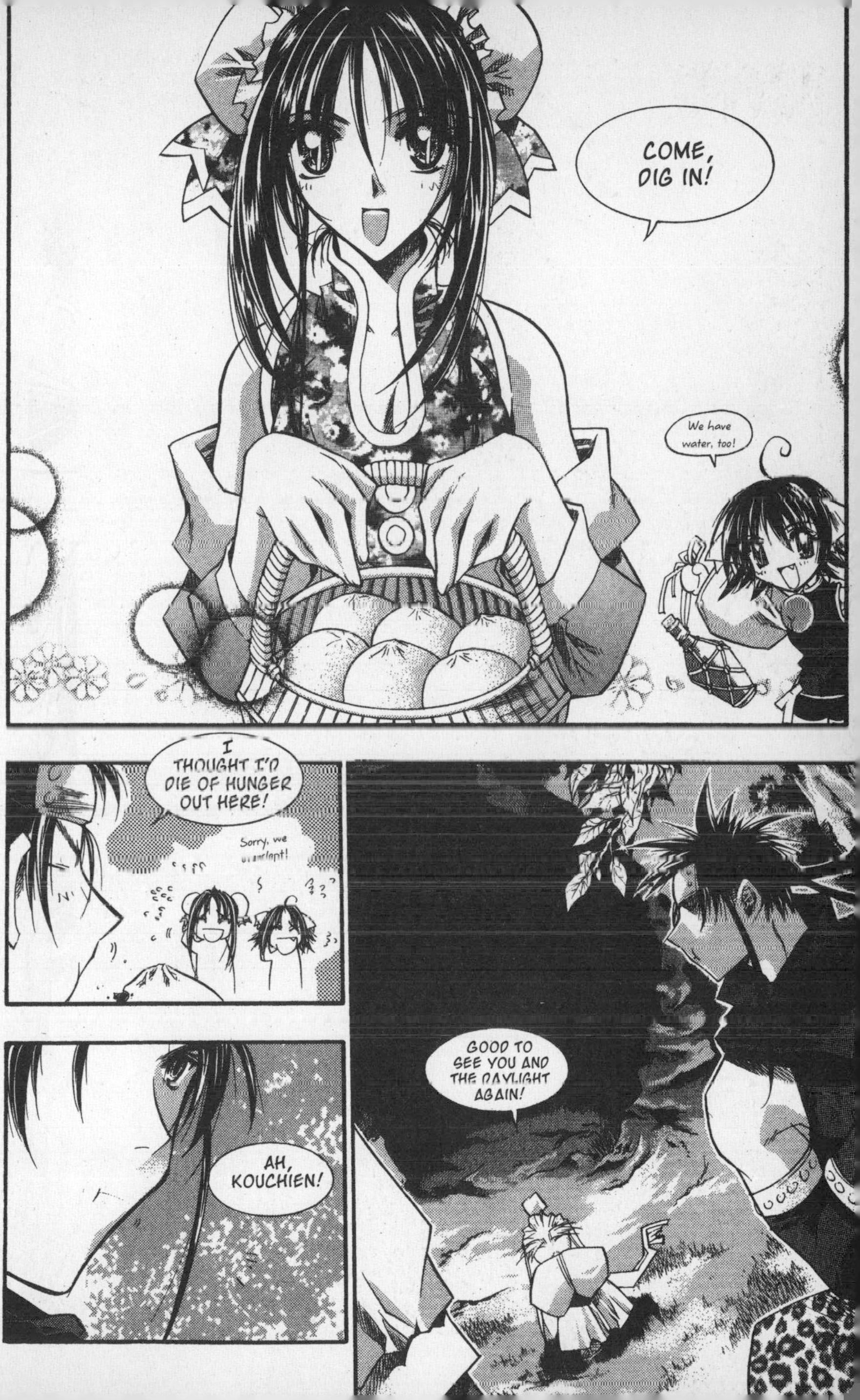
COME, DIG IN!
We have water, too!
I THOUGHT I'D DIE OF HUNGER OUT HERE!
Sorry, we overslept!
AH, KOUCHIEN!
GOOD TO SEE YOU AND THE DAYLIGHT AGAIN!

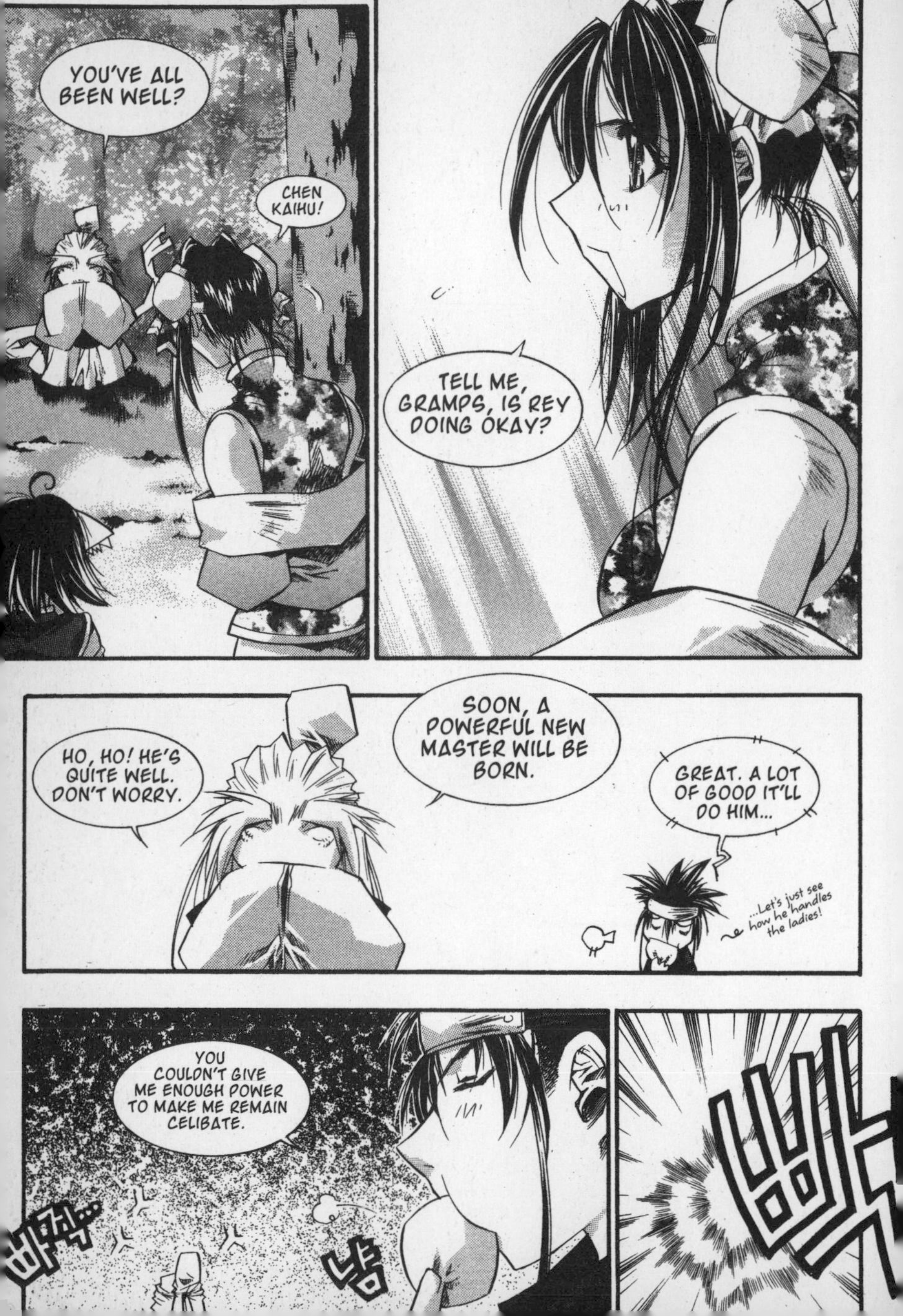
YOU'VE ALL BEEN WELL?
CHEN KAIHU!
TELL ME, GRAMPS, IS REY DOING OKAY?
HO, HO! HE'S QUITE WELL. DON'T WORRY.
SOON, A POWERFUL NEW MASTER WILL BE BORN.
GREAT. A LOT OF GOOD IT'LL DO HIM...
...Let's just see how he handles the ladies!
YOU COULDN'T GIVE ME ENOUGH POWER TO MAKE ME REMAIN CELIBATE.
빠직...
냠
빡

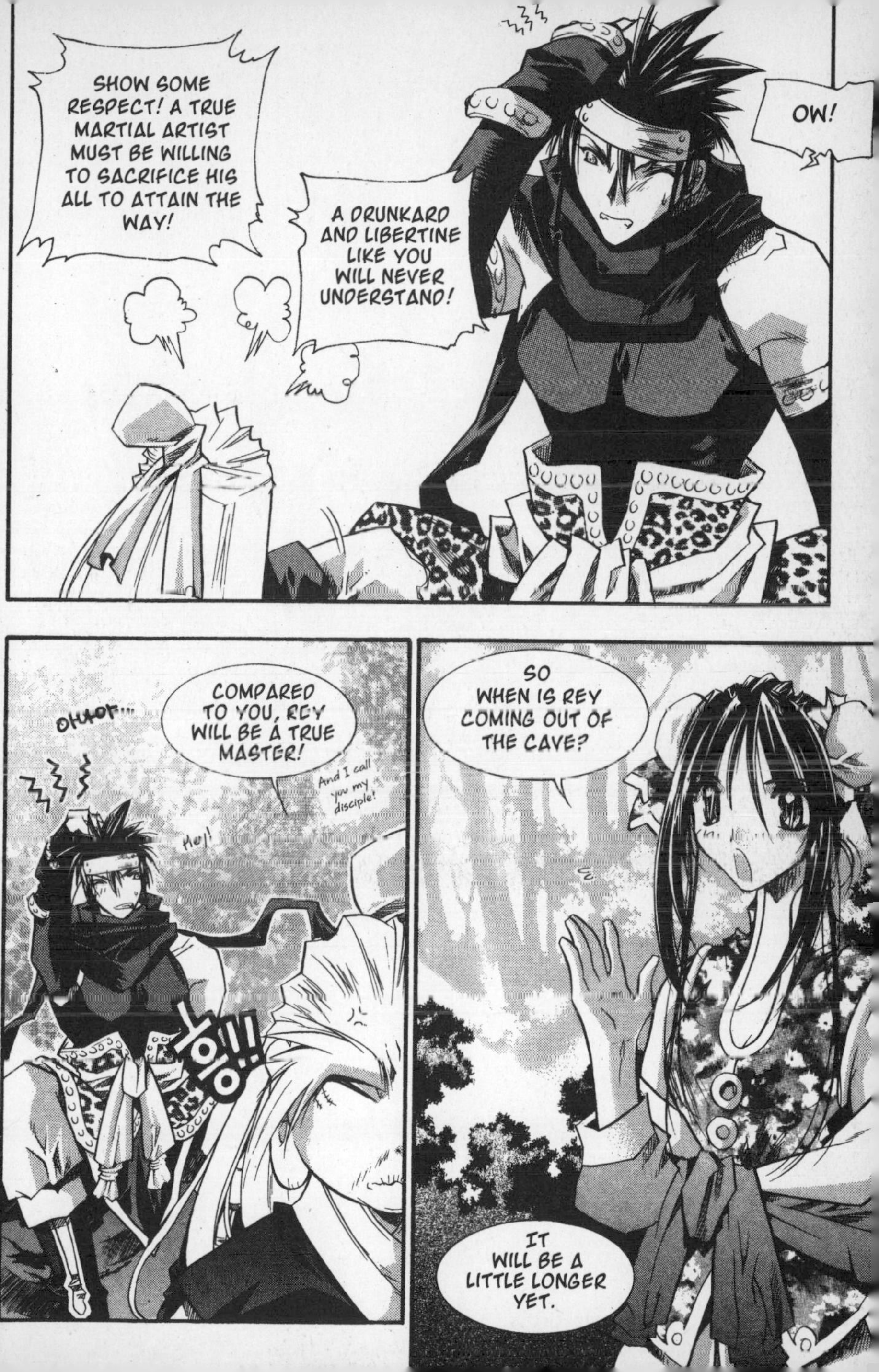
SHOW SOME RESPECT! A TRUE MARTIAL ARTIST MUST BE WILLING TO SACRIFICE HIS ALL TO ATTAIN THE WAY!
A DRUNKARD AND LIBERTINE LIKE YOU WILL NEVER UNDERSTAND!
OW!
COMPARED TO YOU, REY WILL BE A TRUE MASTER!
And I call you my disciple!
Hey!
SO WHEN IS REY COMING OUT OF THE CAVE?
IT WILL BE A LITTLE LONGER YET.

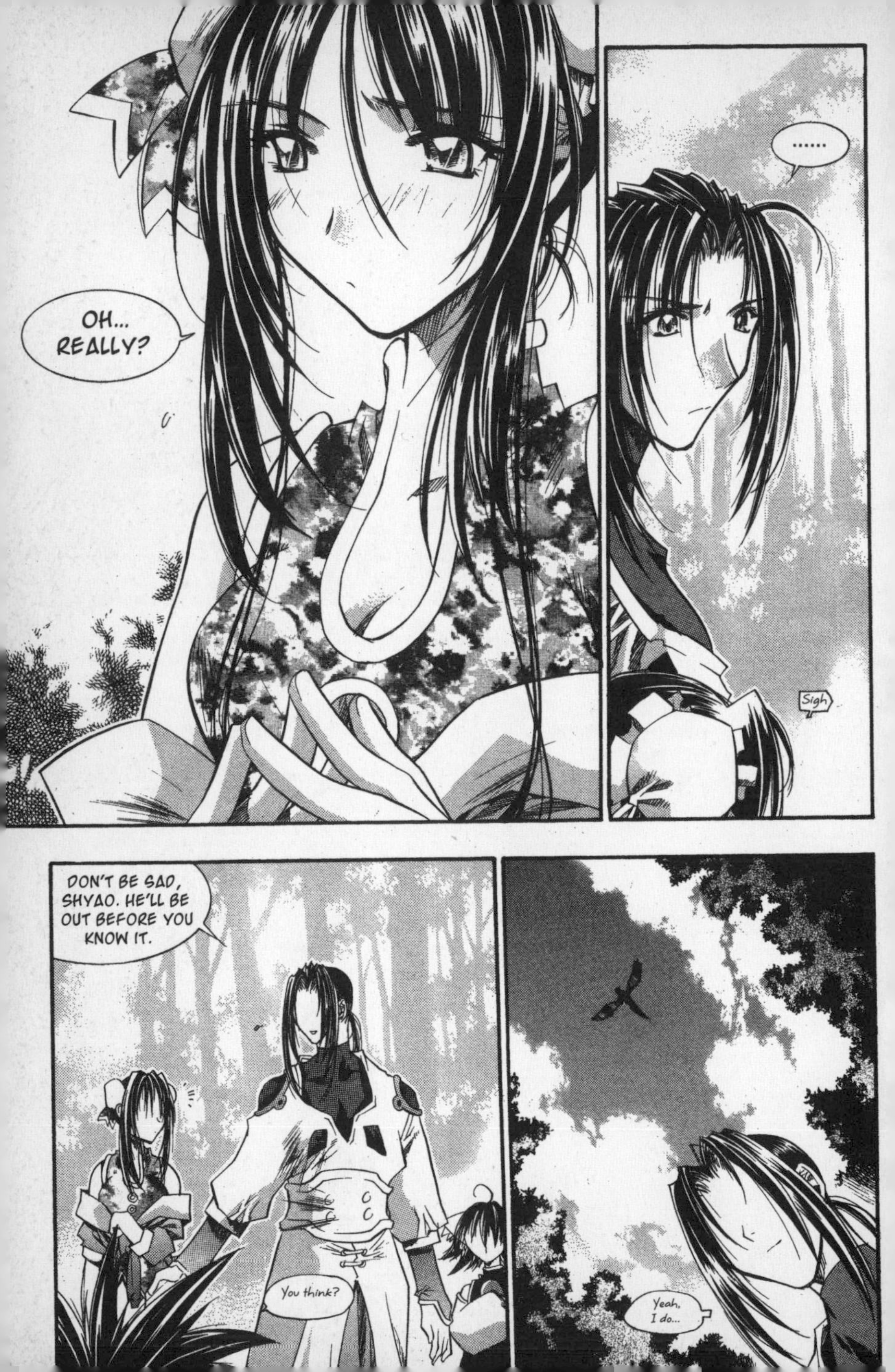
OH... REALLY?
......
Sigh
DON'T BE SAD, SHYAO. HE'LL BE OUT BEFORE YOU KNOW IT.
You think?
Yeah, I do...

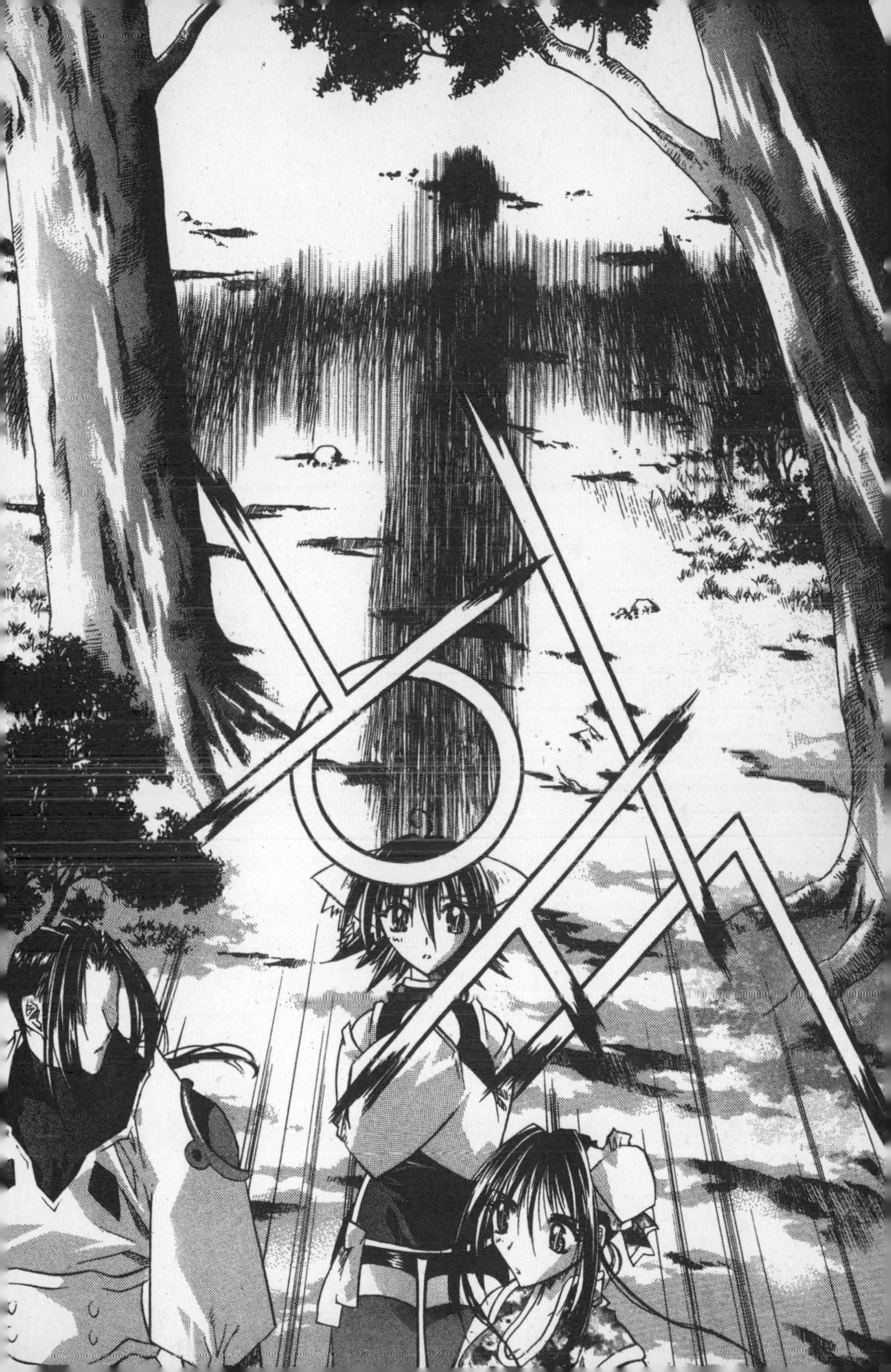

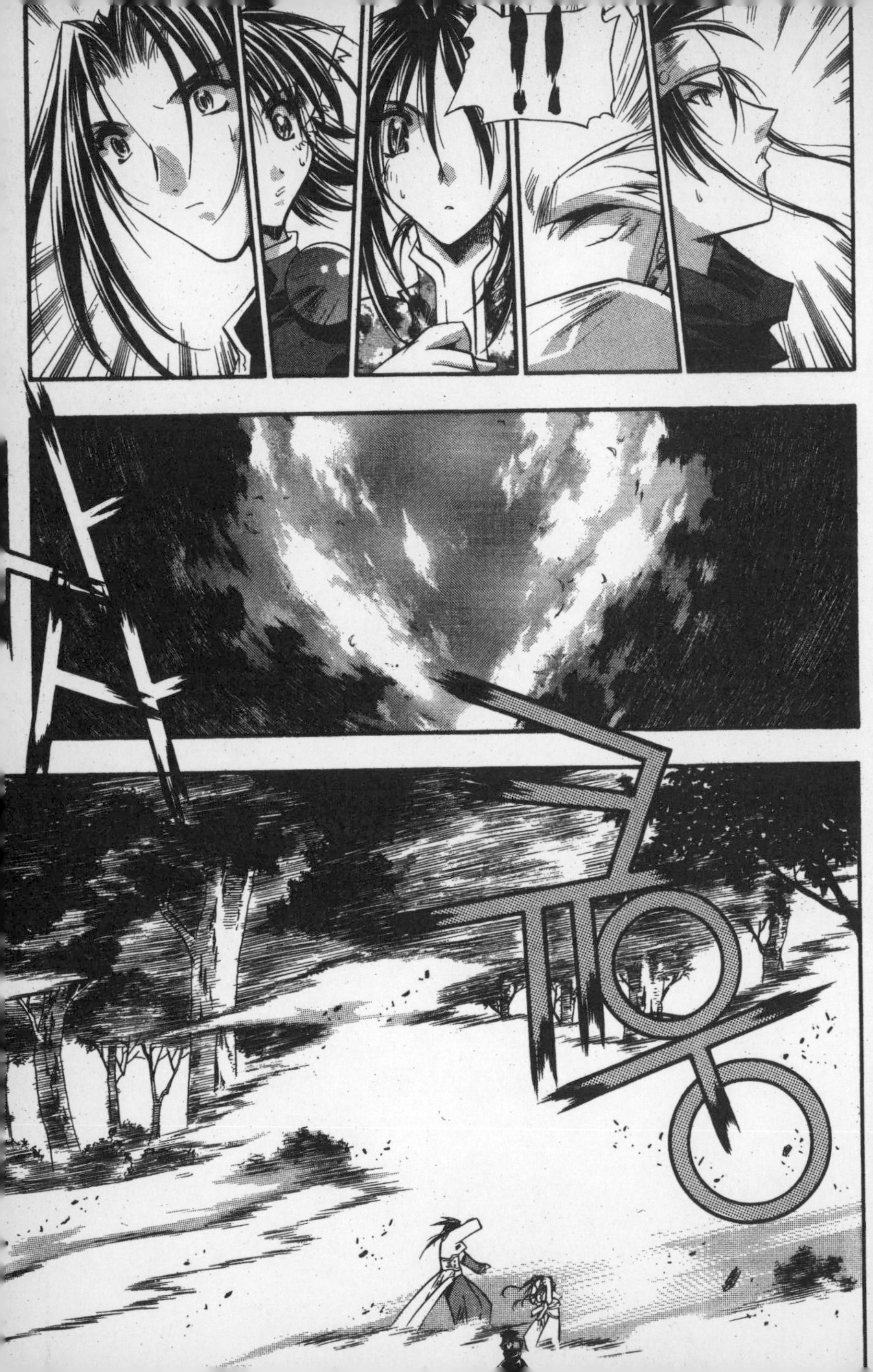
!!

WHAT THE--?!

AACH! MY DUMPLINGS!

LOOK! OVER THERE!

Yow!

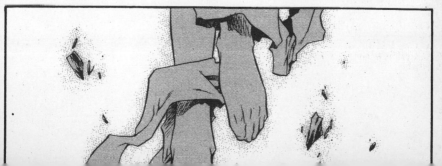

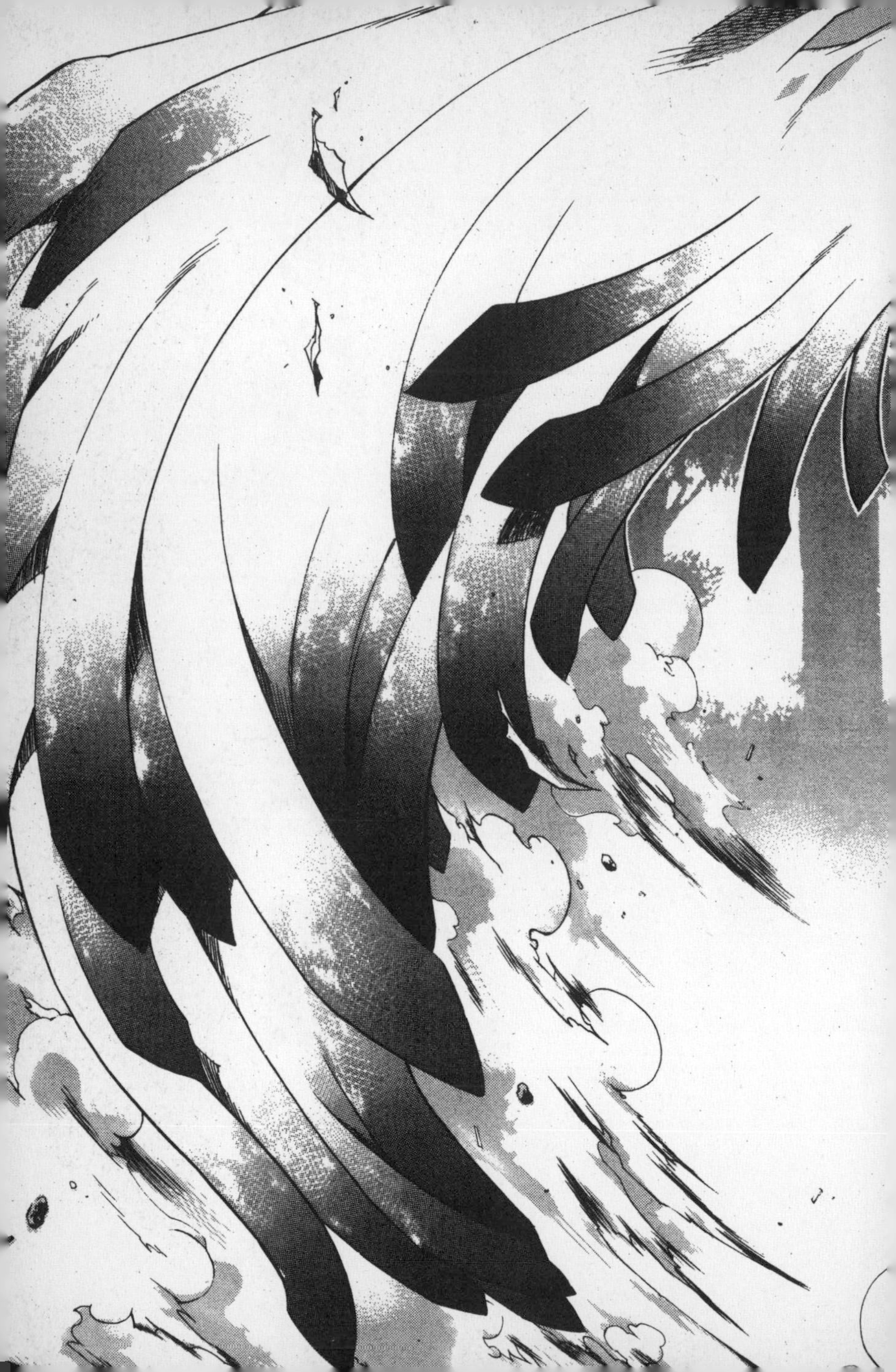

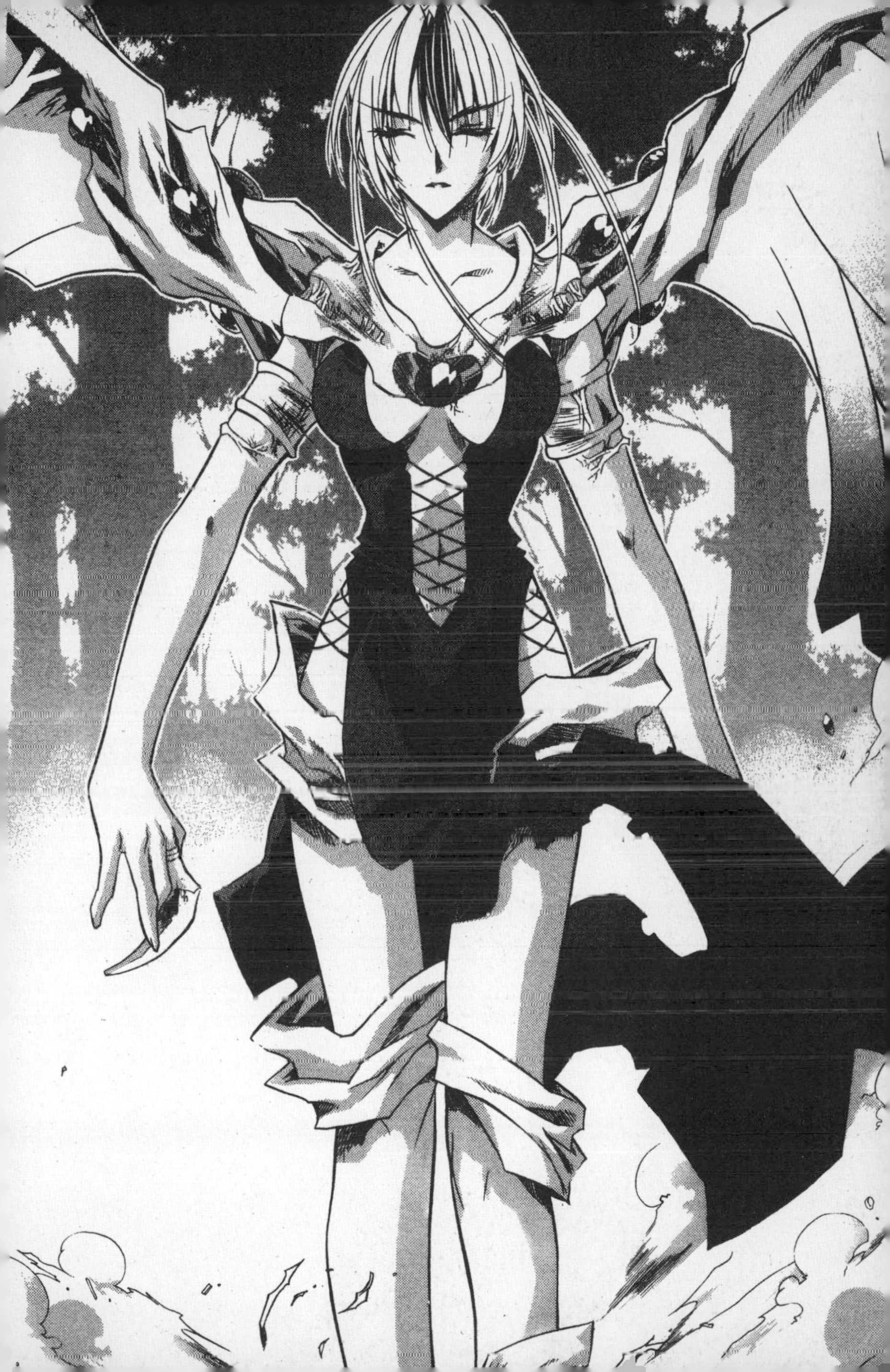

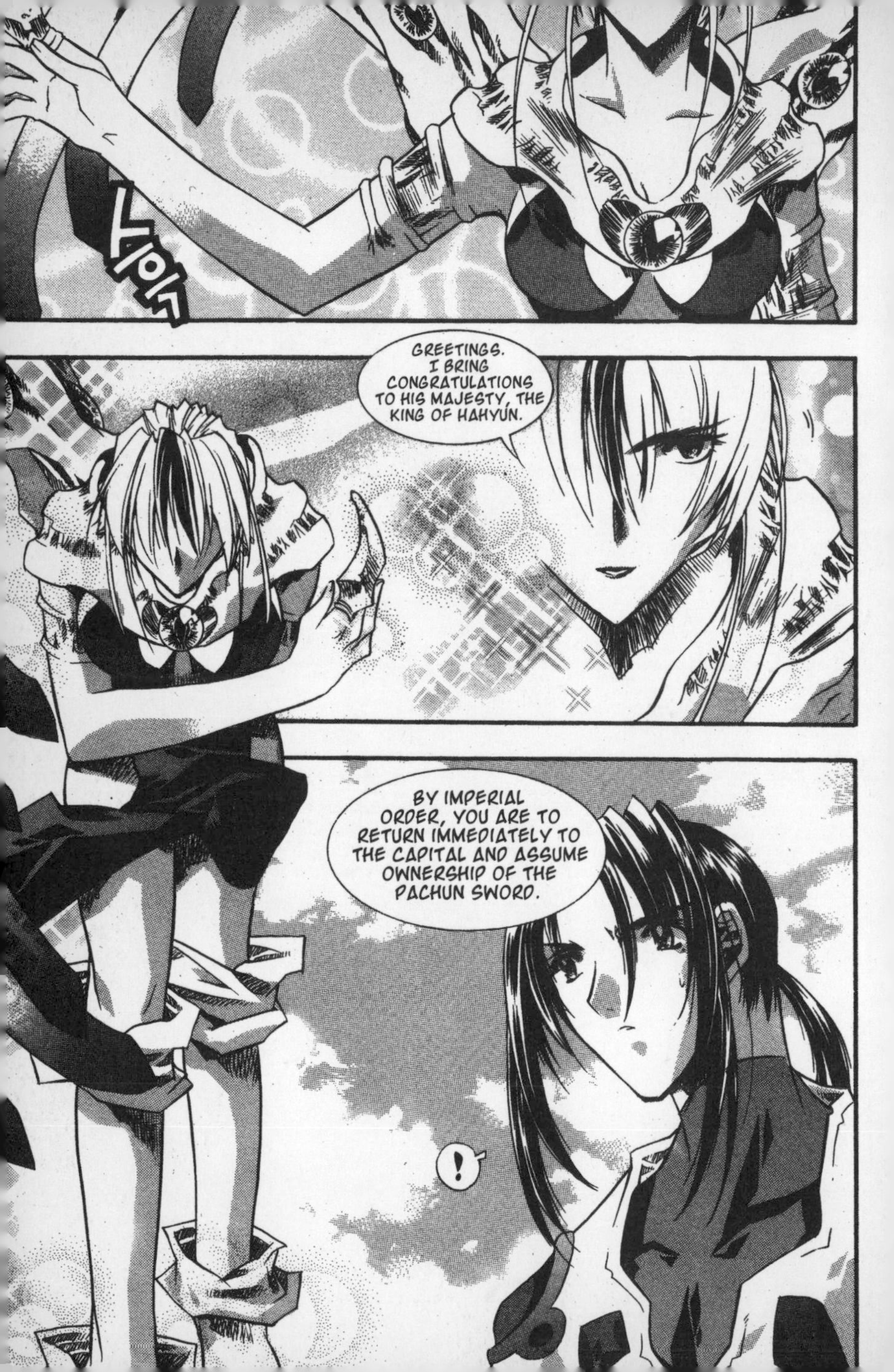
GREETINGS. I BRING CONGRATULATIONS TO HIS MAJESTY, THE KING OF HAHYÚN.
BY IMPERIAL ORDER, YOU ARE TO RETURN IMMEDIATELY TO THE CAPITAL AND ASSUME OWNERSHIP OF THE PACHUN SWORD.
!

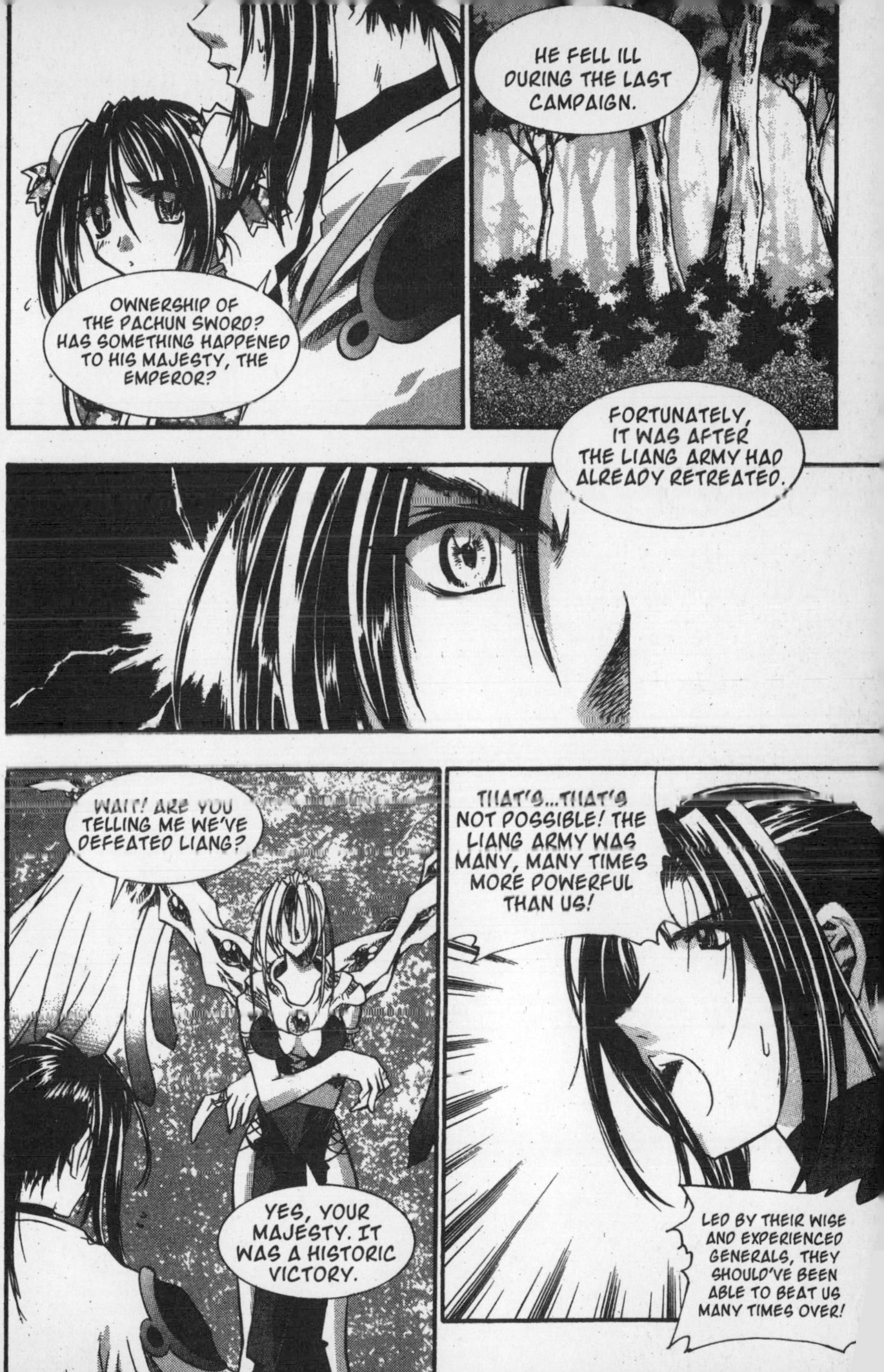

OWNERSHIP OF THE PACHUN SWORD? HAS SOMETHING HAPPENED TO HIS MAJESTY, THE EMPEROR?
HE FELL ILL DURING THE LAST CAMPAIGN.
FORTUNATELY, IT WAS AFTER THE LIANG ARMY HAD ALREADY RETREATED.
WAIT! ARE YOU TELLING ME WE'VE DEFEATED LIANG?
YES, YOUR MAJESTY. IT WAS A HISTORIC VICTORY.
THAT'S...THAT'S NOT POSSIBLE! THE LIANG ARMY WAS MANY, MANY TIMES MORE POWERFUL THAN US!
LED BY THEIR WISE AND EXPERIENCED GENERALS, THEY SHOULD'VE BEEN ABLE TO BEAT US MANY TIMES OVER!

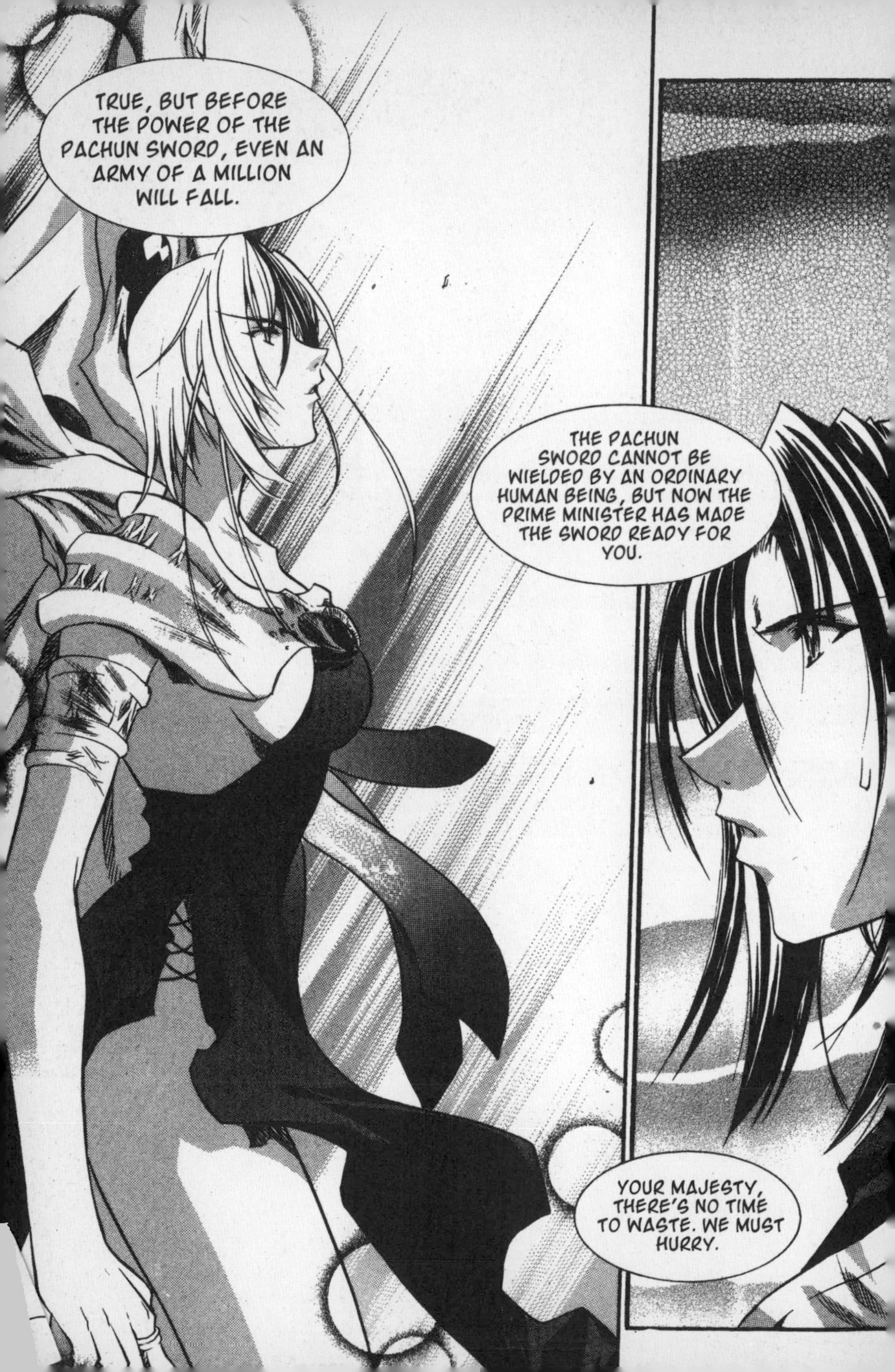
TRUE, BUT BEFORE THE POWER OF THE PACHUN SWORD, EVEN AN ARMY OF A MILLION WILL FALL.
THE PACHUN SWORD CANNOT BE WIELDED BY AN ORDINARY HUMAN BEING, BUT NOW THE PRIME MINISTER HAS MADE THE SWORD READY FOR YOU.
YOUR MAJESTY, THERE'S NO TIME TO WASTE. WE MUST HURRY.

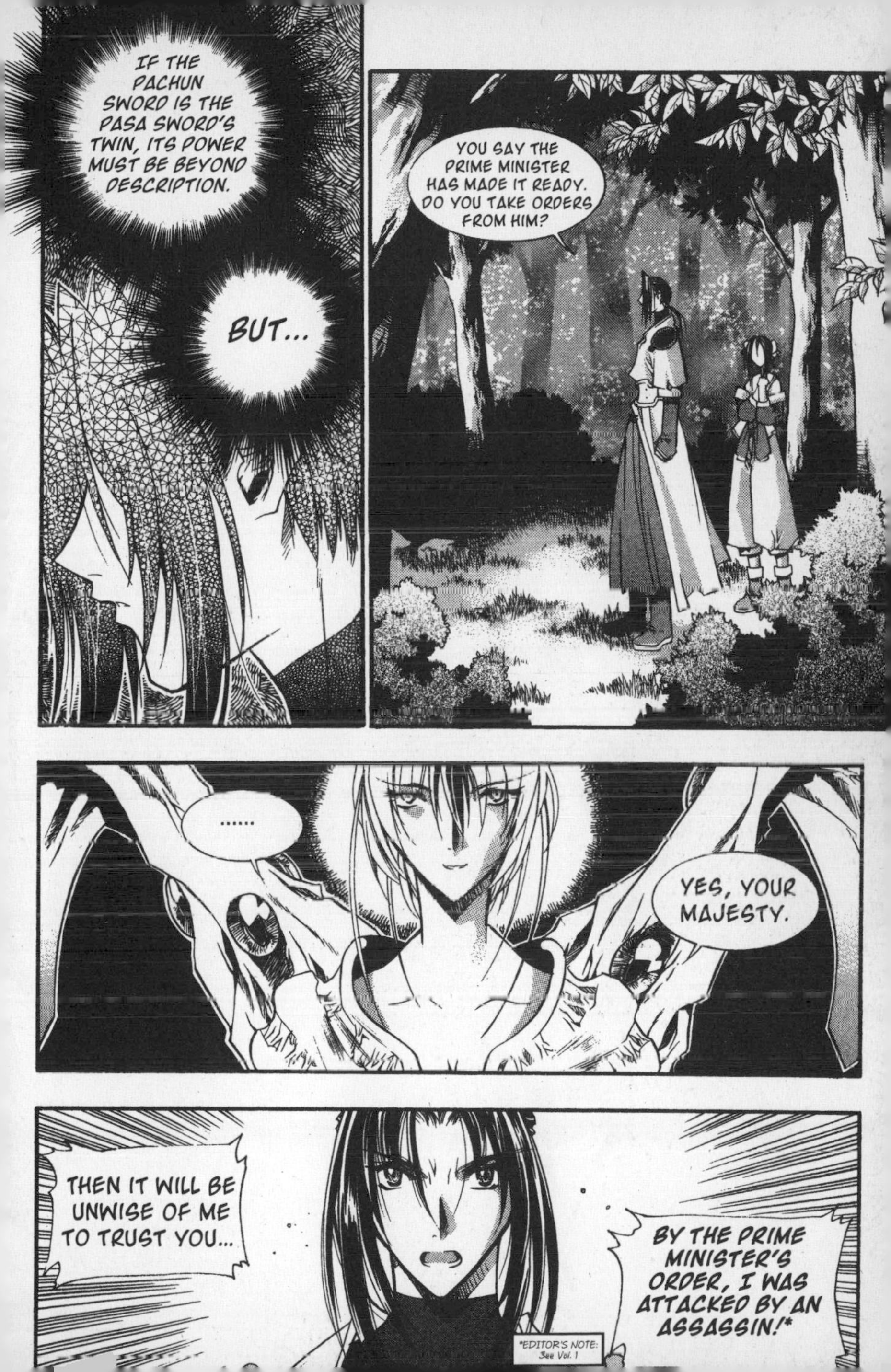
IF THE PACHUN SWORD IS THE PASA SWORD'S TWIN, ITS POWER MUST BE BEYOND DESCRIPTION.
BUT...
YOU SAY THE PRIME MINISTER HAS MADE IT READY. DO YOU TAKE ORDERS FROM HIM?
......
YES, YOUR MAJESTY.
THEN IT WILL BE UNWISE OF ME TO TRUST YOU...
BY THE PRIME MINISTER'S ORDER, I WAS ATTACKED BY AN ASSASSIN!*
*EDITOR'S NOTE: See Vol. 1

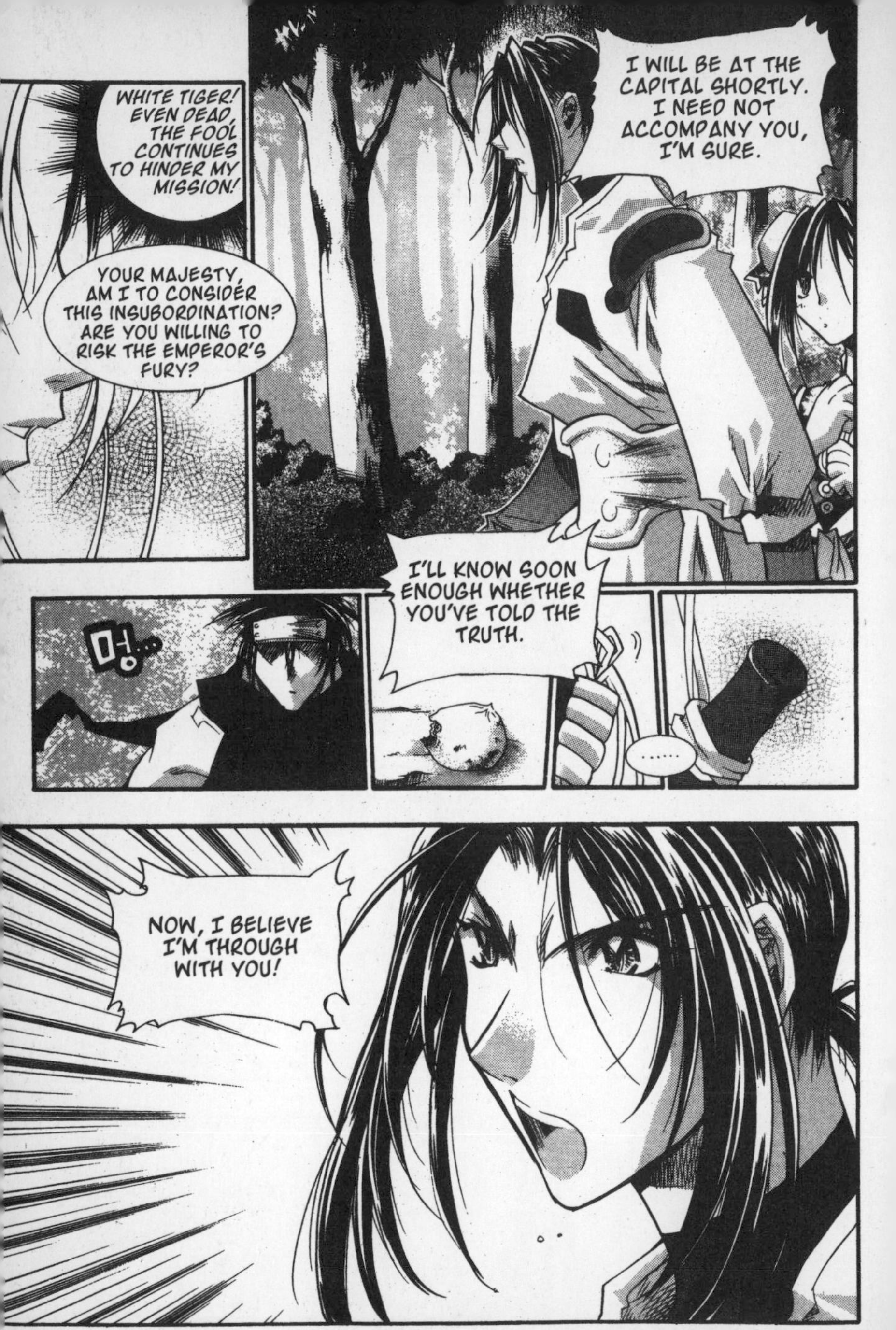
WHITE TIGER! EVEN DEAD, THE FOOL CONTINUES TO HINDER MY MISSION!
YOUR MAJESTY, AM I TO CONSIDER THIS INSUBORDINATION? ARE YOU WILLING TO RISK THE EMPEROR'S FURY?
I WILL BE AT THE CAPITAL SHORTLY. I NEED NOT ACCOMPANY YOU, I'M SURE.
I'LL KNOW SOON ENOUGH WHETHER YOU'VE TOLD THE TRUTH.
멍...
......
NOW, I BELIEVE I'M THROUGH WITH YOU!

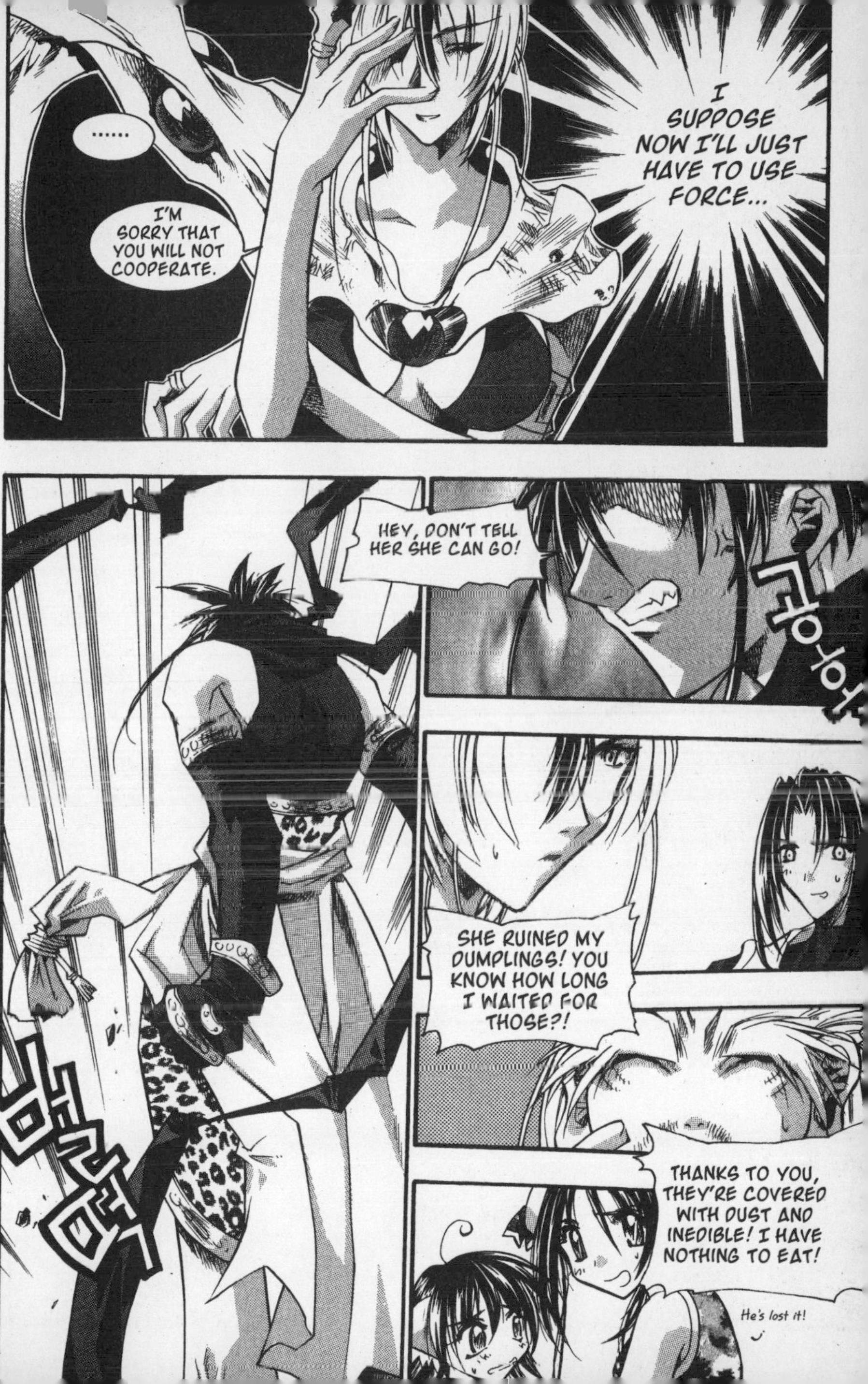
......
I'M SORRY THAT YOU WILL NOT COOPERATE.
I SUPPOSE NOW I'LL JUST HAVE TO USE FORCE...
HEY, DON'T TELL HER SHE CAN GO!
SHE RUINED MY DUMPLINGS! YOU KNOW HOW LONG I WAITED FOR THOSE?!
THANKS TO YOU, THEY'RE COVERED WITH DUST AND INEDIBLE! I HAVE NOTHING TO EAT!
He's lost it!

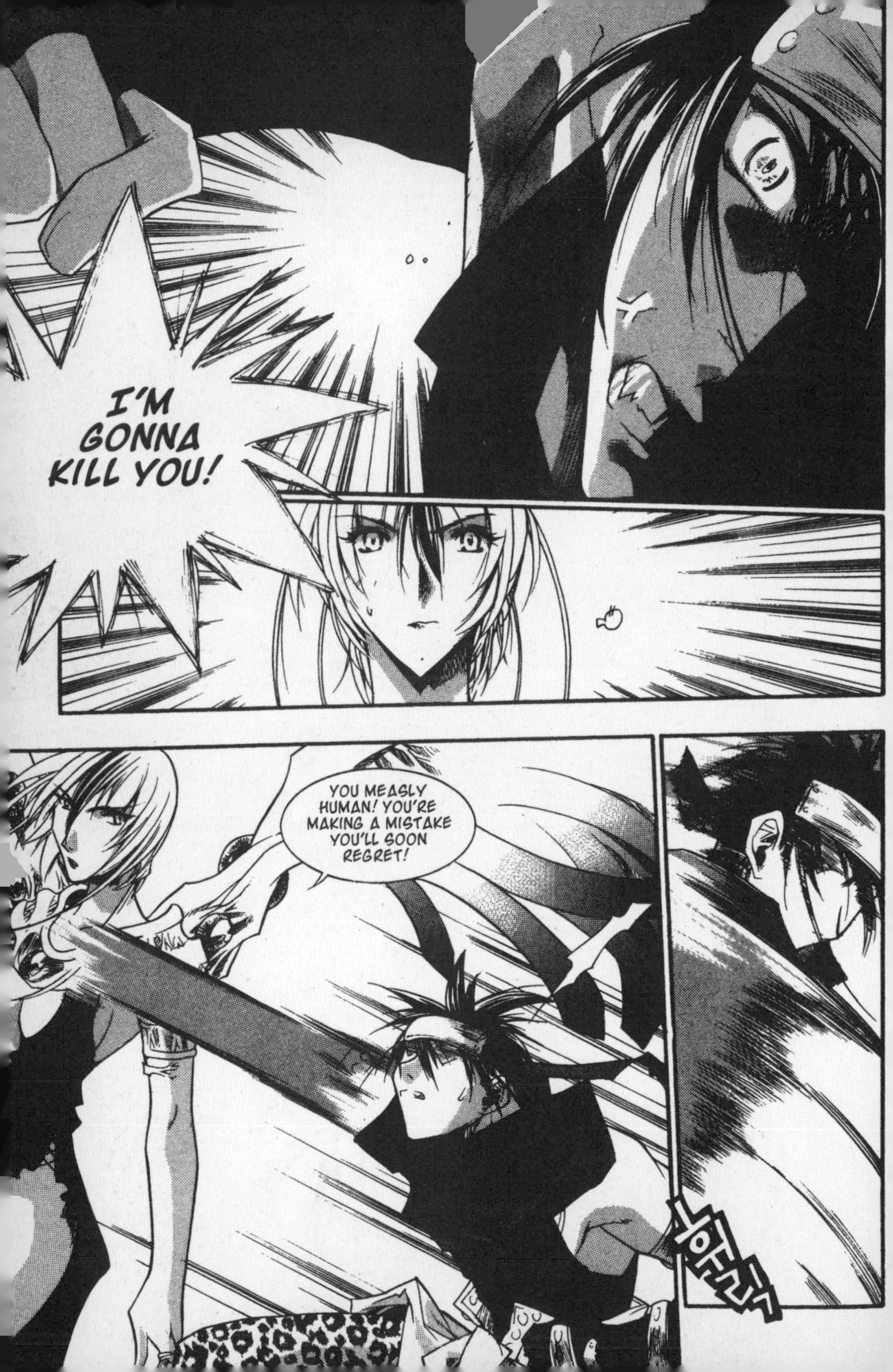
I'M GONNA KILL YOU!
YOU MEASLY HUMAN! YOU'RE MAKING A MISTAKE YOU'LL SOON REGRET!

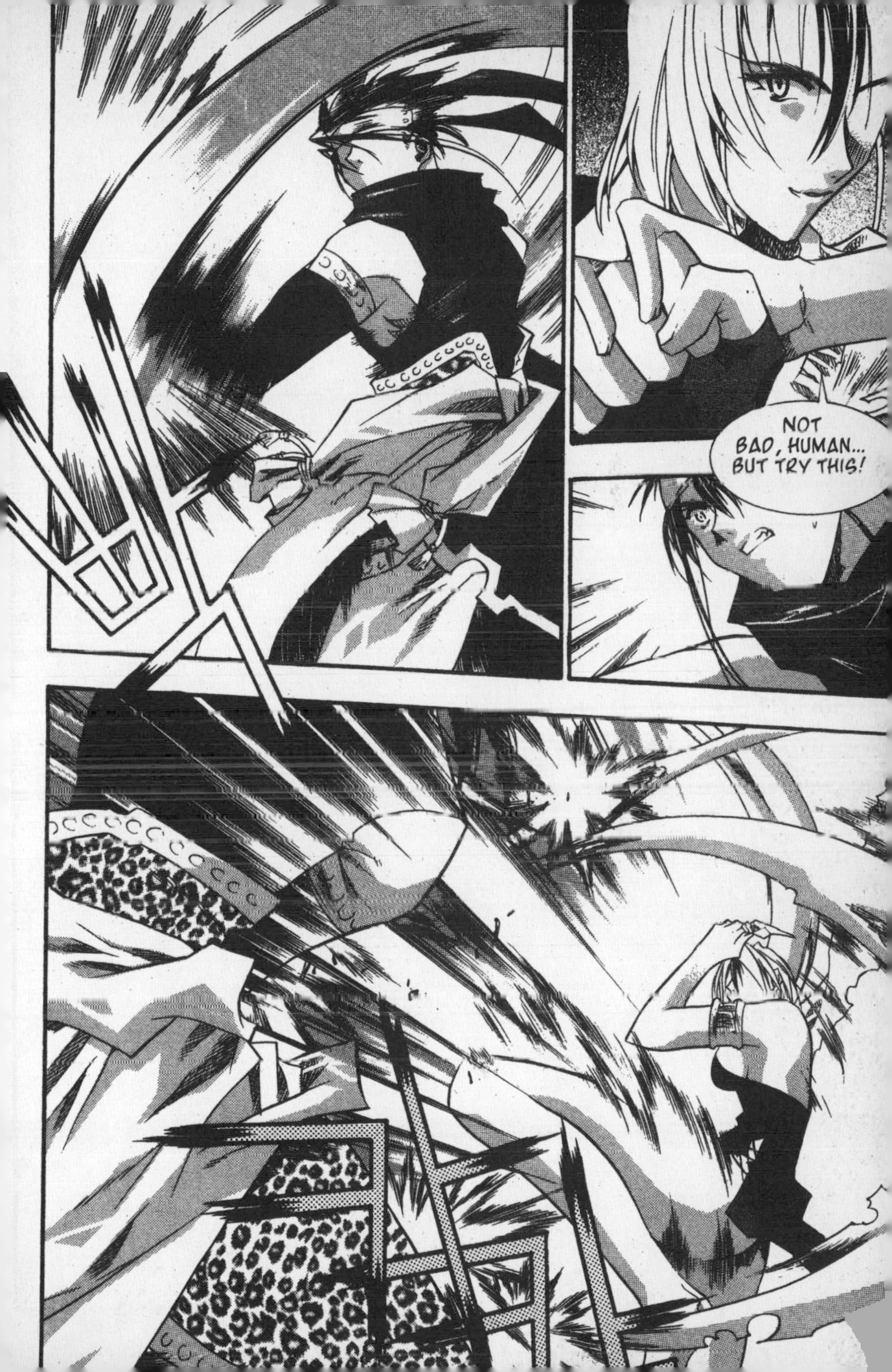
NOT BAD, HUMAN... BUT TRY THIS!

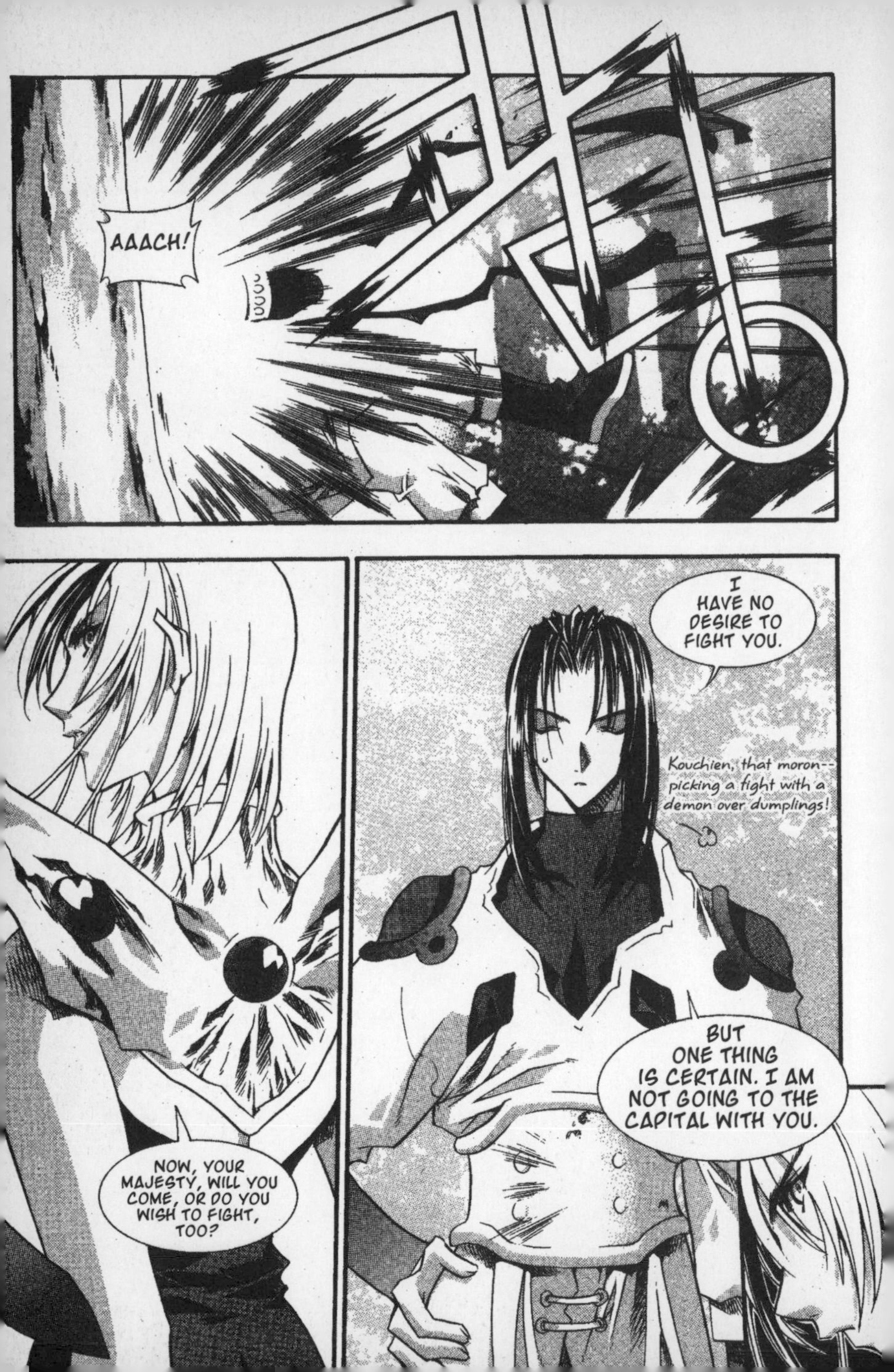
AAACH!
UUUU
NOW, YOUR MAJESTY, WILL YOU COME, OR DO YOU WISH TO FIGHT, TOO?
I HAVE NO DESIRE TO FIGHT YOU.
Kouchien, that moron-- picking a fight with a demon over dumplings!
BUT ONE THING IS CERTAIN. I AM NOT GOING TO THE CAPITAL WITH YOU.

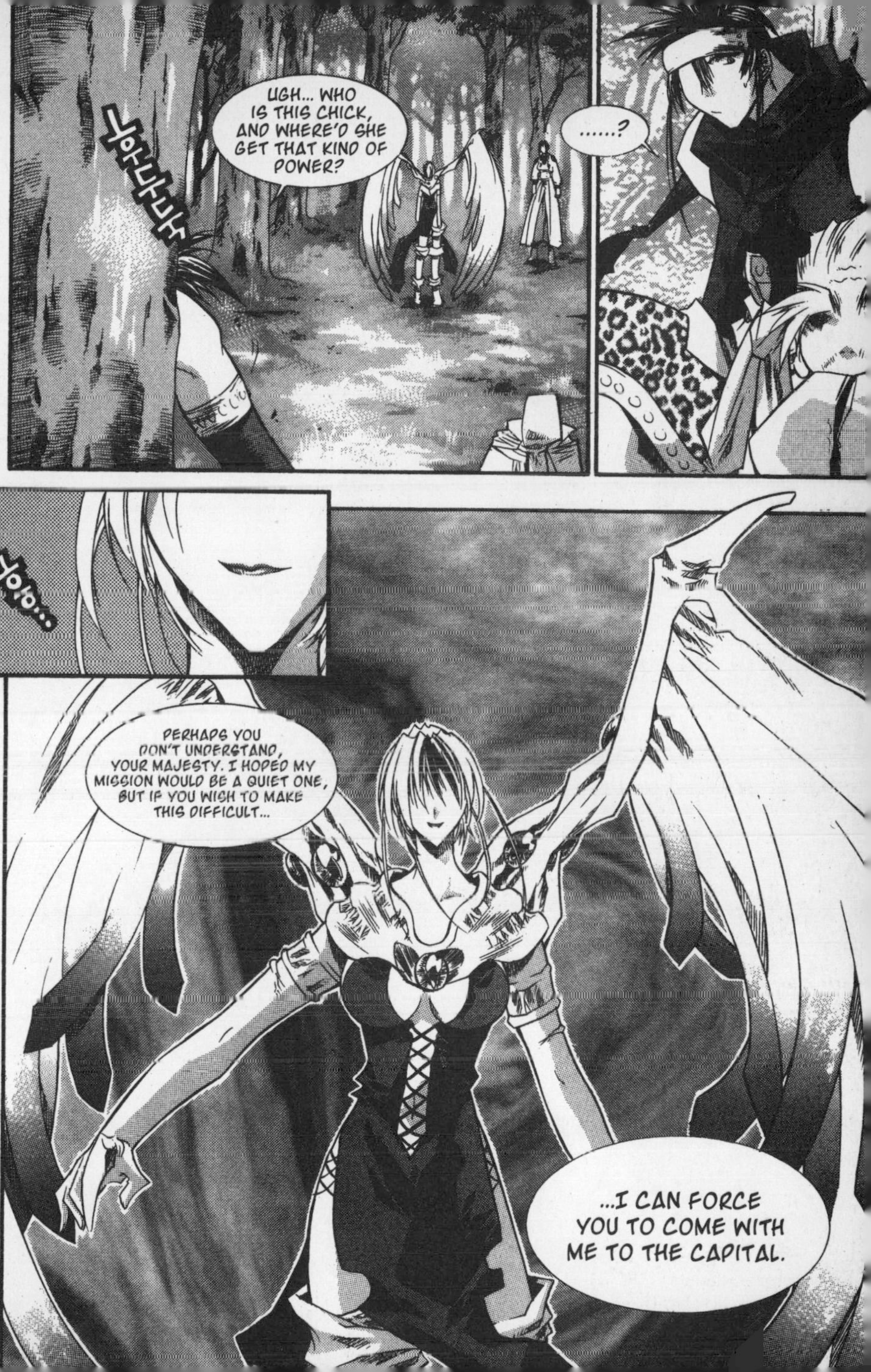
UGH... WHO IS THIS CHICK, AND WHERE'D SHE GET THAT KIND OF POWER?
......?
PERHAPS YOU DON'T UNDERSTAND, YOUR MAJESTY. I HOPED MY MISSION WOULD BE A QUIET ONE, BUT IF YOU WISH TO MAKE THIS DIFFICULT...
...I CAN FORCE YOU TO COME WITH ME TO THE CAPITAL.

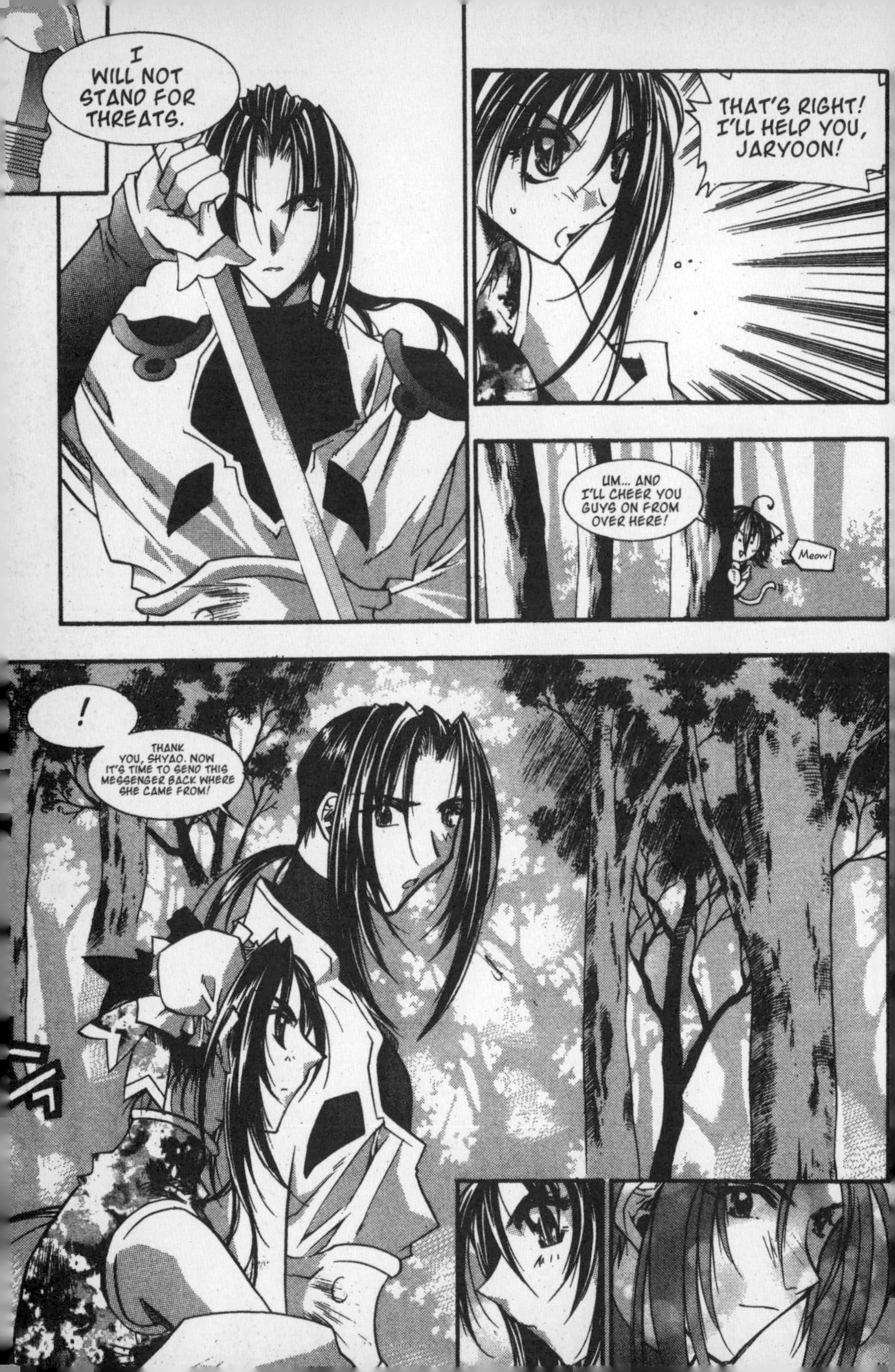
I WILL NOT STAND FOR THREATS.
THAT'S RIGHT! I'LL HELP YOU, JARYOON!
UM... AND I'LL CHEER YOU GUYS ON FROM OVER HERE!
Meow!
!
THANK YOU, SHYAO. NOW IT'S TIME TO SEND THIS MESSENGER BACK WHERE SHE CAME FROM!

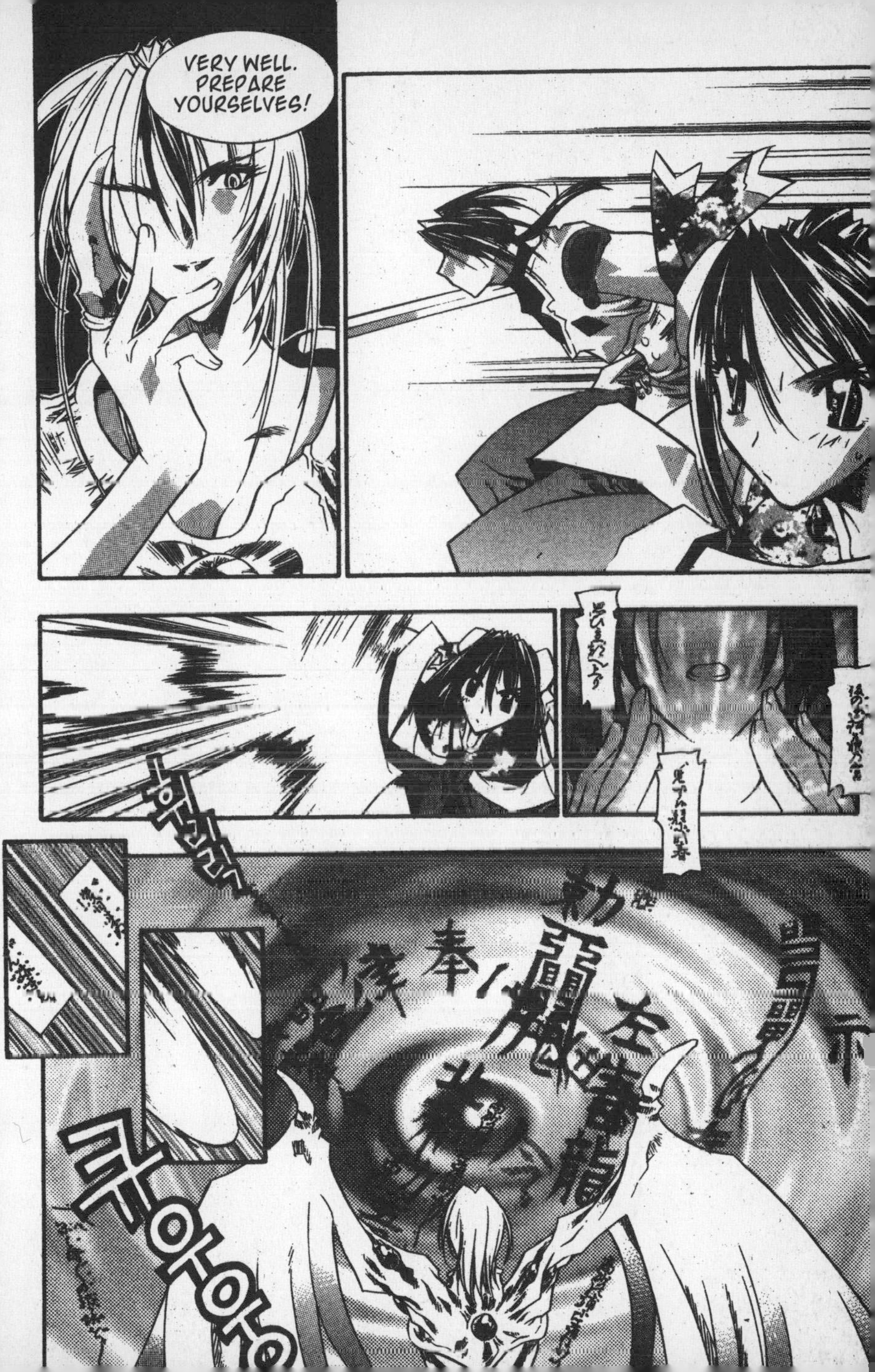
VERY WELL. PREPARE YOURSELVES!

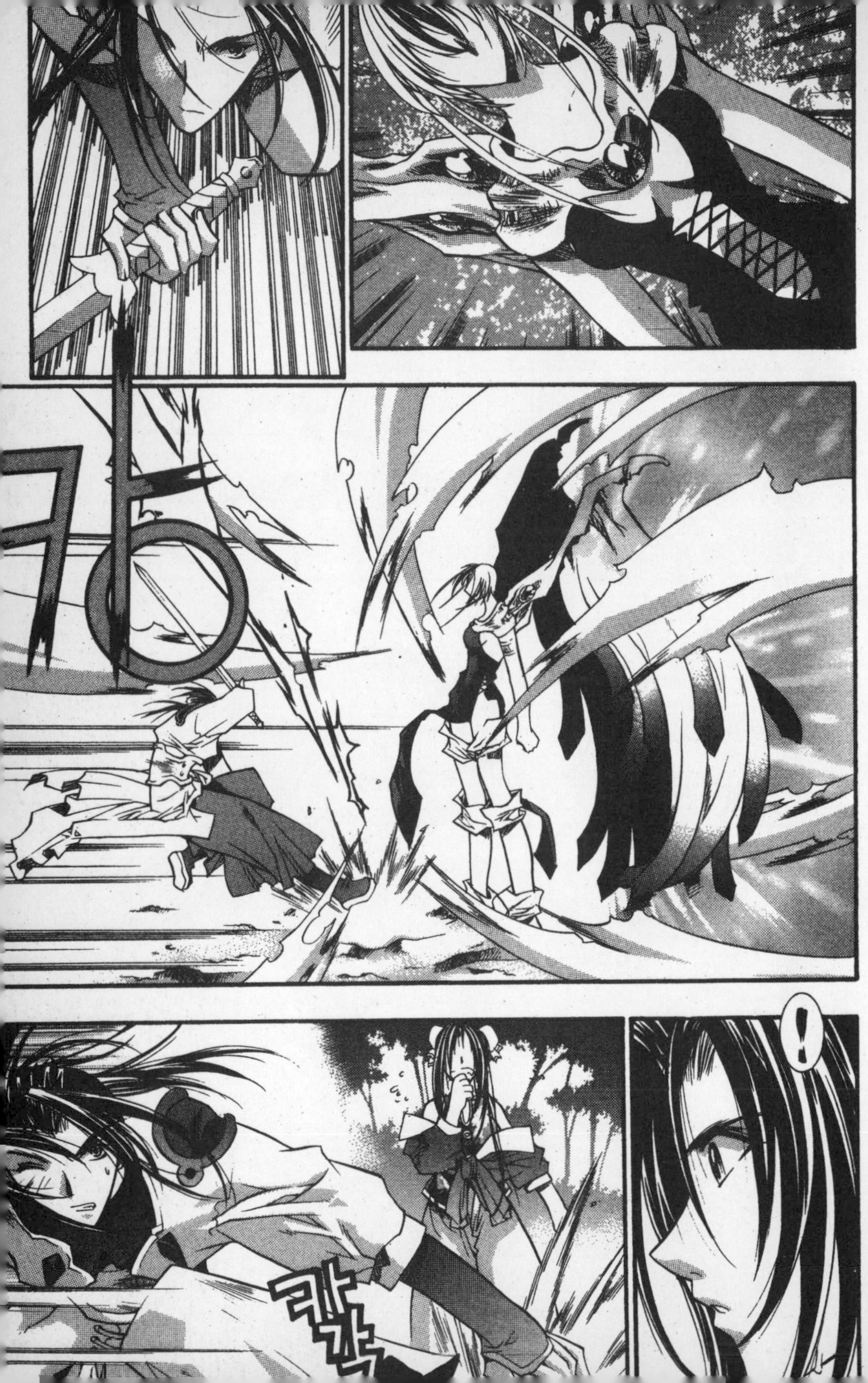
!

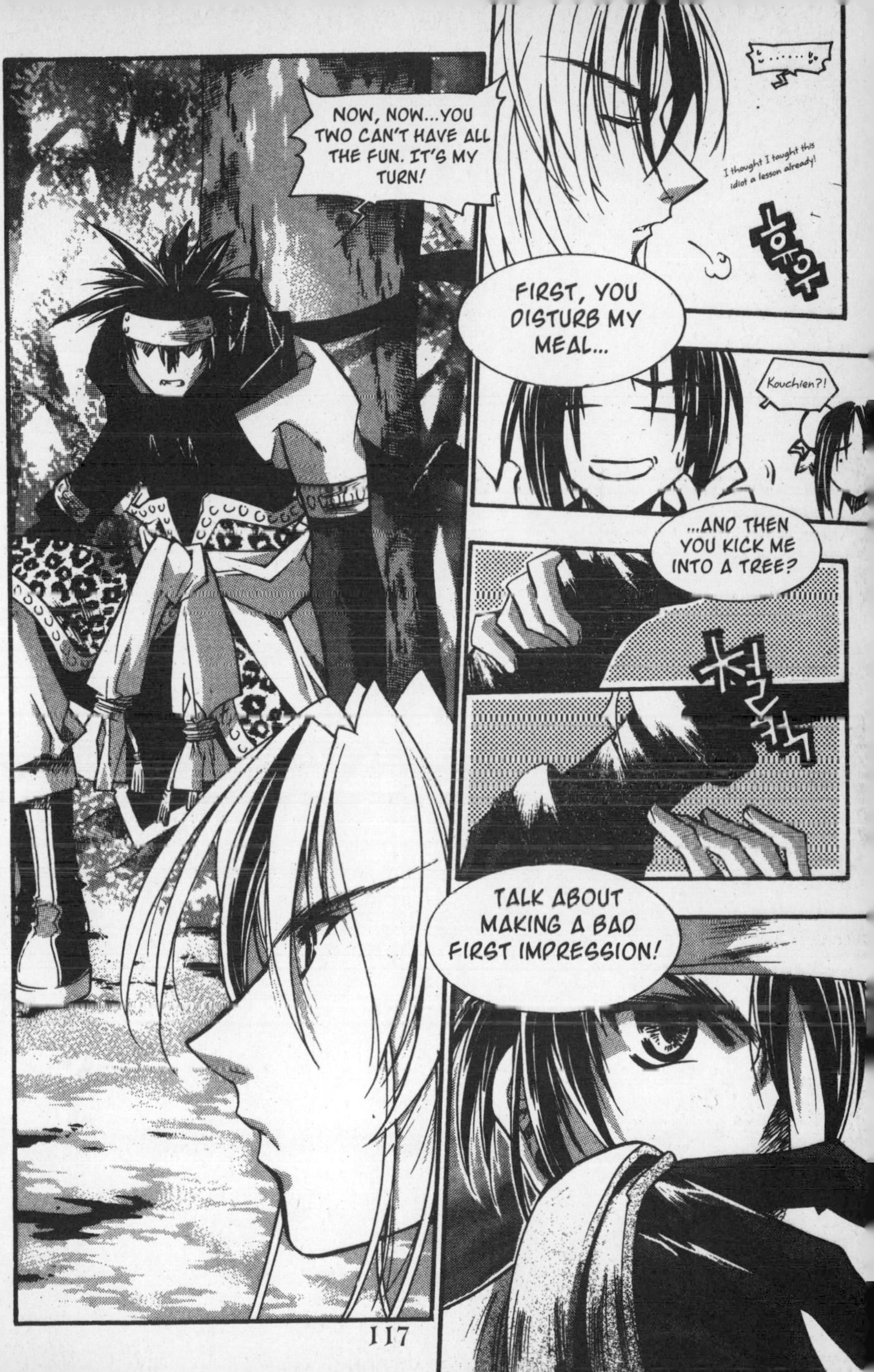
NOW, NOW...YOU TWO CAN'T HAVE ALL THE FUN. IT'S MY TURN!
......
I thought I taught this idiot a lesson already!
FIRST, YOU DISTURB MY MEAL...
Kouchien?!
...AND THEN YOU KICK ME INTO A TREE?
TALK ABOUT MAKING A BAD FIRST IMPRESSION!

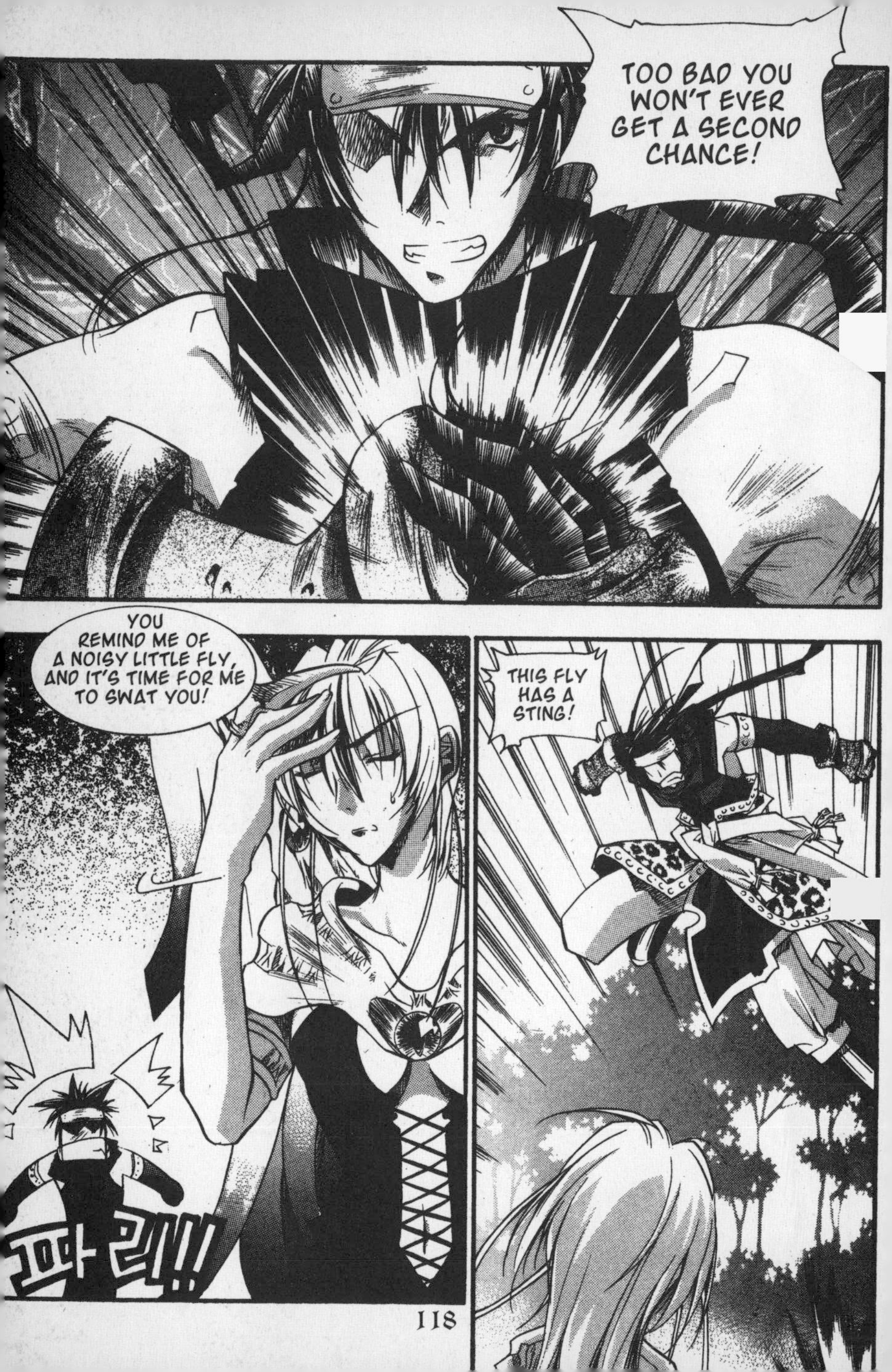
TOO BAD YOU WON'T EVER GET A SECOND CHANCE!
YOU REMIND ME OF A NOISY LITTLE FLY, AND IT'S TIME FOR ME TO SWAT YOU!
파리!!
THIS FLY HAS A STING!

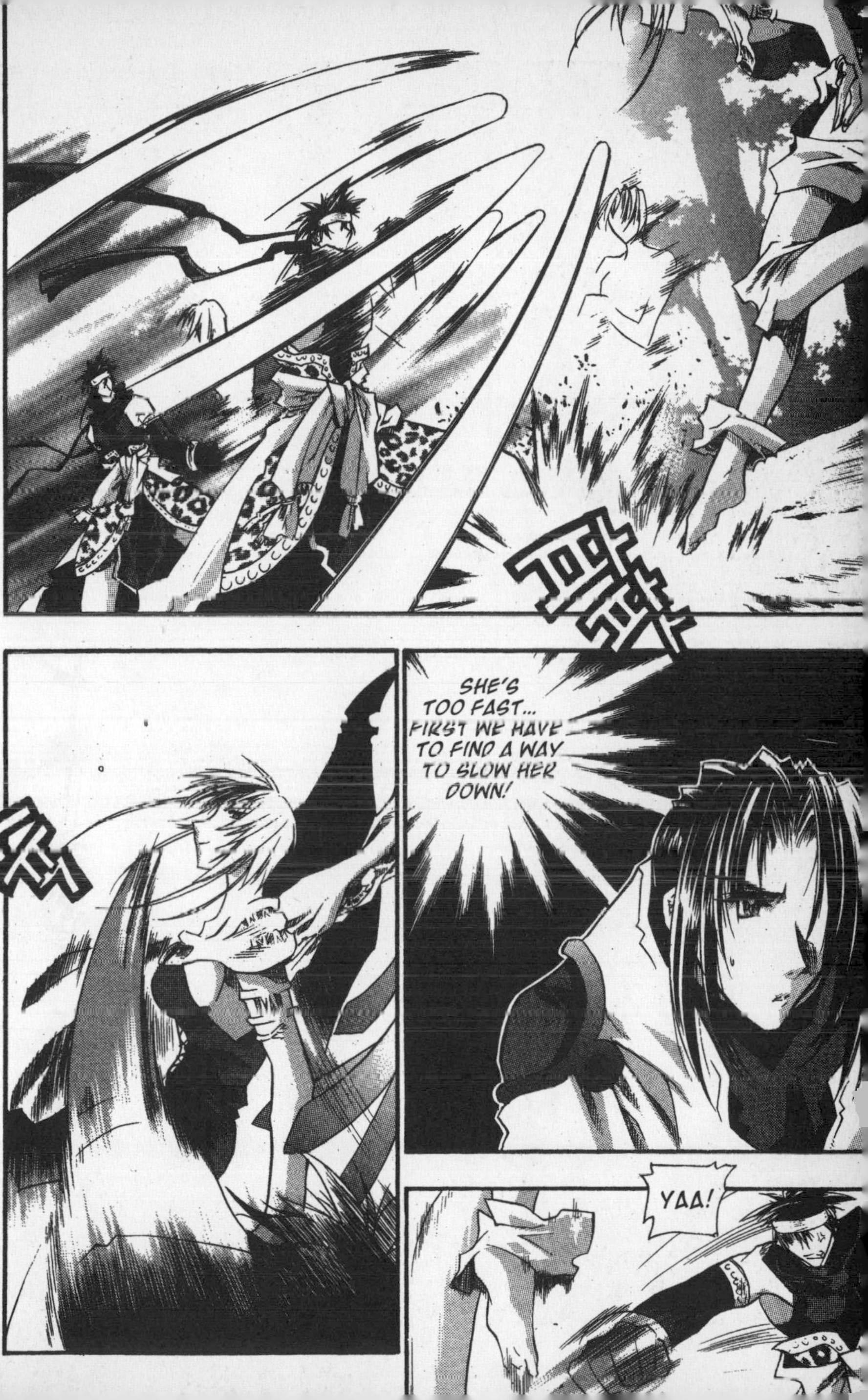
SHE'S TOO FAST... FIRST WE HAVE TO FIND A WAY TO SLOW HER DOWN!
YAA!

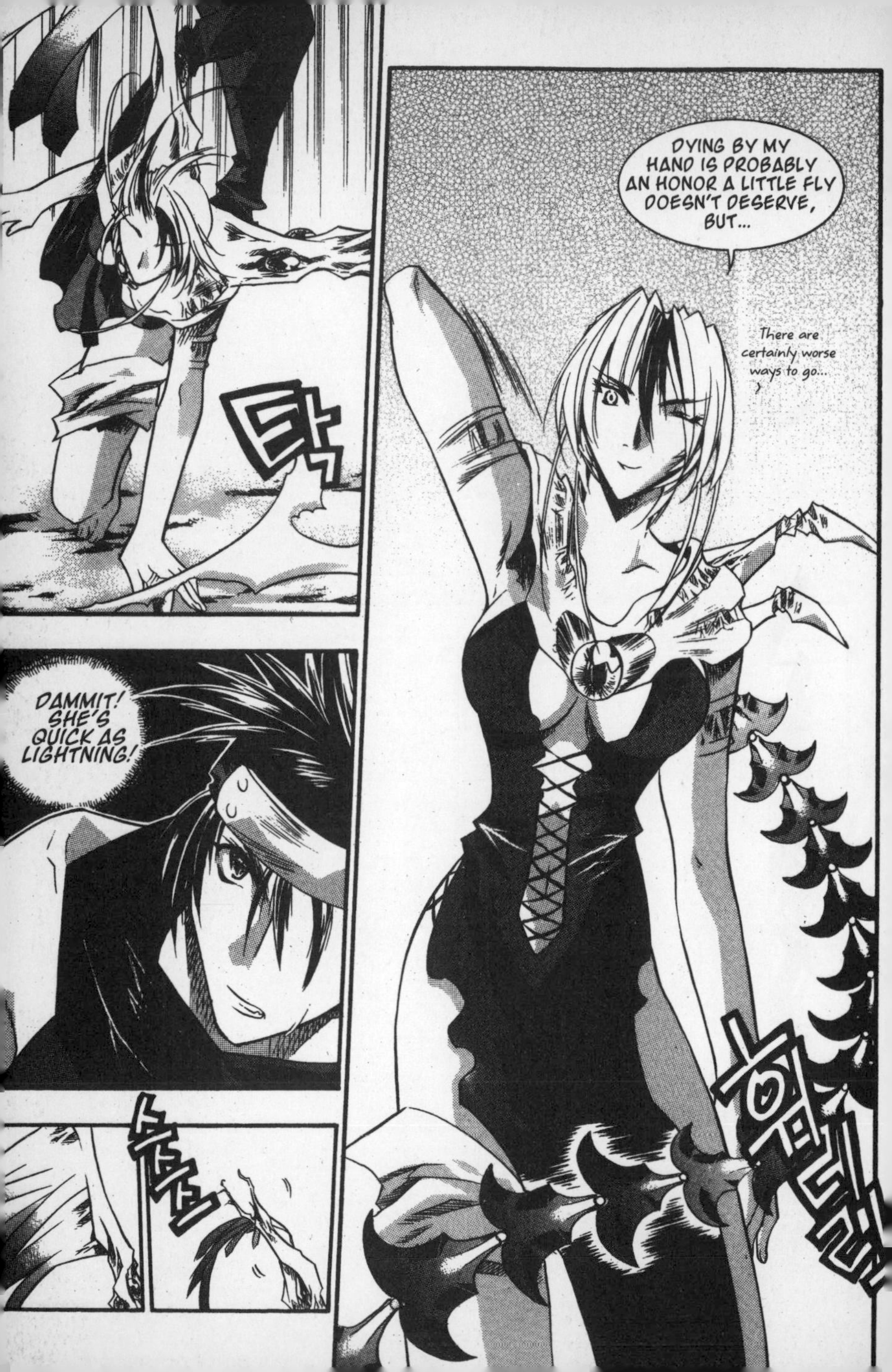
DAMMIT! SHE'S QUICK AS LIGHTNING!
DYING BY MY HAND IS PROBABLY AN HONOR A LITTLE FLY DOESN'T DESERVE, BUT...
There are certainly worse ways to go...

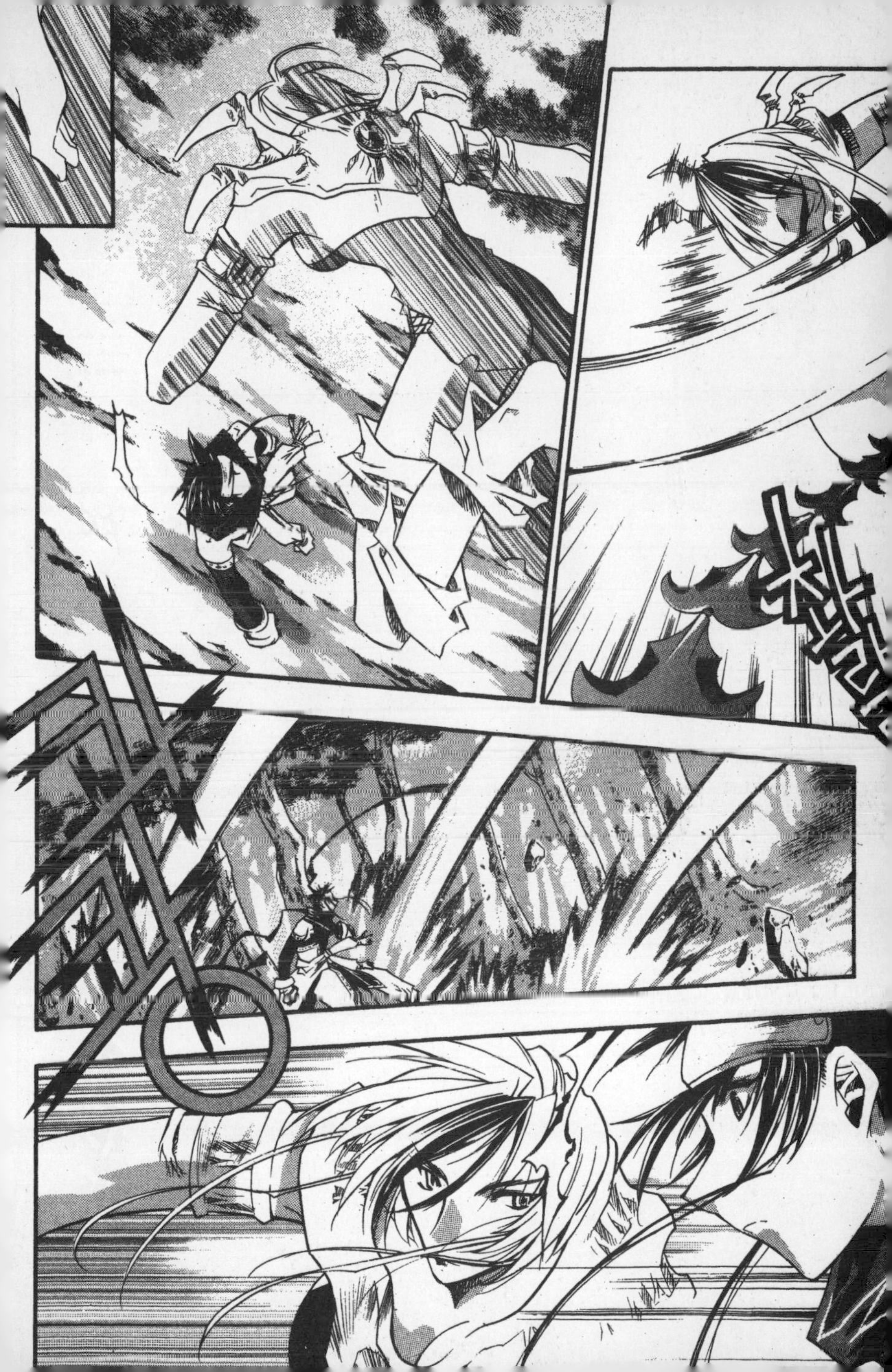

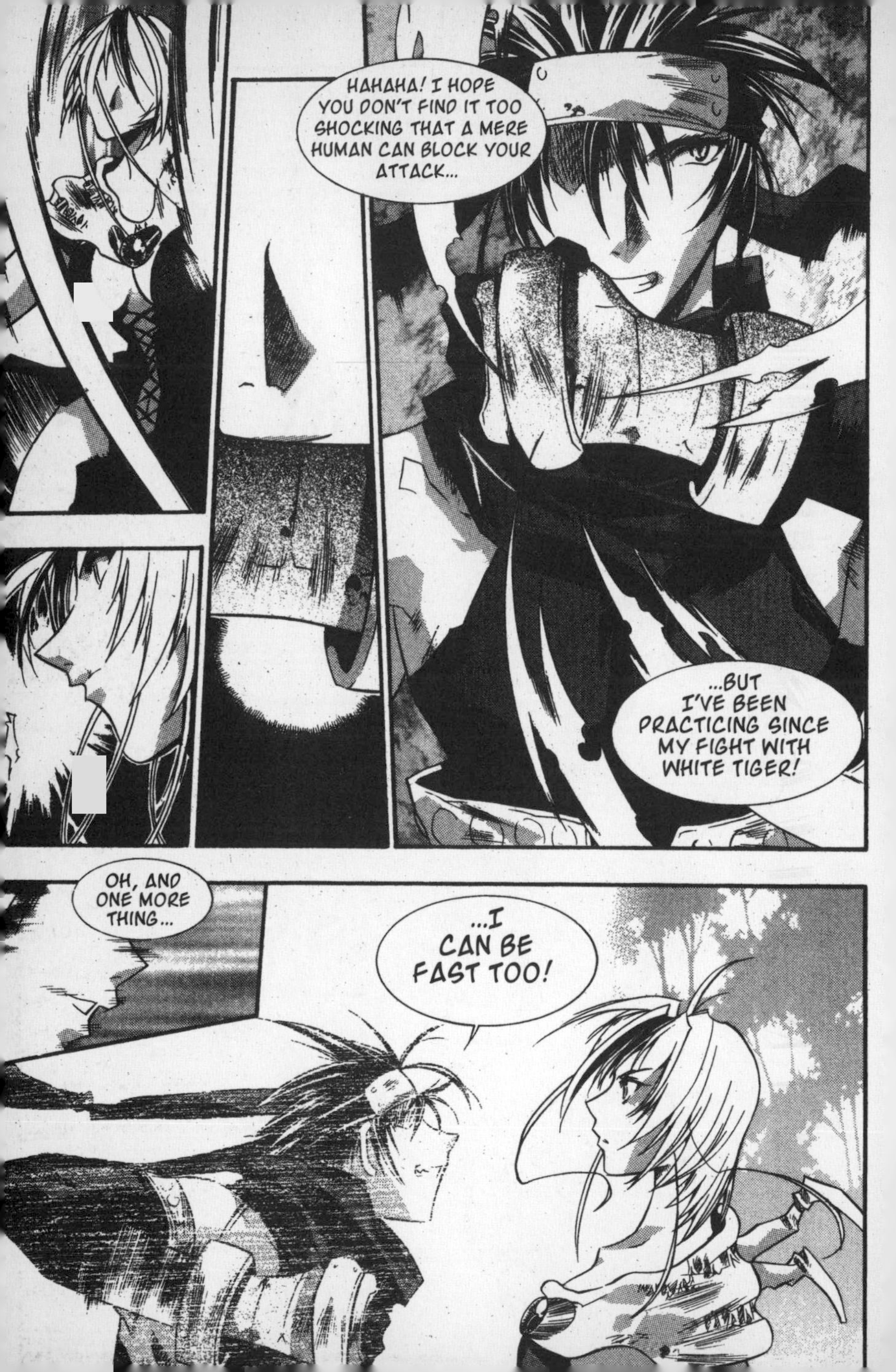
HAHAHA! I HOPE YOU DON'T FIND IT TOO SHOCKING THAT A MERE HUMAN CAN BLOCK YOUR ATTACK...
...BUT I'VE BEEN PRACTICING SINCE MY FIGHT WITH WHITE TIGER!
OH, AND ONE MORE THING...
...I CAN BE FAST TOO!

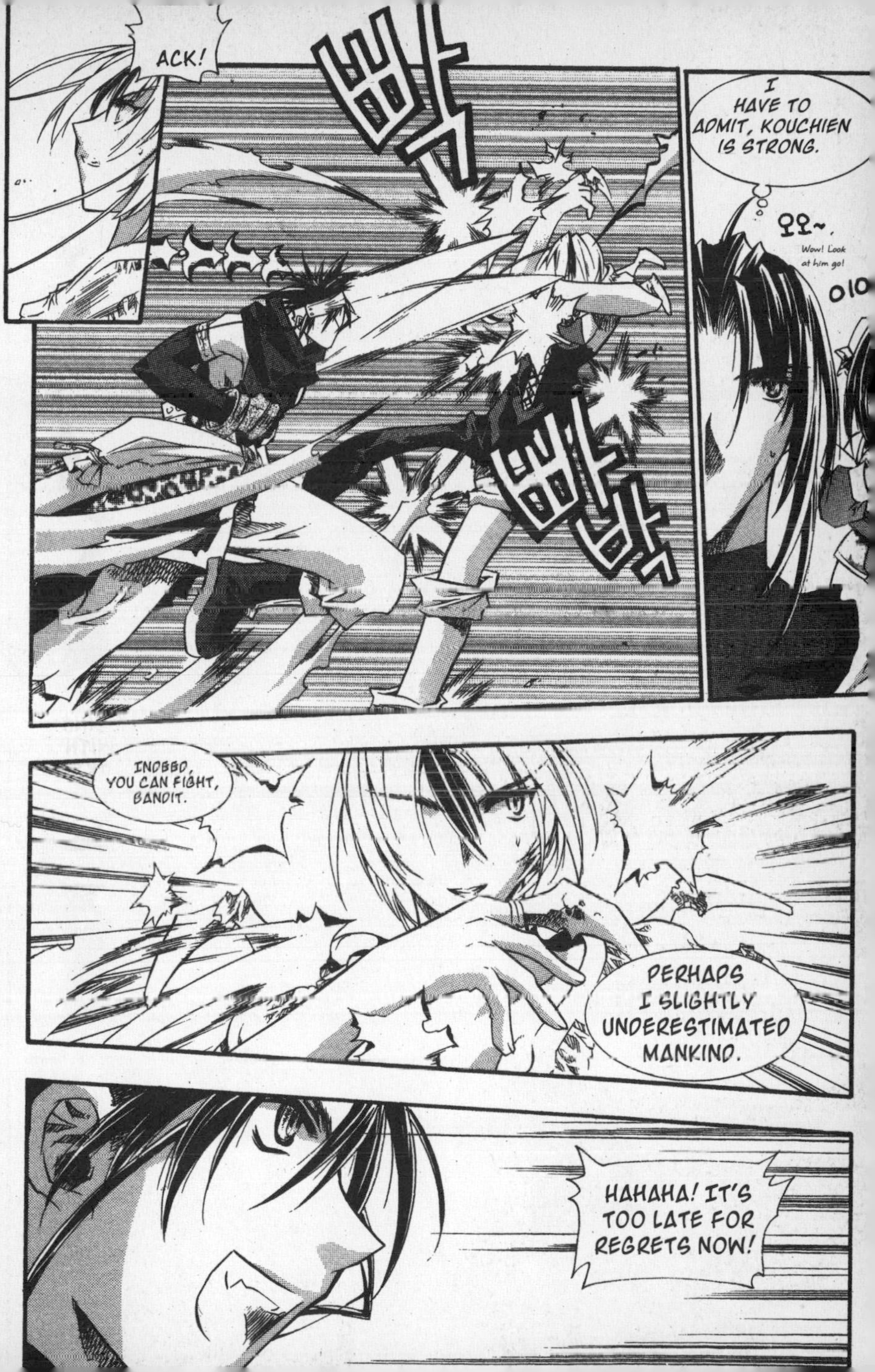
ACK!
I HAVE TO ADMIT, KOUCHIEN IS STRONG.
오오~.
Wow! Look at him go!
INDEED, YOU CAN FIGHT, BANDIT.
PERHAPS I SLIGHTLY UNDERESTIMATED MANKIND.
HAHAHA! IT'S TOO LATE FOR REGRETS NOW!

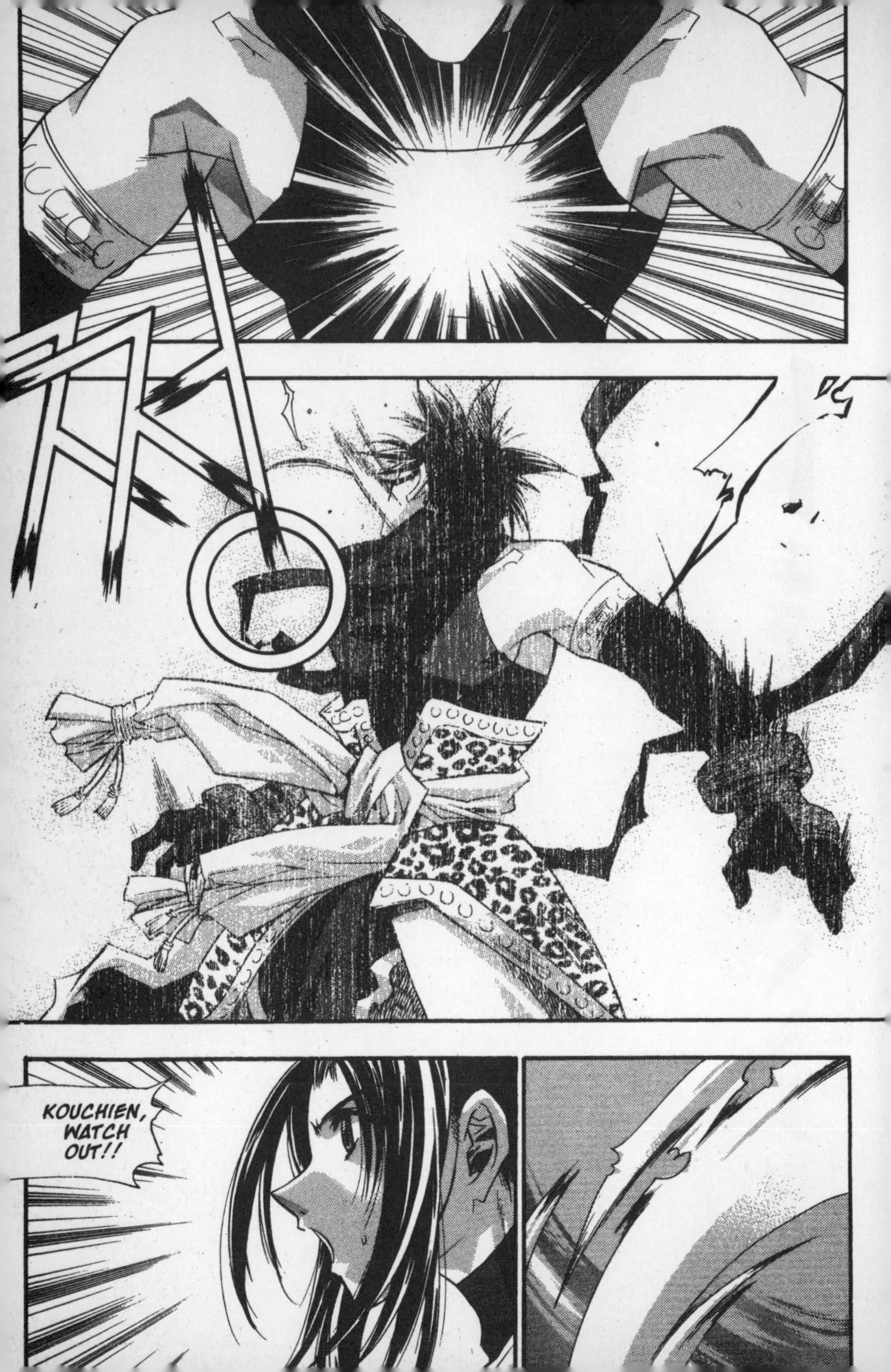
KOUCHIEN, WATCH OUT!!

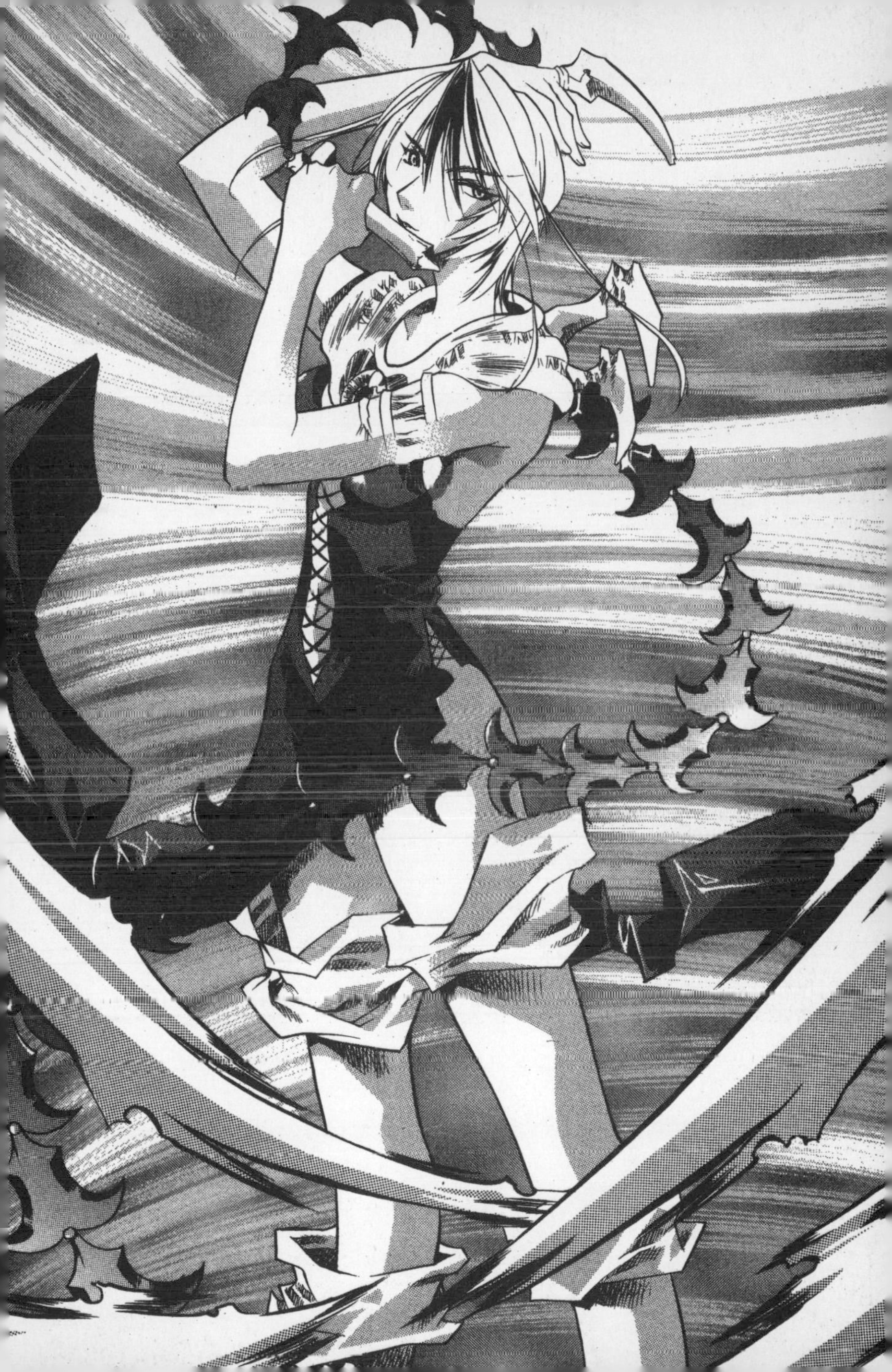

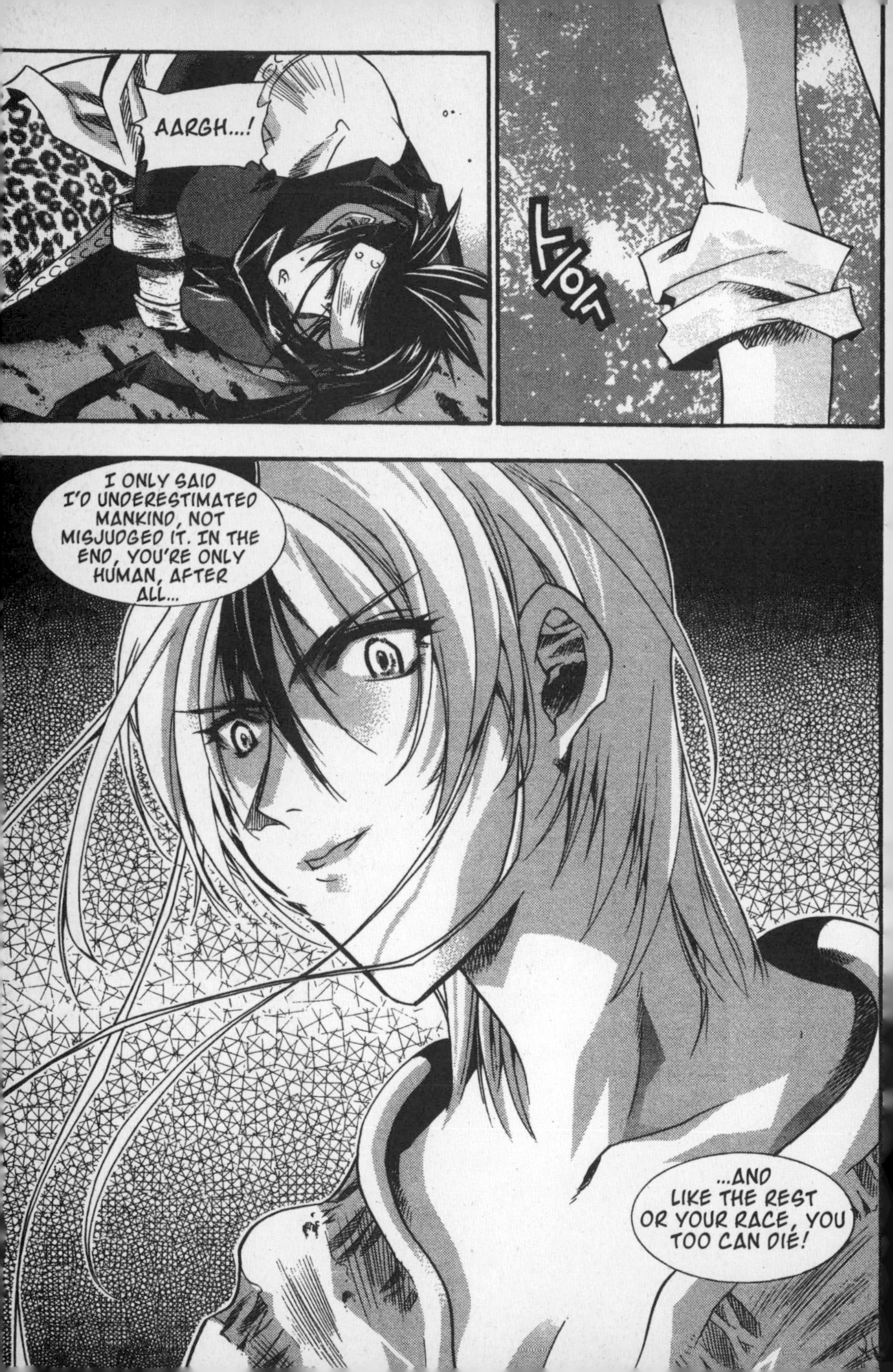
AARGH...!
I ONLY SAID I'D UNDERESTIMATED MANKIND, NOT MISJUDGED IT. IN THE END, YOU'RE ONLY HUMAN, AFTER ALL...
...AND LIKE THE REST OR YOUR RACE, YOU TOO CAN DIE!

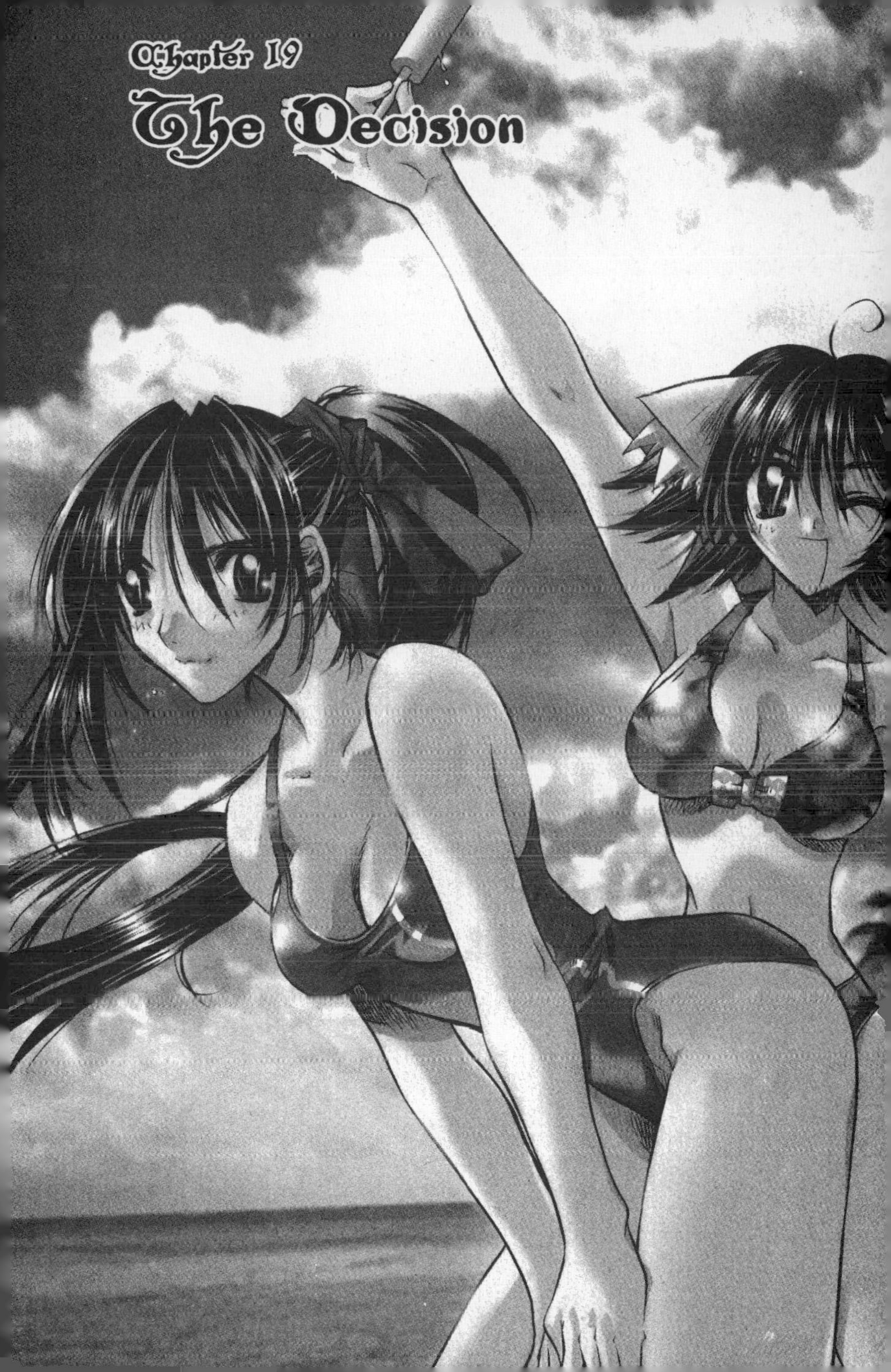
Chapter 19
The Decision

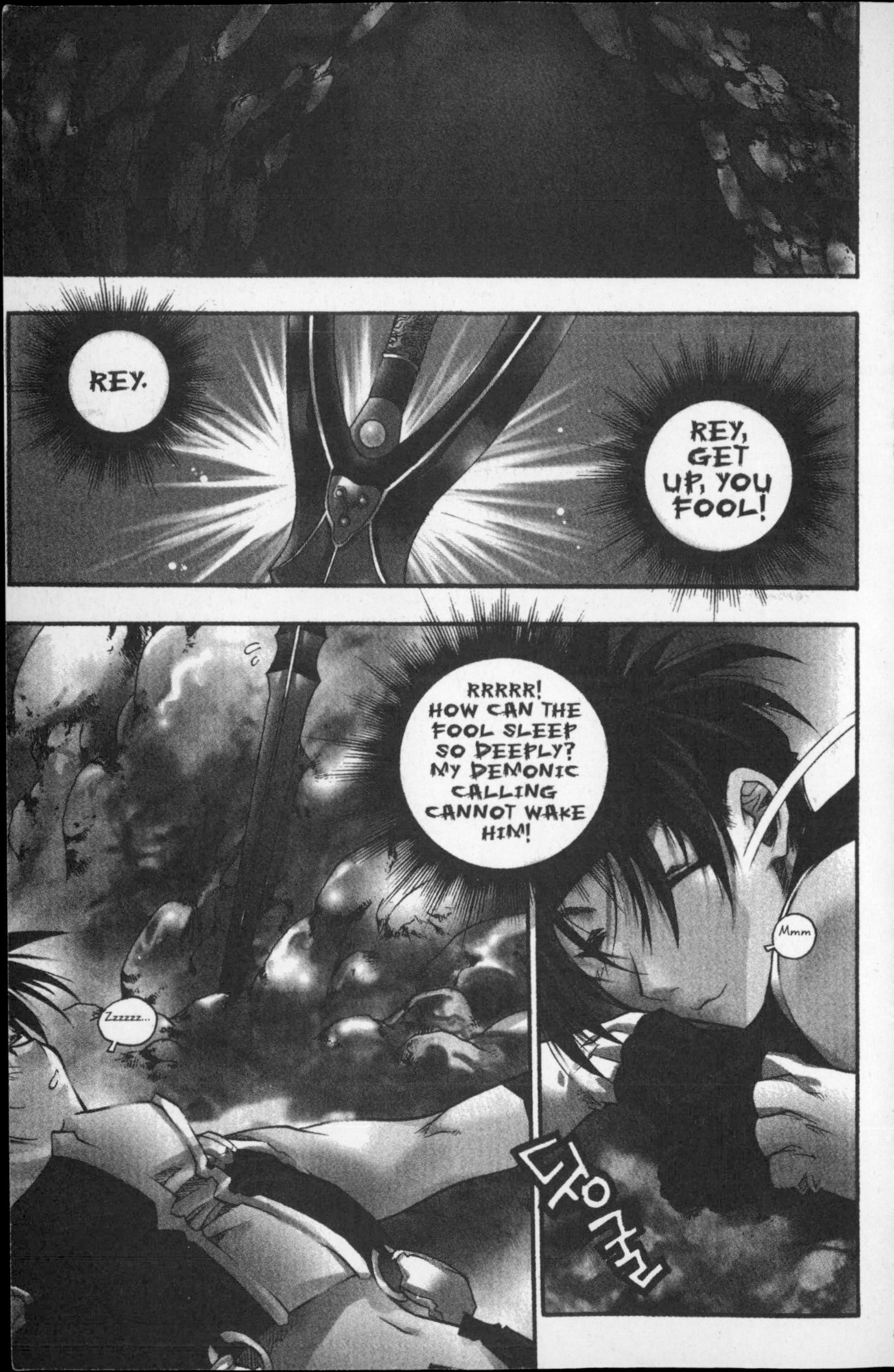
REY.
REY, GET UP, YOU FOOL!
RRRRR! HOW CAN THE FOOL SLEEP SO DEEPLY? MY DEMONIC CALLING CANNOT WAKE HIM!
Mmm
Zzzzzz...

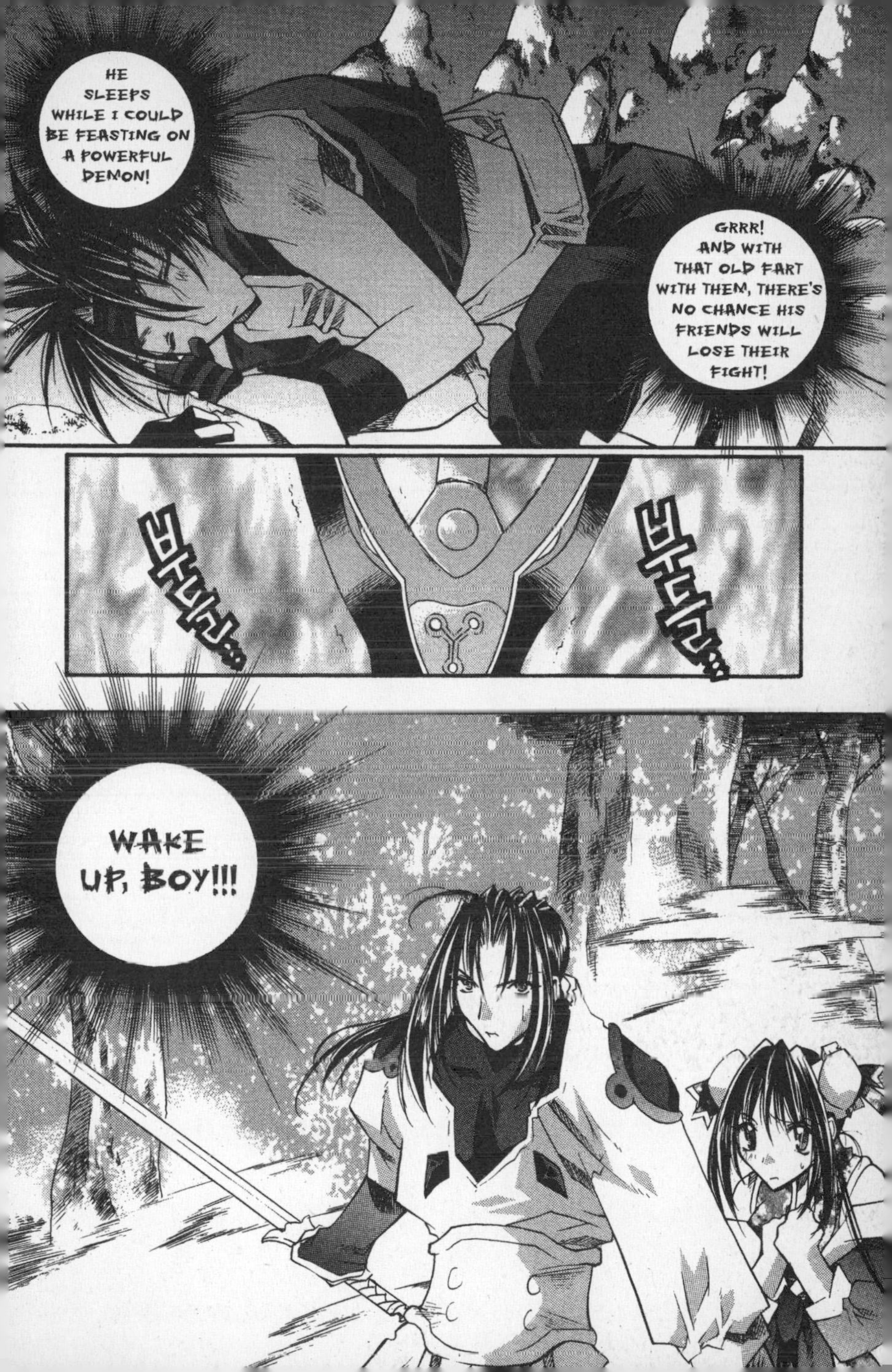
HE SLEEPS WHILE I COULD BE FEASTING ON A POWERFUL DEMON!
GRRR! AND WITH THAT OLD FART WITH THEM, THERE'S NO CHANCE HIS FRIENDS WILL LOSE THEIR FIGHT!
WAKE UP, BOY!!!

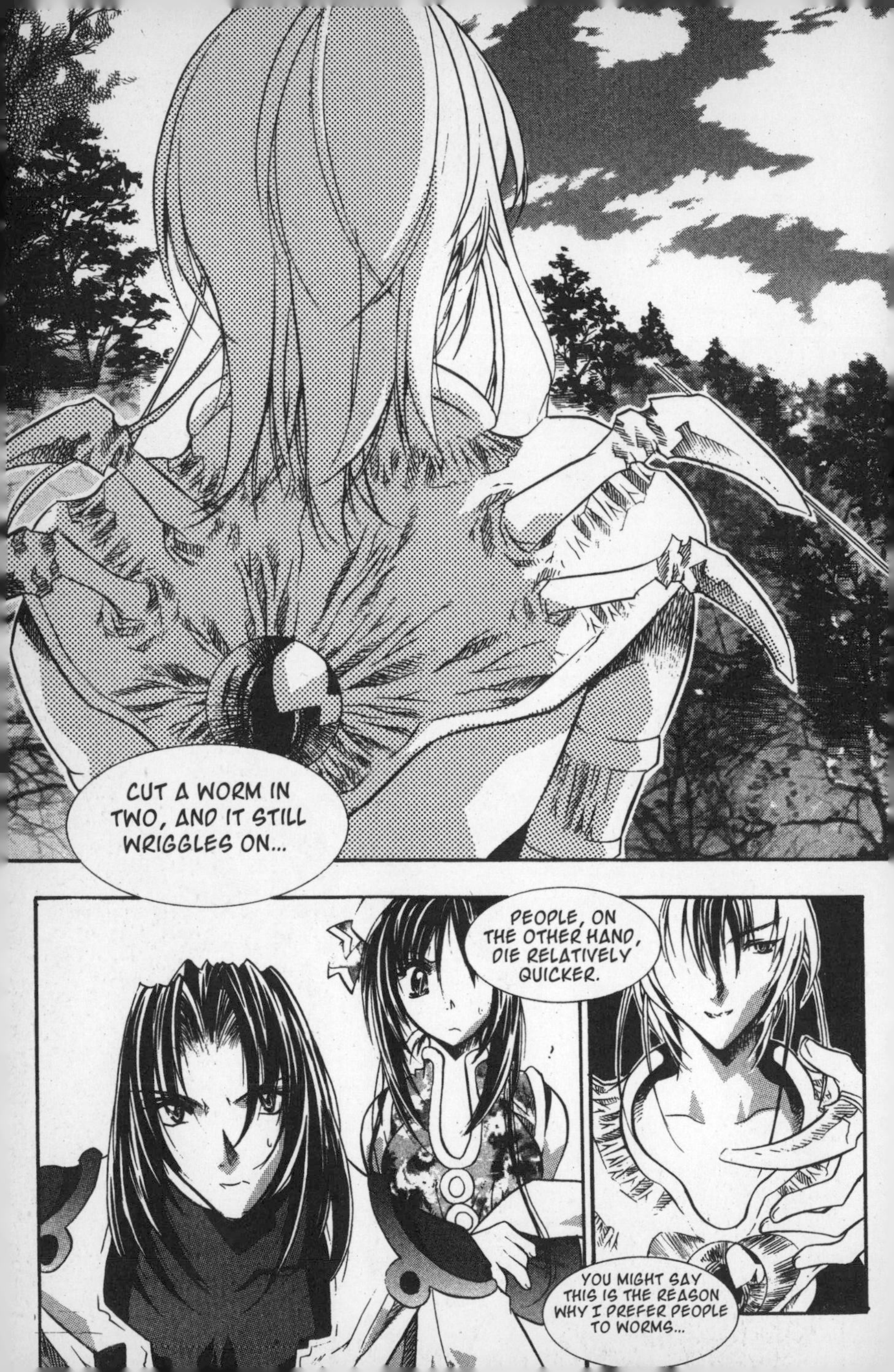
CUT A WORM IN TWO, AND IT STILL WRIGGLES ON...
PEOPLE, ON THE OTHER HAND, DIE RELATIVELY QUICKER.
YOU MIGHT SAY THIS IS THE REASON WHY I PREFER PEOPLE TO WORMS...

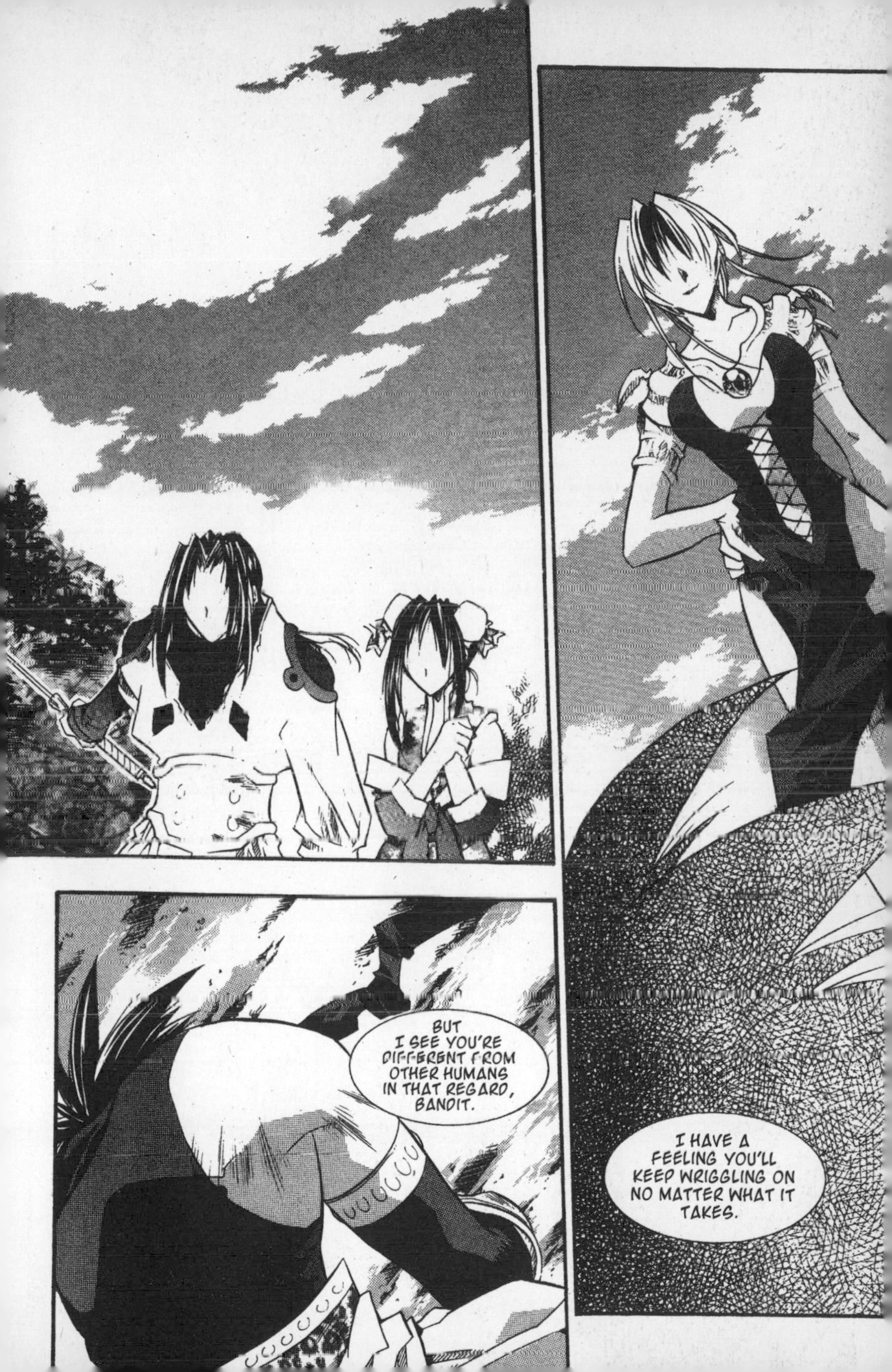
BUT I SEE YOU'RE DIFFERENT FROM OTHER HUMANS IN THAT REGARD, BANDIT.
I HAVE A FEELING YOU'LL KEEP WRIGGLING ON NO MATTER WHAT IT TAKES.

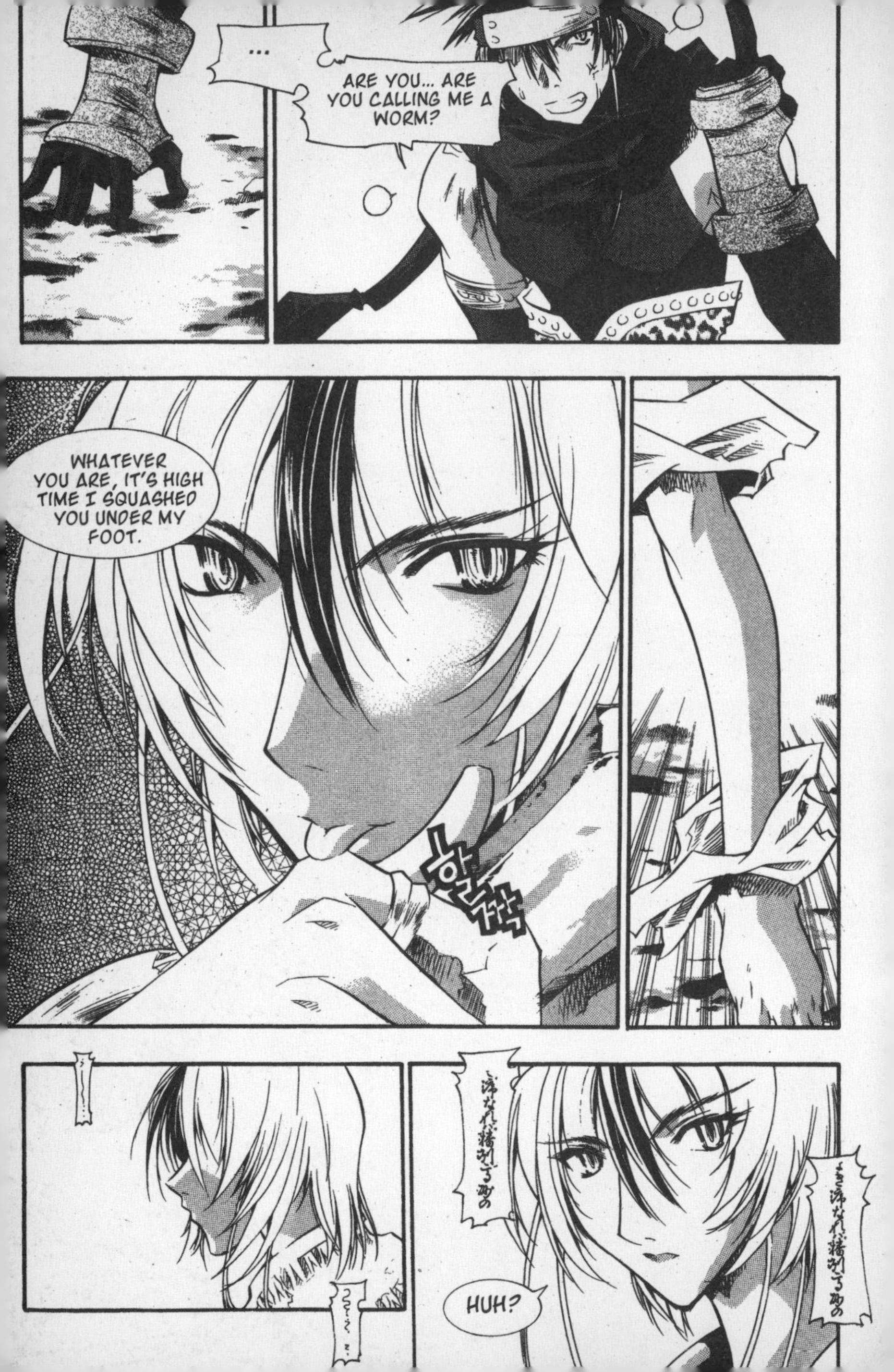
...
ARE YOU... ARE YOU CALLING ME A WORM?
WHATEVER YOU ARE, IT'S HIGH TIME I SQUASHED YOU UNDER MY FOOT.
HUH?

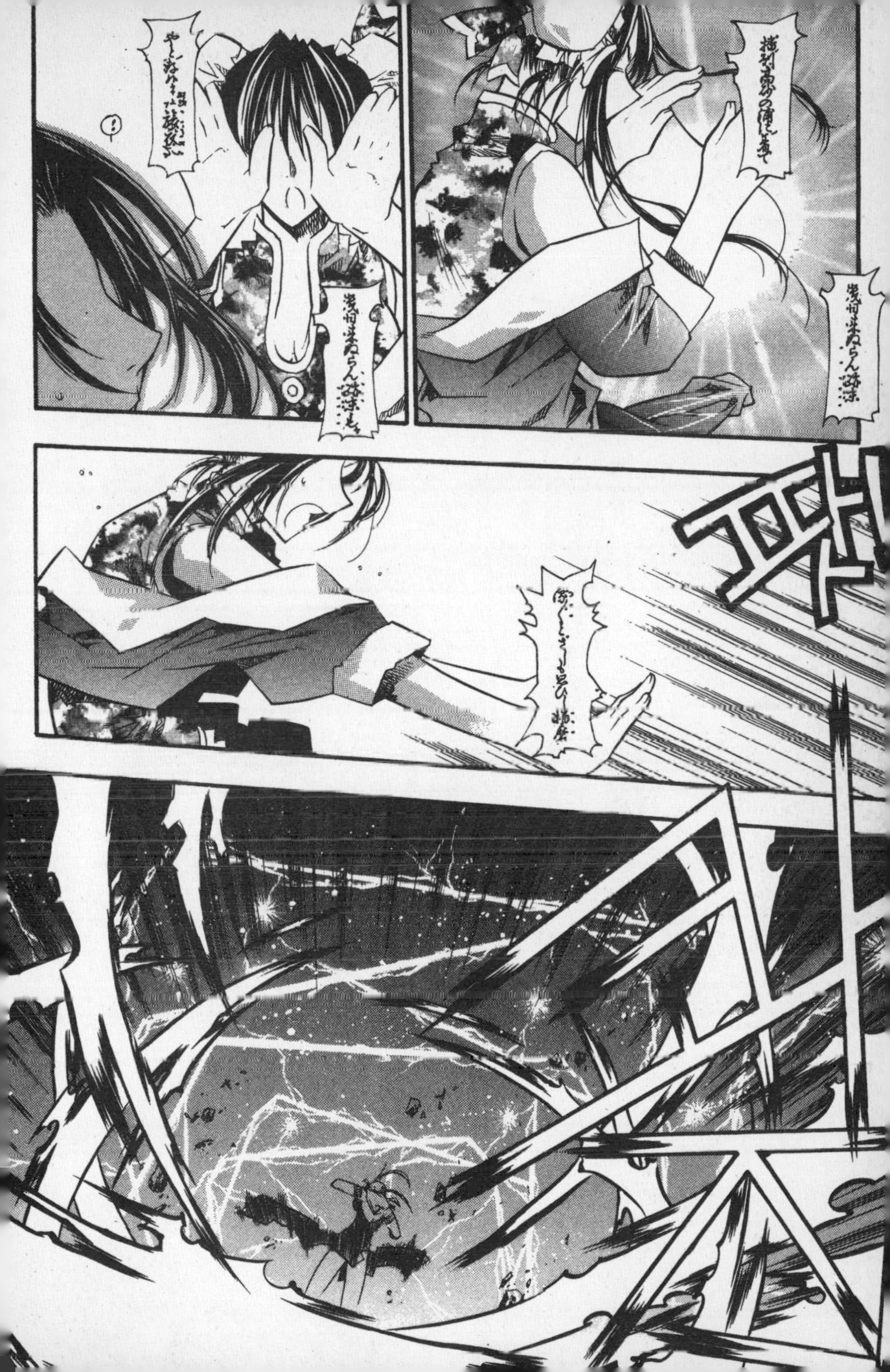
播州高砂の浦に着て

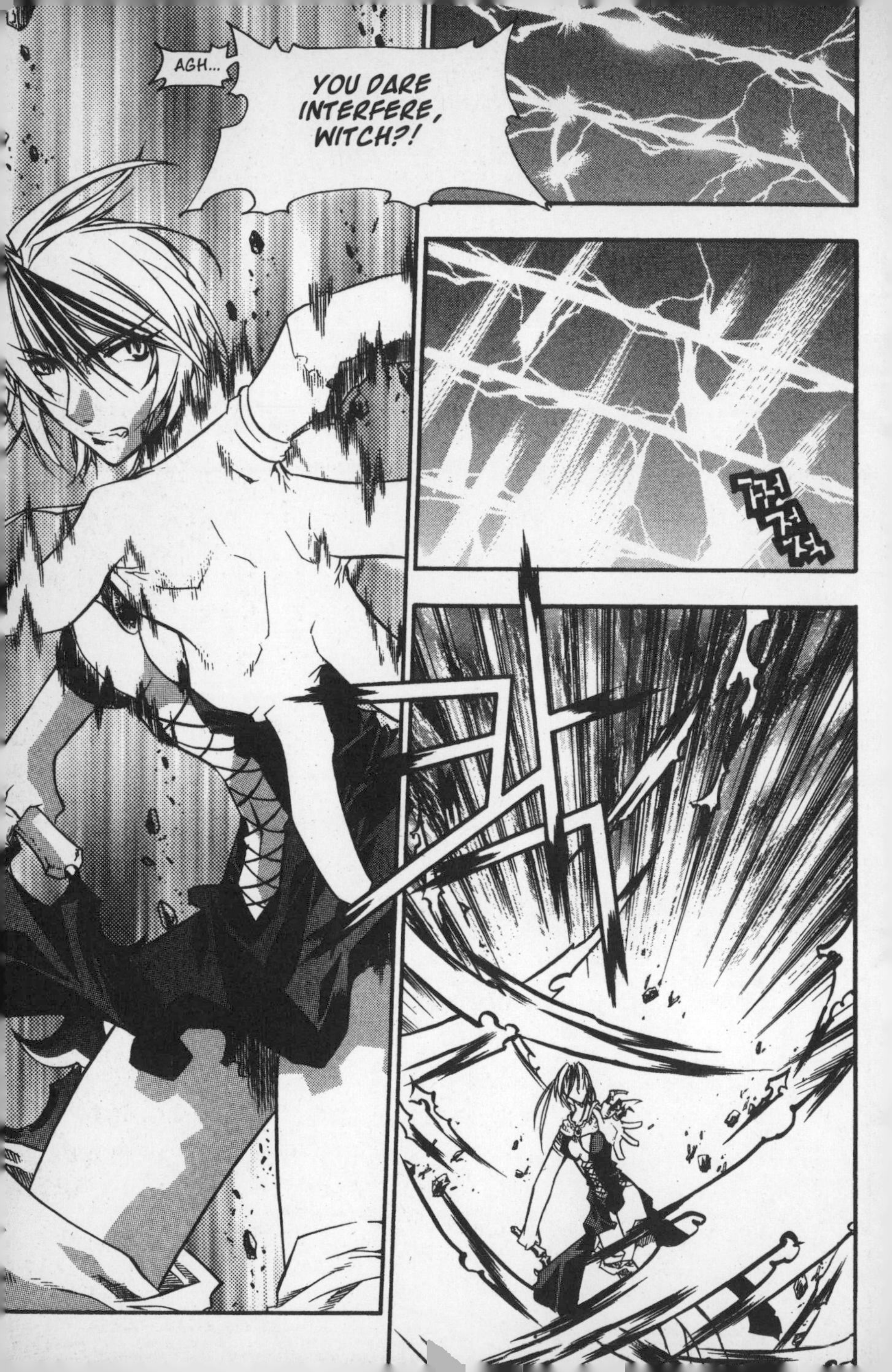
AGH...
YOU DARE INTERFERE, WITCH?!

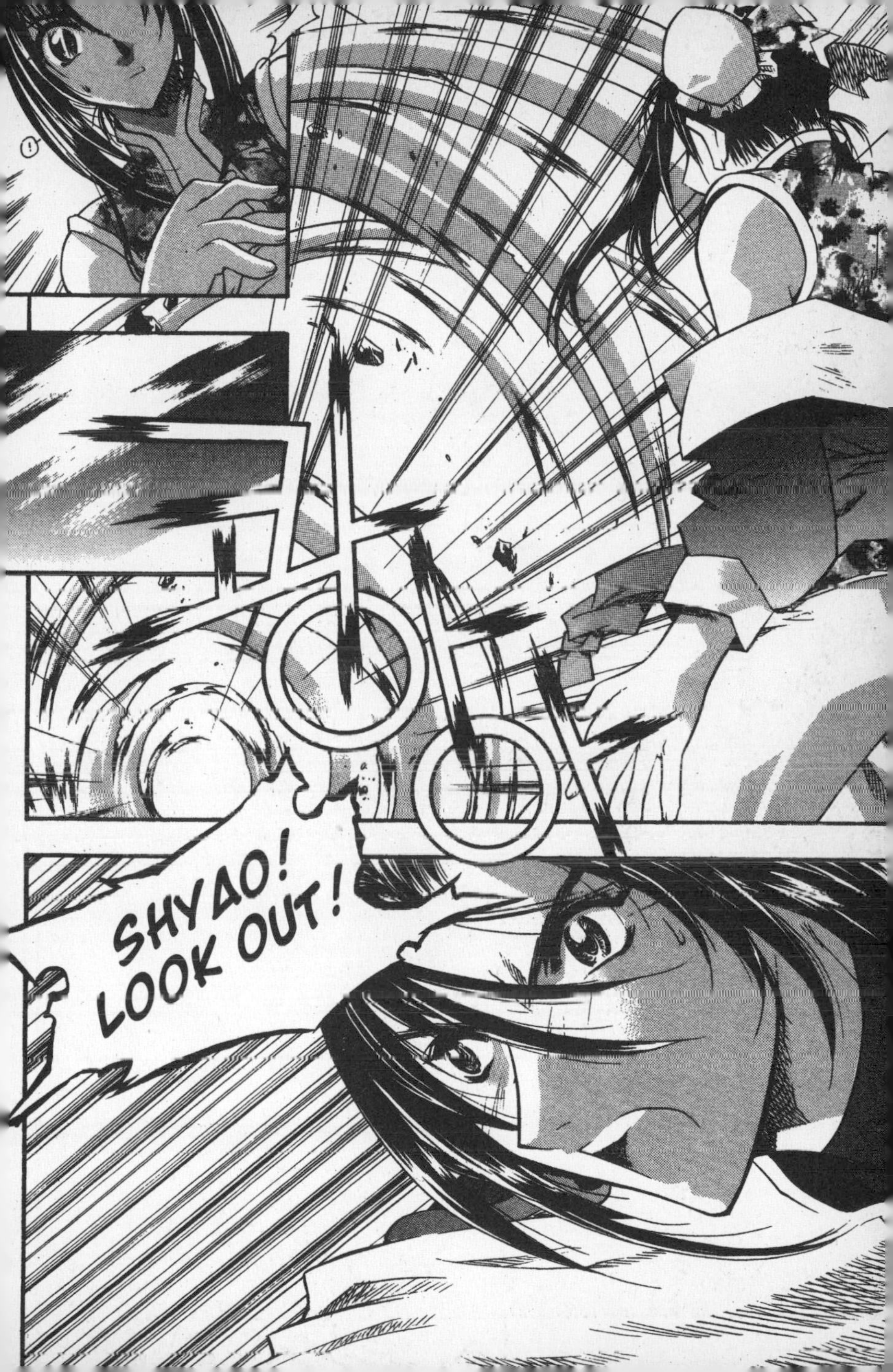
!
SHYAO! LOOK OUT!

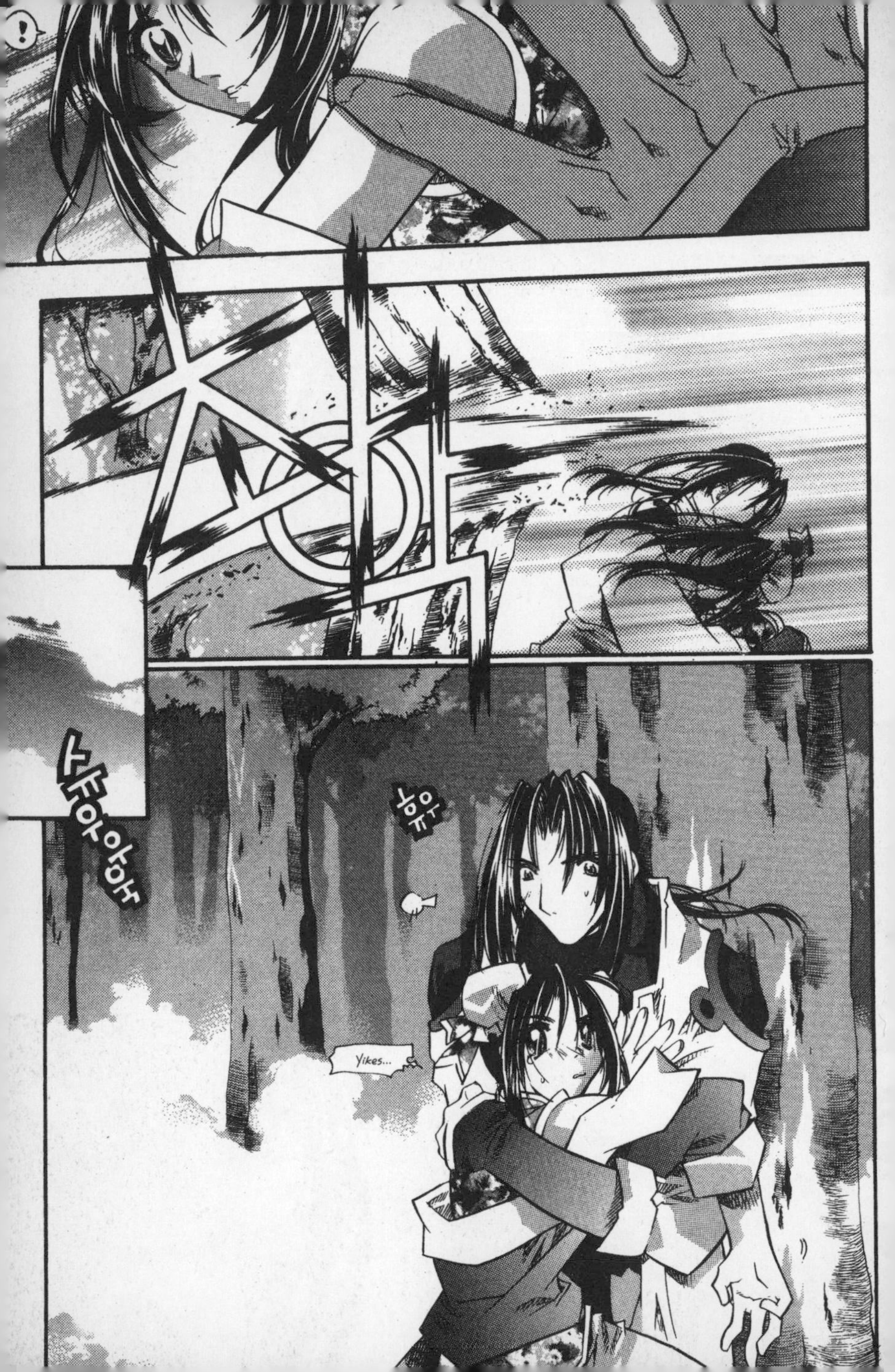
!
Yikes...

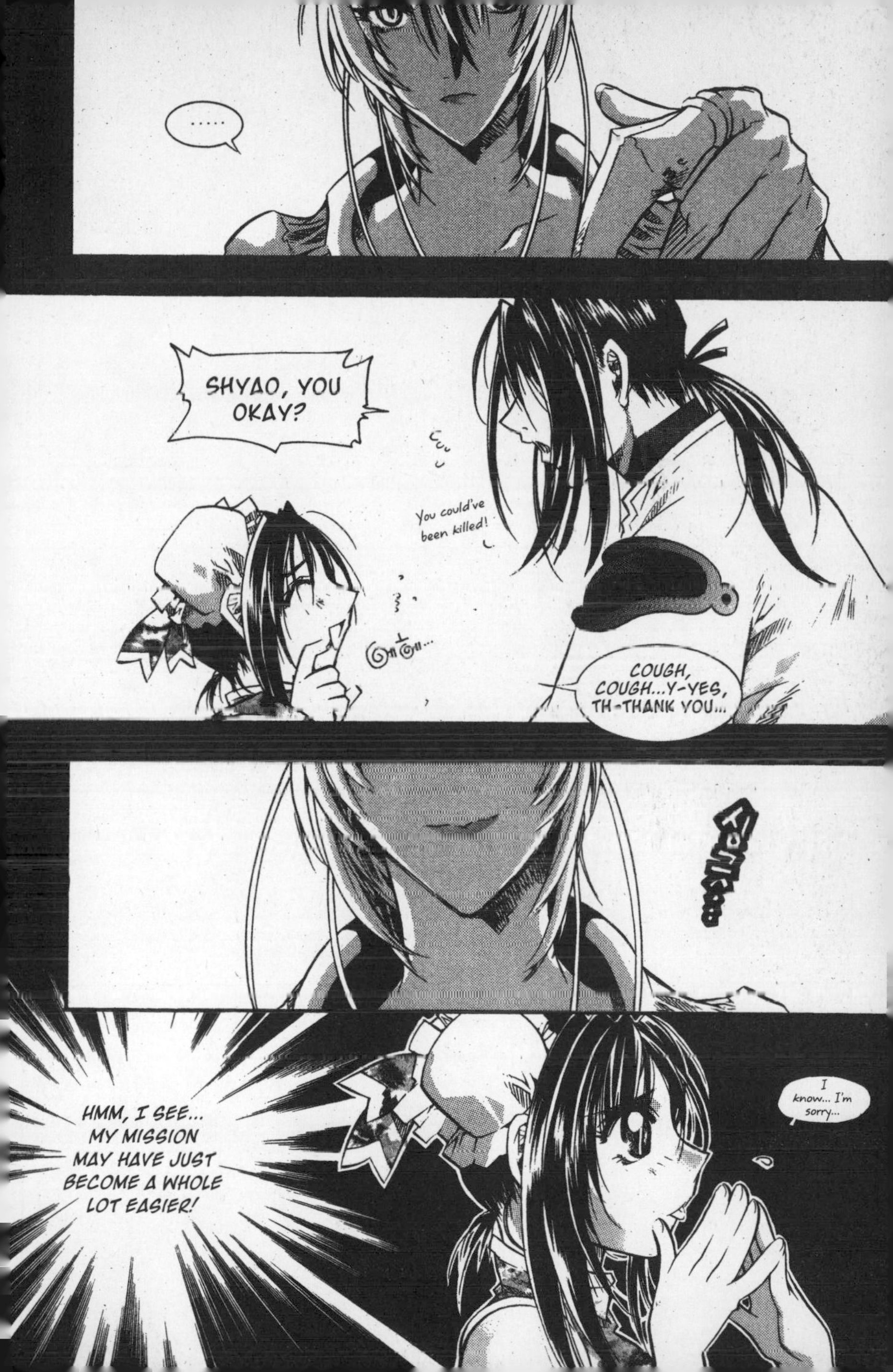
......
SHYAO, YOU OKAY?
You could've been killed!
COUGH, COUGH...Y-YES, TH-THANK YOU...
HMM, I SEE... MY MISSION MAY HAVE JUST BECOME A WHOLE LOT EASIER!
I know... I'm sorry...

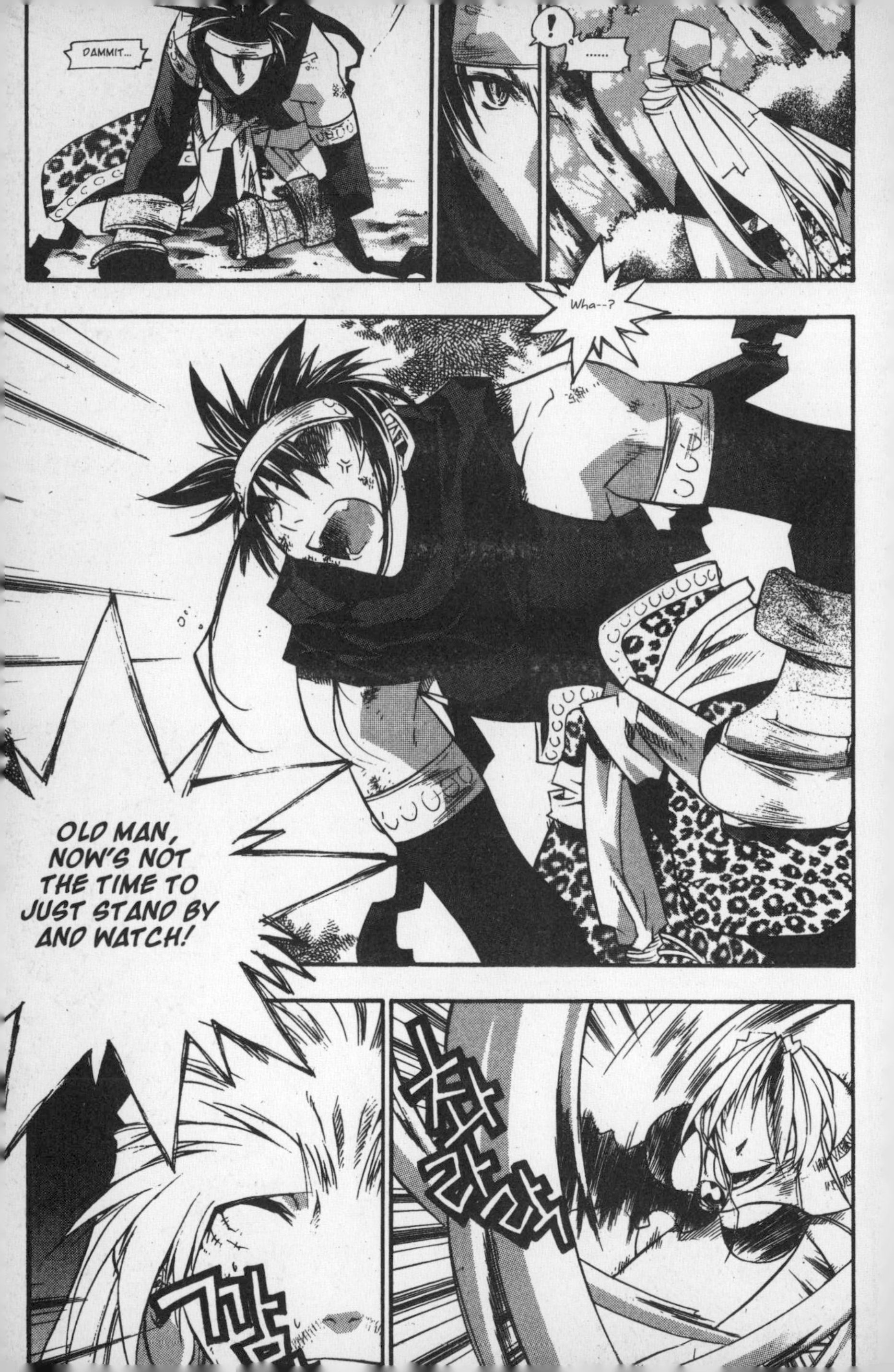
DAMMIT...
!
......
Wha--?
OLD MAN, NOW'S NOT THE TIME TO JUST STAND BY AND WATCH!

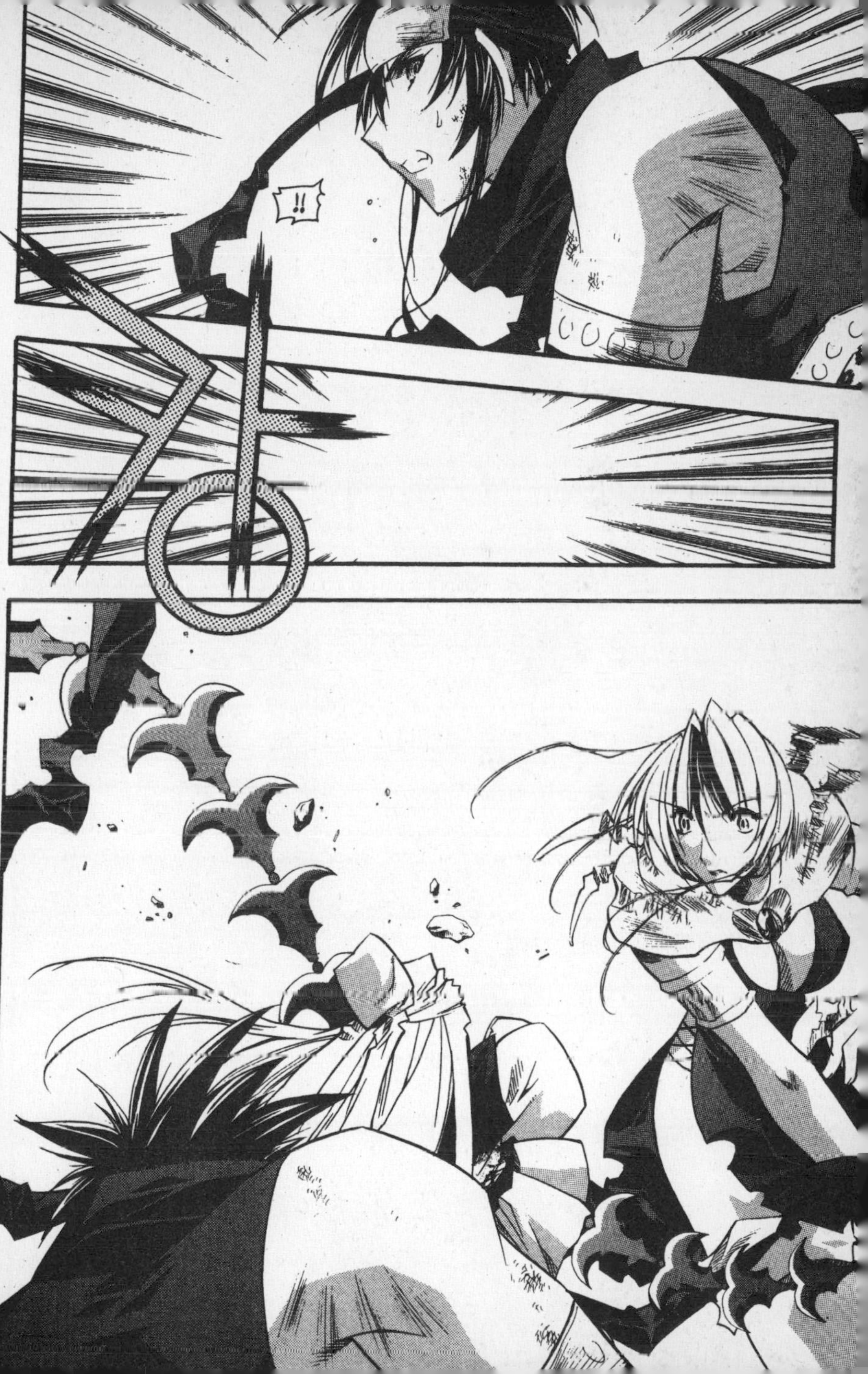
!!

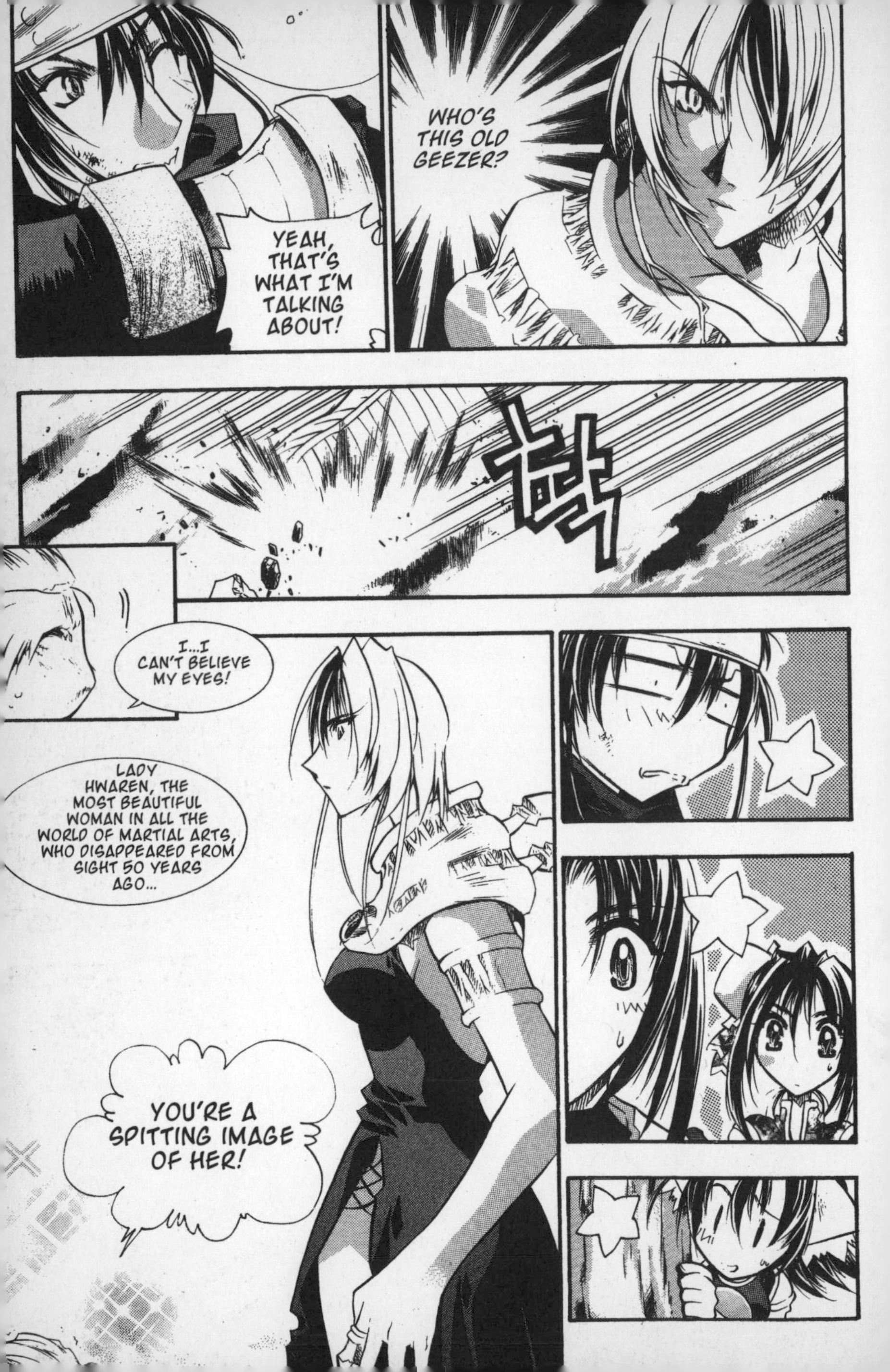
YEAH, THAT'S WHAT I'M TALKING ABOUT!
WHO'S THIS OLD GEEZER?
I...I CAN'T BELIEVE MY EYES!
LADY HWAREN, THE MOST BEAUTIFUL WOMAN IN ALL THE WORLD OF MARTIAL ARTS, WHO DISAPPEARED FROM SIGHT 50 YEARS AGO...
YOU'RE A SPITTING IMAGE OF HER!

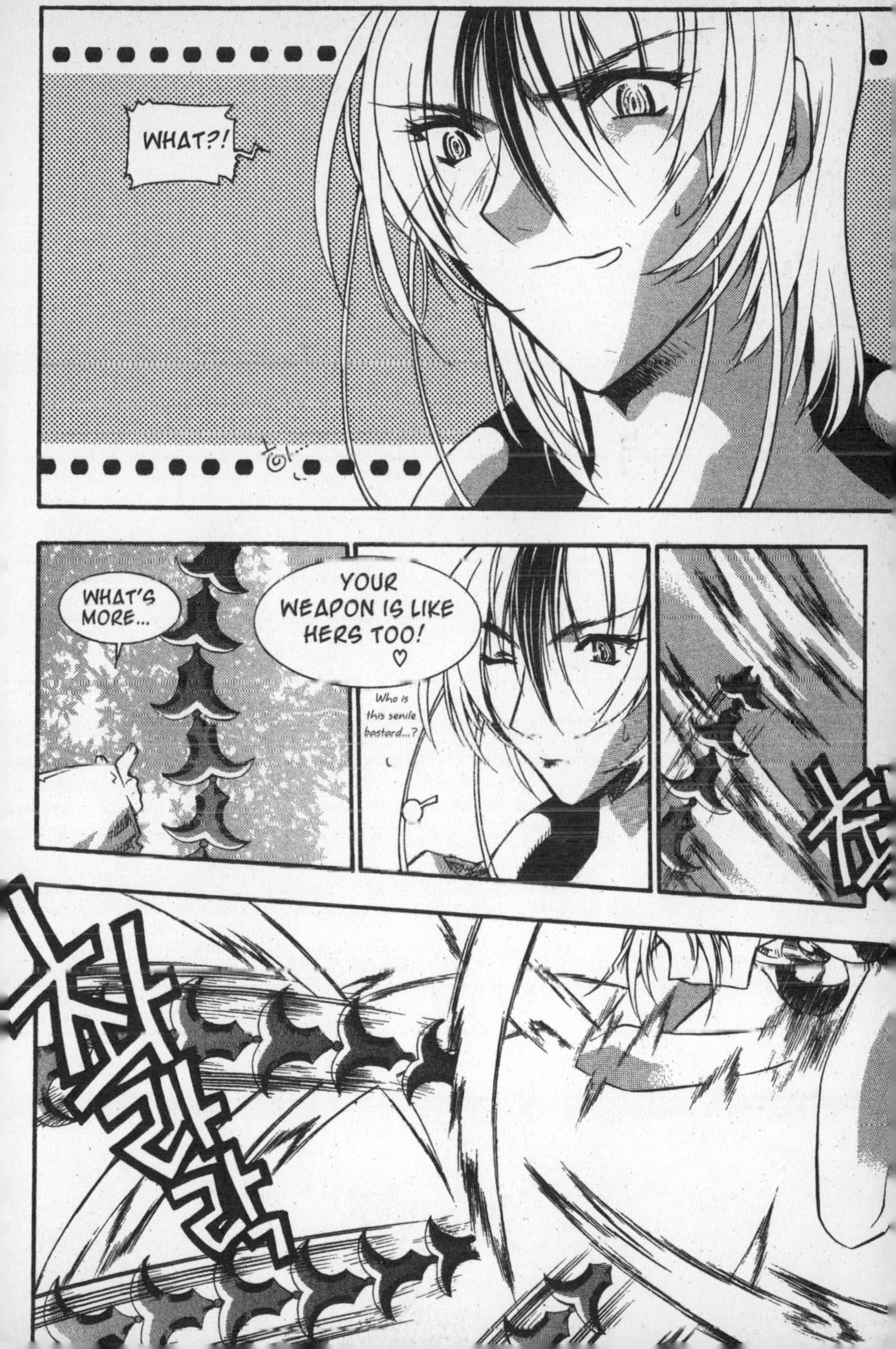
WHAT?!
WHAT'S MORE...
YOUR WEAPON IS LIKE HERS TOO! ♡
Who is this senile bastard...?

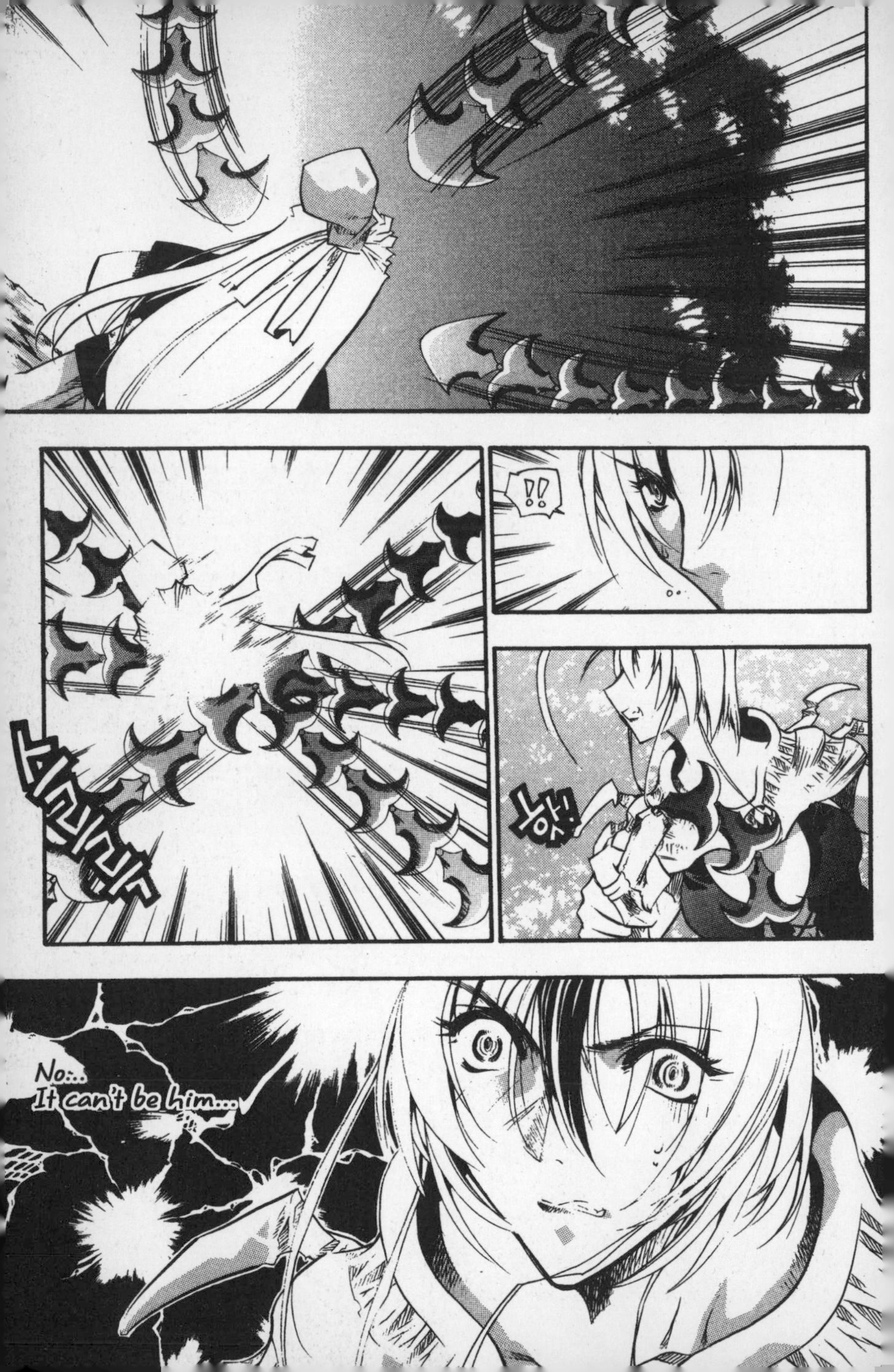
!!
앗!
No...
It can't be him...

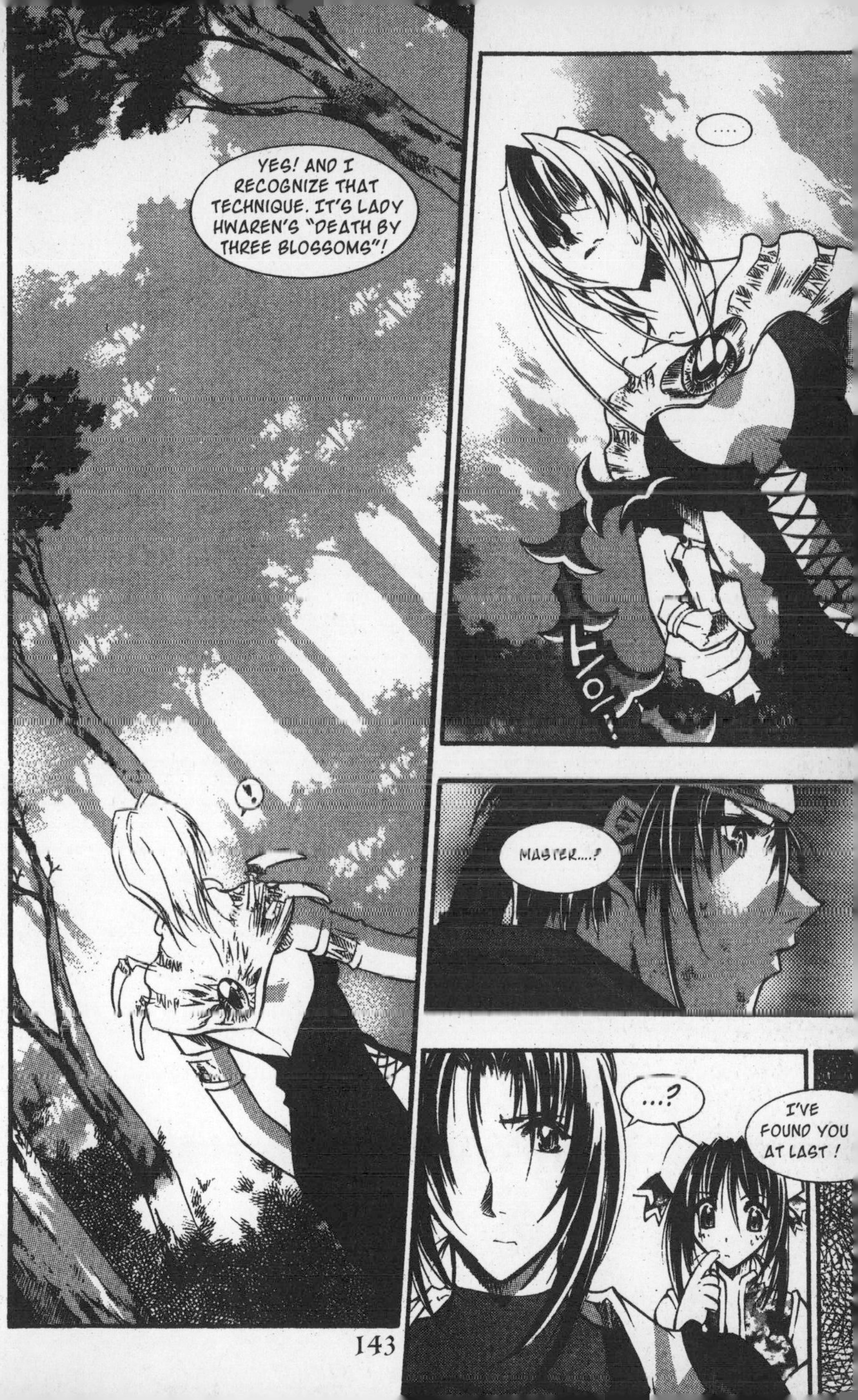
YES! AND I RECOGNIZE THAT TECHNIQUE. IT'S LADY HWAREN'S "DEATH BY THREE BLOSSOMS"!
!
....
MASTER....!
...?
I'VE FOUND YOU AT LAST !

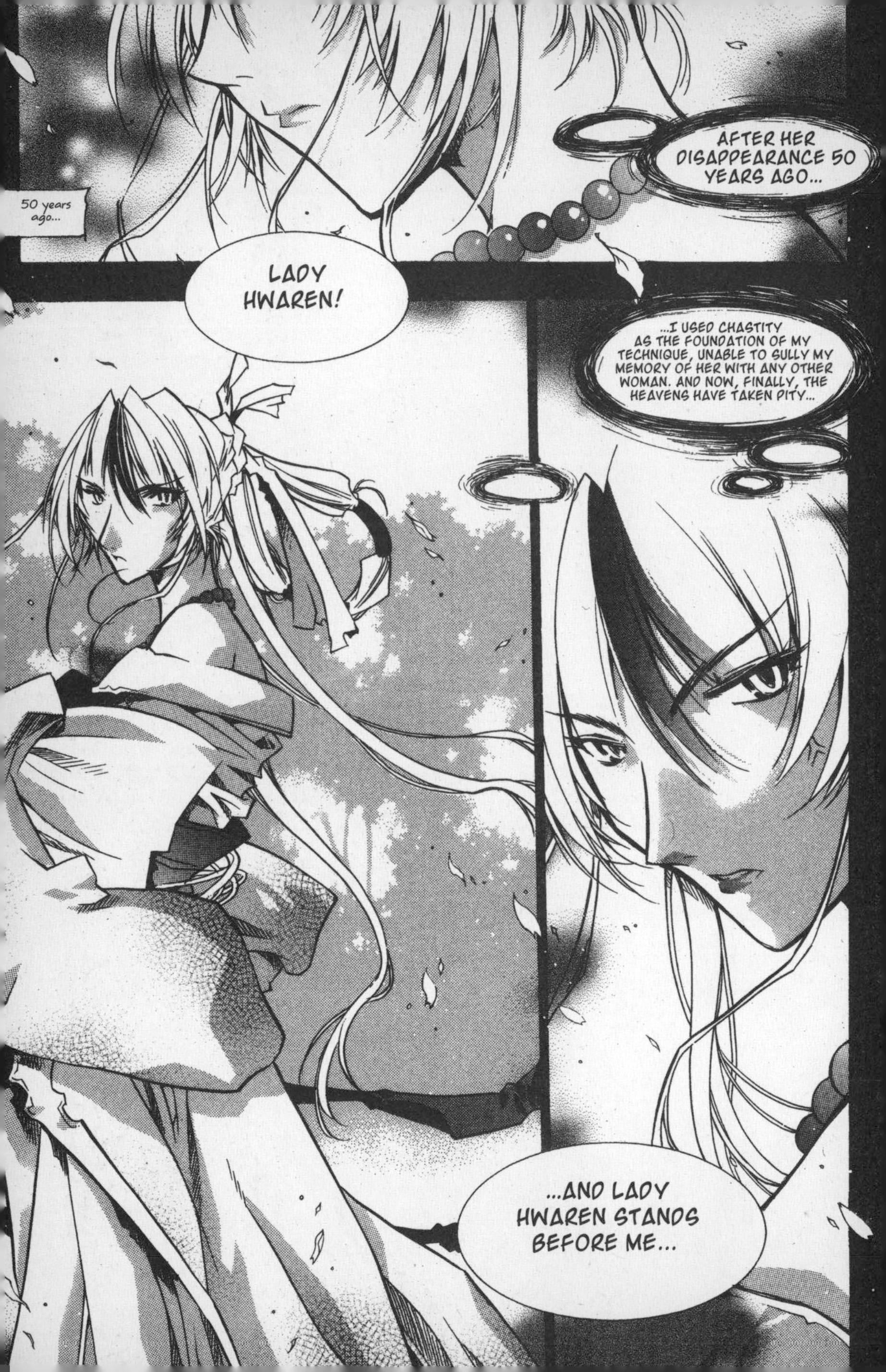
50 years ago...
AFTER HER DISAPPEARANCE 50 YEARS AGO...
LADY HWAREN!
...I USED CHASTITY AS THE FOUNDATION OF MY TECHNIQUE, UNABLE TO SULLY MY MEMORY OF HER WITH ANY OTHER WOMAN. AND NOW, FINALLY, THE HEAVENS HAVE TAKEN PITY...
...AND LADY HWAREN STANDS BEFORE ME...

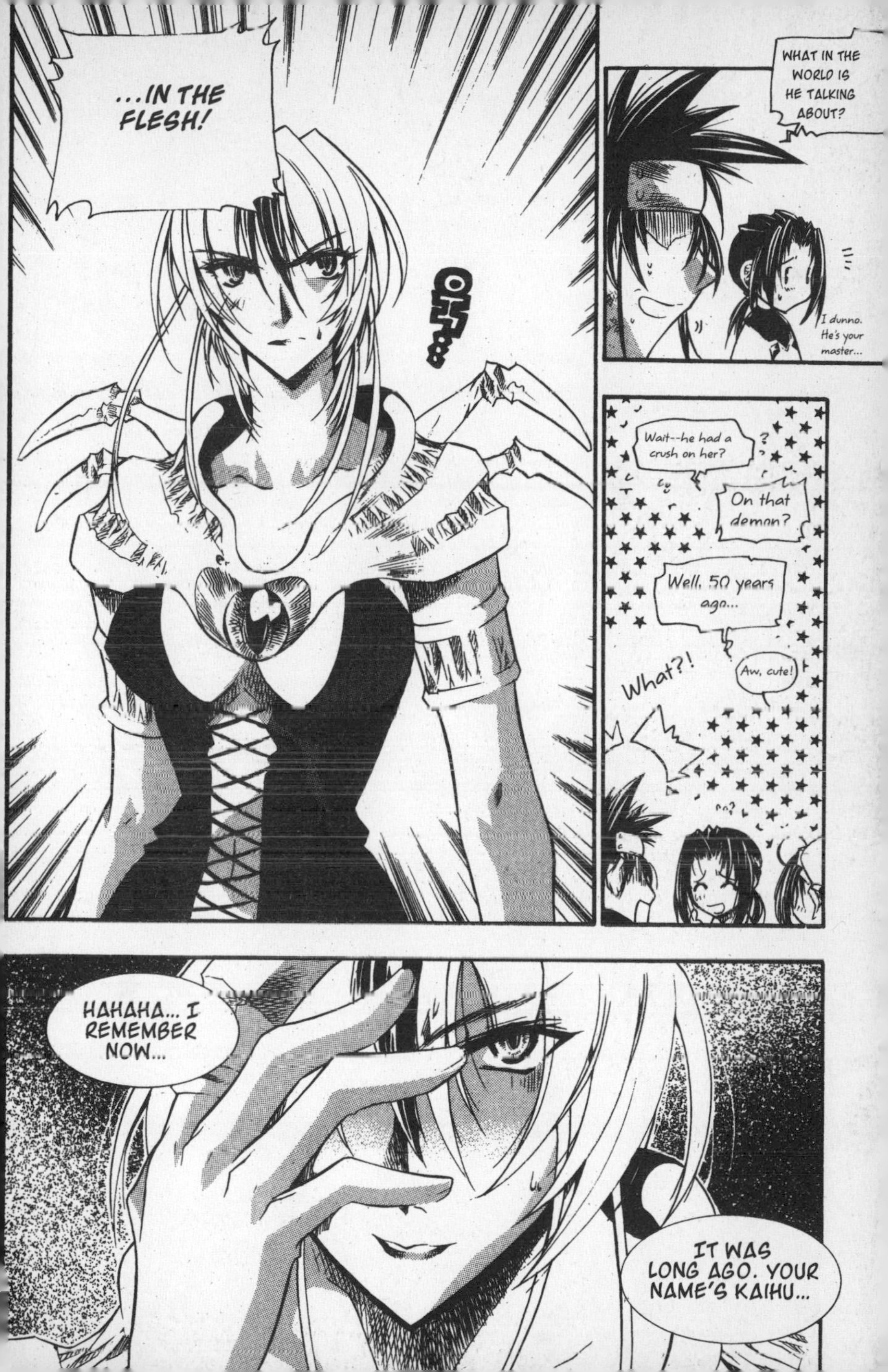
...IN THE FLESH!
OH?...
WHAT IN THE WORLD IS HE TALKING ABOUT?
I dunno. He's your master...
Wait--he had a crush on her?
On that demon?
Well, 50 years ago...
What?!
Aw, cute!
HAHAHA... I REMEMBER NOW...
IT WAS LONG AGO. YOUR NAME'S KAIHU...

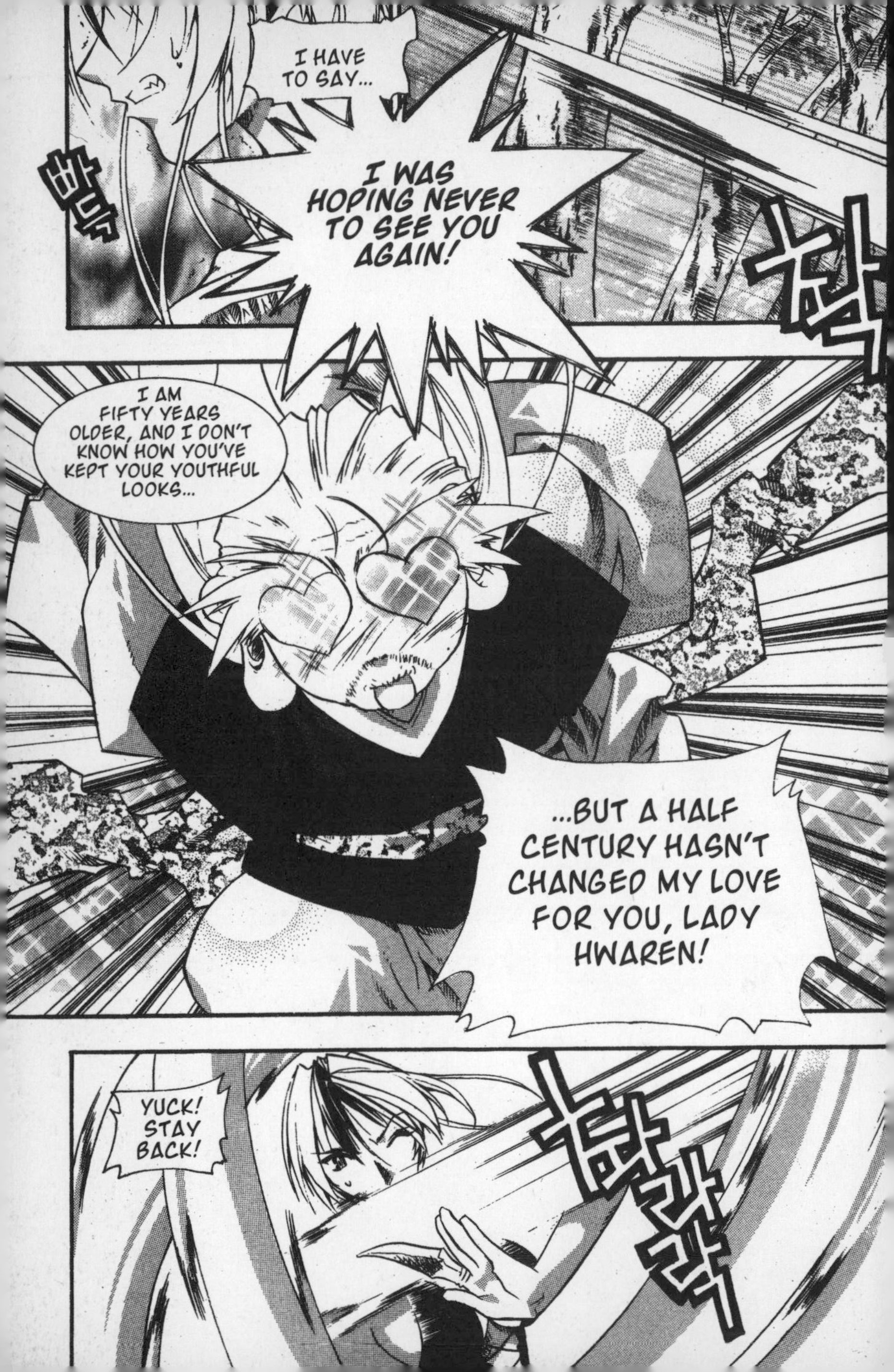
I HAVE TO SAY...
I WAS HOPING NEVER TO SEE YOU AGAIN!
I AM FIFTY YEARS OLDER, AND I DON'T KNOW HOW YOU'VE KEPT YOUR YOUTHFUL LOOKS...
...BUT A HALF CENTURY HASN'T CHANGED MY LOVE FOR YOU, LADY HWAREN!
YUCK! STAY BACK!

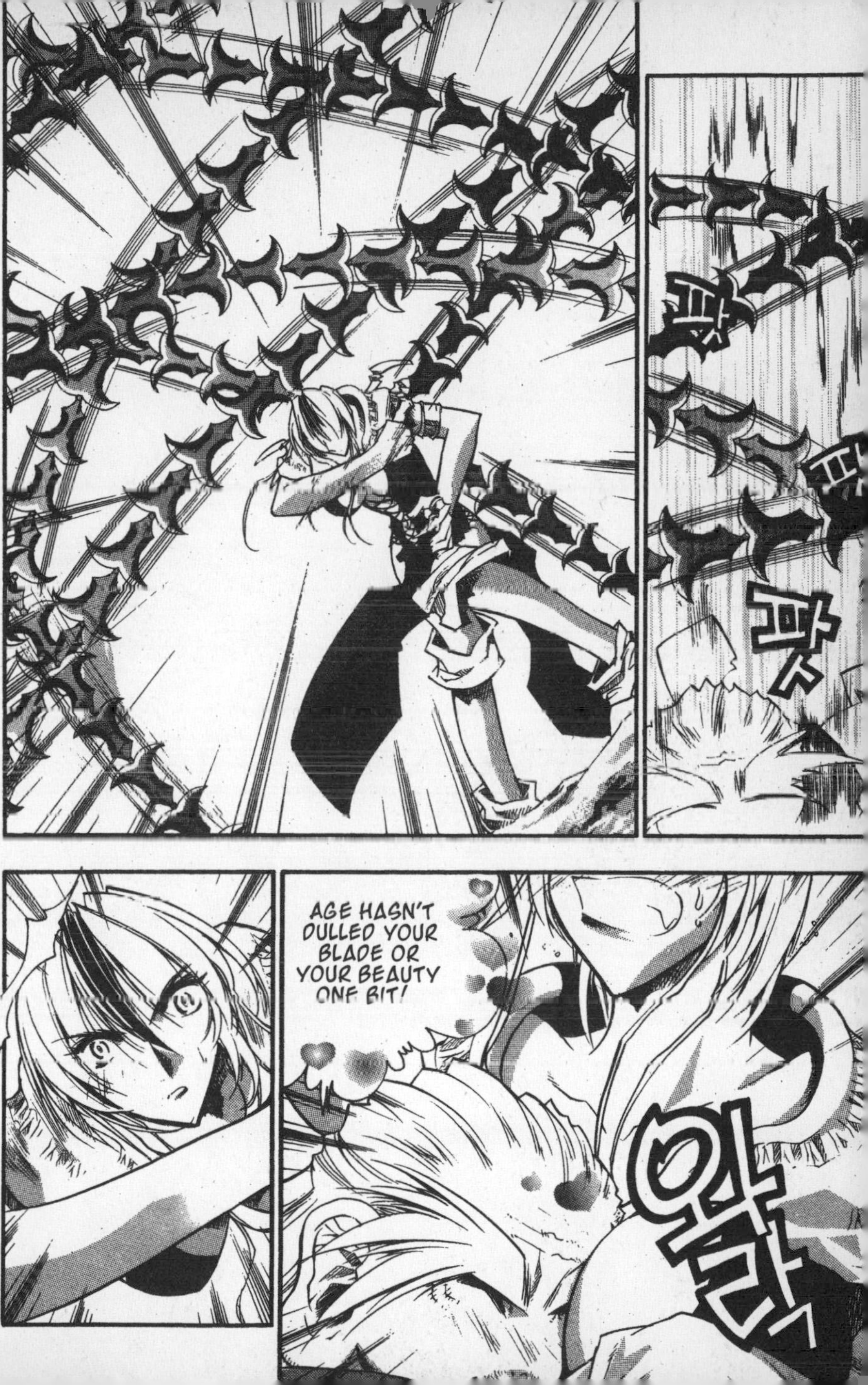
팍
팍
AGE HASN'T DULLED YOUR BLADE OR YOUR BEAUTY ONE BIT!
와락

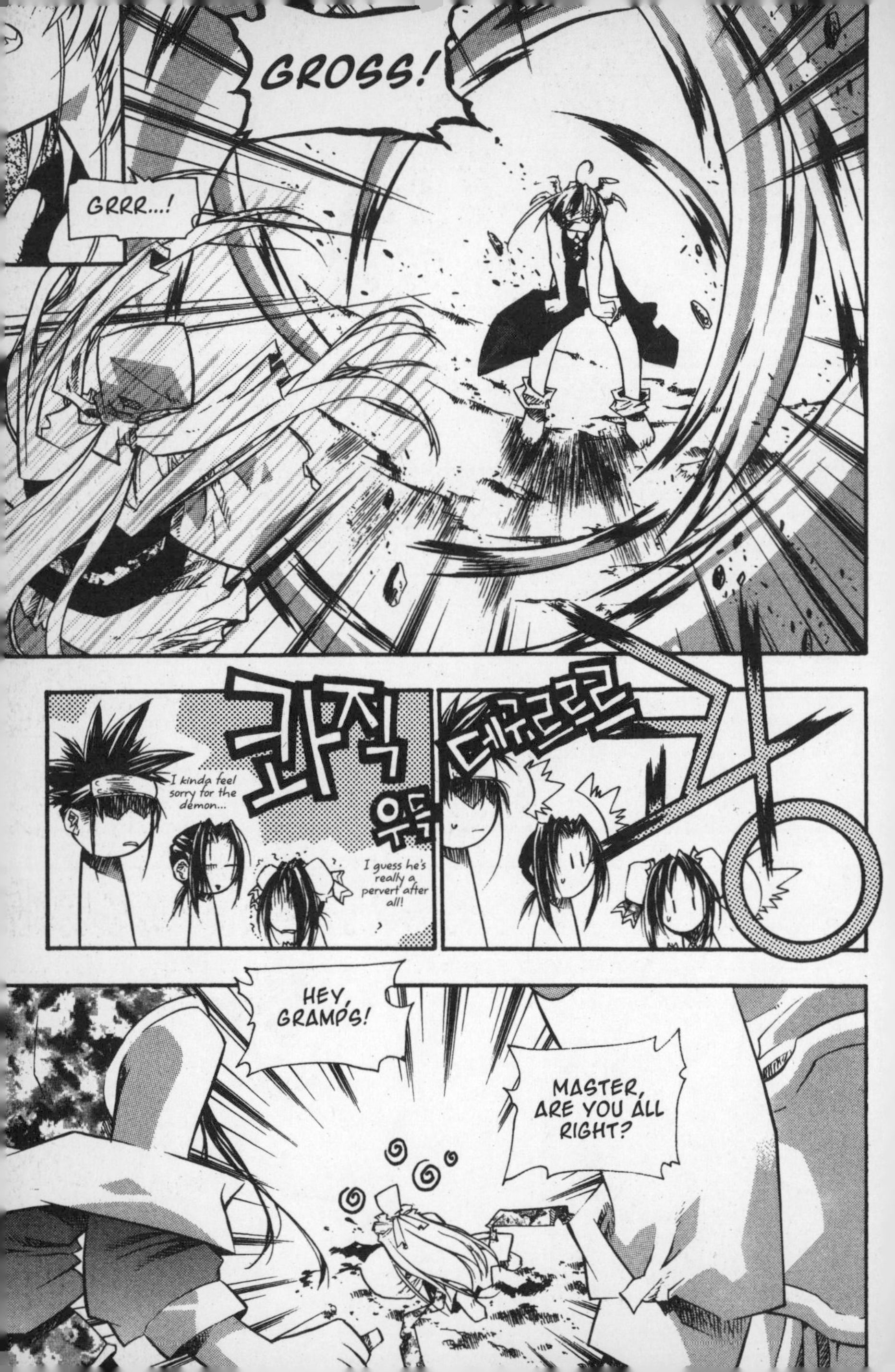
GROSS!
GRRR...!
I kinda feel sorry for the demon...
I guess he's really a pervert after all!
HEY, GRAMPS!
MASTER, ARE YOU ALL RIGHT?

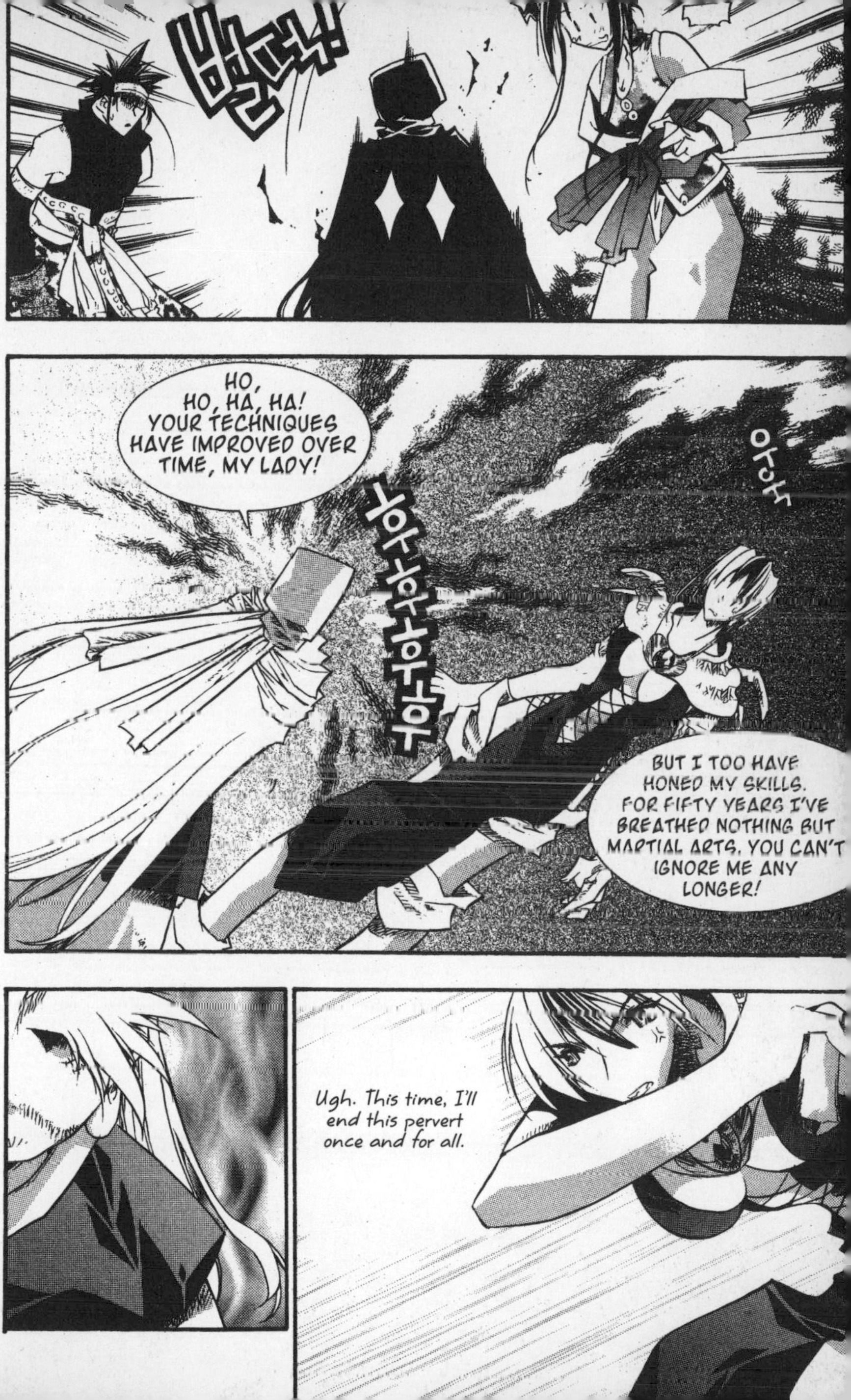
HO, HO, HA, HA! YOUR TECHNIQUES HAVE IMPROVED OVER TIME, MY LADY!
BUT I TOO HAVE HONED MY SKILLS. FOR FIFTY YEARS I'VE BREATHED NOTHING BUT MARTIAL ARTS. YOU CAN'T IGNORE ME ANY LONGER!
Ugh. This time, I'll end this pervert once and for all.

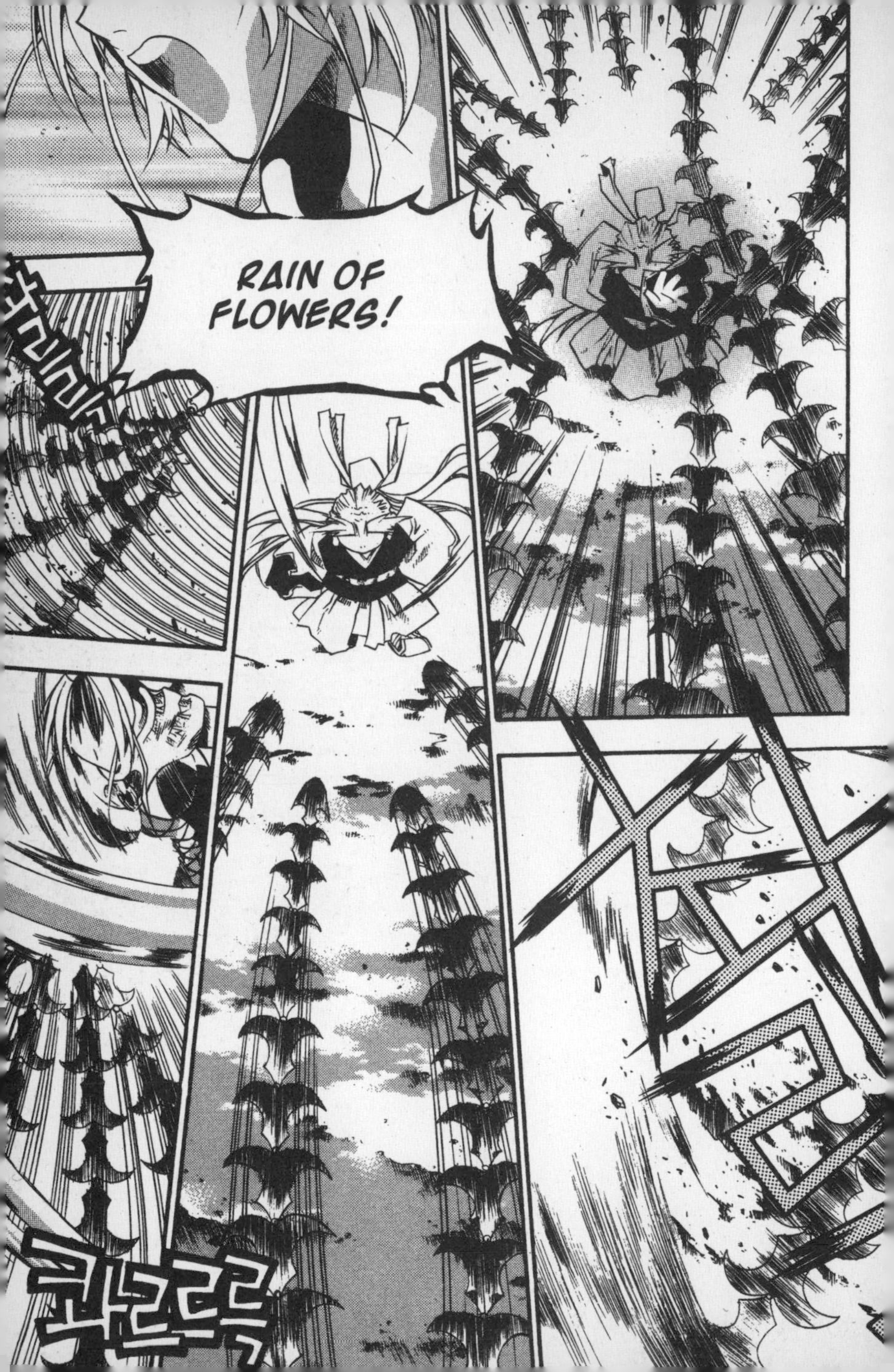
RAIN OF FLOWERS!

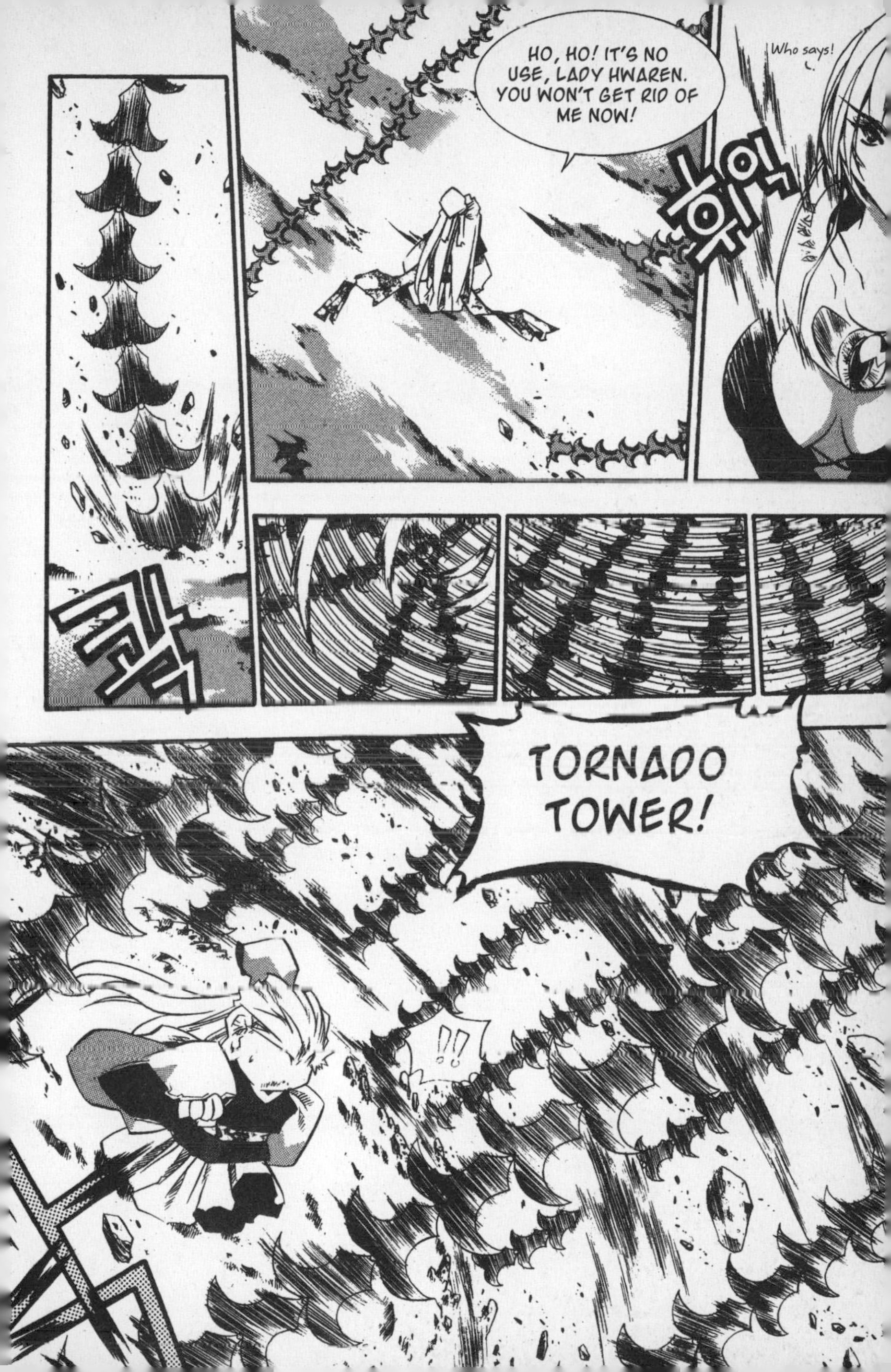
HO, HO! IT'S NO USE, LADY HWAREN. YOU WON'T GET RID OF ME NOW!
Who says!
TORNADO TOWER!
!!

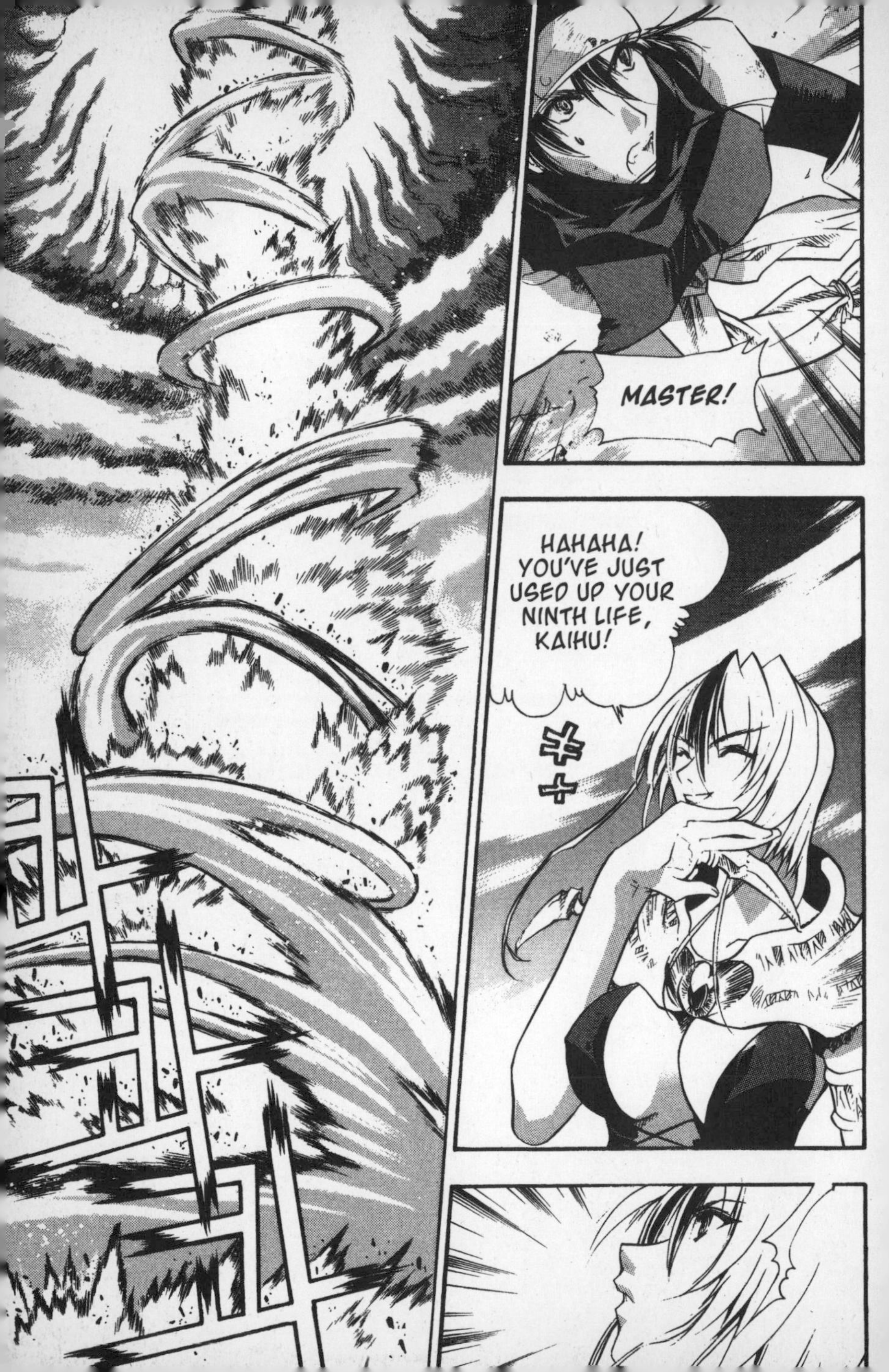
MASTER!
HAHAHA! YOU'VE JUST USED UP YOUR NINTH LIFE, KAIHU!

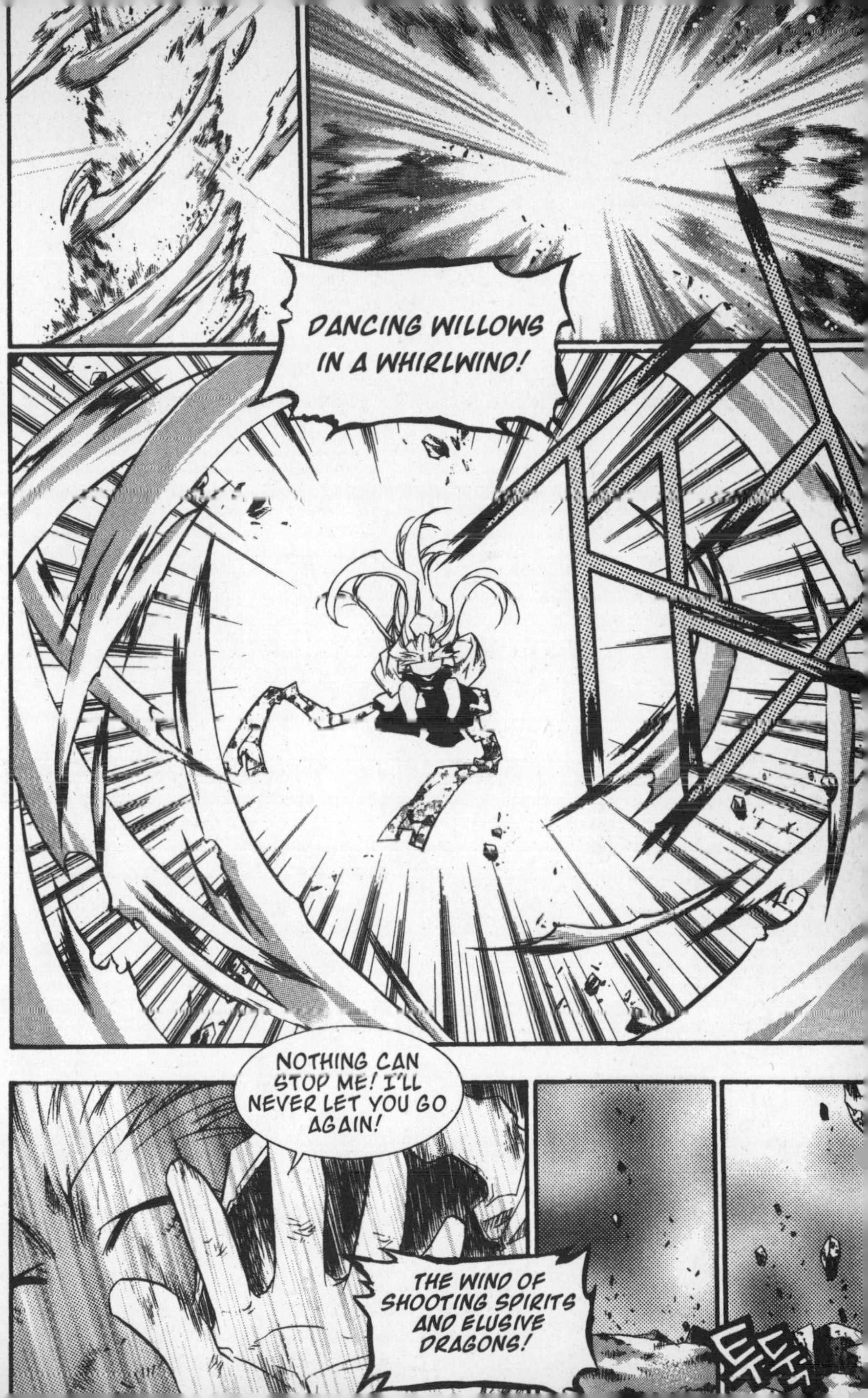
DANCING WILLOWS IN A WHIRLWIND!
NOTHING CAN STOP ME! I'LL NEVER LET YOU GO AGAIN!
THE WIND OF SHOOTING SPIRITS AND ELUSIVE DRAGONS!

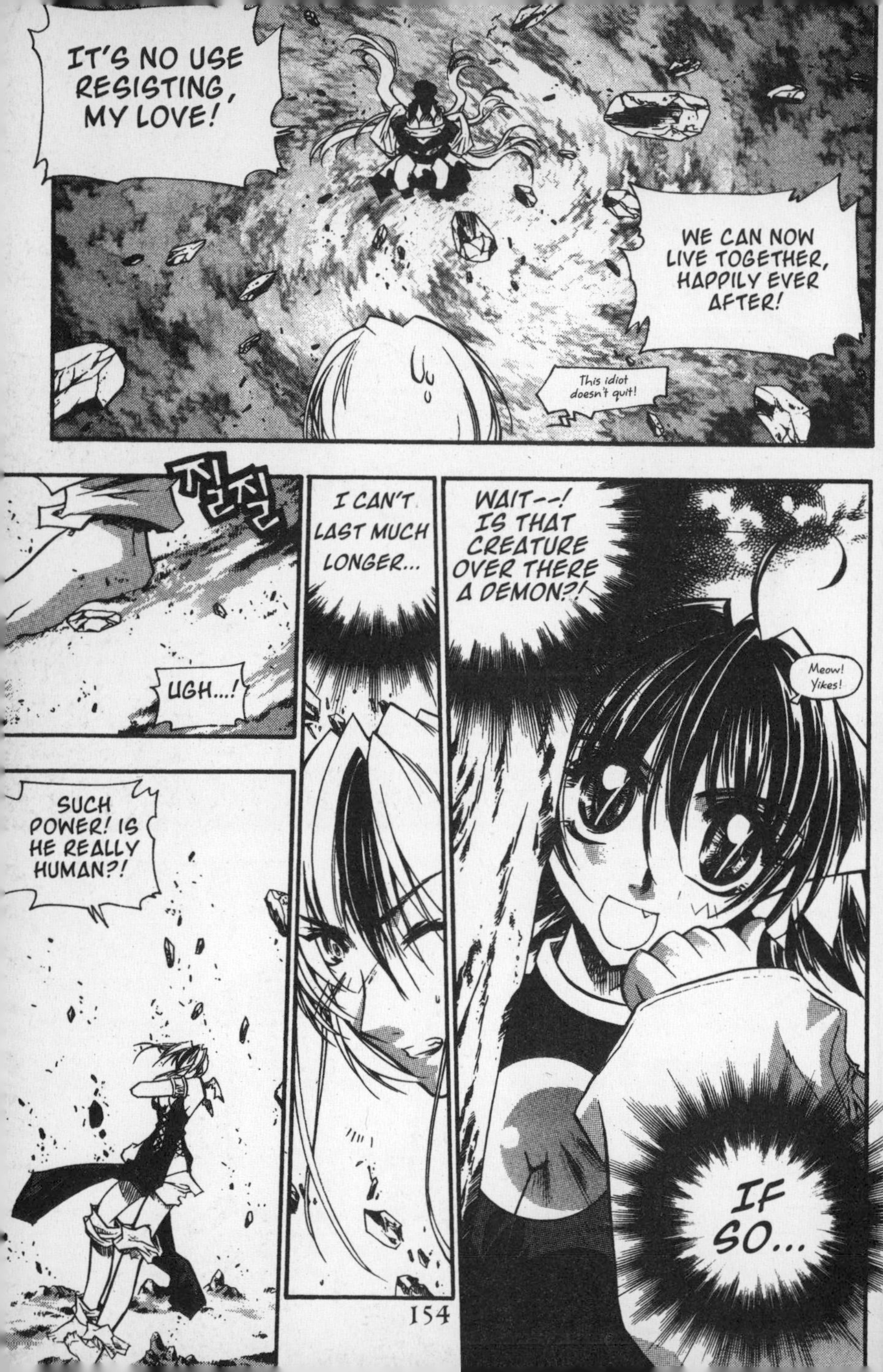
IT'S NO USE RESISTING, MY LOVE!
WE CAN NOW LIVE TOGETHER, HAPPILY EVER AFTER!
This idiot doesn't quit!
진진
UGH...!
SUCH POWER! IS HE REALLY HUMAN?!
I CAN'T LAST MUCH LONGER...
WAIT--! IS THAT CREATURE OVER THERE A DEMON?!
Meow! Yikes!
IF SO...

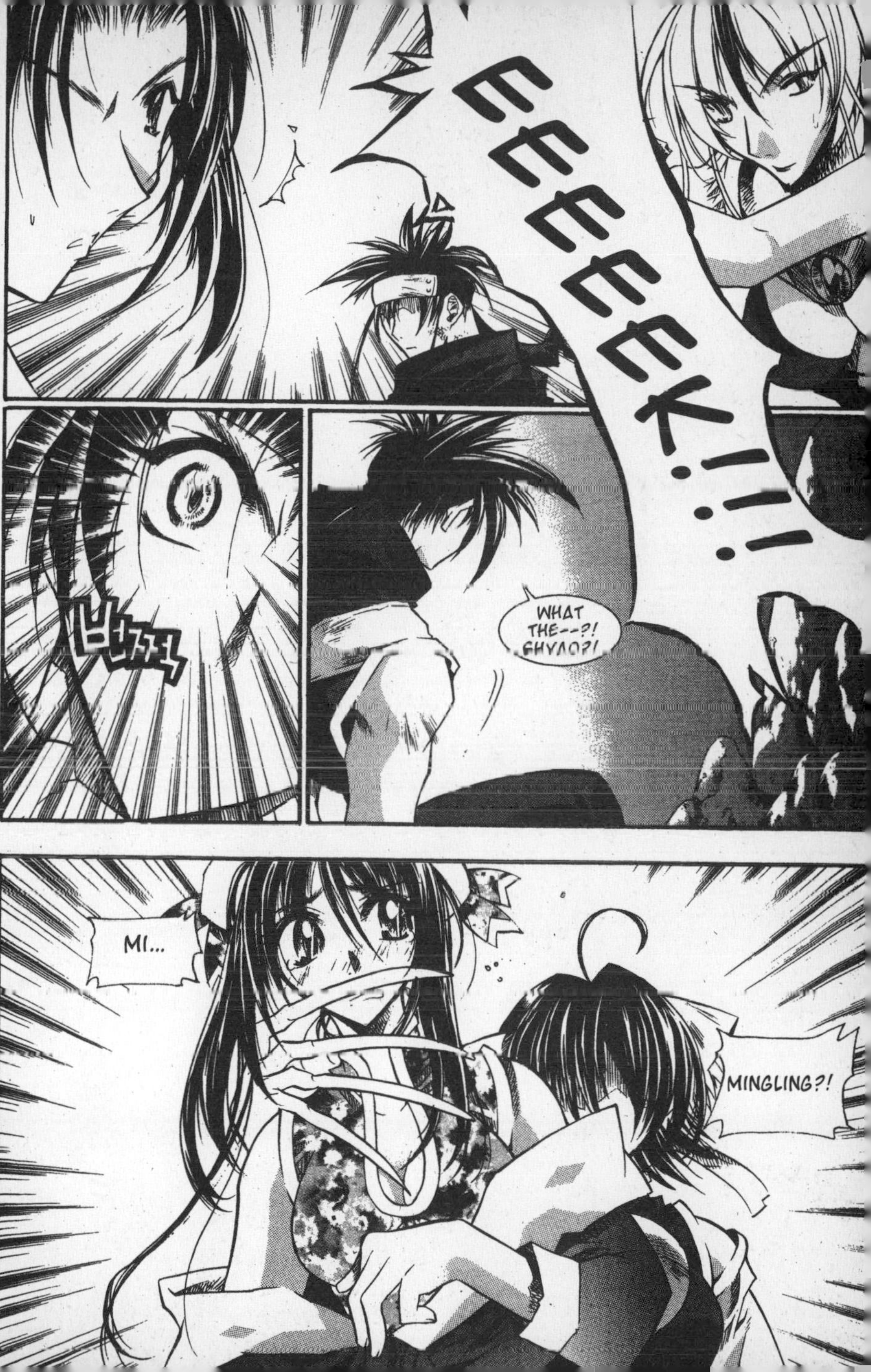
EEEEEEK!!!!
WHAT THE--?! SHYAO?!
MI...
MINGLING?!

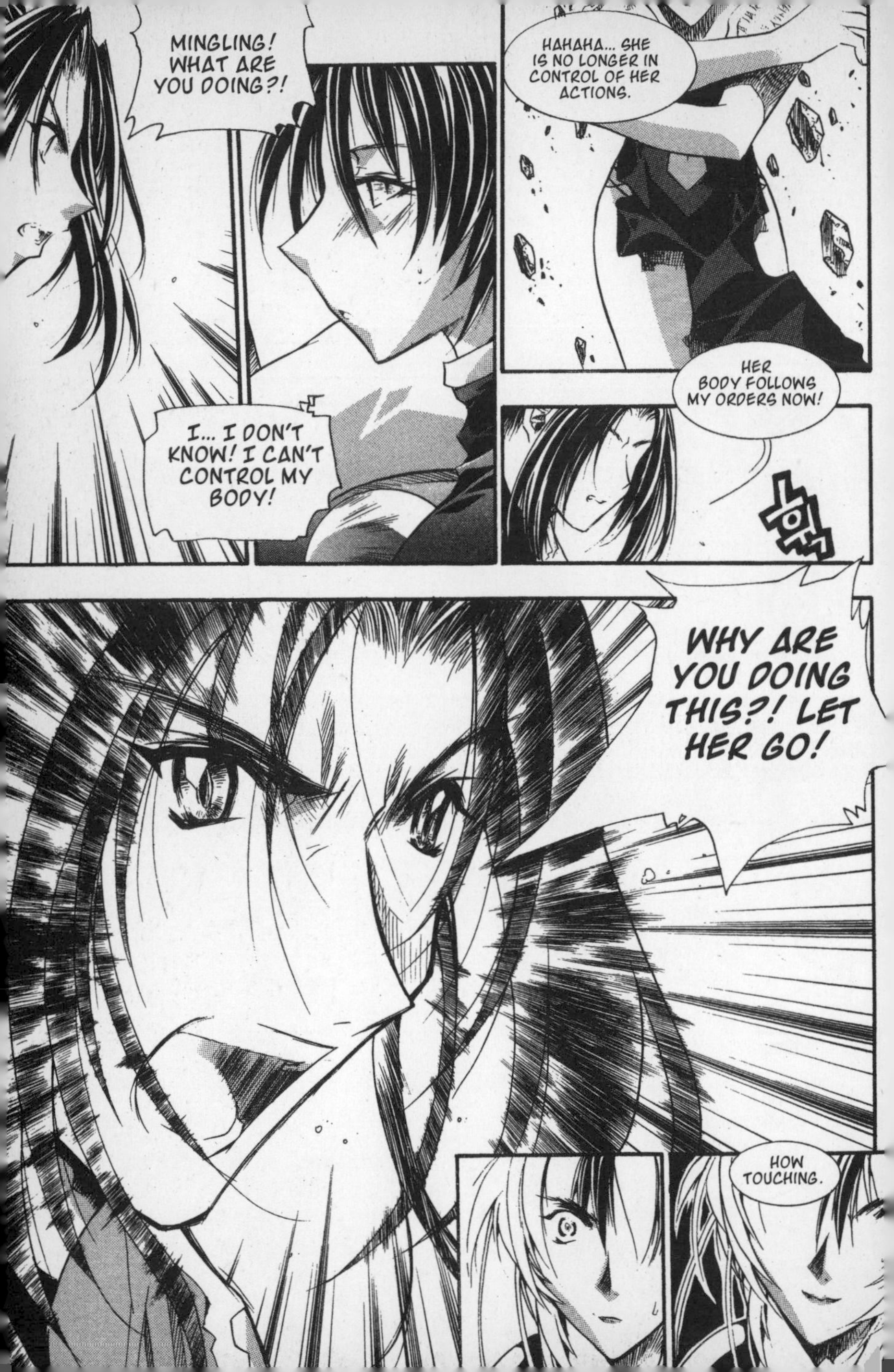
MINGLING! WHAT ARE YOU DOING?!
I... I DON'T KNOW! I CAN'T CONTROL MY BODY!
HAHAHA... SHE IS NO LONGER IN CONTROL OF HER ACTIONS.
HER BODY FOLLOWS MY ORDERS NOW!
WHY ARE YOU DOING THIS?! LET HER GO!
HOW TOUCHING.

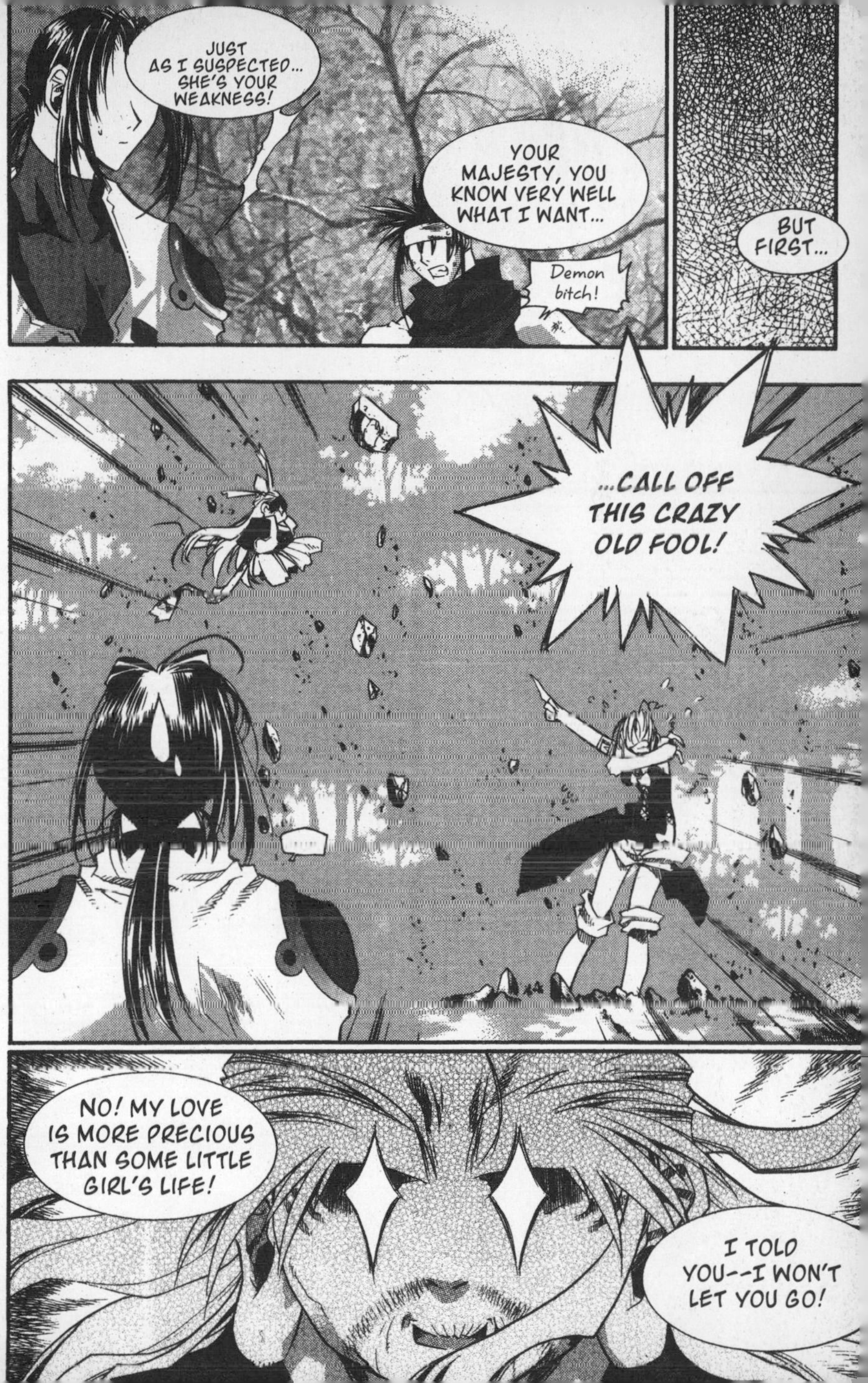
JUST AS I SUSPECTED... SHE'S YOUR WEAKNESS!
YOUR MAJESTY, YOU KNOW VERY WELL WHAT I WANT...
Demon bitch!
BUT FIRST...
...CALL OFF THIS CRAZY OLD FOOL!
NO! MY LOVE IS MORE PRECIOUS THAN SOME LITTLE GIRL'S LIFE!
I TOLD YOU--I WON'T LET YOU GO!

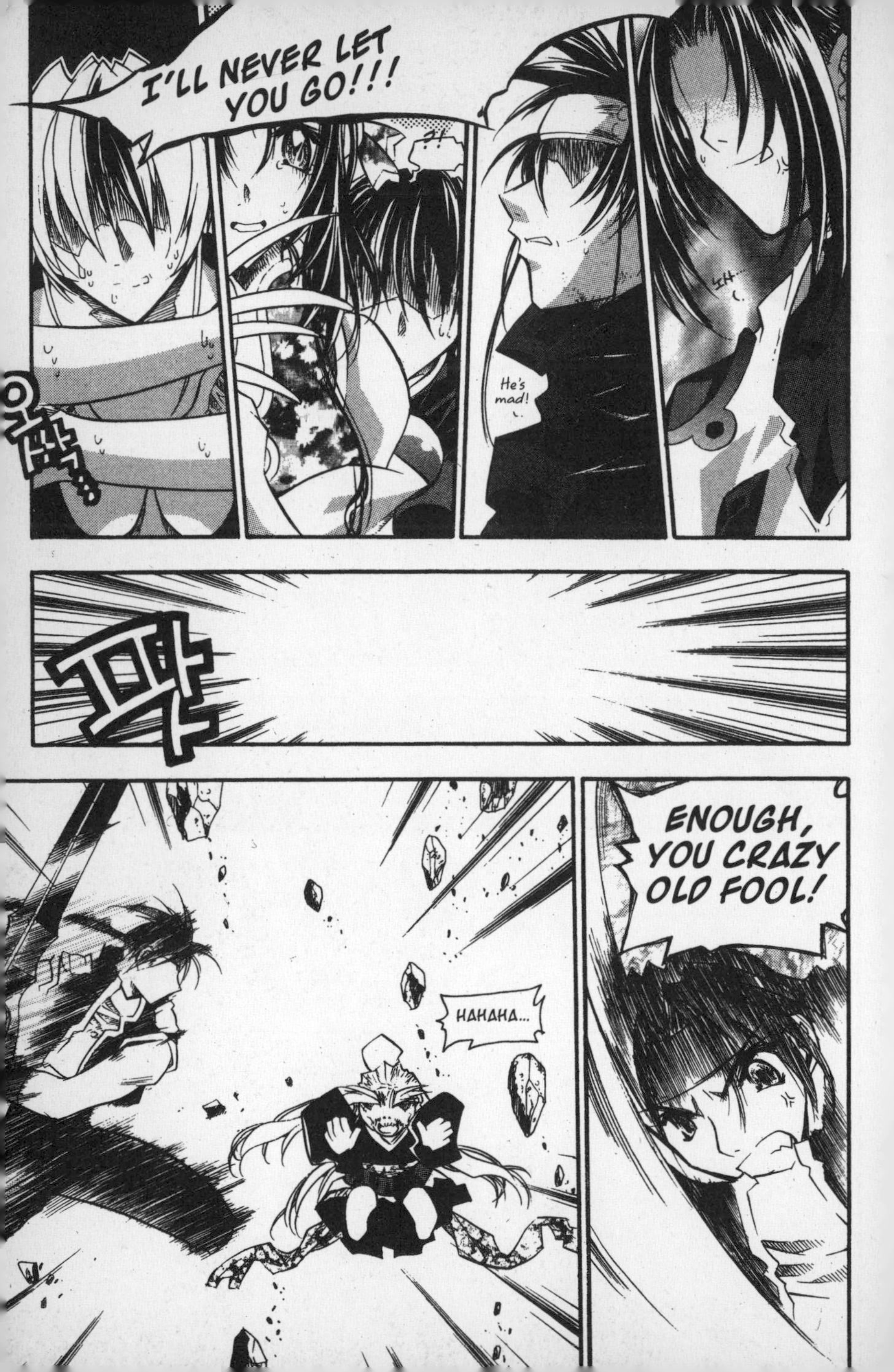
I'LL NEVER LET YOU GO!!!
He's mad!
HAHAHA...
ENOUGH, YOU CRAZY OLD FOOL!

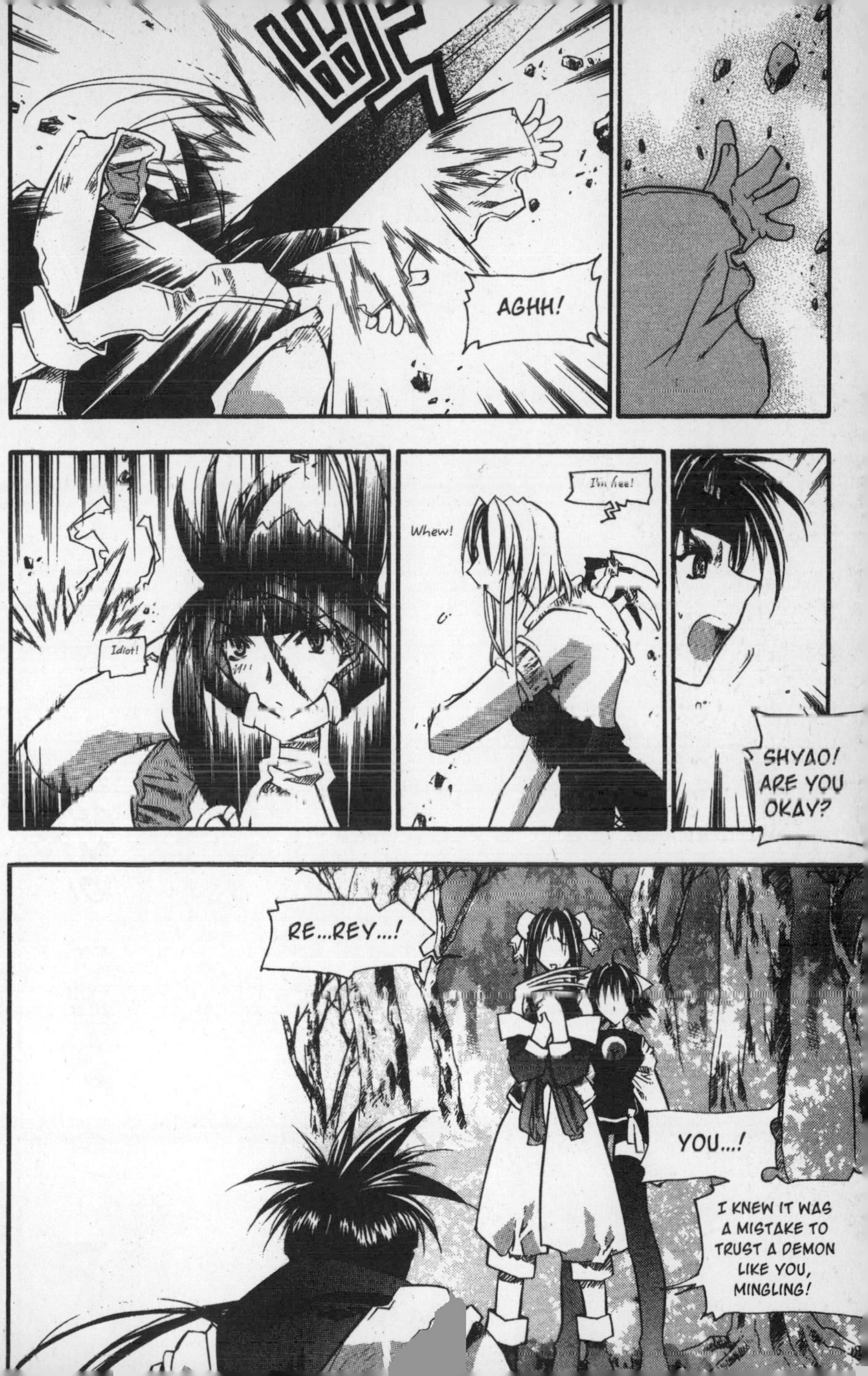
AGHH!
Idiot!
Whew!
I'm free!
SHYAO! ARE YOU OKAY?
RE...REY...!
YOU...!
I KNEW IT WAS A MISTAKE TO TRUST A DEMON LIKE YOU, MINGLING!

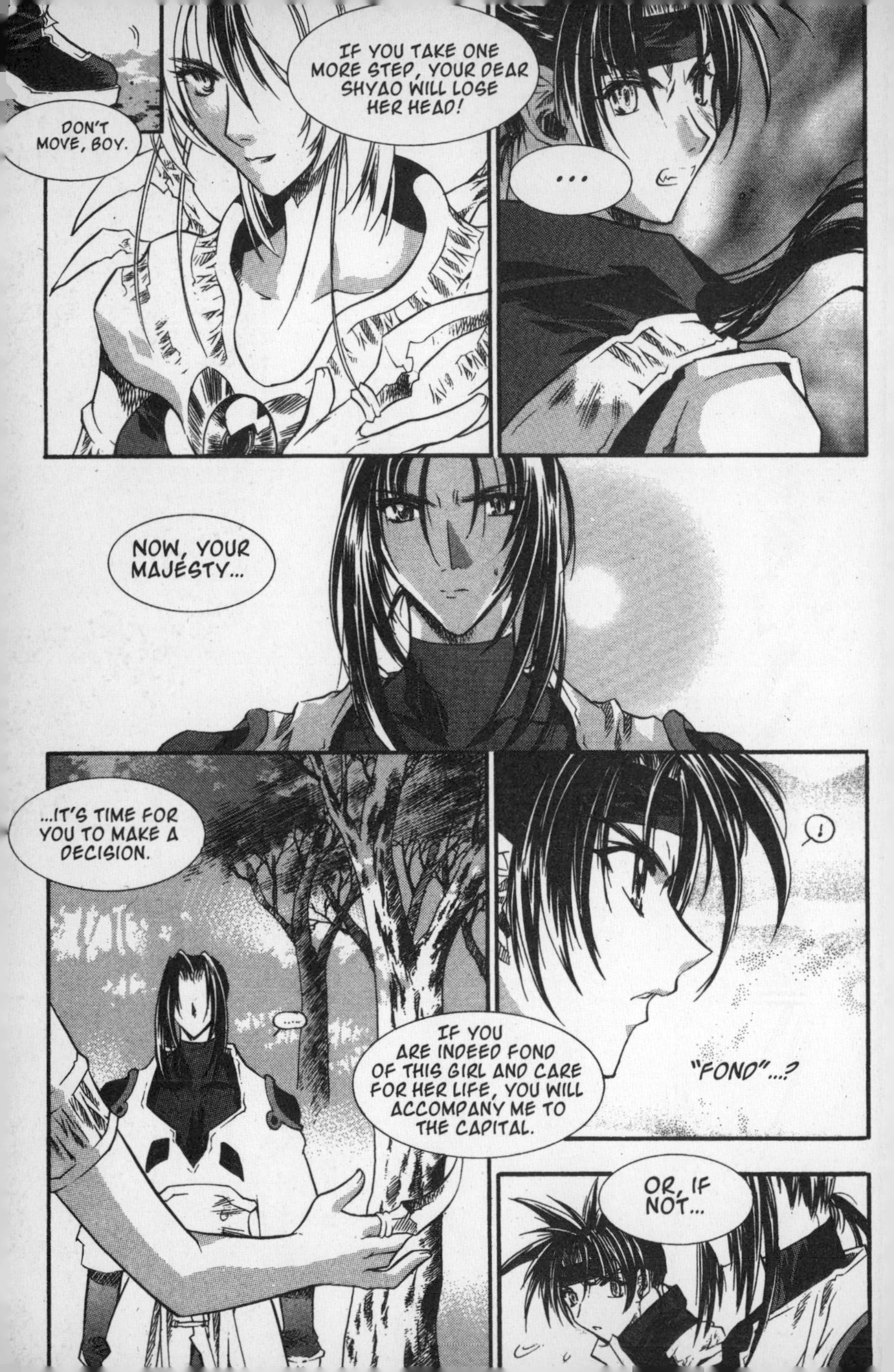
DON'T MOVE, BOY.
IF YOU TAKE ONE MORE STEP, YOUR DEAR SHYAO WILL LOSE HER HEAD!
...
NOW, YOUR MAJESTY...
...IT'S TIME FOR YOU TO MAKE A DECISION.
!
...
IF YOU ARE INDEED FOND OF THIS GIRL AND CARE FOR HER LIFE, YOU WILL ACCOMPANY ME TO THE CAPITAL.
"FOND"...?
OR, IF NOT...

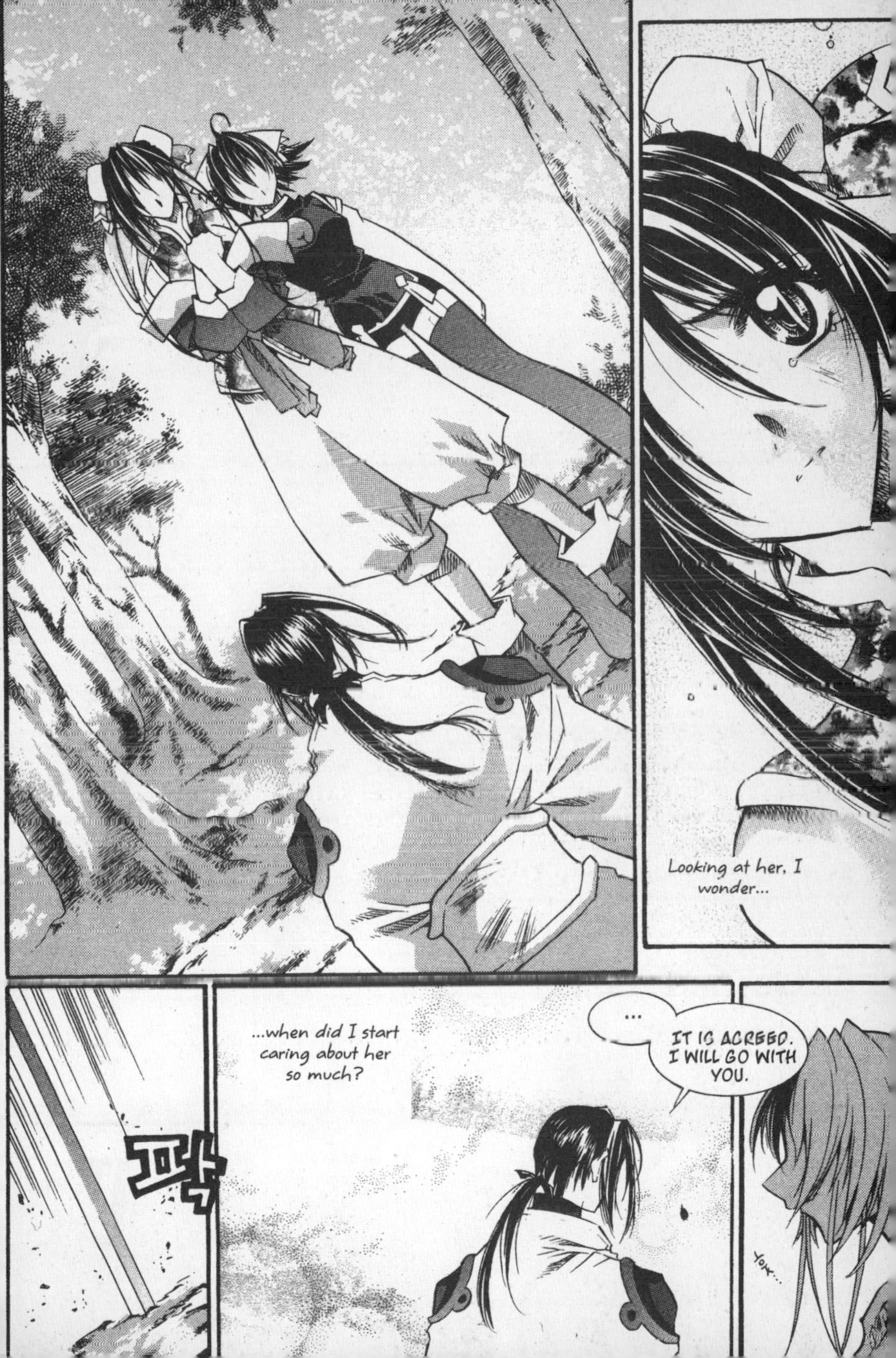
Looking at her, I wonder...
...when did I start caring about her so much?
...
IT IS AGREED. I WILL GO WITH YOU.

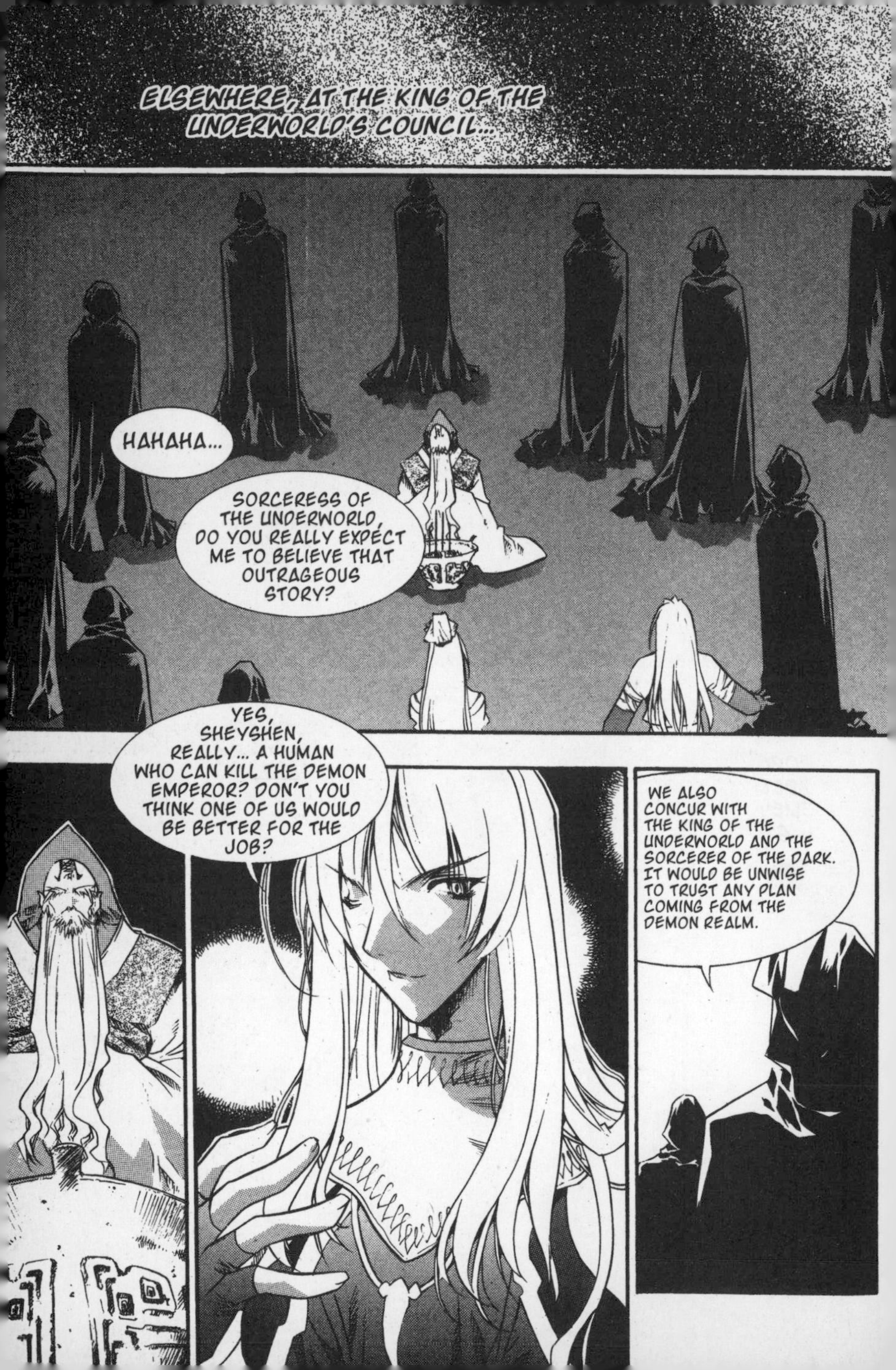
ELSEWHERE, AT THE KING OF THE UNDERWORLD'S COUNCIL...
HAHAHA...
SORCERESS OF THE UNDERWORLD, DO YOU REALLY EXPECT ME TO BELIEVE THAT OUTRAGEOUS STORY?
YES, SHEYSHEN, REALLY... A HUMAN WHO CAN KILL THE DEMON EMPEROR? DON'T YOU THINK ONE OF US WOULD BE BETTER FOR THE JOB?
WE ALSO CONCUR WITH THE KING OF THE UNDERWORLD AND THE SORCERER OF THE DARK. IT WOULD BE UNWISE TO TRUST ANY PLAN COMING FROM THE DEMON REALM.

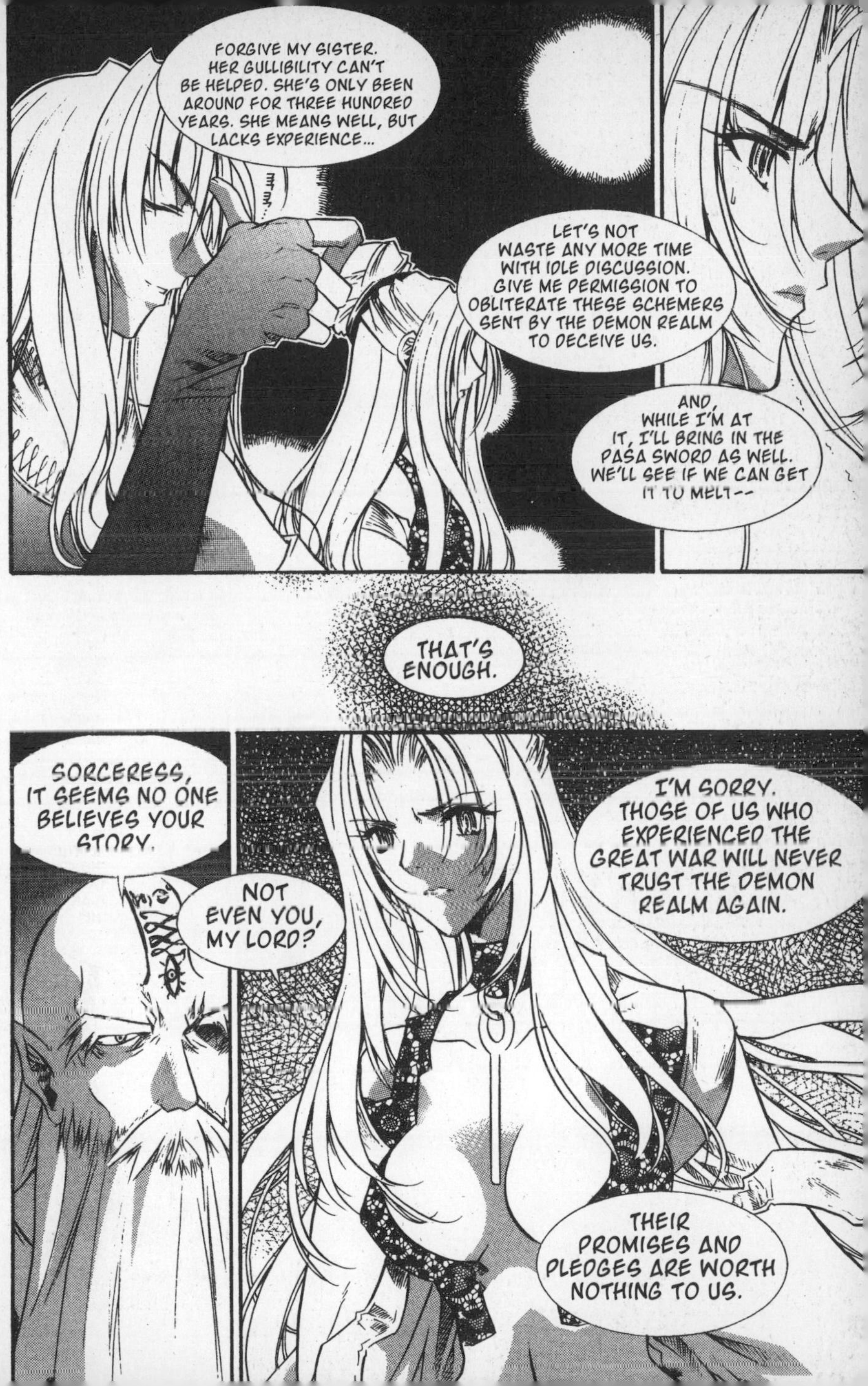
FORGIVE MY SISTER. HER GULLIBILITY CAN'T BE HELPED. SHE'S ONLY BEEN AROUND FOR THREE HUNDRED YEARS. SHE MEANS WELL, BUT LACKS EXPERIENCE...
LET'S NOT WASTE ANY MORE TIME WITH IDLE DISCUSSION. GIVE ME PERMISSION TO OBLITERATE THESE SCHEMERS SENT BY THE DEMON REALM TO DECEIVE US.
AND, WHILE I'M AT IT, I'LL BRING IN THE PASA SWORD AS WELL. WE'LL SEE IF WE CAN GET IT TO MELT--
THAT'S ENOUGH.
SORCERESS, IT SEEMS NO ONE BELIEVES YOUR STORY.
NOT EVEN YOU, MY LORD?
I'M SORRY. THOSE OF US WHO EXPERIENCED THE GREAT WAR WILL NEVER TRUST THE DEMON REALM AGAIN.
THEIR PROMISES AND PLEDGES ARE WORTH NOTHING TO US.

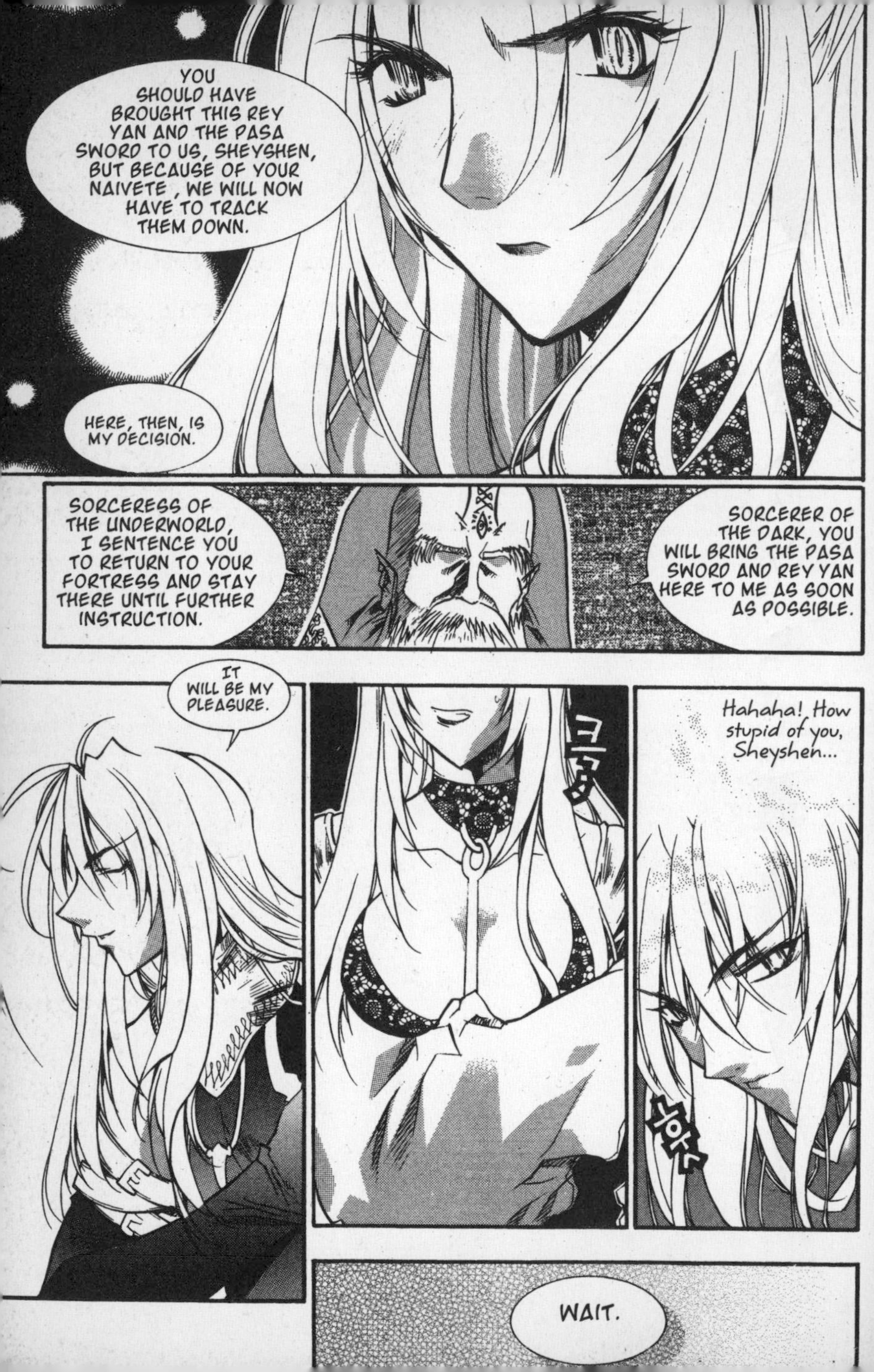
YOU SHOULD HAVE BROUGHT THIS REY YAN AND THE PASA SWORD TO US, SHEYSHEN, BUT BECAUSE OF YOUR NAIVETE , WE WILL NOW HAVE TO TRACK THEM DOWN.
HERE, THEN, IS MY DECISION.
SORCERESS OF THE UNDERWORLD, I SENTENCE YOU TO RETURN TO YOUR FORTRESS AND STAY THERE UNTIL FURTHER INSTRUCTION.
SORCERER OF THE DARK, YOU WILL BRING THE PASA SWORD AND REY YAN HERE TO ME AS SOON AS POSSIBLE.
IT WILL BE MY PLEASURE.
Hahaha! How stupid of you, Sheyshen...
WAIT.

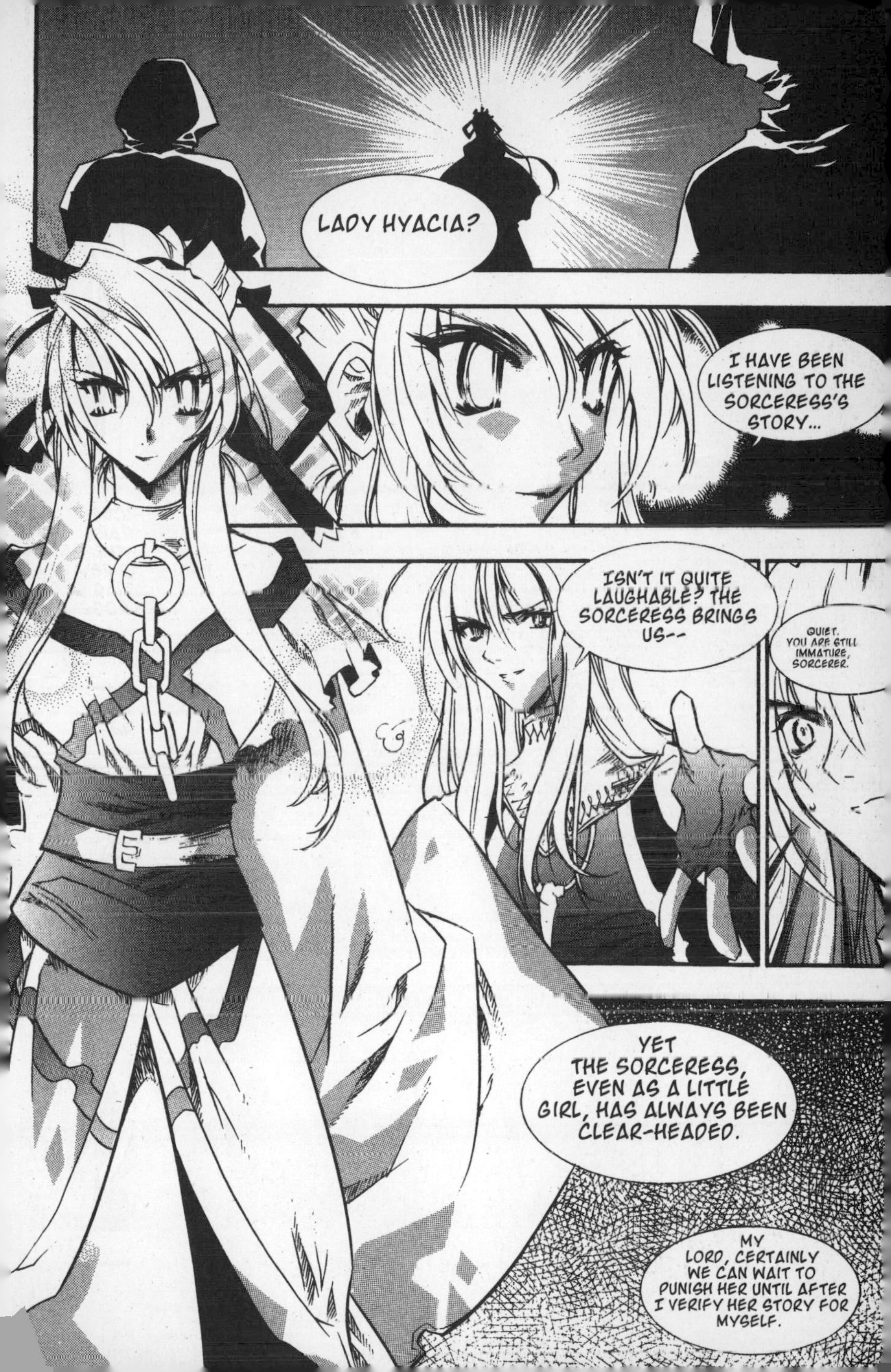
LADY HYACIA?
I HAVE BEEN LISTENING TO THE SORCERESS'S STORY...
ISN'T IT QUITE LAUGHABLE? THE SORCERESS BRINGS US--
QUIET. YOU ARE STILL IMMATURE, SORCERER.
YET THE SORCERESS, EVEN AS A LITTLE GIRL, HAS ALWAYS BEEN CLEAR-HEADED.
MY LORD, CERTAINLY WE CAN WAIT TO PUNISH HER UNTIL AFTER I VERIFY HER STORY FOR MYSELF.

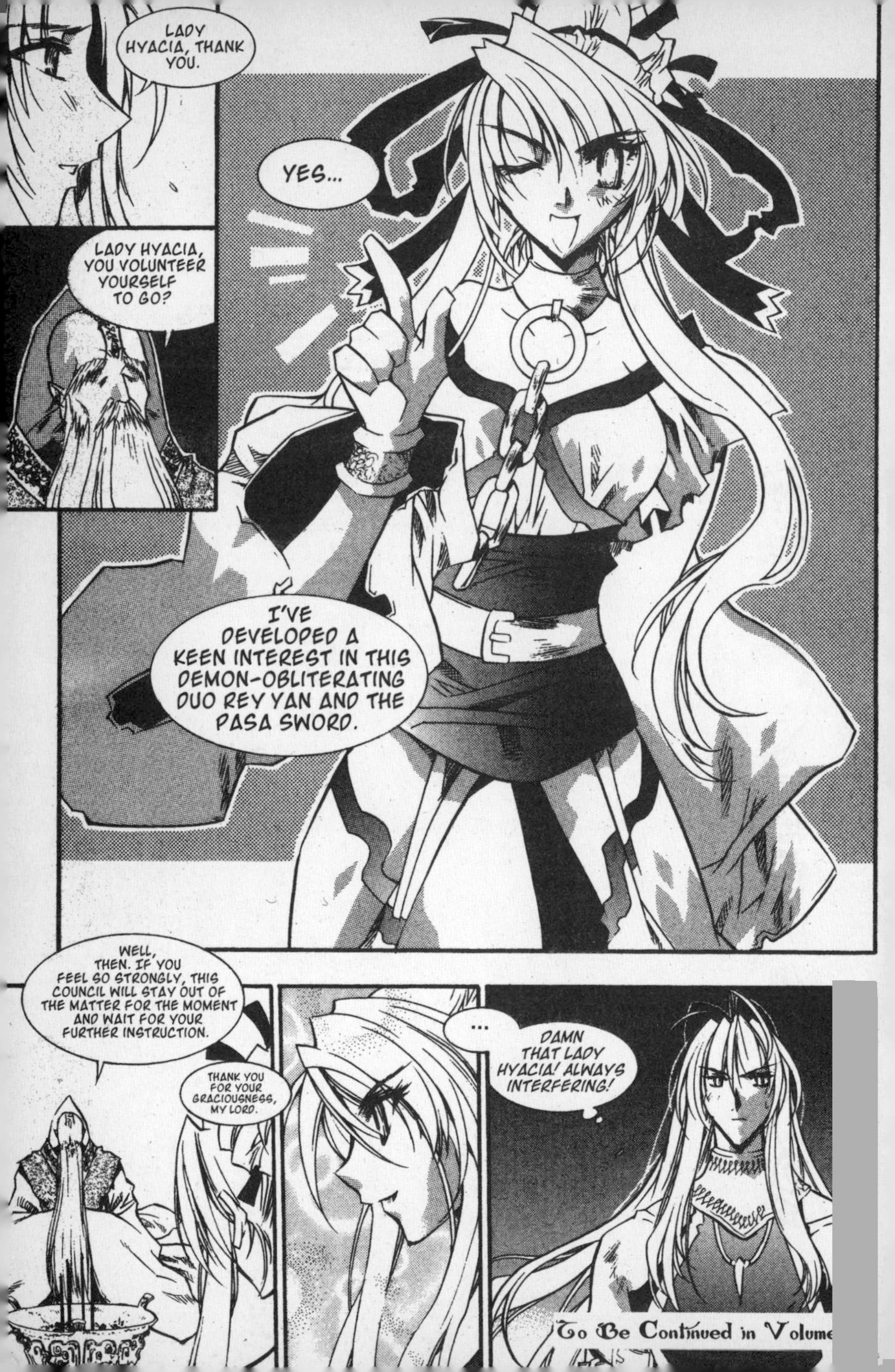
LADY HYACIA, THANK YOU.
YES...
LADY HYACIA, YOU VOLUNTEER YOURSELF TO GO?
I'VE DEVELOPED A KEEN INTEREST IN THIS DEMON-OBLITERATING DUO REY YAN AND THE PASA SWORD.
WELL, THEN. IF YOU FEEL SO STRONGLY, THIS COUNCIL WILL STAY OUT OF THE MATTER FOR THE MOMENT AND WAIT FOR YOUR FURTHER INSTRUCTION.
THANK YOU FOR YOUR GRACIOUSNESS, MY LORD.
...
DAMN THAT LADY HYACIA! ALWAYS INTERFERING!
To Be Continued in Volume

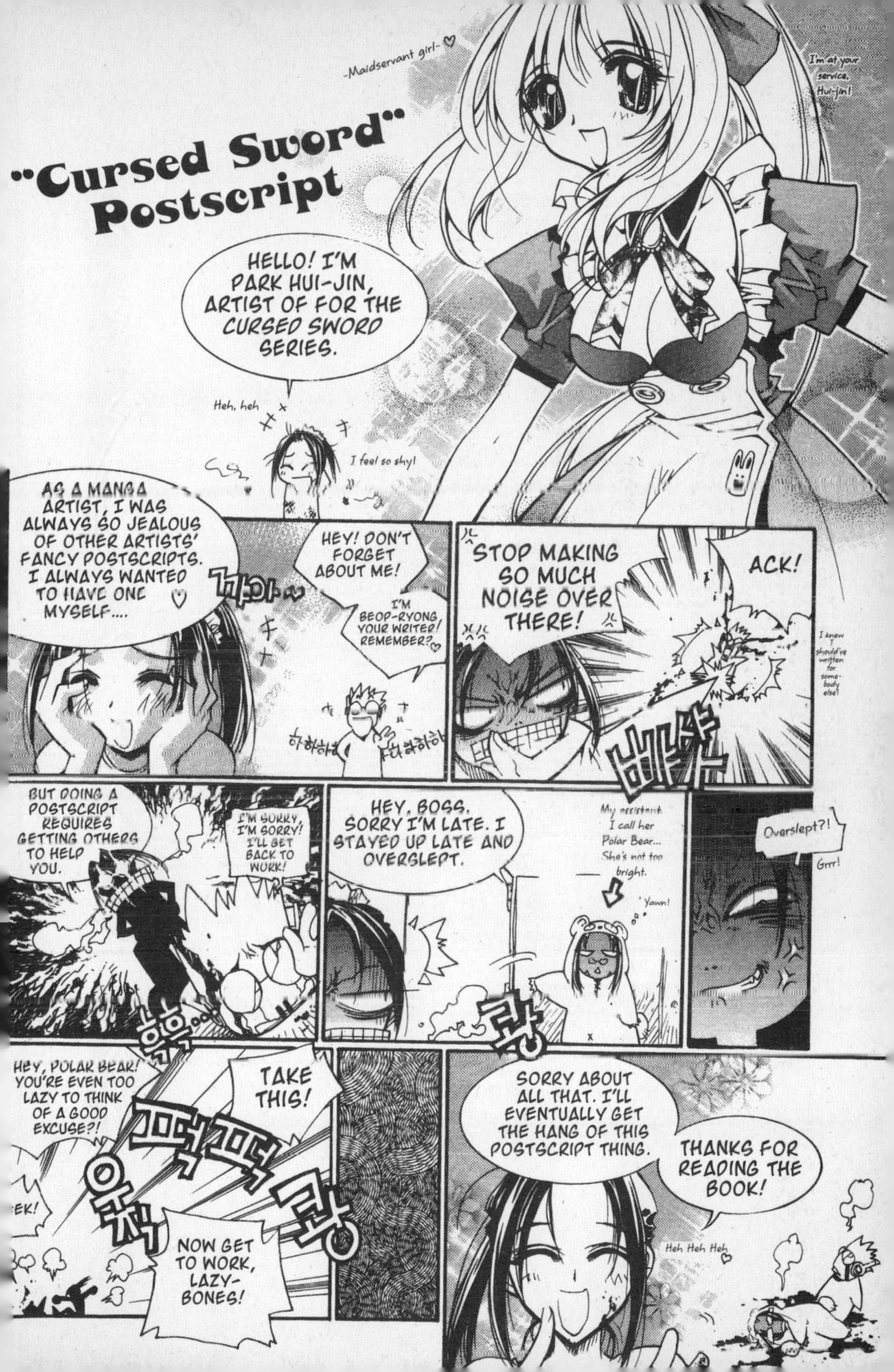
"Cursed Sword" Postscript
-Maidservant girl-♡
I'm at your service, Hui-jin!
HELLO! I'M PARK HUI-JIN, ARTIST OF FOR THE CURSED SWORD SERIES.
Heh, heh
I feel so shy!
AS A MANGA ARTIST, I WAS ALWAYS SO JEALOUS OF OTHER ARTISTS' FANCY POSTSCRIPTS. I ALWAYS WANTED TO HAVE ONE MYSELF....
HEY! DON'T FORGET ABOUT ME!
I'M BEOP-RYONG, YOUR WRITER! REMEMBER?♡
STOP MAKING SO MUCH NOISE OVER THERE!
ACK!
I knew I should've written for somebody else!
BUT DOING A POSTSCRIPT REQUIRES GETTING OTHERS TO HELP YOU.
I'M SORRY, I'M SORRY! I'LL GET BACK TO WORK!
HEY, BOSS. SORRY I'M LATE. I STAYED UP LATE AND OVERSLEPT.
My assistant. I call her Polar Bear... She's not too bright.
Yawn!
Overslept?!
Grrr!
HEY, POLAR BEAR! YOU'RE EVEN TOO LAZY TO THINK OF A GOOD EXCUSE?!
EEK!
TAKE THIS!
NOW GET TO WORK, LAZY-BONES!
SORRY ABOUT ALL THAT. I'LL EVENTUALLY GET THE HANG OF THIS POSTSCRIPT THING.
THANKS FOR READING THE BOOK!
Heh Heh Heh♡

Costume

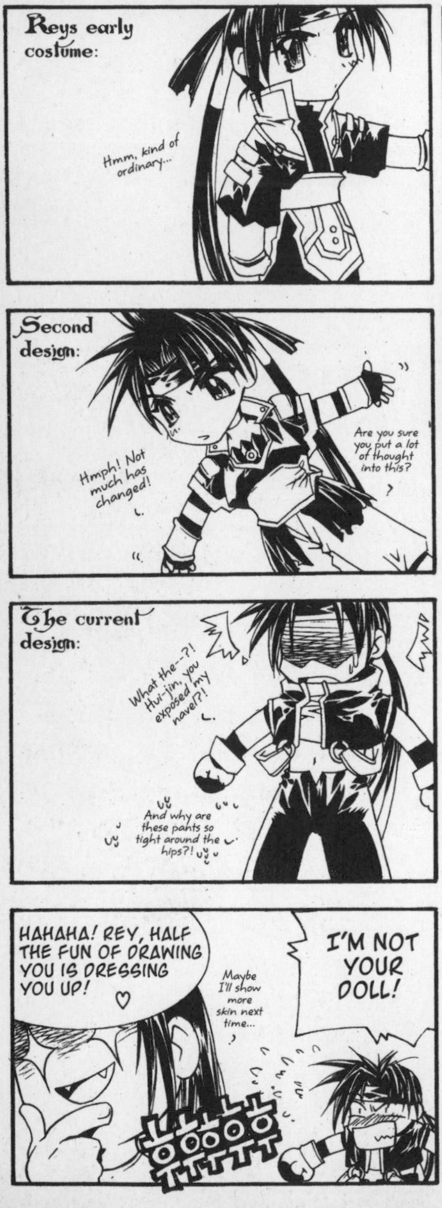
Reys early costume:
Hmm, kind of ordinary...
Second design:
Hmph! Not much has changed!
Are you sure you put a lot of thought into this?
The current design:
What the--?! Hui-jin, you exposed my navel?!
And why are these pants so tight around the hips?!
HAHAHA! REY, HALF THE FUN OF DRAWING YOU IS DRESSING YOU UP! ♡
Maybe I'll show more skin next time...
I'M NOT YOUR DOLL!

Polar Bears Blues

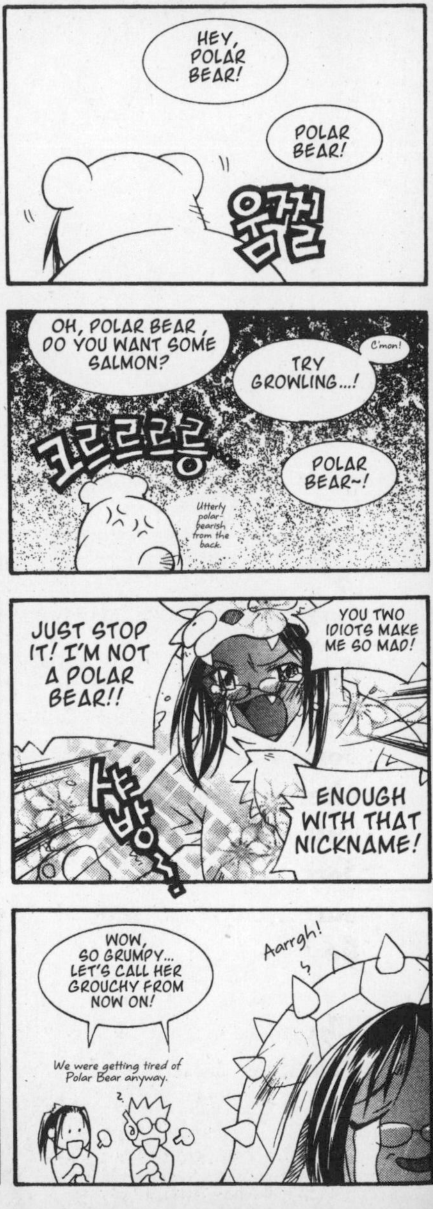
HEY, POLAR BEAR!
POLAR BEAR!
움찔
OH, POLAR BEAR, DO YOU WANT SOME SALMON?
C'mon!
TRY GROWLING...!
크르르르릉...
POLAR BEAR~!
Utterly polar-bearish from the back.
JUST STOP IT! I'M NOT A POLAR BEAR!!
YOU TWO IDIOTS MAKE ME SO MAD!
ENOUGH WITH THAT NICKNAME!
WOW, SO GRUMPY... LET'S CALL HER GROUCHY FROM NOW ON!
Aarrgh!
We were getting tired of Polar Bear anyway.

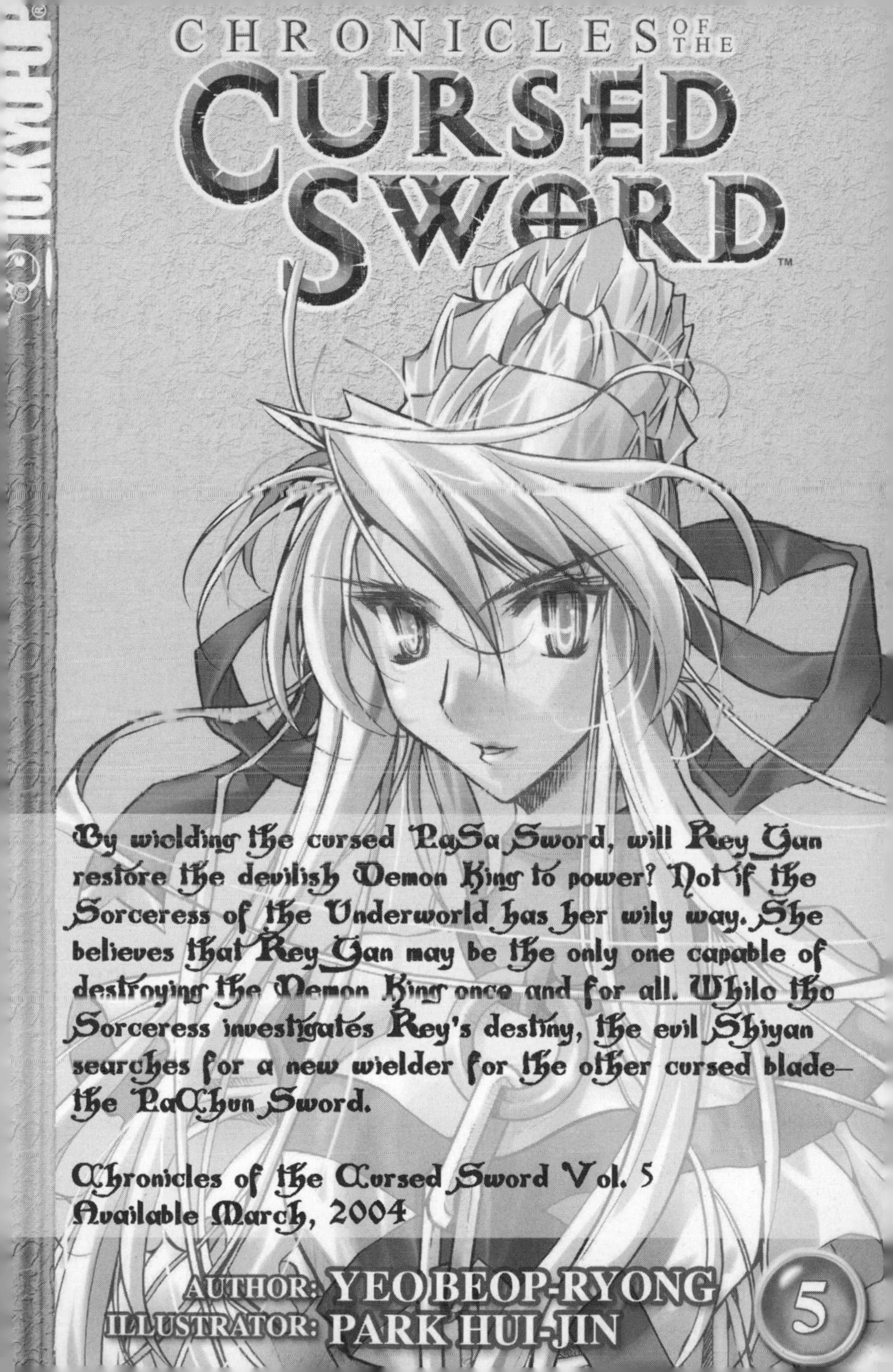
TOKYOPOP
CHRONICLES OF THE CURSED SWORD™
By wielding the cursed PaSa Sword, will Rey Yan restore the devilish Demon King to power? Not if the Sorceress of the Underworld has her wily way. She believes that Rey Yan may be the only one capable of destroying the Demon King once and for all. While the Sorceress investigates Rey's destiny, the evil Shiyan searches for a new wielder for the other cursed blade—the PaChun Sword.
Chronicles of the Cursed Sword Vol. 5
Available March, 2004
AUTHOR: YEO BEOP-RYONG
ILLUSTRATOR: PARK HUI-JIN
5

ALSO AVAILABLE FROM 🐱 TOKYOPOP®

MANGA

.HACK//LEGEND OF THE TWILIGHT
@LARGE
A.I. LOVE YOU February 2004
AI YORI AOSHI January 2004
ANGELIC LAYER
BABY BIRTH
BATTLE ROYALE
BATTLE VIXENS April 2004
BIRTH May 2004
BRAIN POWERED
BRIGADOON
B'TX January 2004
CARDCAPTOR SAKURA
CARDCAPTOR SAKURA: MASTER OF THE CLOW
CARDCAPTOR SAKURA: BOXED SET COLLECTION 1
CARDCAPTOR SAKURA: BOXED SET COLLECTION 2
    March 2004
CHOBITS
CHRONICLES OF THE CURSED SWORD
CLAMP SCHOOL DETECTIVES
CLOVER
COMIC PARTY June 2004
CONFIDENTIAL CONFESSIONS
CORRECTOR YUI
COWBOY BEBOP: BOXED SET THE COMPLETE
    COLLECTION
CRESCENT MOON May 2004
CREST OF THE STARS June 2004
CYBORG 009
DEMON DIARY
DIGIMON
DIGIMON SERIES 3 April 2004
DIGIMON ZERO TWO February 2004
DNANGEL April 2004
DOLL May 2004
DRAGON HUNTER
DRAGON KNIGHTS
DUKLYON: CLAMP SCHOOL DEFENDERS
DV June 2004
ERICA SAKURAZAWA
FAERIES' LANDING January 2004
FAKE
FLCL
FORBIDDEN DANCE
FRUITS BASKET February 2004
G GUNDAM
GATEKEEPERS
GETBACKERS February 2004
GHOST! March 2004
GIRL GOT GAME January 2004
GRAVITATION
GTO

GUNDAM WING
GUNDAM WING: BATTLEFIELD OF PACIFISTS
GUNDAM WING: ENDLESS WALTZ
GUNDAM WING: THE LAST OUTPOST
HAPPY MANIA
HARLEM BEAT
I.N.V.U.
INITIAL D
ISLAND
JING: KING OF BANDITS
JULINE
JUROR 13 March 2004
KARE KANO
KILL ME, KISS ME February 2004
KINDAICHI CASE FILES, THE
KING OF HELL
KODOCHA: SANA'S STAGE
LAMENT OF THE LAMB May 2004
LES BIJOUX February 2004
LIZZIE MCGUIRE
LOVE HINA
LUPIN III
LUPIN III SERIES 2
MAGIC KNIGHT RAYEARTH I
MAGIC KNIGHT RAYEARTH II February 2004
MAHOROMATIC: AUTOMATIC MAIDEN May 2004
MAN OF MANY FACES
MARMALADE BOY
MARS
METEOR METHUSELA June 2004
METROID June 2004
MINK April 2004
MIRACLE GIRLS
MIYUKI-CHAN IN WONDERLAND
MODEL May 2004
NELLY MUSIC MANGA April 2004
ONE April 2004
PARADISE KISS
PARASYTE
PEACH GIRL
PEACH GIRL CHANGE OF HEART
PEACH GIRL RELAUNCH BOX SET
PET SHOP OF HORRORS
PITA-TEN January 2004
PLANET LADDER February 2004
PLANETES
PRIEST
PRINCESS AI April 2004
PSYCHIC ACADEMY March 2004
RAGNAROK
RAGNAROK: BOXED SET COLLECTION 1
RAVE MASTER
RAVE MASTER: BOXED SET March 2004

ALSO AVAILABLE FROM TOKYOPOP

For more information visit www.TOKYOPOP.com

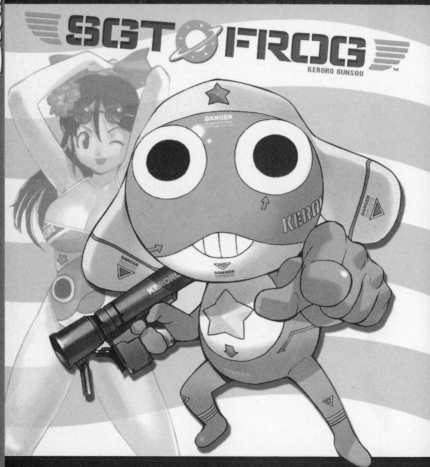

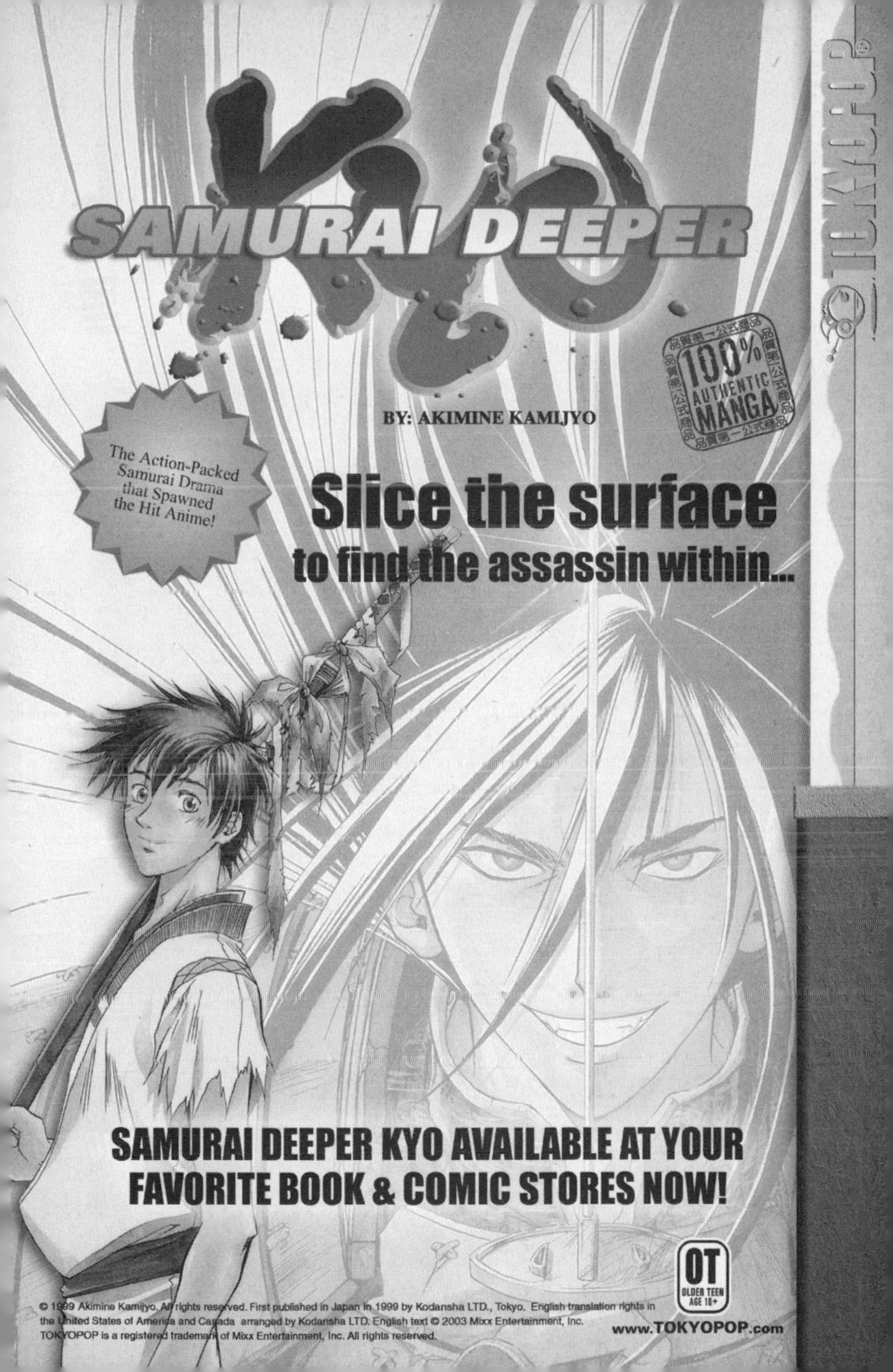

TOKYOPOP
SAMURAI DEEPER
KYO
100% AUTHENTIC MANGA
品質第一公式商品
BY: AKIMINE KAMIJYO
The Action-Packed Samurai Drama that Spawned the Hit Anime!
Slice the surface
to find the assassin within...
SAMURAI DEEPER KYO AVAILABLE AT YOUR FAVORITE BOOK & COMIC STORES NOW!
OT OLDER TEEN AGE 16+
© 1999 Akimine Kamijyo. All rights reserved. First published in Japan in 1999 by Kodansha LTD., Tokyo. English translation rights in the United States of America and Canada arranged by Kodansha LTD. English text © 2003 Mixx Entertainment, Inc. TOKYOPOP is a registered trademark of Mixx Entertainment, Inc. All rights reserved.
www.TOKYOPOP.com

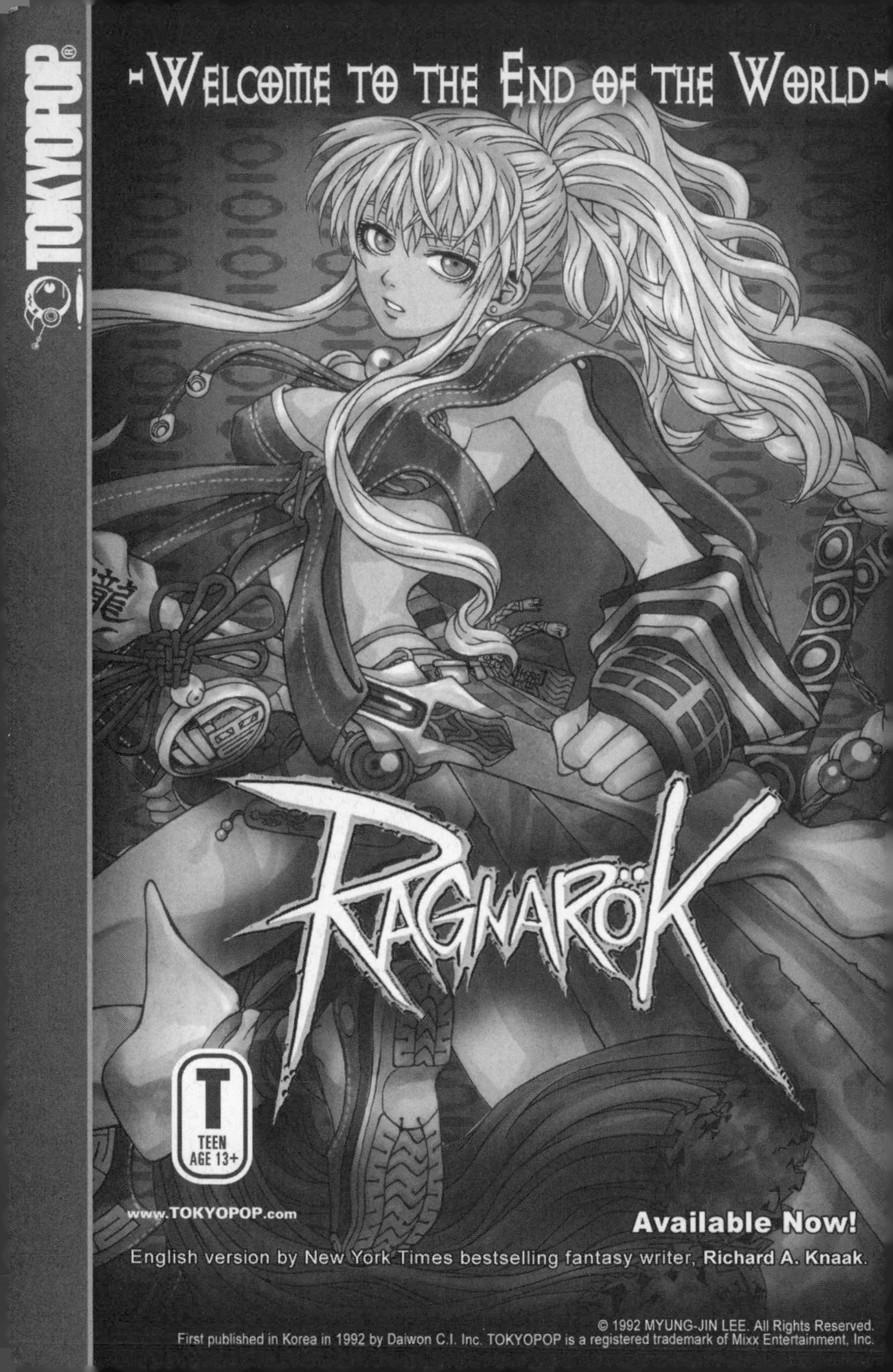

TOKYOPOP®
-WELCOME TO THE END OF THE WORLD-
RAGNARÖK
T
TEEN
AGE 13+
www.TOKYOPOP.com
Available Now!
English version by New York Times bestselling fantasy writer, Richard A. Knaak.
© 1992 MYUNG-JIN LEE. All Rights Reserved.
First published in Korea in 1992 by Daiwon C.I. Inc. TOKYOPOP is a registered trademark of Mixx Entertainment, Inc.

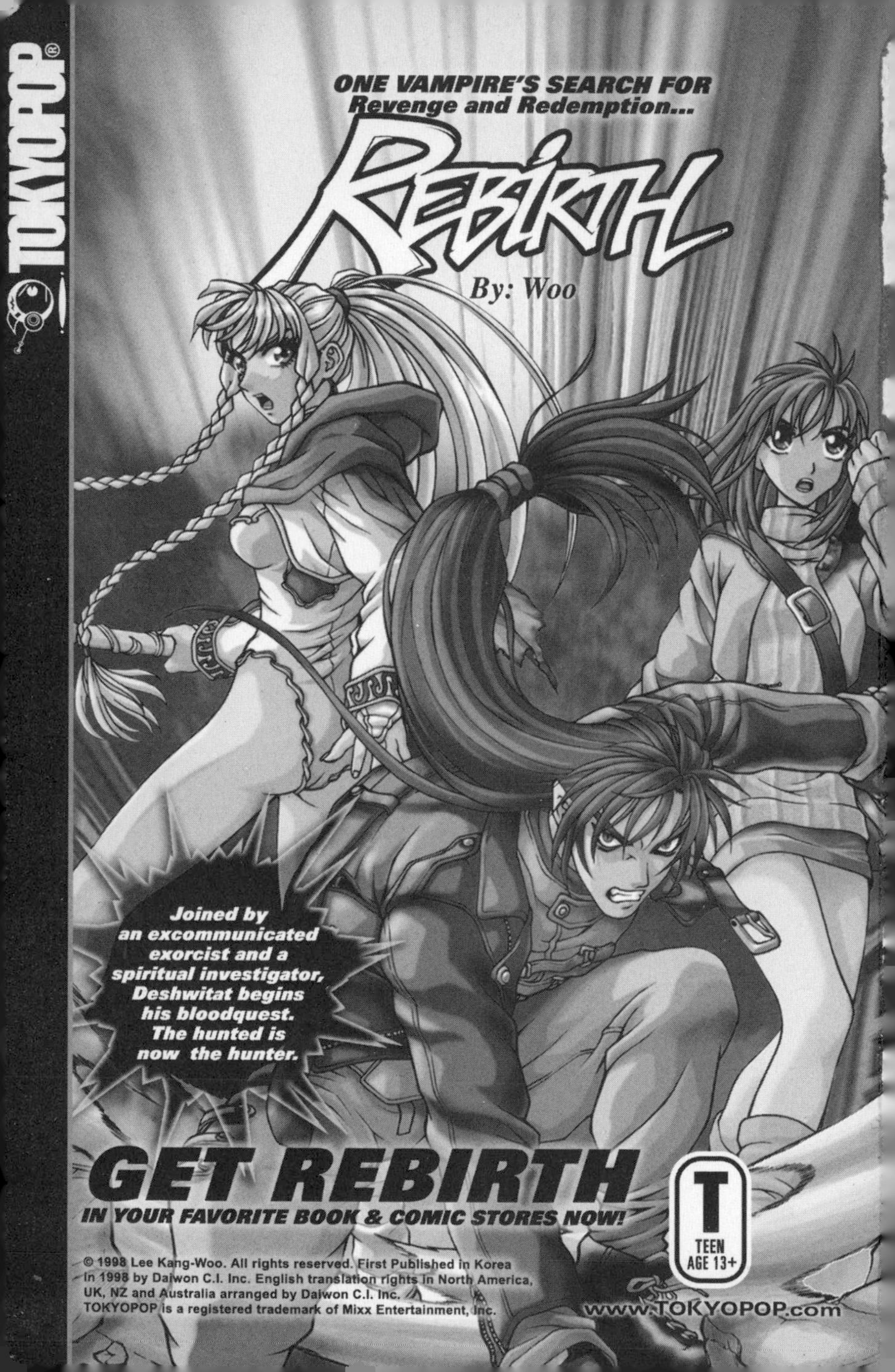